Getting Started With OpenOffice.org 3

ISBN 978-1440451775

Published & distributed by SoHoBooks,
under the terms of the Creative Commons Attrribution 3.0 Licence

Copyright

Authors

Thomas Astleitner
Agnes Belzunce
Richard Detwiler
Regina Henschel
John Kane
Michael Kotsarinis
Ian Laurenson
Alan Madden
Andrew Pitonyak
Iain Roberts
Robert Scott
Barbara M. Tobias
Linda Worthington

Richard Barnes
Daniel Carrera
Spencer E. Harpe
Peter Hillier-Brook
Stefan A. Keel
Peter Kupfer
Dan Lewis
Michel Pinquier
Carol Roberts
Gary Schnabl
Janet M. Swisher
Jean Hollis Weber
Michele Zarri

Feedback

Please direct any comments or suggestions about this document to:
authors@user-faq.openoffice.org

Publisher

Friends of OpenDocument, Inc.
P.O. Box 640, Airlie Beach, QLD 4802, Australia
http://friendsofopendocument.com/

Publication date and software version

Published 25 October 2008. Based on OpenOffice.org 3.0.

Contents

Chapter *1*
Introducing OpenOffice.org

What is OpenOffice.org?

OpenOffice.org (OOo) is both a *software product* and a *community of volunteers* that produces and supports the software.

Note	Because someone else owns the trademark *OpenOffice*, the correct name for both the open-source project and its software is *OpenOffice.org*.

The OpenOffice.org software is a freely available, full-featured office suite.

OOo 3.0 is a major upgrade of an already feature-rich office suite. If you have used previous versions of OOo, please look over the new features list on the OOo wiki.

OOo's native file format is OpenDocument, an open standard format that is being adopted by governments worldwide as a required file format for publishing and accepting documents. OOo can also open and save documents in many other formats, including those used by several versions of Microsoft Office.

OOo includes the following components.

Writer (word processor)

Writer is a feature-rich tool for creating letters, books, reports, newsletters, brochures, and other documents. You can insert graphics and objects from other components into Writer documents. Writer can export files to HTML, XHTML, XML, Adobe's Portable Document

Format (PDF), and several versions of Microsoft Word files. It also connects to your email client.

Calc (spreadsheet)

Calc has all of the advanced analysis, charting and decision-making features expected from a high-end spreadsheet. It includes over 300 functions for financial, statistical, and mathematical operations, among others. The Scenario Manager provides "what if" analyses. Calc generates 2-D and 3-D charts, which can be integrated into other OOo documents. You can also open and work with Microsoft Excel workbooks and save them in Excel format. Calc can export spreadsheets to Adobe's PDF and to HTML.

Impress (presentations)

Impress provides all the common multimedia presentation tools, such as special effects, animation, and drawing tools. It is integrated with the advanced graphics capabilities of OOo's Draw and Math components. Slideshows can be further enhanced with Fontwork's special effects text, as well as sound and video clips. Impress is compatible with Microsoft's PowerPoint file format and can also save your work in numerous graphics formats, including Macromedia Flash (SWF).

Draw (vector graphics)

Draw is a vector drawing tool that can produce everything from simple diagrams or flowcharts to 3-D artwork. Its Smart Connectors feature allows you to define your own connection points. You can use Draw to create drawings for use in any of OOo's other components, and you can create your own clipart and add it to the Gallery. Draw can import graphics from many common formats and save them in over 20 formats including PNG, HTML, PDF, and Flash.

Base (database)

Base provides tools for day-to-day database work within a simple interface. It can create and edit forms, reports, queries, tables, views, and relations, so that managing a connected database is much the same as in other popular database applications. Base provides many new features, such as the ability to analyze and edit relationships from a diagram view. Base incorporates HSQLDB as its default relational database engine. It can also use dBASE, Microsoft Access, MySQL, or Oracle, or any ODBC- or JDBC-compliant database. Base also provides support for a subset of ANSI-92 SQL.

Math (formula editor)

Math is OOo's formula or equation editor. You can use it to create complex equations that include symbols or characters not available in standard font sets. While it is most commonly used to create formulas in other documents, such as Writer and Impress files, Math can also work as a stand-alone tool. You can save formulas in the standard Mathematical Markup Language (MathML) format for inclusion in webpages and other documents not created by OOo.

The advantages of OpenOffice.org

Here are some of the advantages of OpenOffice.org over other office suites:

- **No licensing fees**. OOo is free for anyone to use and distribute at no cost. Many features that are available as extra cost add-ins in other office suites (like PDF export) are free with OOo. There are no hidden charges now or in the future.

- **Open source.** You can distribute, copy, and modify the software as much as you wish, in accordance with either of OOo's Open Source licenses.

- **Cross-platform.** OOo3 runs on several hardware architectures and under multiple operating systems, such as Microsoft Windows, Mac OS X, Linux, and Sun Solaris.

- **Extensive language support**. OOo's user interface is available in over 40 languages, and the OOo project provides spelling, hyphenation, and thesaurus dictionaries in over 70 languages and dialects. OOo also provides support for both Complex Text Layout (CTL) and Right to Left (RTL) layout languages (such as Hindi, Hebrew, and Arabic).

- **Consistent user interface.** All the components have a similar "look and feel," making them easy to use and master.

- **Integration.** The components of OpenOffice.org are well integrated with one another.
  - All the components share a common spelling checker and other tools, which are used consistently across the suite. For example, the drawing tools available in Writer are also found in Calc, with similar but enhanced versions in Impress and Draw.
  - You do not need to know which application was used to create a particular file (for example, you can open a Draw file from Writer).

- **Granularity.** Usually, if you change an option, it affects all components. However, OOo options can be set at a component level or even document level.

- **File compatibility.** In addition to its native OpenDocument formats, OOo includes PDF and Flash export capabilities, as well as support for opening and saving files in many common formats including Microsoft Office, HTML, XML, WordPerfect, and Lotus 123 formats. New in OOo3 (using an extension): the ability to import and edit some PDF files.

- **No vendor lock-in.** OOo3 uses OpenDocument, an XML (eXtensible Markup Language) file format developed as an industry standard by OASIS (Organization for the Advancement of Structured Information Standards). These files can easily be unzipped and read by any text editor, and their framework is open and published.

- **You have a voice.** Enhancements, software fixes, and release dates are community-driven. You can join the community and affect the course of the product you use.

You can read more about OpenOffice.org, its mission, history, licensing, and other organizational information on the OpenOffice.org website.

Minimum requirements

OpenOffice.org 3 requires one of the following operating systems:

- **Microsoft Windows** 98, Windows ME, Windows 2000 (Service Pack 2 or higher), Windows XP, Windows 2003, or Windows Vista
- **GNU/Linux** Kernel version 2.2.13 and glibc 2.2.0 or newer
- **Mac OS X** 10.4.x, X11 required; Mac OS X 10.5+ without X11
- **Solaris** version 8 or higher

Some OpenOffice.org features (wizards and the HSQLDB database engine) require that the Java Runtime Environment (JRE) be installed on your computer. Although OOo will work fine without Java support, some features will not be available. You can download OOo with or without JRE included. If you have a slow machine and do not often need the features requiring JRE, you can try to disable it to speed up the loading of the program.

For a more detailed (and up-to-date) listing of requirements, see http://www.openoffice.org/dev_docs/source/sys_reqs_30.html.

How to get the software

Many new computers come with OpenOffice.org installed. In addition, most Linux distributions, such as Ubuntu, include OpenOffice.org.

If you need to install it yourself, it's very easy to do. You can download the OpenOffice.org installation package from the project's home page (http://www.openoffice.org/) or by using a Peer to Peer client such as BitTorrent. Instructions for BitTorrent are here: http://distribution.openoffice.org/p2p/

The installation package is approximately 150MB. People with slow Internet connections may prefer to purchase a copy on a CD or DVD from a third-party distributor. The project maintains a list of distributors: http://distribution.openoffice.org/cdrom/sellers.html, but the distributors are not connected with, nor endorsed by, OpenOffice.org.

How to install the software

Information on installing and setting up OpenOffice.org on the various supported operating systems is given here: http://download.openoffice.org/ common/instructions.html

You can also download the more detailed *Setup Guide* (in several languages) from http://documentation. openoffice.org/setup_guide2/index.html

How to get help

This book and the other OOo user guides and help and user support systems assume that you are familiar with your computer and basic functions such as starting a program, opening and saving files.

Help system

OOo comes with an extensive Help system. This is your first line of support for using OOo.

To display the full Help system, press *F1* or select **OpenOffice.org Help** from the Help menu. In addition, you can choose whether to activate tooltips, extended tips, and the Help Agent (using **Tools > Options > General**).

If tooltips are enabled, place the mouse pointer over any of the icons to see a small box ("tooltip") with a brief explanation of the icon's function. For a more detailed explanation, select **Help > What's This?** and hold the pointer over the icon.

Free online support

The OpenOffice.org community not only develops software, but provides free, volunteer-based support. Users of OOo can get comprehensive online support from community venues such as newsgroups, forums, or mailing lists. There are also numerous websites run by users that offer free tips and tutorials.

Free OpenOffice.org support	
Users Mailing List	Free community support provided by a network of hundreds of experienced users. You must be subscribed to post messages. To subscribe, send a blank email to users-subscribe@openoffice.org List archives are here: http://www.openoffice.org/servlets/ SummarizeList? listName=users
Documentation Project	Templates, user guides, how-tos, and other documentation. http://documentation.openoffice.org/ See also the Documentation wiki, http://wiki.services.openoffice.org/wiki/ Documentation
Native Language Project	Information, resources, and mail lists in your language. http://projects.openoffice.org/native-lang.html
Mac Support	Support for installing and using OOo on Mac OS X. http://porting.openoffice.org/mac/index.html
OpenOffice.org Community Forum	Extensive discussion forum for OpenOffice.org issues from setup to advanced programming features. http://user.services.openoffice.org/en/forum/

Free OpenOffice.org support	
OpenOffice.org Macro Information	Andrew Pitonyak, the author of *OpenOffice.org Macros Explained*, maintains this site which provides extensive documentation on OOo's macro capability. Many good referral links are also provided: http://www.pitonyak.org/oo.php

Read more about the support options for OOo at http://support.openoffice.org/index.html

Paid support and training

Alternatively, you can pay for support services. Service contracts can be purchased from a vendor or consulting firm specializing in OpenOffice.org.

OOo is supported by Sun Microsystems, Inc. under the Sun Software Support program, which includes two levels of support that cover extended business hours or around-the-clock service for mission-critical deployments. http://www.sun.com/service/support/software/openoffice/index.html

A list of independent consultants and the services they offer, listed alphabetically by region and then by country, is provided on the OpenOffice.org website. http://bizdev.openoffice.org/consultants.html

Extensions and add-ons

Several websites provide extensions and add-ons to enhance OpenOffice.org. The following table lists a few of these websites. See Chapter 14 (Customizing OpenOffice.org) for more information.

Free OOo templates, artwork, add-ons, and other resources	
OpenOffice.org Extensions	The official respository for extensions to OOo. Most are free, but some are not. http://extensions.services.openoffice.org/
OOExtras	Provides templates, samples, and macros in several languages. http://ooextras.sourceforge.net/

Free OOo templates, artwork, add-ons, and other resources	
OOoMacros	A repository for OOo macros and addons and documentation about writing macros or extending OOo. http://www.ooomacros.org/
Open Clip Art Library	An archive of clip art that can be used for free for any use. http://www.openclipart.org/

Starting OpenOffice.org

The most common way to launch any component of OOo is by using the system menu, the standard menu from which most applications are started. On Windows, it is called the Start menu. On GNOME, it is called the Applications menu. On KDE it is identified by the KDE logo. On Mac OS X, it is the Applications menu.

When OOo was installed on your computer, in most cases a menu entry for each component was added to your system menu. (If you are using a Mac, see note below.) The exact name and location of these menu entries depends on the operating system and graphical user interface.

Note for Mac users

You should see the OpenOffice.org icon in the Applications folder. When you double-click this icon, a text document opens in Writer. To open the other components (Draw, Calc, Impress, Base), go to the File menu of the Writer window and select the component you want.

OOo does not automatically put a shortcut icon on the desktop, but you can add one if you wish. If you don't know how to add shortcut icons for launching programs, please consult the help for your operating system.

Starting from an existing document

You can start OOo by double-clicking the filename of an OOo document in a file manager such as Windows Explorer. The appropriate component of OOo will start and the document will be loaded.

Note for Windows users

If you have associated Microsoft Office file types with OOo, then when you double-click on a *.doc (Word) file, it opens in Writer; *.xls (Excel) files open in Calc, and *.ppt (Powerpoint) files open in Impress.

If you did not associate the file types, then when you double-click on a Microsoft Word document, it opens in Microsoft Word (if Word is installed on your computer), Excel files open in Excel, and Powerpoint files open in Powerpoint.

You can use another method to open Microsoft Office files in OOo and save in those formats from OOo. See "Opening an existing document" on page 16 for more information.

Using the Quickstarter under Windows

The Quickstarter is an icon that is placed in the Windows system tray during system startup. It indicates that OpenOffice.org has been loaded and is ready to use. (The Quickstarter loads library .DLL files required by OOo, thus shortening the startup time for OOo components by about half.) If the Quickstarter is disabled, see "Reactivating the Quickstarter" if you want to enable it.

Using the Quickstarter icon

Right-click the **Quickstarter** icon in the system tray to open a pop-up menu from which you can open a new document, open the Templates and Documents dialog, or choose an existing document to open. You can also double-click the **Quickstarter** icon to display the Templates and Documents dialog.

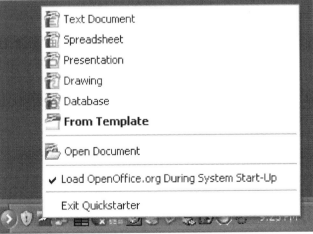

Figure 1: Quickstarter popup menu

Disabling the Quickstarter

To close the Quickstarter, right-click on the icon in the system tray, and then click **Exit Quickstarter** on the pop-up menu. The next time the computer is restarted, the Quickstarter will be loaded again.

To prevent OpenOffice.org from loading during system startup, deselect the **Load OpenOffice.org during system start-up** item on the pop-up menu. You might want to do this if your computer has insufficient memory, for example.

Reactivating the Quickstarter

If the Quickstarter has been disabled, you can reactivate it by selecting the **Load OpenOffice.org during system start-up** checkbox in **Tools > Options > OpenOffice.org > Memory**.

Using the Quickstarter in Linux

Some installations of OpenOffice.org under Linux have a Quickstarter that looks and acts like the one described above for Windows (the checkbox on the Memory page is labeled **Enable systray quickstarter**).

Preloading OOo under Linux/KDE

In Linux/KDE, you can use KDocker to have OOo loaded and ready for use at startup. KDocker is not part of OOo; it is a generic "systray app docker" that is helpful if you open OOo often.

Starting from the command line

You may want to start OOo from the command line (using the keyboard instead of the mouse). Why? Well, by using the command line, you have more control over what happens when OOo is started. For example, using the command line, you can tell Writer to load a document and print it immediately, or to start without showing the splash screen.

Note   Most users will never need to do this.

There is more than one way to start OOo from the command line, depending on whether you have installed a customized version or the standard download from the OOo website.

If you installed using the download on the OOo website, you can start Writer by typing at the command line:

```
soffice -writer
```
or

```
swriter
```

Writer will start and create a new document. Likewise, you can start other OOo components from the command line:

Type of document	Component	Command-line option
Text	Writer	`-writer`
Spreadsheet	Calc	`-calc`
Drawing	Draw	`-draw`
Presentation	Impress	`-impress`
Formula	Math	`-math`
Web page	Writer	`-web`

To see a list of options you can use when starting Writer at the command line, type:

```
soffice -?
```

Below is a list of some of the more popular options.

Option	Description
`-help`	Get a complete list of options.
`-nologo`	Do not show the startup screen.
`-show <odp-file>`	Start presentation immediately.
`-view <documents ...>`	Open documents in viewer (read-only) mode.
`-minimized`	Start OOo minimized.
`-norestore`	Suppress restart/restore after fatal errors.
`-invisible`	No startup screen, no default document and no UI. This is useful for third-party applications that use functionality provided by OOo.

If you have a customized version of OOo (such as the one provided by Linux Mandrake or Gentoo), you can start Writer by typing at the command line:

```
oowriter
```

Note	Although the command syntax differs, the effect is identical: it starts OOo with an empty Writer document.

Parts of the main window

The main window is similar in each component of OOo, although some details vary. See the component chapters in this book for descriptions of those details.

Common features include the menu bar, standard toolbar, and formatting toolbar at the top of the window and the status bar at the bottom.

Menu bar

The *Menu bar* is located across the top of the screen, just below the Title bar. When you choose one of the menus, a submenu drops down to show commands.

- **File** contains commands that apply to the entire document such as Open, Save, and Export as PDF.
- **Edit** contains commands for editing the document such as Undo and Find & Replace. It also contains commands to cut, copy and paste selected parts of your document.
- **View** contains commands for controlling the display of the document such as Zoom and Web Layout.
- **Insert** contains commands for inserting elements into your document such as Header, Footer, and Picture.
- **Format** contains commands, such as Styles and Formatting and AutoFormat, for formatting the layout of your document.
- **Table** shows all commands to insert and edit a table in a text document.
- **Tools** contains functions such as Spelling and Grammar, Customize, and Options.
- **Window** contains commands for the display window.
- **Help** contains links to the OpenOffice.org Help file, What's This?, and information about the program.

Toolbars

OOo has several types of toolbars: docked, floating, and tear-off. Docked toolbars can be moved to different locations or made to float, and floating toolbars can be docked.

The top docked toolbar (default position) is called the *Standard toolbar*. The Standard toolbar is consistent across the OpenOffice.org applications.

The second toolbar across the top (default location) is the *Formatting toolbar*. It is a context-sensitive bar that shows the relevant tools in response to the cursor's current position or selection. For example, when the cursor is on a graphic, the Formatting bar provides tools for formatting graphics; when the cursor is in text, the tools are for formatting text.

Displaying or hiding toolbars

To display or hide toolbars, choose **View > Toolbars**, then click on the name of a toolbar in the list. An active toolbar shows a checkmark beside its name. Tear-off toolbars are not listed in the View menu.

Submenus and tear-off toolbars

Toolbar icons with a small triangle to the right will display *submenus*, *tear-off toolbars*, and other ways of selecting things, depending on the icon.

Figure 2 shows a tear-off toolbar from the Drawing toolbar.

The tear-off toolbars can be floating or docked along an edge of the screen or in one of the existing toolbar areas. To move a floating tear-off toolbar, drag it by the title bar. See "Moving toolbars" below.

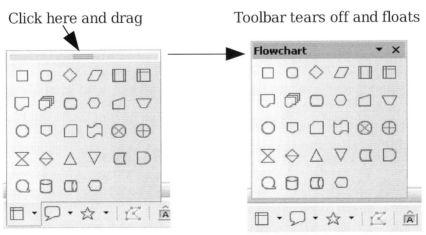

Figure 2: Example of a tear-off toolbar

Moving toolbars

To move a docked toolbar, place the mouse pointer over the toolbar handle, hold down the left mouse button, drag the toolbar to the new location, and then release the mouse button (Figure 3).

To move a floating toolbar, click on its title bar and drag it to a new location (Figure 4).

Handle of docked toolbar

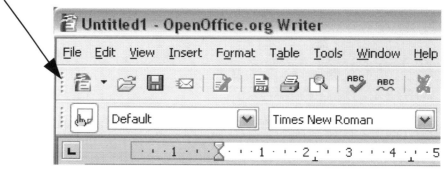

Figure 3: Moving a docked toolbar

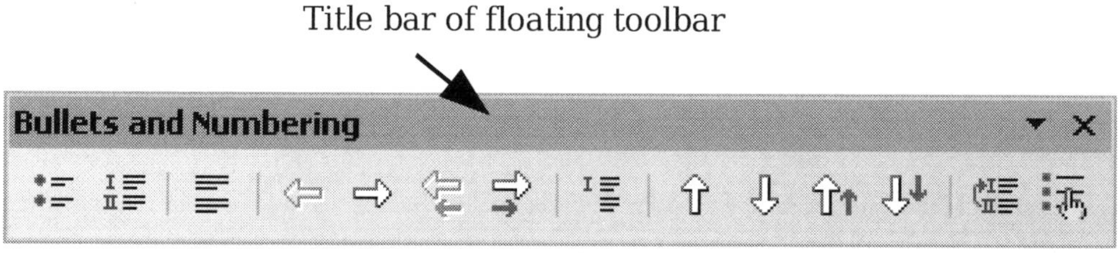

Title bar of floating toolbar

Figure 4: Moving a floating toolbar

Floating toolbars

OOo includes several additional context-sensitive toolbars, whose defaults appear as floating toolbars in response to the cursor's current position or selection. For example, when the cursor is in a table, a floating *Table* toolbar appears, and when the cursor is in a numbered or bullet list, the *Bullets and Numbering* toolbar appears. You can dock these toolbars to the top, bottom, or side of the window, if you wish (see "Moving toolbars" on page 14).

Docking/floating windows and toolbars

Toolbars and some windows, such as the Navigator and the Styles and Formatting window, are dockable. You can move, re-size or dock them to an edge.

To dock a window or toolbar, do one of the following:

- Click on the title bar of the floating window and drag it to the side until you see the outline of a box appear in the main window, then release the window. This method depends on your system's window manager settings, so it may not work for you.

- Hold down the *Control* key and double-click on a vacant part of the floating window to dock it in its last position. If that does not work, try double-clicking without using the *Control* key.

To undock a window, hold down the *Control* key and double-click on a vacant part of the docked window.

Figure 5: Docking a window

Note	The Styles and Formatting window can also be docked or undocked by using *Control+double-click* on the gray area next to the icons at the top of the window.

Customizing toolbars

You can customize toolbars in several ways, including choosing which icons are visible and locking the position of a docked toolbar. You can also add icons and create new toolbars, as described in Chapter 14.

To access a toolbar's customization options, use the down-arrow at the end of the toolbar or on its title bar (see Figure 6).

Toolbar customization icons

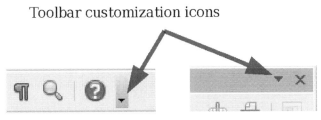

Figure 6: Customizing toolbars

To show or hide icons defined for the selected toolbar, choose **Visible Buttons** from the drop-down menu. Visible icons have a checkmark next to them. Click on icons to select or deselect them.

Right-click (context) menus

You can quickly access many menu functions by right-clicking on a paragraph, graphics, or other object. A context menu will pop up. Often the context menu is the fastest and easier way to reach a function. If you're not sure where in the menus or toolbars a function is located, you can often find it by right-clicking.

Starting a new document

You can create a new, blank document in OOo in several ways.

When OOo is open but no document is open (for example if you close all the open documents but leave the program running), a Welcome screen is shown. Click one of the icons to open a new document of that type, or click the Templates icon to start a new document using a template.

You can also start a new document in one of the following ways. If a document is already open in OOo, the new document opens in a new window.

- Use **File > New** and choose the type of document.
- Use the arrow next to the **New** button on the main toolbar. From the drop-down menu, select the type of document to be created.
- Press *Control+N* on the keyboard.
- Use **File > Wizards** for some types of documents.

Opening an existing document

When no document is open, the Welcome screen provides an icon for opening an existing document.

You can also open an existing document in one of the following ways. If a document is already open in OOo, the second document opens in a new window.

- Click **File > Open**.
- Click the **Open** button on the main toolbar.
- Press *Control+O* on the keyboard.

In each case, the Open dialog appears. Select the file you want, and then click **Open**.

In the Open dialog, you can reduce the list of files by selecting the type of file you are looking for. For example, if you choose **Text documents** as the file type, you will only see documents Writer can open (including .odt, .doc, .txt); if you choose **Spreadsheets**, you will see .ods, .xsl, and other files that Calc opens.

You can also open an existing document that is in an OpenDocument format by double-clicking on the file's icon on the desktop or in a file manager such as Windows Explorer.

If you have associated Microsoft Office file formats with OOo, you can also open these files by double-clicking on them.

Note	Under Microsoft Windows you can use either the OOo Open and Save As dialogs or the ones provided by Microsoft Windows. See "Using the Open and Save As dialogs" on page 18.

Saving documents

To save a new document:

1) Choose **File > Save**.
2) When the Save As dialog appears, enter the file name and verify the file type (if applicable).

To save an open document with the current file name, choose **File > Save**. This will overwrite the last saved state of the file.

Password protection

To protect an entire document from being viewable without a password, use the option on the Save As dialog to enter a password. This option is only available for files saved in OpenDocument formats or the older OpenOffice.org 1.x formats.

1) On the Save As dialog, select the checkbox beside **Save with password**, and then click **Save.** You will receive a prompt.
2) Type the same password in the **Password** field and the **Confirm** field, and then click **OK.** If the passwords match, the document is saved password protected. If the passwords do not match, you receive the prompt to enter the password again.

Enter Password

			OK
Password			Cancel
Confirm			Help

Note　Passwords must contain a minimum of 5 characters. Until you have entered 5 characters, the **OK** button remains inactive.

OOo uses a very strong encryption mechanism which makes it almost impossible to recover the contents of a document in case you lose the password.

Saving a document automatically

You can choose to have OpenOffice.org save files for you automatically. Automatic saving, like manual saving, overwrites the last saved state of the file. To set up automatic file saving:

1) Choose **Tools > Options > Load/Save > General**.
2) Mark **Save AutoRecovery information every**, and set the time interval.

Renaming and deleting files

You can rename or delete files within the OOo dialogs, just as you can in your usual file manager. However, you cannot copy or paste files within the dialogs.

Using the Open and Save As dialogs

You can choose whether to use the OpenOffice.org Open and Save As dialogs or the ones provided by your operating system. To view or change which type of dialog OpenOffice.org uses:

1) Choose **Tools > Options > OpenOffice.org > General**.
2) Select the **Use OpenOffice.org dialogs** checkbox.

This section discusses the OpenOffice.org Open and Save As dialogs. See Figure 7 for an example of the Save As dialog; the Open dialog is similar.

The three buttons in the top right of the OOo Open and Save As dialogs are, from left to right:

- Go **Up One Level** in the folder (directory) hierarchy. This is a long-click button if you want to go up higher than just one level.
- **Create New Folder**.
- **View Menu**.

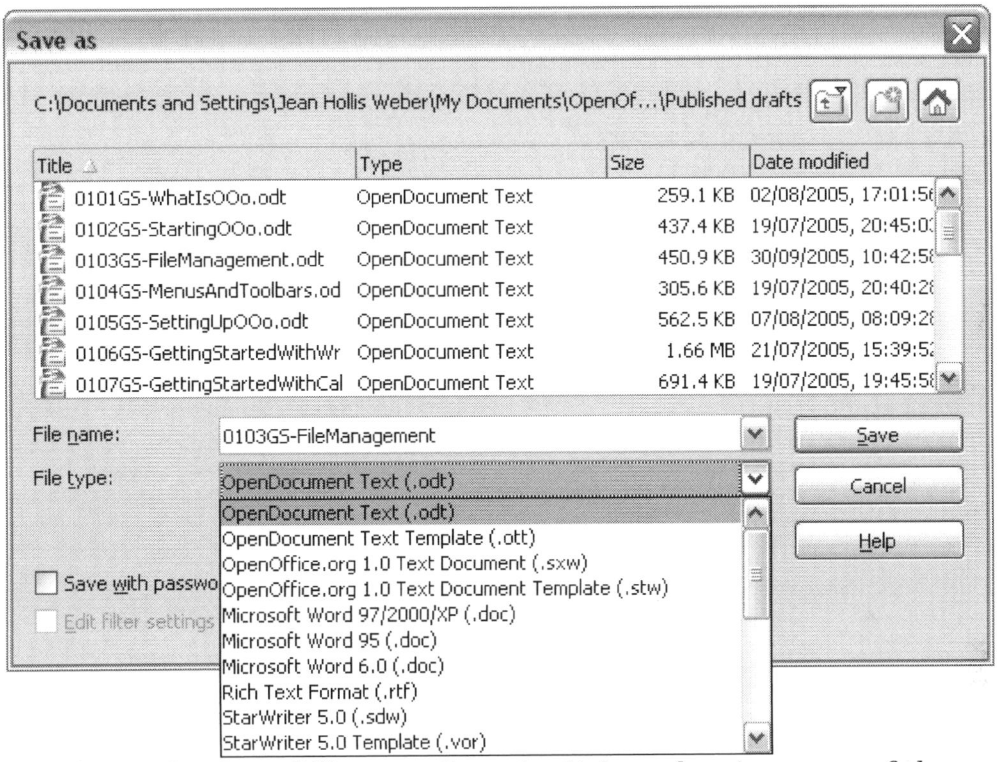

Figure 7: The OpenOffice.org Save As dialog, showing some of the Save formats

For OpenOffice.org documents that have been saved with more than one version, use the version drop-down to select which version you wish to open in read-only mode. For Microsoft Office documents, only the current version can be opened.

Use the **File type** field to specify the type of file to be opened or the format of the file to be saved.

The **Read-only** checkbox opens the file for reading and printing only. Consequently, most of the toolbars disappear, and most menu options are disabled. An **Edit File** button is displayed on the Standard toolbar to open the file for editing.

It is possible to open files from the Web using URLs.

Using the Navigator

The Navigator displays all objects contained in a document, collected into categories. For example, in Writer it displays Headings, Tables, Text frames, Notes, Graphics, Bookmarks, and other items (see Figure 8.

Figure 8: The Navigator in Writer

In Calc it shows Sheets, Range Names, Database Ranges, Graphics, Drawing Objects, and other items. In Impress and Draw it shows Slides, Pictures, and other items. Click the + sign by any of the categories to display the list of objects in that category.

To open the Navigator, click its icon on the Standard toolbar, or press *F5*, or choose **Edit > Navigator** on the main menu bar. You can dock the Navigator to either side of the main OOo window or leave it floating (see "Docking/floating windows and toolbars" on page 14).

To hide the list of categories and show only the toolbars at the top,

click the **List Box On/Off** icon . Click this icon again to show the list box.

The Navigator provides several convenient ways to move around a document and find items in it:

- When a category is showing the list of objects in it, double-click on an object to jump directly to that object's location in the document. Objects are much easier to find if you have given them names when creating them, instead of keeping OOo's default graphics1, graphics2, Table1, Table2, and so on—which may not correspond to the position of the object in the document.

   If you only want to see the content in a certain category, highlight the category and click the **Content View** icon. Until you click the icon again, only the objects of that category will be displayed.

- Click the 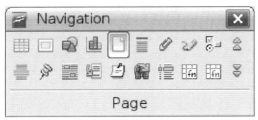 icon (second from the left at the top of the Navigator) to display the Navigation toolbar (Figure 9). Here you can pick one of the categories and use the **Previous** and **Next** icons to move from one item to the next. This is particularly helpful for finding items like bookmarks and indexes, which can be difficult to see. The names of the icons (shown in the tooltips) change to match the selected category; for example, **Next Graphic** or **Next Bookmark**.

Figure 9: Navigation toolbar

- To jump to a specific page in the document, type its page number in the box at the top of the Navigator.

A bit of experimentation with the other icons will demonstrate their functions. Some component-specific uses are described in the chapters on Writer and the other components.

Closing a document

To close a document, click **File > Close**.

You can also close a document by clicking on the **Close** icon on the document window. This button looks like the red X shown in Figure 10.

If more than one OOo window is open, each window looks like the sample shown on the left in Figure 10. Closing this window leaves the other OOo windows open.

If only one OOo window is open, it looks like the sample shown on the right in Figure 10. Notice the small black X below the large red X. Clicking the small X closes the document but leaves OOo open. Clicking the large red X closes OOo completely.

Figure 10. Close icons

If the document has not been saved since the last change, a message box is displayed. Choose whether to save or discard your changes.

- **Save**: The document is saved and then closed.

- **Discard**: The document is closed, and all modifications since the last save are lost.

- **Cancel**: Nothing happens, and you return to the document.

Caution

Not saving your document could result in the loss of recently made changes, or worse still, your entire file.

Closing OpenOffice.org

To close OOo completely, click **File > Exit,** or close the last open document as described in "Closing a document" on page 21.

If all the documents have been saved, OOo closes immediately. If any documents have been modified but not saved, a warning message appears. Follow the procedure in "Closing a document" to save or discard your changes.

Chapter *2*
Setting up OpenOffice.org

Choosing options to suit the way you work

Choosing options for all of OOo

This section covers some of the settings that apply to all the components of OpenOffice.org. For information on settings not discussed here, see the online help.

Click **Tools > Options**. The list in the left-hand box varies depending on which component of OOo is open. The illustrations in this chapter show the list as it appears when a Writer document is open.

Click the + sign to the left of *OpenOffice.org* in the left-hand section of the Options – OpenOffice.org dialog. A list of subsections drops down. Selecting an item of the subsection causes the right-hand side of the dialog to display the relevant options.

Figure 11: OpenOffice.org Options

Note	The **Back** button has the same effect on all pages of the Options dialog. It resets the options to the values that were in place when you opened OpenOffice.org.

User Data options

Because OOo's revision features mark your changes and comments with the name or initials stored in User Data, you will want to ensure that your name and initials appear there.

In the Options dialog, click **OpenOffice.org > User Data**.

Fill in the form (shown in Figure 12), or amend or delete any existing incorrect information.

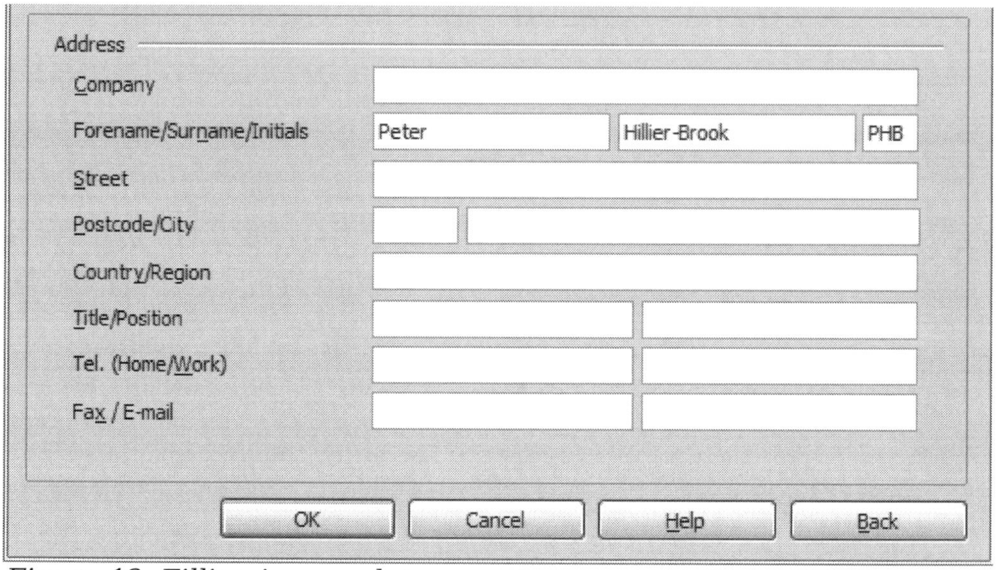

Figure 12: Filling in user data

General options

In the Options dialog, click **OpenOffice.org > General**. The options on this page are described below.

Help - Tips

When *Help Tips* are active, one or two words will appear when you hold the cursor over an icon or field on the main OOo window, without clicking.

Help - Extended tips

When *Extended tips* are active, a brief description of the function of a particular icon or menu command or a field on a dialog appears when you hold the cursor over that item.

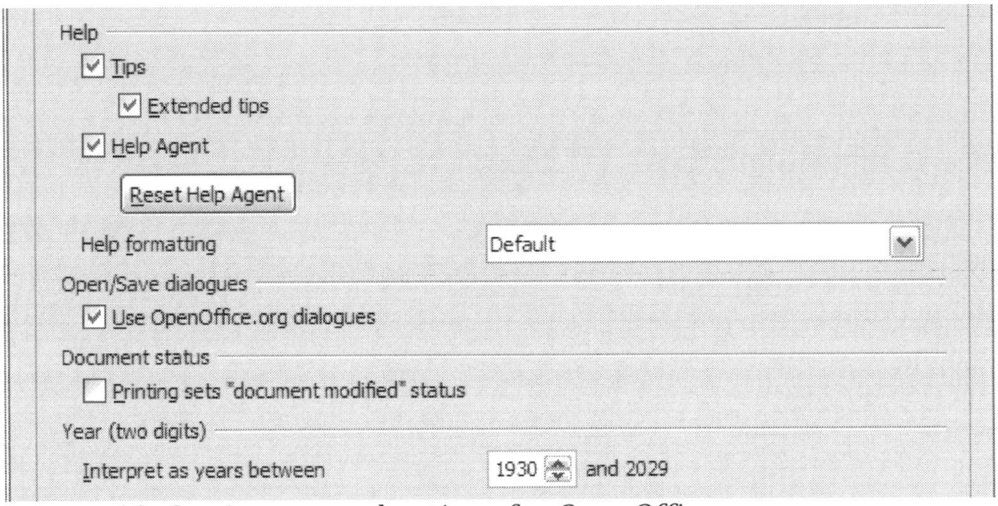

Figure 13: Setting general options for OpenOffice.org

Help Agent

To turn off the *Help Agent* (similar to Microsoft's Office Assistant), deselect this option. To restore the default Help Agent behavior, click **Reset Help Agent**.

Help formatting

High contrast is an operating system setting that changes the system color scheme to improve readability. To display Help in high contrast (if your computer's operating system supports this), choose one of the high-contrast style sheets from the pull-down list. For Windows XP, the high-contrast style options are as described below.

High-contrast style	Visual effect
Default	Black text on white background
High Contrast #1	Yellow text on black background
High Contrast #2	Green text on black background
High Contrast Black	White text on black background
High Contrast White	Black text on white background

Open/Save dialogs

To use the standard Open and Save dialogs for your operating system, deselect the **Use OpenOffice.org dialogs** option. When this option is selected, the Open and Save dialogs supplied with OpenOffice.org will be used. See Chapter 1 (Introducing OpenOffice.org) for more about the OOo Open and Save dialogs.

Document status

Choose whether printing a document counts as changing the document. If this option is selected, then the next time you close the document after printing, the print date is recorded in the document properties as a change and you will be prompted to save the document again, even if you did not make any other changes.

Year (two digits)

Specifies how two-digit years are interpreted. For example, if the two-digit year is set to 1930, and you enter a date of 1/1/30 or later into your document, the date is interpreted as 1/1/1930 or later. An "earlier" date is interpreted as being in the following century; that is, 1/1/20 is interpreted as 1/1/2020.

Memory options

In the Options dialog, click **OpenOffice.org > Memory**. Some considerations:

- More memory can make OpenOffice.org faster and more convenient (for example, more undo steps require more memory); but the trade-off is less memory available for other applications and you could run out of memory altogether.

- To load the Quickstarter (an icon on the desktop or in the system tray) when you start your computer, select the option near the bottom of the dialog. This makes OpenOffice.org start faster; the trade-off is OOo uses some memory even when not being used. This option (called **Enable systray quickstarter**) is not available on all operating systems.

Undo		
Number of steps	100	
Graphics cache		
Use for OpenOffice.org	9	MB
Memory per object	2.4	MB
Remove from memory after	00:10	hh:mm
Cache for inserted objects		
Number of objects	20	
OpenOffice.org Quickstarter		
☑ Load OpenOffice.org during system start-up		

Figure 14: Choosing Memory options for the OOo applications

View options

The choices of View options affect the way the document window looks and behaves.

In the Options dialog, click **OpenOffice.org > View**. On the page displayed (Figure 15), set the options to suit your personal preferences. Some options are described below.

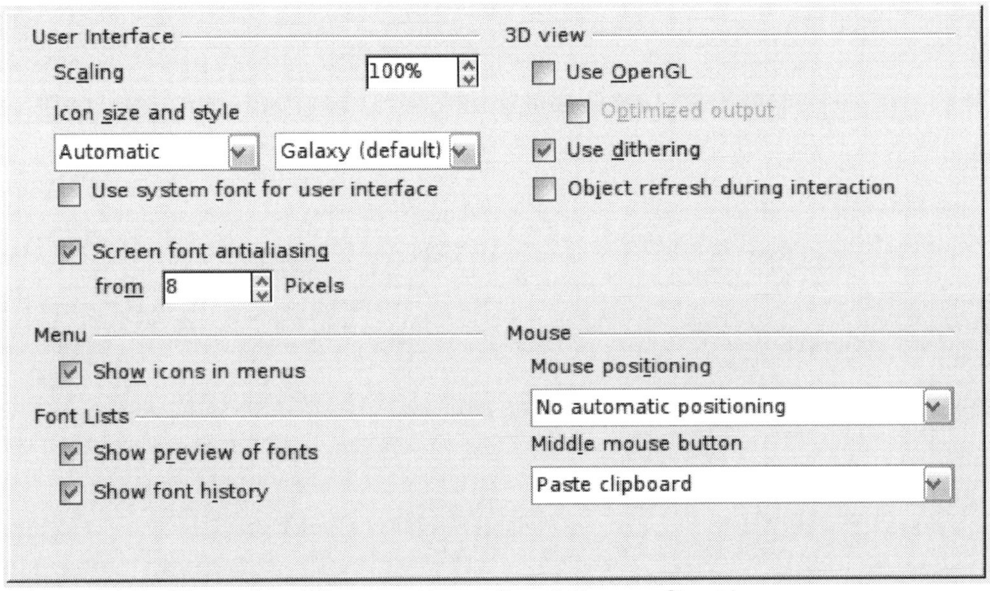

Figure 15: Choosing View options for OOo applications

User Interface – Scaling

If the text in the help files or on the menus of the OOo user interface is too small or too large, you can change it by specifying a scaling factor. Sometimes a change here can have unexpected results, depending on the screen fonts available on your system. However, it does not affect the actual font size of the text in your documents.

User Interface – Icon size and style

The first box specifies the display size of toolbar icons (Automatic, Small, or Large). The Automatic icon size option uses the setting for your operating system. The second box specifies the icon set (theme); here the Automatic option uses an icon set compatible with your operating system and choice of desktop: for example, KDE or Gnome on Linux.

User Interface – Use system font for user interface

If you prefer to use the system font (the default font for your computer and operating system), instead of the font provided by OOo, for the user interface, select this option.

User interface – Screen font antialiasing

(Not available in Windows.) Select this option to smooth the screen appearance of text. Enter the smallest font size to apply antialiasing.

Menu – icons in menus

Select this option if you want icons as well as words to be visible in menus.

Font Lists - Show preview of fonts

When you select this option, the font list looks like Figure 16, Left, with the font names shown as an example of the font; with the option deselected, the font list shows only the font names, not their formatting (Figure 16, Right). The fonts you will see listed are those that are installed on your system.

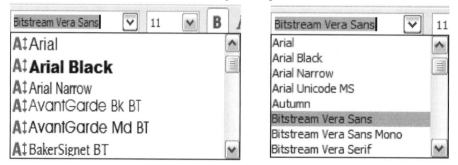

Figure 16. Font list (Left) With preview; (Right) Without preview

Font Lists - Show font history

When you select this option, the last five fonts you have assigned to the current document are displayed at the top of the font list.

3D view – Use OpenGL

Specifies that all 3D graphics from Draw and Impress will be displayed in your system using OpenGL-capable hardware. If your system does not have OpenGL-capable hardware, this setting will be ignored.

3D view – Use OpenGL – Optimized output

Select this option for optimized OpenGL output. Disable the optimization in case of graphical errors of 3D output.

3D view – Use dithering

The **Use dithering** option uses dithering to display additional colors when the computer's graphics system offers less than the optimal 16 million (24-bit) colors. Dithering creates the illusion of new colors and shades by varying the pattern of color pixels. Varying the patterns of black and white dots, for instance, produces different shades of gray.

Note	Internally, 3-D graphics are always created with 16 million colors (24-bit color depth) and dithering can be used to compensate when fewer actual colors are available. Without dithering, several bits of color information would be omitted, leading to significantly reduced image quality.

3D view – Object refresh during interaction

Specifies that if you rotate or move a 3-D object, the full display is rotated or moved and not a grid frame.

Tip	Press *Shift+Control+R* to restore or refresh the view of the current document.

Mouse positioning

Specifies if and how the mouse pointer will be positioned in newly opened dialogs.

Middle mouse button

Defines the function of the middle mouse button.

- **Automatic scrolling** – dragging while pressing the middle mouse button shifts the view.

- **Paste clipboard** – pressing the middle mouse button inserts the contents of the "Selection clipboard" at the cursor position.

   The "Selection clipboard" is independent of the normal clipboard that you use by **Edit > Copy/Cut/Paste** or their respective keyboard shortcuts. Clipboard and the "Selection clipboard" can contain different contents at the same time.

Function	*Clipboard*	*Selection clipboard*
Copy content	**Edit > Copy** *Control+C*	Select text, table, or object.
Paste content	**Edit > Paste** *Control+V* pastes at the cursor position.	Clicking the middle mouse button pastes at the mouse pointer position.
Pasting into another document	No effect on the clipboard contents.	The last marked selection is the content of the selection clipboard.

Print options

Set the print options to suit your default printer and your most common printing method.

In the Options dialog, click **OpenOffice.org > Print**.

In the *Printer warnings* section near the bottom of the page (Figure 17). Here you can choose whether to be warned if the paper size or orientation specified in your document does not match the paper size or orientation available for your printer. Having these warnings turned on can be quite helpful, particularly if you work with documents produced by people in other countries where the standard paper size is different from yours.

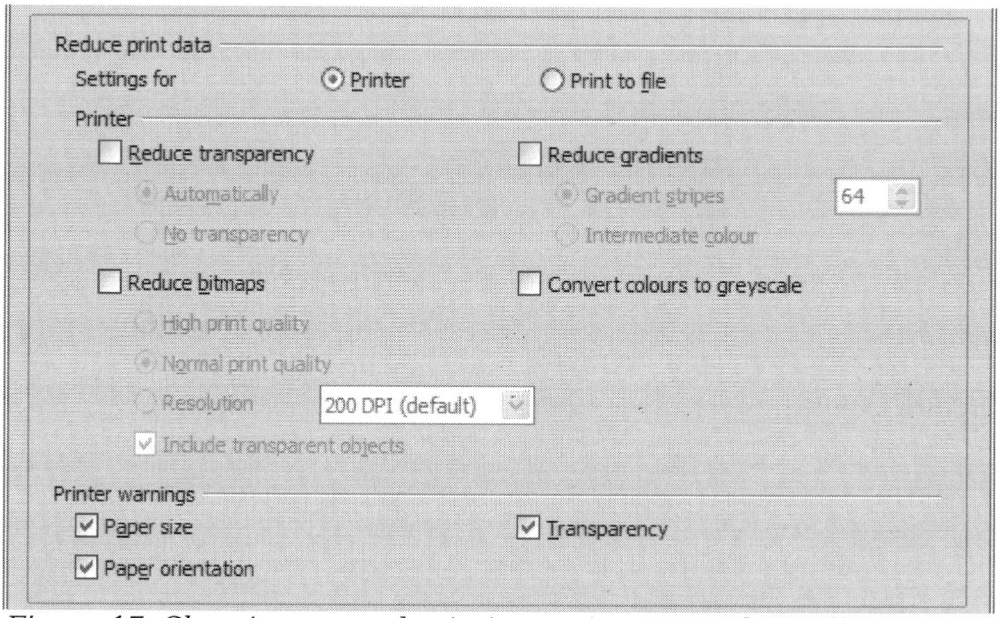

Reduce print data		
Settings for	⦿ Printer	○ Print to file
Printer		
☐ Reduce transparency		☐ Reduce gradients
⦿ Automatically		⦿ Gradient stripes 64
○ No transparency		○ Intermediate colour
☐ Reduce bitmaps		☐ Convert colours to greyscale
○ High print quality		
⦿ Normal print quality		
○ Resolution 200 DPI (default)		
☑ Include transparent objects		
Printer warnings		
☑ Paper size		☑ Transparency
☑ Paper orientation		

Figure 17: Choosing general printing options to apply to all OOo components

---

Tip	If your printouts are coming out incorrectly placed on the page or chopped off at the top, bottom, or sides, or the printer is refusing to print, the most likely cause is page size incompatibility.

Path options

You can change the location of files associated with, or used by, OpenOffice.org to suit your working situation. In a Windows system, for example, you might want to store documents by default somewhere other than My Documents.

In the Options dialog, click **OpenOffice.org > Paths**.

To make changes, select an item in the list shown in Figure 18 and click **Edit**. On the Select Paths dialog (not shown), add or delete folders as required, and then click **OK** to return to the Options dialog. Note that some items have at least two paths listed: one to a shared folder (which might be on a network) and one to a user-specific folder (normally on the user's personal computer).

Tip	You can use the entries in the OpenOffice.org – Paths dialog to compile a list of files, such as those containing AutoText, that you need to back up or copy to another computer.

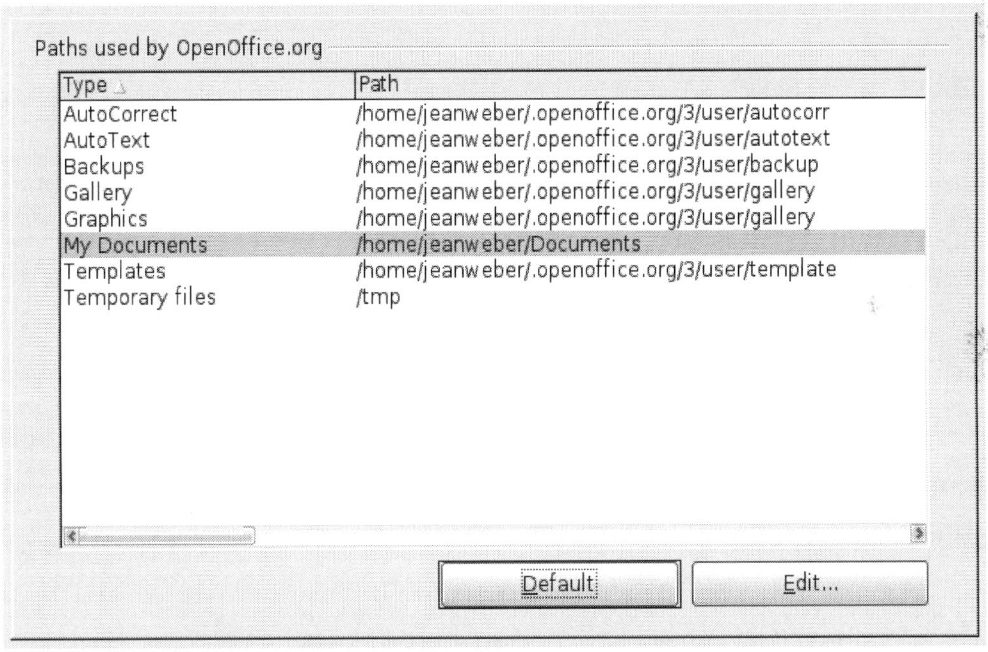

Figure 18: Viewing the paths of files used by OpenOffice.org

Color options

On the *OpenOffice.org – Colors* page (Figure 19), you can specify colors to use in OOo documents. You can select a color from a color table, edit an existing color, or define new colors. These colors will then be available in color selection palettes in OOo.

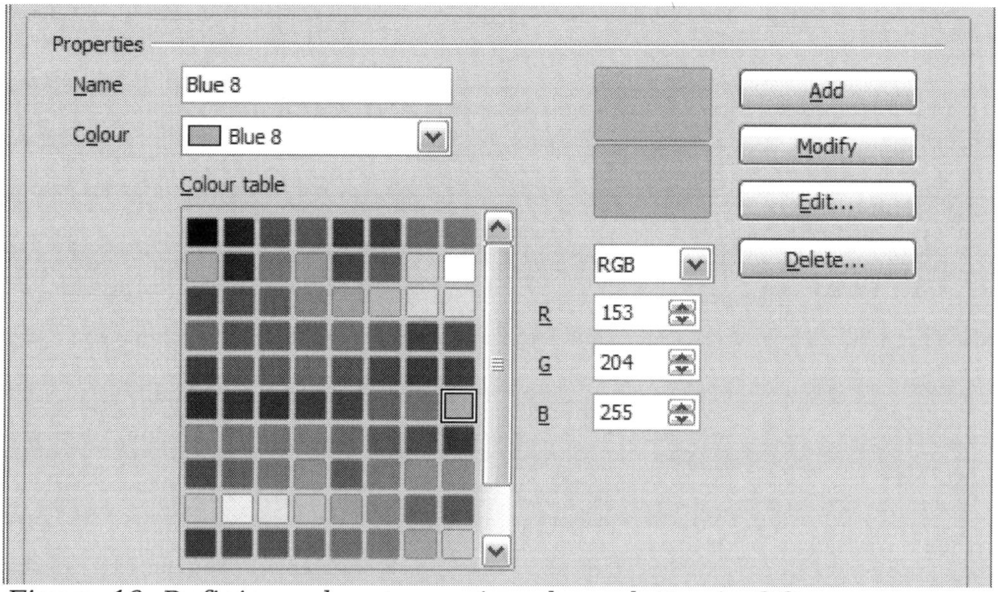

Figure 19: Defining colors to use in color palettes in OOo

Font options

You can define replacements for any fonts that might appear in your documents. If you receive from someone else a document containing fonts that you do not have on your system, OpenOffice.org will substitute fonts for those it does not find. You might prefer to specify a different font from the one the program chooses.

On the *OpenOffice.org > Fonts* page (Figure 20):

- Select the **Apply Replacement Table** option.

- Select or type the name of the font to be replaced in the **Font** box. (If you do not have this font on your system, it will not appear in the drop-down list in this box, so you need to type it in.)

- In the **Replace with** box, select a suitable font from the drop-down list of fonts installed on your computer.

The checkmark to the right of the **Replace with** box turns green. Click on this checkmark. A row of information now appears in the larger box below the input boxes. Select the options under **Always** and **Screen**.

In the bottom section of the page, you can change the typeface and size of the font used to display source code such as HTML and Basic (in macros).

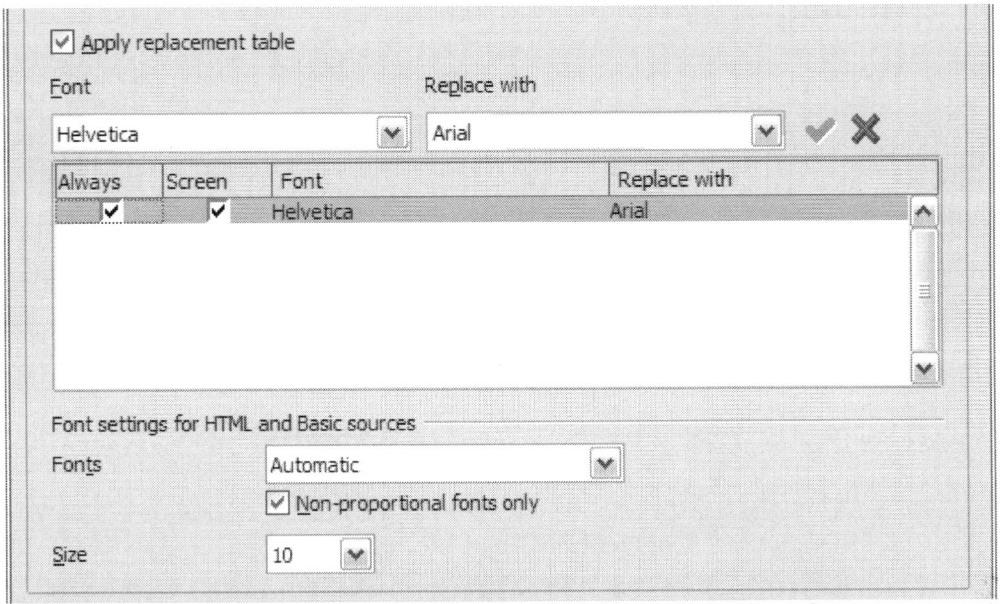

Figure 20: Defining a font to be substituted for another font

Security options

Use the *OpenOffice.org – Security* page (Figure 21) to choose security options for saving documents and for opening documents that contain macros.

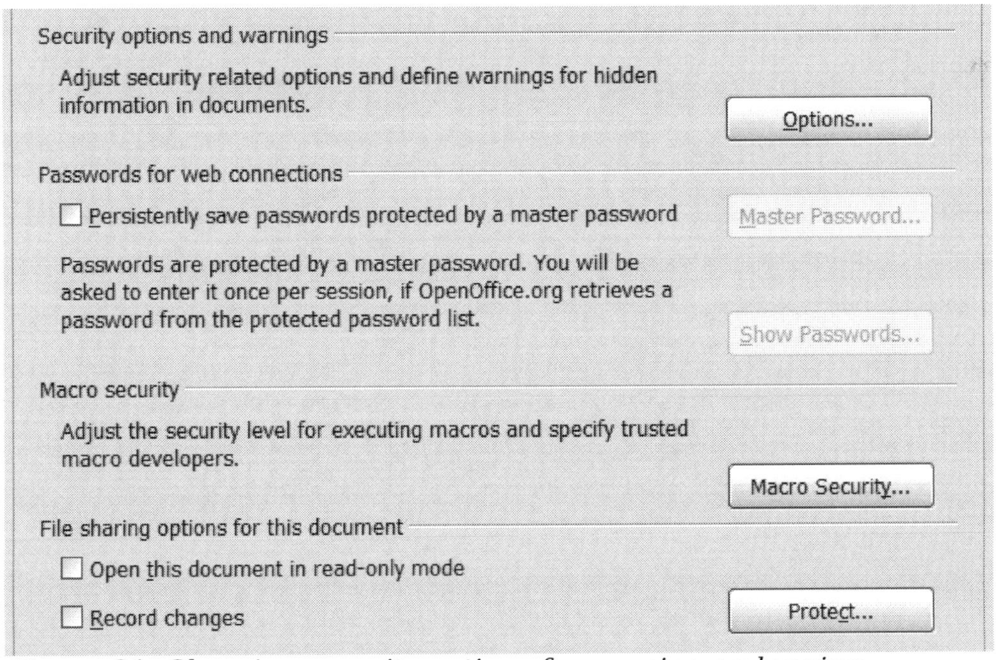

Figure 21: Choosing security options for opening and saving documents

Security options and warnings

If you record changes, save multiple versions, or include hidden information or notes in your documents, and you do not want some of the recipients to see that information, you can set warnings to remind you to remove this information, or you can have OOo remove some information automatically. Note that (unless removed) much of this information is retained in a file whether the file is in OpenOffice.org's default OpenDocument format, or has been saved to other formats, including PDF.

Click the **Options** button to open a separate dialog with specific choices (Figure 22).

Remove personal information on saving. Select this option to always remove user data from the file properties when saving the file. To manually remove personal information from specific documents, deselect this option and then use the **Delete** button under **File > Properties > General**.

Ctrl-click required to follow hyperlinks. In older versions of OOo, clicking on a hyperlink in a document opened the linked document. Now you can choose whether to keep this behavior (by unchecking this box). Many people find creation and editing of documents easier when accidental clicks on links do not activate the links.

The other options on this dialog should be self-explanatory.

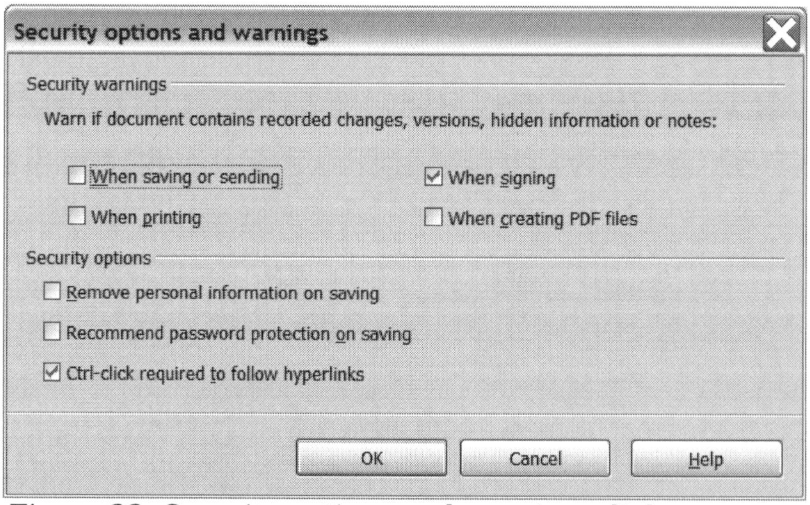

Figure 22: Security options and warnings dialog

Macro security

Click the **Macro Security** button to open the Macro Security dialog (not shown here), where you can adjust the security level for executing macros and specify trusted sources.

File sharing options for this document

Select the **Open this document in read-only mode** option to restrict this document to be opened in read-only mode only. This option protects the document against accidental changes. It is still possible to edit a copy of the document and save that copy with the same name as the original.

Select the **Record changes** option to enable recording changes. This is the same as Edit > Changes > Record. To allow other users of this document to apply changes, but prevent them from disabling change recording, click the **Protect** buton and enter a password.

Appearance options

Writing, editing, and page layout are often easier to do when you can see as much as possible of what is going on in your document. You may wish to make visible such items as text, table, and section boundaries (in Writer documents), page breaks in Calc, and grid lines in Draw or Writer. In addition, you might prefer different colors (from OOo's defaults) for such items as note indicators or field shadings.

On the *OpenOffice.org – Appearance* page (Figure 23), you can specify which items are visible and the colors used to display various items.

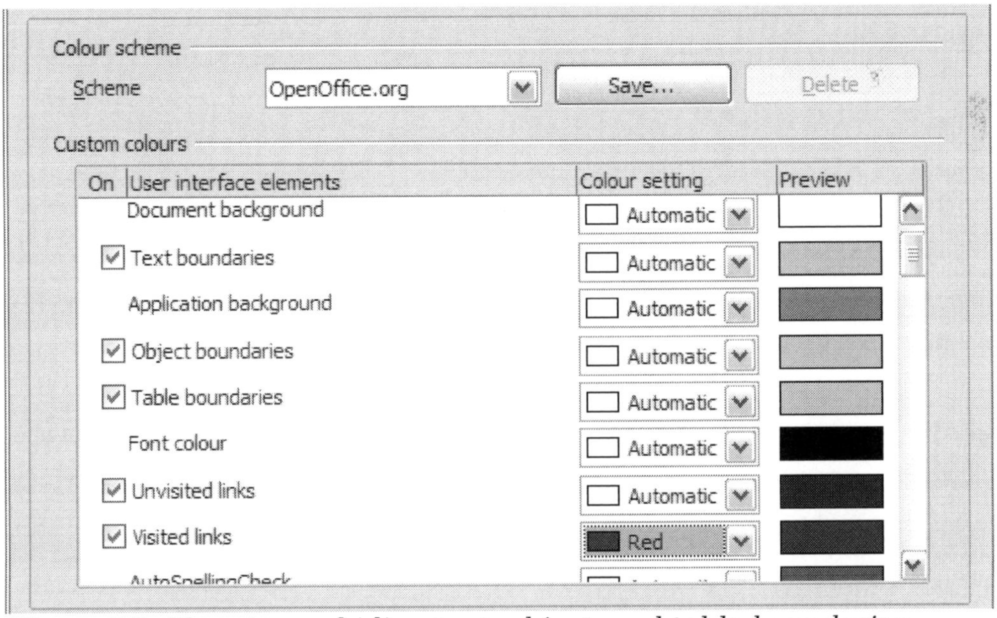

Figure 23: Showing or hiding text, object, and table boundaries

- To show or hide items such as text boundaries, select or deselect the options next to the names of the items.

- To change the default colors for items, click the down-arrow in the *Color Setting* column by the name of the item and select a color from the pop-up box.

- To save your color changes as a color scheme, click **Save,** type a name in the *Scheme* box; then click **OK**.

Accessibility options

Accessibility options include whether to allow animated graphics or text, how long help tips remain showing, some options for high contrast display, and a way to change the font for the user interface of the OpenOffice.org program (see Figure 24).

Accessibility support relies on Sun Microsystems Java technology for communications with assistive technology tools. See "Java options" below. The *Support assistive technology tools* option is not shown on all OOo installations. See *Assistive Tools in OpenOffice.org* in the Help for other requirements and information.

Select or deselect the options as required.

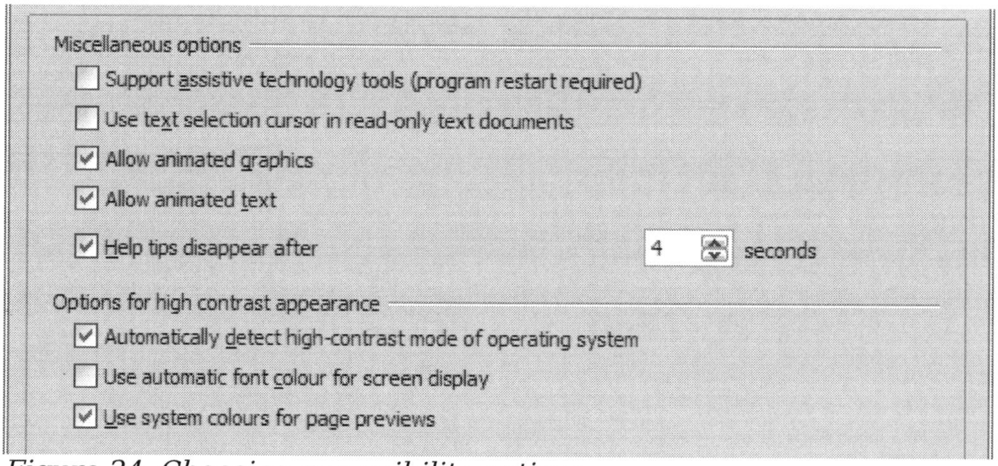

Figure 24: Choosing accessibility options

Java options

If you install or update a Java Runtime Environment (JRE) after you install OpenOffice.org, or if you have more than one JRE installed on your computer, you can use the *OpenOffice.org – Java options* page (Figure 25) to choose the JRE for OOo to use.

If you are a system administrator, programmer, or other person who customizes JRE installations, you can use the Parameters and Class Path pages (reached from the Java page) to specify this information.

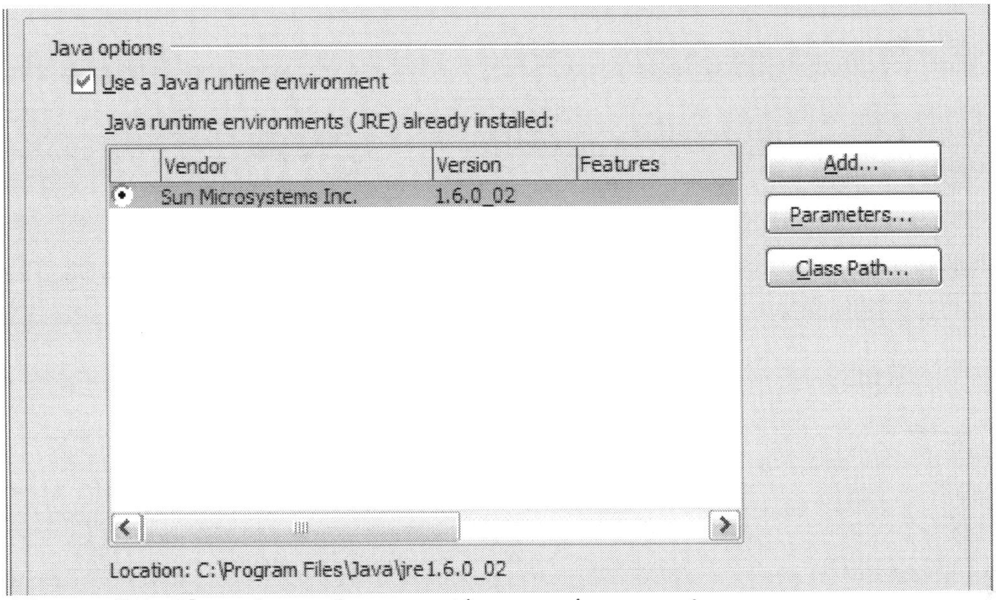

Figure 25: Choosing a Java runtime environment

If you do not see anything listed in the middle of the page, wait a few minutes while OOo searches for JREs on the hard disk.

If OOo finds one or more JREs, it will display them there. You can then select the **Use a Java runtime environment** option and (if necessary) choose one of the JREs listed.

Online Update options

On the *OpenOffice.org – Online Update* page (Figure 26), you can choose whether and how often to have OOo check the OOo website for program updates. If the **Check for updates automatically** option is selected, an icon appears at the right-hand end of the menu bar when an update is available. Click this icon to open a dialog where you can choose to download the update.

If the **Download updates automatically** option is selected, the download starts when you click the icon. To change the download destination, click the **Change** button and select the required folder in the file browser window.

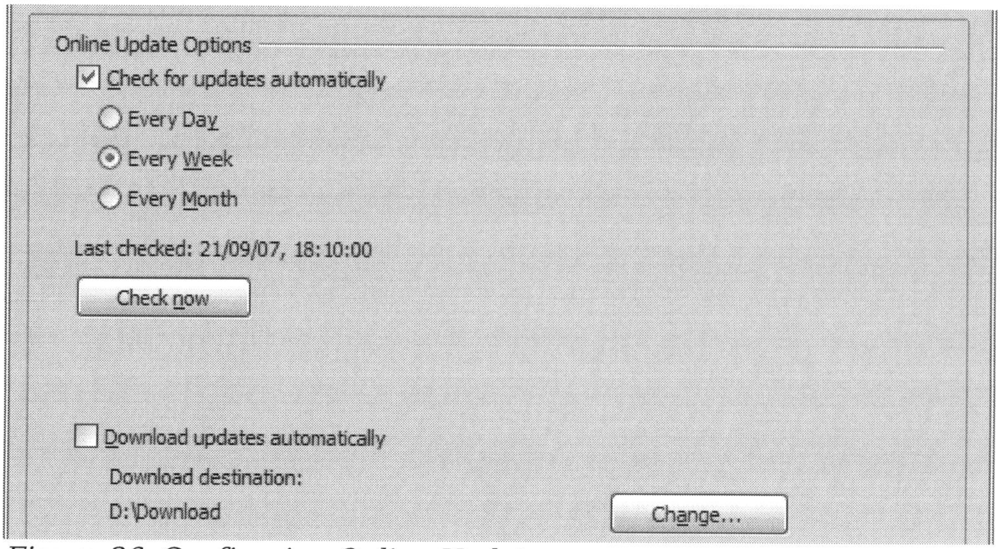

Figure 26: Configuring Online Update

Choosing options for loading and saving documents

You can set the Load/Save options to suit the way you work.

Figure 27: Load/Save options

General Load/Save options

If the Options dialog is not already open, click **Tools > Options**. Click the + sign to the left of **Load/Save**. Choose **Load/Save > General**.

Most of the choices on the *Load/Save – General* page (Figure 28) are familiar to users of other office suites. Some items of interest are described below.

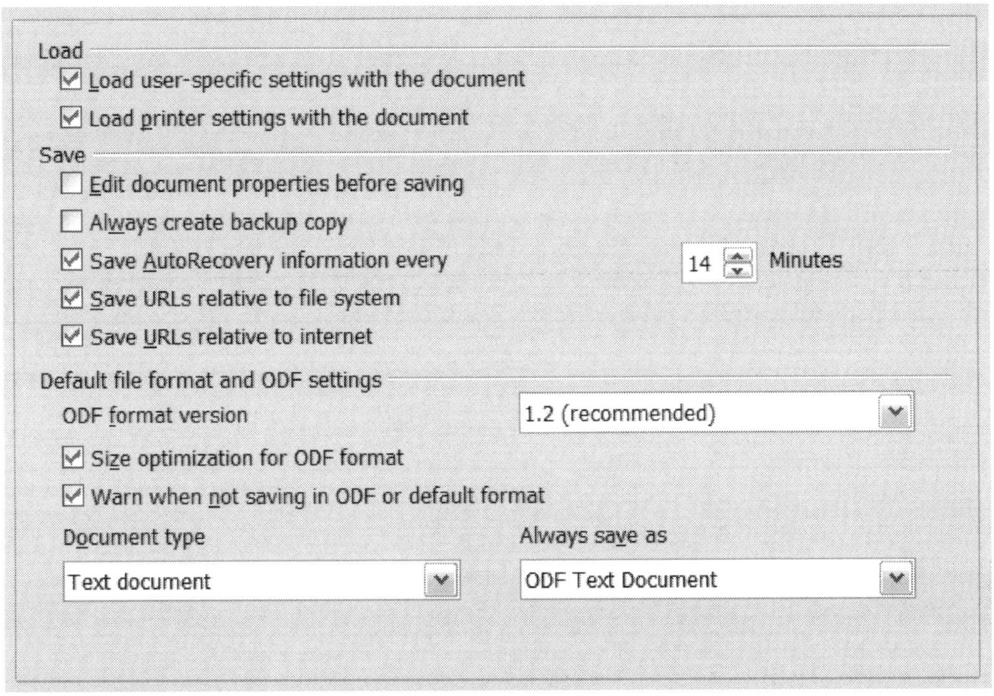

Figure 28. Choosing Load and Save options

Load user-specific settings with the document

When you save a document, certain settings are saved with it. For example, your choice (in the options for OOo Writer) of how to update links is affected by the **Load user-specific settings** option. Some settings (printer name, data source linked to the document) are always loaded with a document, whether or not this option is selected.

If you select this option, these document settings are overruled by the user-specific settings of the person who opens it. If you deselect this option, the user's personal settings do not overrule the settings in the document.

Load printer settings with the document

If this option is **not** selected, the printer settings that are stored with the document are ignored when you print it using the **Print File Directly** icon. The default printer in your system will be used instead.

Edit document properties before saving

If you select this option, the Document Properties dialog pops up to prompt you to enter relevant information the first time you save a new document (or whenever you use **Save As**).

Save AutoRecovery information every

Note that AutoRecovery in OpenOffice.org overwrites the original file. If you have also chosen **Always create backup copy**, the original file then overwrites the backup copy. If you have this set, recovering your document after a system crash will be easier; but recovering an earlier version of the document may be harder.

Save URLs relative to file system / internet

Relative addressing to a file system is only possible if the source document and the referenced document are both on the same drive. A relative address always starts from the directory in which the current document is located. It is recommended to save relatively if you want to create a directory structure on an Internet server.

Default file format and ODF settings

ODF format version. OpenOffice.org by default saves documents in OpenDocument Format (ODF) version 1.2. While this allows for improved functionality, there may be backwards compatibility issues. When a file saved in ODF 1.2 is opened in an earlier version of OpenOffice.org (using ODF 1.0/1.1), some of the advanced features may be lost. Two notable examples are cross-references to headings and the formatting of numbered lists. If you plan to share documents with people who are still using older versions of OpenOffice.org, it is recommended that you save the document using ODF version 1.0/1.1.

Size optimization for ODF format. OpenOffice.org documents are XML files. When you select this option, OOo writes the XML data without indents and line breaks. If you want to be able to read the XML files in a text editor in a structured form, deselect this option.

Document type. If you routinely share documents with users of Microsoft Word, you might want to change the **Always save as** attribute for text documents to one of the Word formats.

VBA Properties Load/Save options

On the *Load/Save – VBA Properties* page (Figure 29), you can choose whether to keep any macros in MSOffice documents that are opened in OOo.

- If you choose **Save original Basic code**, the macros will not work in OOo but are retained if you save the file into Microsoft Office format.

- If you choose **Load Basic code to edit**, the changed code is saved in an OOo document but is not retained if you save into an MSOffice format.

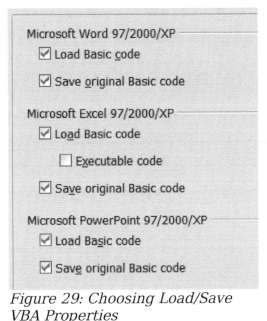

*Figure 29: Choosing Load/Save
VBA Properties*

- If you are importing a Microsoft Excel file containing VBA code, you can select the option **Executable code**. Whereas normally the code is preserved but rendered inactive (if you inspect it with the StarBasic IDE you will notice that it is all commented), with this option the code is ready to be executed.

Microsoft Office Load/Save options

On the *Load/Save – Microsoft Office* page (Figure 30), you can choose what to do when importing and exporting Microsoft Office OLE objects (linked or embedded objects or documents such as spreadsheets or equations).

Select the [L] options to convert Microsoft OLE objects into the corresponding OpenOffice.org OLE objects when a Microsoft document is loaded into OOo (mnemonic: "L" for "load").

Select the [S] options to convert OpenOffice.org OLE objects into the corresponding Microsoft OLE objects when a document is saved in a Microsoft format (mnemonic: "S" for "save").

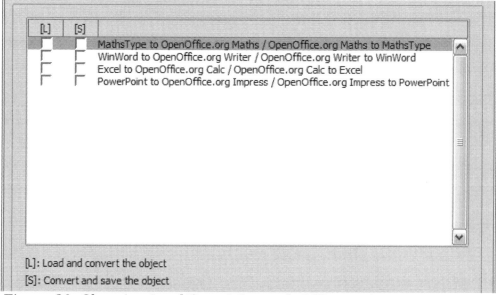

Figure 30: Choosing Load/Save Microsoft Office options

HTML compatibility Load/Save options

Choices made on the *Load/Save – HTML Compatibility* page (Figure 31) affect HTML pages imported into OpenOffice.org and those exported from OOo. See *HTML documents; importing/exporting* in the Help for more information.

Font sizes			Import
Size 1	7	⬍	☐ Use 'English (USA)' locale for numbers
Size 2	10	⬍	☐ Import unknown HTML tags as fields
Size 3	12	⬍	☐ Ignore font settings
Size 4	14	⬍	Export
Size 5	18	⬍	Netscape Navigator ⌄
Size 6	24	⬍	☐ OpenOffice.org Basic
Size 7	36	⬍	☑ Display warning
			☐ Print layout
			☑ Copy local graphics to Internet
			Character set Western Europe (Windows-12! ⌄

Figure 31. Choosing HTML compatibility options

Font sizes

Use these fields to define the respective font sizes for the HTML <font size=1> to <font size=7> tags, if they are used in the HTML pages. (Many pages no longer use these tags.)

Import - Use 'English (USA)' locale for numbers

When importing numbers from an HTML page, the decimal and thousands separator characters differ according to the locale of the HTML page. The clipboard, however, contains no information about the locale. If this option is **not** selected, numbers will be interpreted according to the **Language - Locale setting** in **Tools > Options > Language Settings > Languages** (see page 44). If this option is selected, numbers will be interpreted as for the English (USA) locale.

Import - Import unknown HTML tags as fields

Select this option if you want tags that are not recognized by OOo to be imported as fields. For an opening tag, an HTML_ON field will be created with the value of the tag name. For a closing tag, an HTML_OFF will be created. These fields will be converted to tags in the HTML export.

Import - Ignore font settings

Select this option to have OOo ignore all font settings when importing. The fonts that were defined in the HTML Page Style will be used.

Export

To optimize the HTML export, select a browser or HTML standard from the **Export** box. If OpenOffice.org Writer is selected, specific OpenOffice.org Writer instructions are exported.

Export - OpenOffice.org Basic

Select this option to include OOo Basic macros (scripts) when exporting to HTML format. You must activate this option *before* you create the OpenOffice.org Basic macro; otherwise the script will not be inserted. OpenOffice.org Basic macros must be located in the header of the HTML document. Once you have created the macro in the OpenOffice.org Basic IDE, it appears in the source text of the HTML document in the header.

If you want the macro to run automatically when the HTML document is opened, choose **Tools > Customize > Events**. See Chapter 13 (Getting Started with Macros) for more information.

Export - Display warning

When the **OpenOffice.org Basic** option (see above) is *not* selected, the **Display warning** option becomes available. If the **Display warning** option is selected, then when exporting to

HTML a warning is shown that OpenOffice.org Basic macros will be lost.

Export - Print layout
Select this option to export the print layout of the current document as well. The HTML filter supports CSS2 (Cascading Style Sheets Level 2) for printing documents. These capabilities are only effective if print layout export is activated.

Export - Copy local graphics to Internet
Select this option to automatically upload the embedded pictures to the Internet server when uploading using FTP.

Export - Character set
Select the appropriate character set for the export.

Choosing language settings

You may need to do several things to set the language settings to what you want:

- Install the required dictionaries
- Change some locale and language settings
- Choose spelling options

Install the required dictionaries

OOo3 automatically installs several dictionaries with the program. To add other dictionaries, use **Tools > Language > More Dictionaries Online**. OOo will open your default web browser to a page containing links to additional dictionaries that you can install. Follow the prompts to install them.

Change locale and language settings

You can change some details of the locale and language settings that OOo uses for all documents, or for specific documents.

In the Options dialog, click **Language Settings > Languages**.

Figure 32: Language Setting Options

On the right-hand side of the *Language Settings – Languages* page (Figure 33), change the *User interface, Locale setting, Default currency*, and *Default languages for documents* as required. In the example, English (UK) has been chosen for all the appropriate settings.

If you want the language (dictionary) setting to apply to the current document only, instead of being the default for all new documents, select the option labelled *For the current document only*.

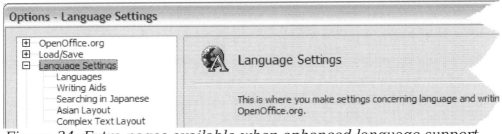

Figure 33: Choosing language options

If necessary, select the options to enable support for Asian languages (Chinese, Japanese, Korean) and support for CTL (complex text layout) languages such as Hindi, Thai, Hebrew, and Arabic. If you choose either of these options, the next time you open this dialog, you will see some extra choices under Language Settings, as shown in Figure 34. These choices (*Searching in Japanese, Asian Layout*, and *Complex Text Layout*) are not discussed here.

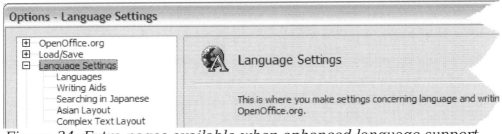

Figure 34: Extra pages available when enhanced language support options are selected

Choose spelling options

To choose the options for checking spelling, click **Language Settings > Writing Aids**. In the *Options* section of the page (Figure 35), choose the settings that are useful for you. Some considerations:

- If you do not want spelling checked while you type, deselect **Check spelling as you type** and select **Do not mark errors**. (To find the second item, scroll down in the Options list.)

- If you use a custom dictionary that includes words in all upper case and words with numbers (for example, AS/400), select **Check uppercase words** and **Check words with numbers**.

- **Check special regions** includes headers, footers, frames, and tables when checking spelling.

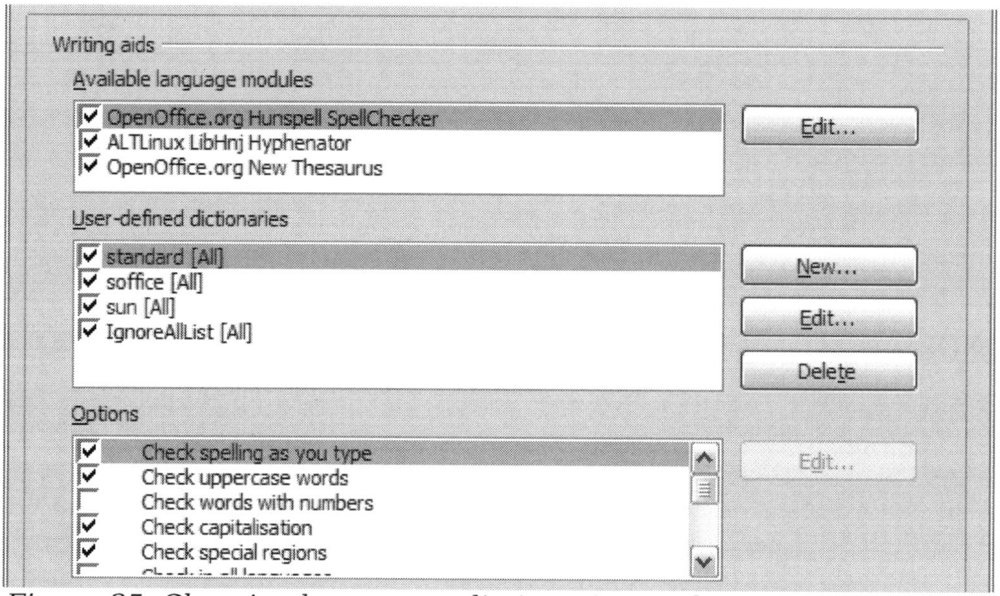

Figure 35: Choosing languages, dictionaries, and options for checking spelling

Here you can also check which user-defined (custom) dictionaries are active by default, and add or remove dictionaries, by clicking the **New** or **Delete** buttons.

Choosing Internet options

Use the Internet Options pages to define search engines and save proxy settings for use with OpenOffice.org.

If you are using a Netscape or Mozilla browser (such as Firefox), you can enable the Mozilla Plug-in so you can open OOo files in your browser, print them, save them, and work with them in other ways.

If you are using a Unix- or Linux-based operating system (including Mac OS X), an additional page of E-mail options is available, where you can specify the e-mail program to use when you send the current document as e-mail (Figure 36). Under Windows the operating system's default e-mail program is always used.

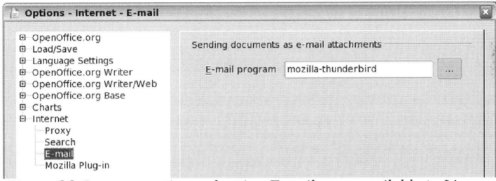

Figure 36: Internet options, showing E-mail page available to Linux users.

Controlling OOo's AutoCorrect functions

Some people find some or all of the items in OOo's AutoCorrect function annoying because they change what you type when you do not want it changed. Many people find some of the AutoCorrect functions quite helpful; if you do, then select the relevant options. But if you find unexplained changes appearing in your document, this is a good place to look to find the cause.

To open the AutoCorrect dialog, click **Tools > AutoCorrect**. (You need to have a document open for this menu item to appear.)

In Writer, this dialog has five tabs, as shown below. In other components of OOo, the dialog has only four tabs.

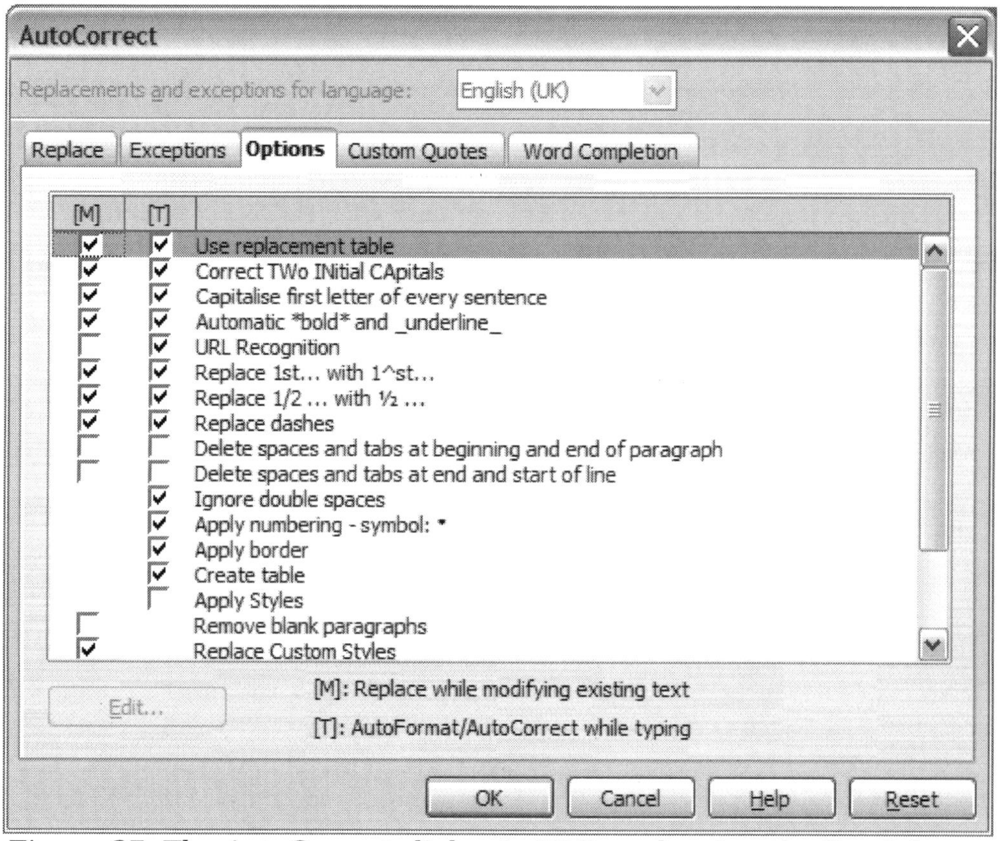

Figure 37: The AutoCorrect dialog in Writer, showing the five tabs and some of the choices

Chapter 3
Using Styles and Templates

What is a template?

A *template* is a model that you use to create other documents. For example, you can create a template for business reports that has your company's logo on the first page. New documents created from this template will all have your company's logo on the first page.

Templates can contain anything that regular documents can contain, such as text, graphics, a set of styles, and user-specific setup information such as measurement units, language, the default printer, and toolbar and menu customization.

All documents in OpenOffice.org (OOo) are based on templates. You can create a specific template for any document type (text, spreadsheet, drawing, presentation). If you do not specify a template when you start a new document, then the document is based on the default template for that type of document. If you have not specified a default template, OOo uses the blank template for that type of document that is installed with OOo. See "Setting a default template" on page 65 for more information.

What are styles?

A *style* is a set of formats that you can apply to selected pages, text, frames, and other elements in your document to quickly change their appearance. When you apply a style, you apply a whole group of formats at the same time.

Many people manually format paragraphs, words, tables, page layouts, and other parts of their documents without paying any attention to styles. They are used to writing documents according to *physical* attributes. For example, you might specify the font family, font size, and any formatting such as bold or italic.

Styles are *logical* attributes. Using styles means that you stop saying "font size 14pt, Times New Roman, bold, centered", and you start saying "Title" because you have defined the "Title" style to have those characteristics. In other words, styles means that you shift the emphasis from what the text (or page, or other element) looks like, to what the text *is*.

Styles help improve consistency in a document. They also make major formatting changes easy. For example, you may decide to change the indentation of all paragraphs, or change the font of all titles. For a long document, this simple task can be prohibitive. Styles make the task easy.

In addition, styles are used by OpenOffice.org for many processes, even if you are not aware of them. For example, Writer relies on heading styles (or other styles you specify) when it compiles a table of contents. Some common examples of style use are given in "Examples of style use" on page 70.

OpenOffice.org supports the following types of styles:

- *Page styles* include margins, headers and footers, borders and backgrounds. In Calc, page styles also include the sequence for printing sheets.

- *Paragraph styles* control all aspects of a paragraph's appearance, such as text alignment, tab stops, line spacing, and borders, and can include character formatting.

- *Character styles* affect selected text within a paragraph, such as the font and size of text, or bold and italic formats.

- *Frame styles* are used to format graphic and text frames, including wrapping type, borders, backgrounds, and columns.

- *Numbering styles* apply similar alignment, numbering or bullet characters, and fonts to numbered or bulleted lists.

- *Cell styles* include fonts, alignment, borders, background, number formats (for example, currency, date, number), and cell protection.

- *Graphics styles* in drawings and presentations include line, area, shadowing, transparency, font, connectors, dimensioning, and other attributes.

- *Presentation styles* include attributes for font, indents, spacing, alignment, and tabs.

Different styles are available in the various components of OOo, as listed in Table 1.

OpenOffice.org comes with many predefined styles. You can use the styles as provided, modify them, or create new styles, as described in this chapter.

Table 1. Styles available in OOo components

Style Type	Writer	Calc	Draw	Impress
Page	√	√		
Paragraph	√			
Character	√			
Frame	√			
Numbering	√			
Cell		√		
Presentation			√	√
Graphics	(included in Frame styles)		√	√

Applying styles

OpenOffice.org provides several ways for you to select styles to apply.

Using the Styles and Formatting window

1) Click the **Styles and Formatting** icon located at the left-hand end of the object bar, or click **Format > Styles and Formatting**, or press *F11*. The Styles and Formatting window shows the types of styles available for the OOo component you are using. Figure 38 shows the window for Writer, with Page Styles visible.

    You can move this window to a convenient position on the screen or dock it to an edge (hold down the *Ctrl* key and drag it by the title bar to where you want it docked).

2) Click on one of the icons at the top left of the Styles and Formatting window to display a list of styles in a particular category.

3) To apply an existing style (except for character styles), position the insertion point in the paragraph, frame, or page, and then

double-click on the name of the style in one of these lists. To apply a character style, select the characters first.

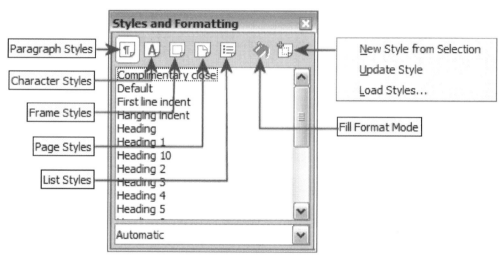

Figure 38: The Styles and Formatting window for Writer, showing paragraph styles.

Using Fill Format mode

Use Fill Format to apply a style to many different areas quickly without having to go back to the Styles and Formatting window and double-click every time. This method is quite useful when you need to format many scattered paragraphs, cells, or other items with the same style.

1) Open the Styles and Formatting window and select the style you want to apply.

2) Click the **Fill Format mode** icon 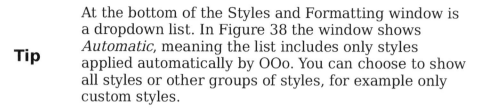.

3) To apply a paragraph, page, or frame style, hover the mouse over the paragraph, page, or frame and click. To apply a character style, hold down the mouse button while selecting the characters, Clicking on a word applies the character style for that word. Repeat step 3 until you made all the changes for that style.

4) To quit Fill Format mode, click the **Fill Format mode** icon again or press the *Esc* key.

Caution	When this mode is active, a right-click anywhere in the document undoes the last Fill Format action. Be careful not to accidentally right-click and thus undo actions you want to keep.

Using the Apply Style list

After you have used a style at least once in a document, the style name appears on the Apply Style list at the left-hand end of the Formatting toolbar, next to the Styles and Formatting icon.

You can open this list and click once on the style you want, or you can use the up and down arrow keys to move through the list and then press *Enter* to apply the highlighted style.

Tip	Select **More...** at the bottom of the list to open the Styles and Formatting window.

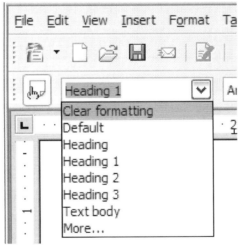

Figure 39: The Apply Style list on the Formatting toolbar.

Using keyboard shortcuts

Some keyboard shortcuts for applying styles are predefined. For example, in Writer *Control+0* applies the *Text body* style, *Control+1* applies the *Heading 1* style, and *Control+2* applies the *Heading 2* style. You can modify these shortcuts and create your own; see Chapter 14 (Customizing OpenOffice.org) for instructions.

Modifying styles

OpenOffice.org provides several ways to modify styles (both the predefined styles and custom styles that you create):

- Changing a style using the Style dialog
- Updating a style from a selection
- Use AutoUpdate (paragraph and frame styles only)
- Load or copy styles from another document or template

Tip	Any changes you make to a style are effective only in the current document. To change styles in more than one document, you need to change the template or copy the styles into the other documents as described on page 57.

Changing a style using the Style dialog

To change an existing style using the Style dialog, right-click on the required style in the Styles and Formatting window and select **Modify** from the pop-up menu.

The Style dialog displayed depends on the type of style selected. Each style dialog has several tabs. See the chapters on styles in the user guides for details.

Updating a style from a selection

To update a style from a selection:

1) Open the Styles and Formatting window.
2) In the document, select an item that has the format you want to adopt as a style.

Caution ⚠	Make sure that there are unique properties in this paragraph. For example, if there are two different font sizes or font styles, that particular property will remain the same as before.

3) In the Styles and Formatting window, select the style you want to update (single-click, not double-click), then long-click on the arrow next to the **New Style from Selection** icon and click on **Update Style**.

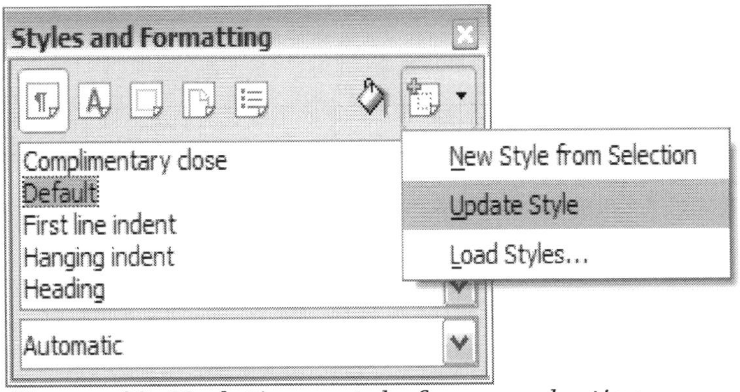

Figure 40: Updating a style from a selection.

Using AutoUpdate

AutoUpdate applies to paragraph and frame styles only. If the AutoUpdate option is selected on the Organizer page of the Paragraph Style or Frame Style dialog, applying direct formatting to a paragraph or frame using this style in your document automatically updates the style itself.

Tip	If you are in the habit of manually overriding styles in your document, be sure that AutoUpdate is **not** enabled.

Updating styles from a document or template

You can update styles by copying or loading them from a template or another document. See "Copying and moving styles" on page 57.

Creating new (custom) styles

You may want to add some new styles. You can do this in two ways:

* Creating a new style using the Style dialog
* Creating a new style from a selection

Creating a new style using the Style dialog

To create a new style using the Style dialog, right-click in the Styles and Formatting window and select **New** from the pop-up menu.

If you want your new style to be linked with an existing style, first select that style and then right-click and select **New**.

If you link styles, then when you change the base style (for example, by changing the font from Times to Helvetica), all the linked styles will change as well. Sometimes this is exactly what you want; other times you do not want the changes to apply to all the linked styles. It pays to plan ahead.

The dialogs and choices are the same for defining new styles and for modifying existing styles. See the chapters on styles in the user guides for details.

Creating a new style from a selection

You can create a new style by copying an existing style. This new style applies only to this document; it will not be saved in the template.

1) Open the Styles and Formatting window and choose the type of style you want to create.
2) In the document, select the item you want to save as a style.
3) In the Styles and Formatting window, click on the **New Style from Selection** icon.
4) In the Create Style dialog, type a name for the new style. The list shows the names of existing custom styles of the selected type. Click **OK** to save the new style.

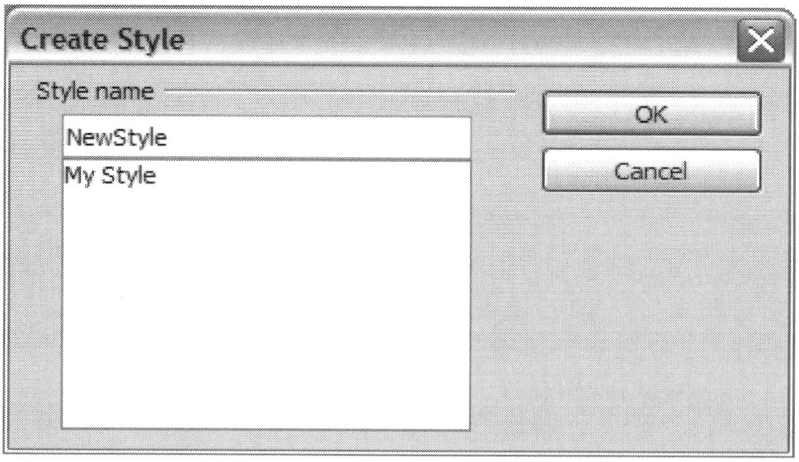

Figure 41: Naming a new style created from a selection.

Dragging and dropping to create a style

You can drag and drop a text selection into the Styles and Formatting window to create a new style.

Writer

Select some text and drag it to the Styles and Formatting window. If Paragraph Styles are active, the paragraph style will be added to the list. If Character Styles are active, the character style will be added to the list.

Calc

Drag a cell selection to the Styles and Formatting window to create cell styles.

Draw/Impress

Select and drag drawing objects to the Styles and Formatting window to create graphics styles.

Copying and moving styles

You can copy or move styles from one template or document into another template or document, in two ways:

* Using the Template Management dialog
* Loading styles from a template or document

Using the Template Management dialog

To copy or move styles using the Template Management dialog:

1) Click **File > Templates > Organize**.

2) In the Template Management dialog (Figure 42), set the lists at the bottom to either Templates or Documents, as needed. The default is Templates on the left and Documents on the right.

Tip	To load styles from a file that is not open, click the **File** button. When you return to this dialog, both lists show the selected file as well as all the currently open documents.

3) Open the folders and find the templates from and to which you want to copy. Double-click on the name of the template or document, and then double-click the Styles icon to show the list of individual styles (Figure 43).

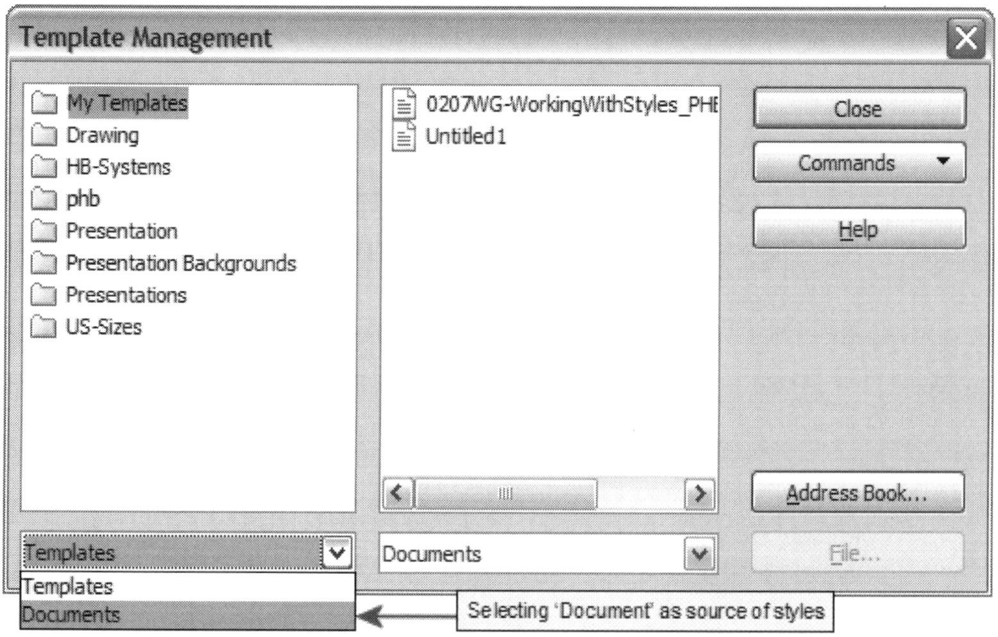

Figure 42: Choosing to copy styles from a document, not a template.

4) To *copy* a style, hold down the *Ctrl* key and drag the name of the style from one list to the other.

Caution

If you do not hold down the *Control* key when dragging, the style will be moved from one list to the other. The style will be deleted from the list you are dragging it from.

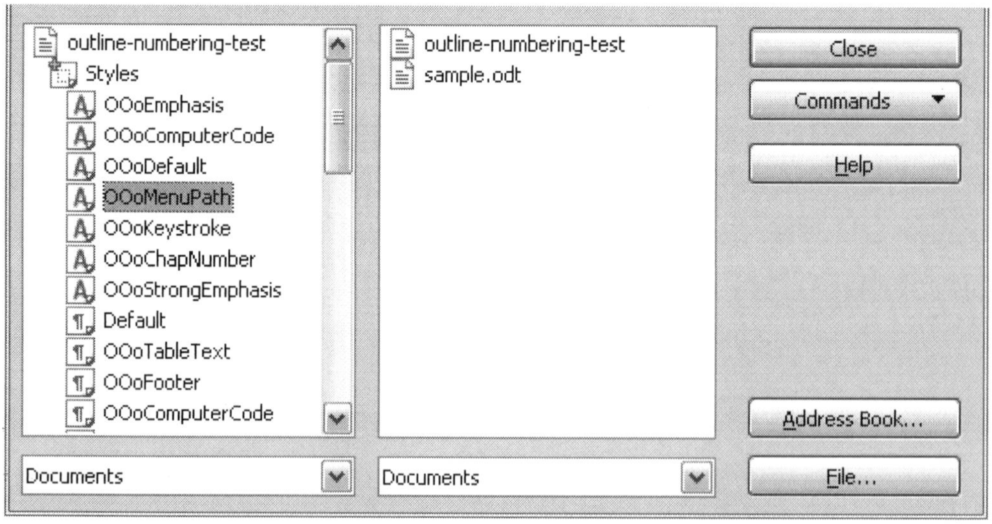

Figure 43: Copying a style from one document to another.

---

5) Repeat for each style you want to copy. If the receiving template or document hasmany styles, you may not see any change unless you scroll down in the list. When you are finished, click **Close**.

Loading styles from a template or document

You can copy styles by loading them from a template or another document:

1) Open the document you want to copy styles into.

2) In the Styles and Formatting window, long-click on the arrow next to the **New Style from Selection** icon, and then click on **Load Styles** (see Figure 40).

3) On the Load Styles dialog (Figure 44), find and select the template you want to copy styles from.

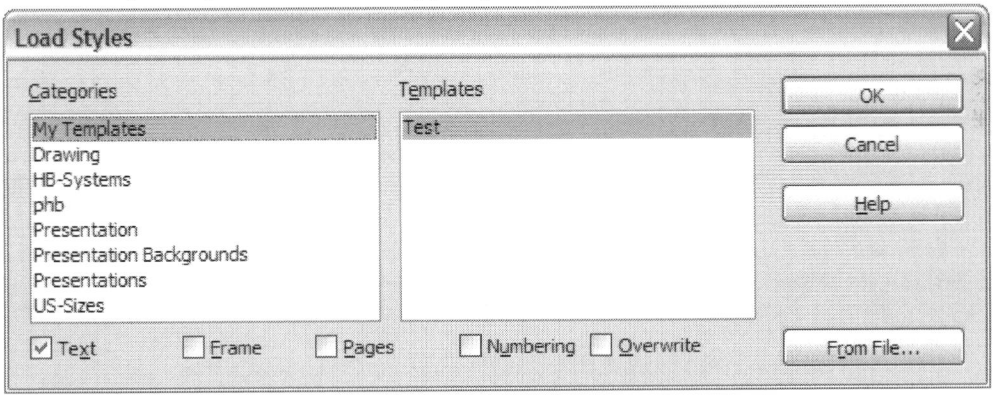

Load Styles

Categories

My Templates
Drawing
HB-Systems
phb
Presentation
Presentation Backgrounds
Presentations
US-Sizes

Templates

Test

OK

Cancel

Help

☑ Text   ☐ Frame   ☐ Pages   ☐ Numbering   ☐ Overwrite   From File...

Figure 44. Copying styles from a template into the open document

4) Select the categories of styles to be copied. Select **Overwrite** if you want the styles being copied to replace any styles of the same names in the document you're copying them into.

5) Click **OK** to copy the styles. You will not see any change on screen.

Note	To copy the styles from another document, click the **From File** button to open a window from which you can select the required document.

Caution ⚠	If your document has a table of contents, and if you have used custom styles for headings, the heading levels associated with outline levels (in **Tools > Outline Numbering**) will revert to the defaults of Heading 1, Heading 2, and so on when you load styles this . You will need to change these back to your custom heading styles. This is a bug.

Deleting styles

You cannot remove (delete) any of OOo's predefined styles from a document or template, even if they are not in use.

You can remove any user-defined (custom) styles; but before you do, you should make sure the styles are not in use. If an unwanted style is in use, you will want to replace it with a substitute style.

To delete unwanted styles, right-click on them (one at a time) in the Styles and Formatting window and click **Delete** on the pop-up menu.

If the style is in use, you receive a warning message.

Caution	Make sure the style is not in use before deletion. Otherwise, all objects with that style will return to the default style and retain their formatting as manual formatting. This can be a problem in a long document.

If the style is not in use, you receive a confirmation message; click **Yes**.

Using a template to create a document

To use a template to create a document:

1) From the main menu, choose **File > New > Templates and Documents.** The Templates and Documents dialog opens. (See Figure 45.)

2) In the box on the left, click the **Templates** icon if it is not already selected. A list of template folders appears in the center box.

3) Double-click the folder that contains the template that you want to use. A list of all the templates contained in that folder appears in the center box.

4) Select the template that you want to use. You can preview the selected template or view the template's properties:

   • To preview the template, click the **Preview** icon. A preview of the template appears in the box on the right.

   • To view the template's properties, click the **Document Properties** icon. The template's properties appear in the box on the right.

5) Click **Open.** The Templates and Documents dialog closes and a new document based on the selected template opens in OOo.

You can then edit and save the new document just as you would any other document.

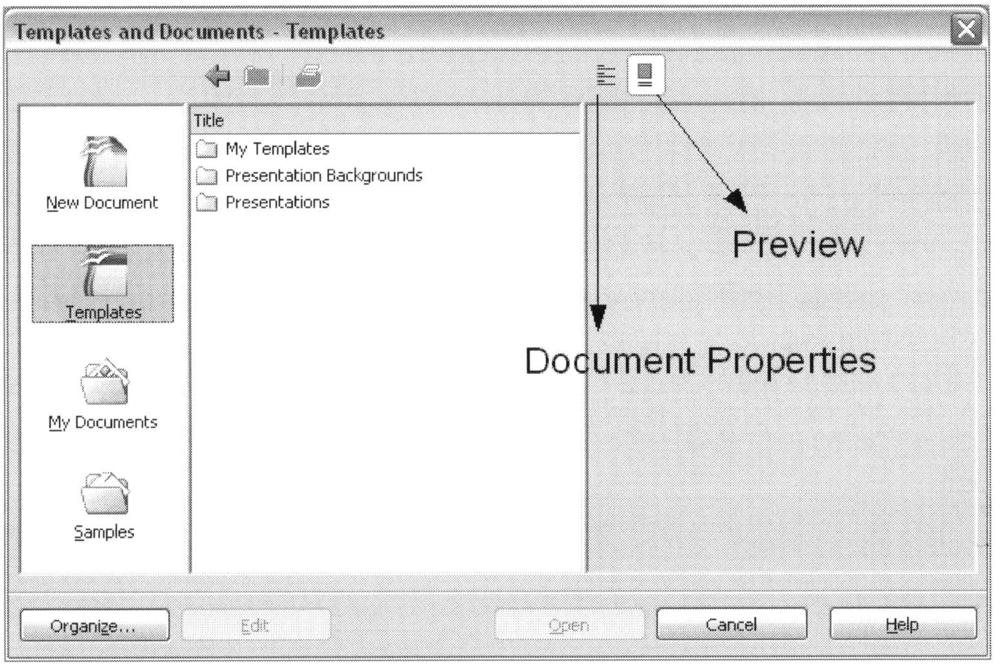

Figure 45: Templates and Documents window.

Creating a template

You can create your own templates in two ways: from a document, and using a wizard.

Creating a template from a document

To create a template from a document:

1) Open a new or existing document of the type you want to make into a template (text document, spreadsheet, drawing, presentation).

2) Add the content and styles that you want.

3) From the main menu, choose **File > Templates > Save.** The Templates dialog opens (see Figure 46).

4) In the **New template** field, type a name for the new template.

5) In the **Categories** list, click the category to which you want to assign the template. The category you choose has no effect on the template itself; it is simply the folder in which you save the template. Choosing an appropriate category makes it easier to find the template easily when you want to use it. For example,

you might save Impress templates under the **Presentations** category.

To learn more about template folders, see "Organizing templates" on page 68.

6) Click **OK** to save the new template.

Figure 46: Saving a new template.

Any settings that can be added to or modified in a document can be saved in a template. For example, below are some of the settings (although not a full list) that can be included in a Writer document and then saved as a template for later use:

- Printer settings: which printer, single sided / double sided, and paper size, and so on

- Styles to be used, including character, page, frame, numbering and paragraph styles

- Format and settings regarding indexes, tables, bibliographies, table of contents

Templates can also contain predefined text, saving you from having to type it every time you create a new document. For example, a letter template may contain your name, address and salutation.

You can also save menu and toolbar customizations in templates; see Chapter 14 (Customizing OpenOffice.org) for more information.

Creating a template using a wizard

You can use wizards to create templates for letters, faxes, agendas, presentations, and Web pages.

For example, the Fax Wizard guides you through the following choices:

- Type of fax (business or personal)
- Document elements like the date, subject line (business fax), salutation, and complementary close
- Options for sender and recipient information (business fax)
- Text to include in the footer (business fax)

To create a template using a wizard:

1) From the main menu, choose **File > Wizards >** [type of template required].

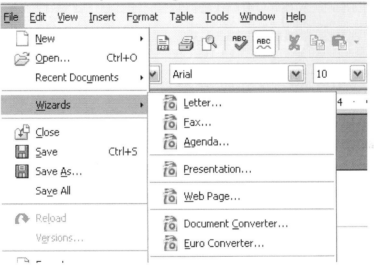

Figure 47. Creating a template using a wizard

2) Follow the instructions on the pages of the wizard. This process is slightly different for each type of template, but the format is very similar.

3) In the last section of the wizard, you can specify the name and location for saving the template. The default location is your user templates directory, but you can choose a different location if you prefer.

4) Finally, you have the option of creating a new document from your template immediately, or manually changing the template. For future documents, you can re-use the template created by the wizard, just as you would use any other template.

Editing a template

You can edit a template's styles and content, and then, if you wish, you can reapply the template's styles to documents that were created from that template. (Note that you can only reapply styles. You cannot reapply content.)

To edit a template:

1) From the main menu, choose **File > Templates > Organize.** The Template Management dialog opens (see Figure 48).

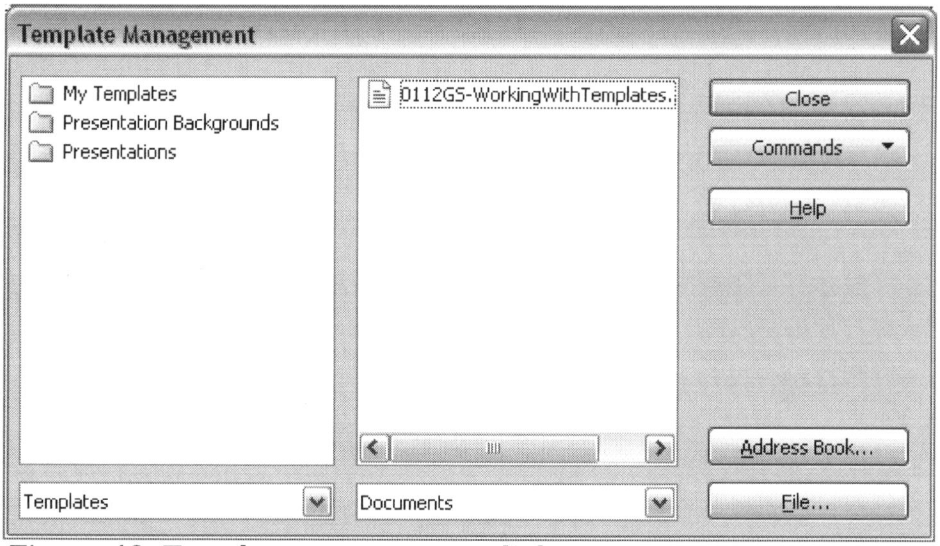

Figure 48: Template management dialog

2) In the box on the left, double-click the folder that contains the template that you want to edit. A list of all the templates contained in that folder appears underneath the folder name.

3) Select the template that you want to edit.

4) Click the **Commands** button and choose **Edit** from the drop-down menu.

5) Edit the template just as you would any other document. To save your changes, choose **File > Save** from the main menu.

Updating a document from a changed template

The next time you open a document that was created from the changed template, the message in Figure 49 appears.

Click **Yes** to apply the template's changed styles to the document. Click **No** if you do not want to apply the template's changed styles to the document. Whichever option you choose, the message box closes and the document opens in OOo.

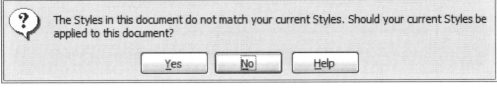

Figure 49. Apply current styles message

Adding templates using the Extension Manager

The Extension Manager provides an easy way to install collections of templates, graphics, macros, or other add-ins that have been "packaged" into files with a .OXT extension. See Chapter 14 (Customizing OpenOffice.org) for more about the Extension Manager.

This Web page lists many of the available extensions: http://extensions.services.openoffice.org/.

To install an extension, follow these steps:

1) Download an extension package and save it anywhere on your computer.

2) In OOo, select **Tools > Extension Manager** from the menu bar. In the Extension Manager dialog, click **Add**.

3) A file browser window opens. Find and select the package of templates you want to install and click **Open**.The package begins installing. You may be asked to accept a license agreement.

4) When the package installation is complete, the templates are available for use through **File > New > Templates and Documents** and the extension is listed in the Extension Manager.

Setting a default template

If you create a document by choosing **File > New > Text Document** (or **Spreadsheet**, **Presentation**, or **Drawing**) from the main menu, OOo creates the document from the Default template for that type of document. You can, however, set a custom template to be the default. You can reset the default later if you choose.

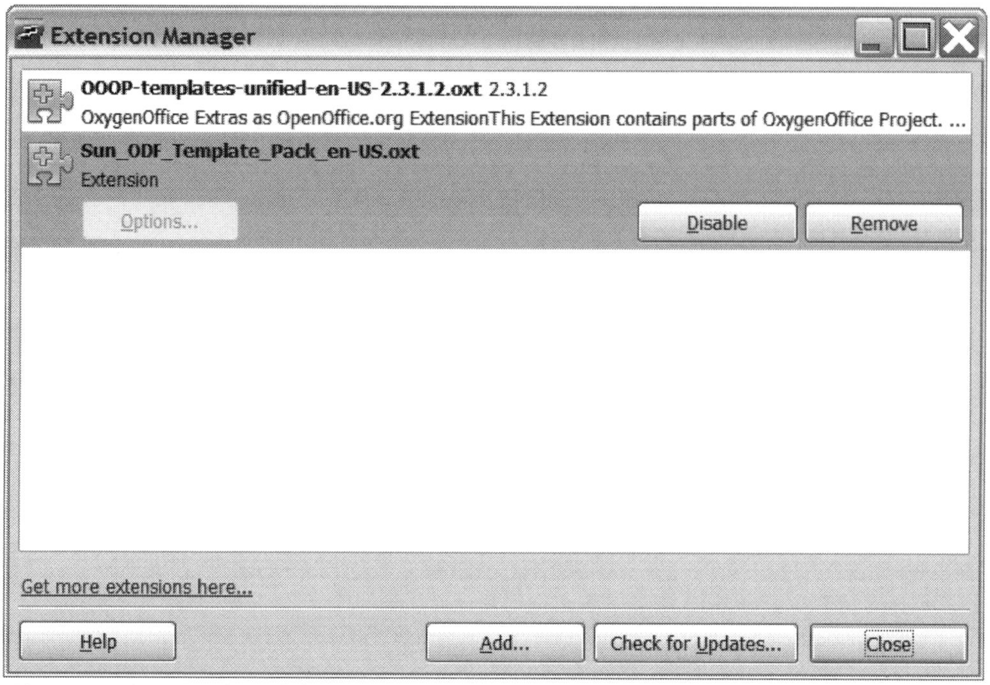

Figure 50: Newly-added package of templates.

Setting a custom template as the default

You can set any template to be the default, as long as it is in one of the folders displayed in the Template Management dialog.

To set a custom template as the default:

1) From the main menu, choose **File > Templates > Organize.** The Template Management dialog opens.

2) In the box on the left, select the folder containing the template that you want to set as the default, then select the template.

3) Click the **Commands** button and choose **Set As Default Template** from the drop-down menu.

The next time that you create a document by choosing **File > New,** the document will be created from this template.

Although many important settings can be changed in the Options dialog (see Chapter 2), for example default fonts and page size, more advanced settings (such as page margins) can only be changed by replacing the default template with a new one.

Resetting the default template

To re-enable OOo's Default template for a document type as the default:

1) In the Template Management dialog, click any folder in the box on the left.

2) Click the **Commands** button and choose **Reset Default Template** from the drop-down menu.

The next time that you create a document by choosing **File > New,** the document will be created from OOo's Default template for that document type.

Associating a document with a different template

At times you might want to associate a document with a different template, or perhaps you're working with a document that did not start from a template.

One of the major advantages of using templates is the ease of updating styles in more than one document, as described on page 64. If you update styles by loading a new set of styles from a different template (as described on page 59), the document has no association with the template from which the styles were loaded—so you cannot use this method. What you need to do is associate the document with the different template.

You can do this in two ways. In both cases, for best results the names of styles should be the same in the existing document and the new template. If they are not, you will need to use Search and Replace to replace old styles with new ones. See Chapter 4 (Getting Started with Writer) for more about replacing styles using Search and Replace.

Method 1
This method includes any graphics and wording (such as legal notices) that exists in the new template, as well as including styles. If you don't want this material, you need to delete it.

1) Use **File > New > Templates and Documents**. Choose the template you want. If the template has unwanted text or graphics in it, delete them.

2) Open the document you want to change. (It opens in a new window.) Press *Control+A* to select everything in the document. Paste into the blank document created in step 1.

3) Update the table of contents, if there is one. Save the file.

Method 2

This method does not include any graphics or text from the new template; it simply includes styles from the new template and establishes an association between the template and the document.

1) Download the Template Changer extension from http://extensions.services.openoffice.org/ and install it as described on page 65.

2) Close and reopen OpenOffice.org. Now the **File > Templates** menu has two new choices: *Assign Template (current document)* and *Assign Template (folder)*.

3) Open the document whose template you want to change. Choose **File > Templates > Assign Template (current document)**.

4) In the Select Template window, find and select the required template and click **Open**.

5) Save the document. If you now look in **File > Properties**, you will see the new template listed at the bottom of the General page.

Organizing templates

OOo can only use templates that are in OOo template folders. You can create new OOo template folders and use them to organize your templates, and import templates into those folders. For example, you might have one template folder for report templates and another for letter templates. You can also export templates.

To begin, choose **File > Templates > Organize** from the main menu. The Template Management dialog opens.

Note	All the actions made by the **Commands** button in the Template Management dialog can be made as well by right-clicking on the templates or the folders.

Creating a template folder

To create a template folder:

1) In the Template Management dialog, click any folder.

2) Click the **Commands** button and choose **New** from the drop-down menu. A new folder called *Untitled* appears.

3) Type a name for the new folder, and then press *Enter*. OOo saves the folder with the name that you entered.

Deleting a template folder

You cannot delete template folders supplied with OOo or installed using the Extension Manager; you can only delete template folders that you have created.

To delete a template folder:

1) In the Template Management dialog, select the folder that you want to delete.

2) Click the **Commands** button and choose **Delete** from the drop-down menu. A message box appears and asks you to confirm the deletion. Click **Yes.**

Moving a template

To move a template from one template folder to another template folder:

1) In the Template Management dialog, double-click the folder that contains the template you want to move. A list of the templates contained in that folder appears underneath the folder name.

2) Click the template that you want to move and drag it to the desired folder. If you do not have the authority to delete templates from the source folder, this action *copies* the template instead of moving it.

Deleting a template

You cannot delete templates supplied with OOo or installed using the Extension Manager; you can only delete templates that you have created or imported.

To delete a template:

1) In the Template Management dialog, double-click the folder that contains the template you want to delete. A list of the templates contained in that folder appears underneath the folder name.

2) Click the template that you want to delete.

3) Click the **Commands** button and choose **Delete** from the drop-down menu. A message box appears and asks you to confirm the deletion. Click **Yes.**

Importing a template

If the template that you want to use is in a different location, you must import it into an OOo template folder.

To import a template into a template folder:

1) In the Template Management dialog, select the folder into which you want to import the template.

2) Click the **Commands** button and choose **Import Template** from the drop-down menu. A standard file browser window opens.

3) Find and select the template that you want to import and click **Open.** The file browser window closes and the template appears in the selected folder.

4) If you want, type a new name for the template, and then press *Enter.*

Exporting a template

To export a template from a template folder to another location:

1) In the Template Management dialog, double-click the folder that contains the template you want to export. A list of the templates contained in that folder appears underneath the folder name.

2) Click the template that you want to export.

3) Click the **Commands** button and choose **Export Template** from the drop-down menu. The Save As window opens.

4) Find the folder into which you want to export the template and click **Save**.

Examples of style use

The following examples of common use of page and paragraph styles are taken from Writer. There are many other ways to use styles; see the guides for the various components for details.

Defining a different first page for a document

Many documents, such as letters and reports, have a first page that is different from the other pages in the document. For example, the first page of a letterhead typically has a different header, or the first page of a report might have no header or footer, while the other pages do. With OOo, you can define the *page style* for the first page and specify the style for the following pages to be applied automatically.

As an example, we can use the *First Page* and *Default* page styles that come with OOo. Figure 51 shows what we want to happen: the first page is to be followed by the default page, and all the following pages are to be in the *Default* page style. Details are in Chapter 4 (Formatting Pages) in the *Writer Guide*.

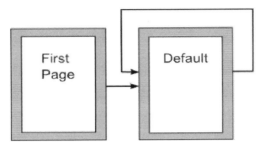

Figure 51: Flow of page styles

Dividing a document into chapters

In a similar way, you can divide a document into chapters. Each chapter might start with the *First Page* style, with the following pages using the *Default* page style, as above. At the end of the chapter, insert a manual page break and specify the next page to have the *First Page* style to start the next chapter, as shown in Figure 52.

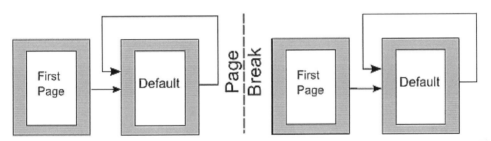

Figure 52: Dividing a document into chapters using page styles

Changing page orientation within a document

A Writer document can contain pages in more than one orientation. A common scenario is to have a landscape page in the middle of a document, whereas the other pages are in a portrait orientation. This can also be done with page breaks and page styles.

Different headers on right and left pages

Page styles can be set up to have the facing left and right pages *mirrored* or only right (first pages of chapters are often defined to be right-page only) or only left. When you insert a header on a page style set up for mirrored pages or right-and-left pages, you can have the contents of the header be the same on all pages or be different on the right and left pages. For example, you can put the page number on the left-hand edge of the left pages and on the right-hand edge of the right pages, put the document title on the right-hand page only, or make other changes.

Controlling page breaks automatically

Writer automatically flows text from one page to the next. If you do not like the default settings, you can change them. For example, you can require a paragraph to start on a new page or column and specify the style of the new page. A typical use is for chapter titles to always start on a new right-hand (odd-numbered) page.

Compiling an automatic table of contents

To compile an automatic table of contents, first apply styles to the headings you want to appear in the contents list, then use **Tools > Outline Numbering** to tell Writer which styles go with which level in the table of contents. See Chapter 4 for more information.

Defining a sequence of styles

You can set up one paragraph style so that when you press *Enter* at the end of that paragraph, the following paragraph automatically has the style you wish applied to it. For example, you could define a *Heading 1* paragraph to be followed by a *Text Body* paragraph. A more complex example would be: *Title* followed by *Author* followed by *Abstract* followed by *Heading 1* followed by *Text Body*. By setting up these sequences, you can avoid manually applying styles in most cases.

Chapter *4*
Getting Started with Writer

Word processing with OpenOffice.org

What is Writer?

Writer is the word processor component of OpenOffice.org (OOo). In addition to the usual features of a word processor (spell checking, thesaurus, hyphenation, autocorrect, find and replace, automatic generation of tables of contents and indexes, mail merge and others), Writer provides these important features:

- Templates and styles (see Chapter 3)
- Powerful page layout methods, including frames, columns, and tables
- Embedding or linking of graphics, spreadsheets, and other objects
- Built-in drawing tools
- Master documents—to group a collection of documents into a single document
- Change tracking during revisions
- Database integration, including a bibliography database
- Export to PDF, including bookmarks (see Chapter 10)
- And many more

These features are covered in detail in the *Writer Guide*.

The Writer interface

The main Writer workspace is shown in Figure 53. The menus and toolbars are described in Chapter 1 (Introducing OpenOffice.org).

Some other features of the Writer interface are covered in this chapter.

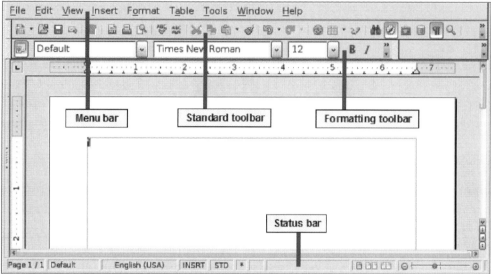

Figure 53: The main Writer workspace in Print Layout view

Status bar

The Writer status bar provides information about the document and convenient ways to quickly change some document features. From left to right, the fields are as follows.

Page number

Shows the current page number, the sequence number of the current page (if different), and the total number of pages in the document. For example, if you restarted page numbering at 1 on the third page, its page number is 1 and its sequence number is 3.

To jump to the location of a bookmark, right-click on this field. A list of bookmarks pops up; click on the required one.

To jump to a specific page in the document, double-click in this field. The Navigator opens. Click in the Page Number field and type the required page number.

Page style

Shows the style of the current page. To change the page style, right-click on this field. A list of page styles pops up; choose a different style by clicking on it.

To edit the page style, double-click on this field. The Page Style dialog opens.

Language

Shows the language for the selected text.

Click to open a menu where you can choose another language for the selected text or for the paragraph where the cursor is located. You can also choose **None** to exclude the text from spellchecking or choose **More…** to open the Character dialog.

Insert mode

Click to toggle between *Insert* and *Overwrite* modes when typing.

Selection mode

Click to toggle between STD (*Standard*), EXT (*Extend*), ADD (*Add*) and BLK (*Block*) selection. EXT is an alternative to *Shift+click* when selecting text. See "Working with text" on page 79 for more information about ADD and BLK.

Digital signature

If the document has been digitally signed, an icon  shows in this part of the Status bar. You can double-click the icon to view the certificate.

Section or object information

When the cursor is on a section or object (such as a picture), information about that item appears in this field. For details, consult the Help or the *Writer Guide*.

View layout

Click the appropriate icon to change between single page, side-by-side, and book layout views (Figure 54). You can edit the document in any view.

Zoom

To change the view magnification, drag the Zoom slider or click on the + and – signs or click on the slider itself. You can also right-click on the zoom level percentage to select a magnification value. Zoom interacts with the selected view layout to determine how many pages are visible in the document window.

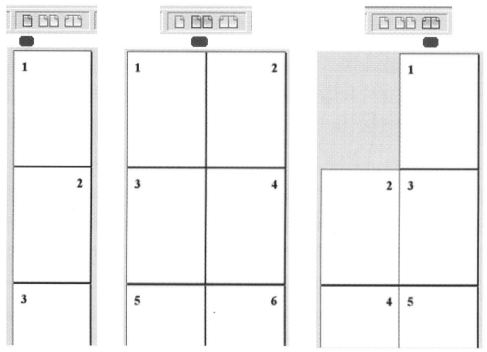

Figure 54: View layouts: single, side-by-side, book.

Document views

Writer has several ways to view a document: Print Layout, Web Layout, and Full Screen. To access these and other choices, go to the **View** menu and click on the required view. (When in Full Screen view, press the *Esc* key to return to either Print or Web Layout view.)

When in Web Layout, you can use the Zoom slider on the Status bar, as described above. In Print Layout, you can use both the Zoom slider and the View Layout icons on the Status bar.

You can also choose **View > Zoom** from the menu bar to display the Zoom & View Layout dialog (see Figure 55), where you can set the same options as on the Status bar. In Web Layout view, most of the choices are not available.

Moving quickly through a document

In addition to the navigation features of the Status bar (described above), you can use the main Navigator window and the Navigation toolbar as described in Chapter 1 (Introducing OpenOffice.org).

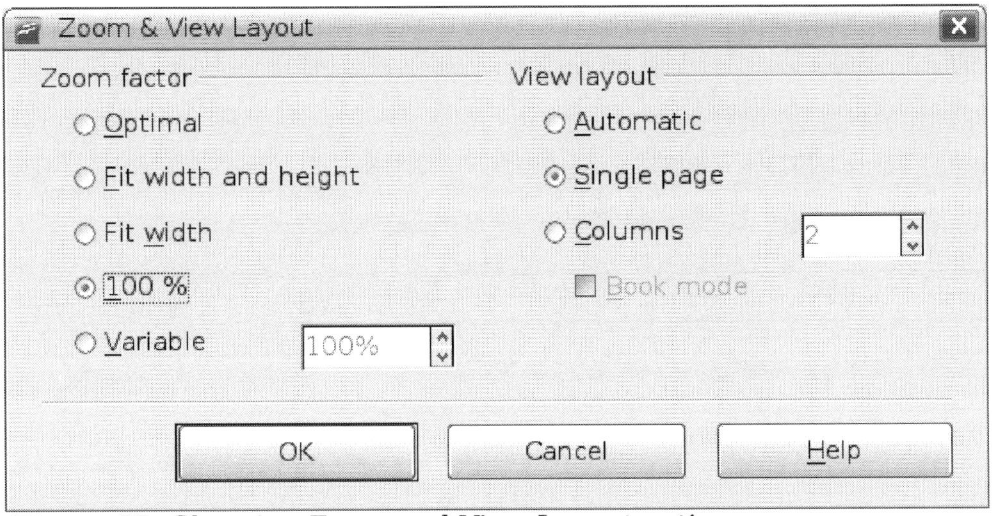

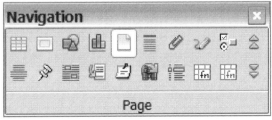

Figure 55: Choosing Zoom and View Layout options.

In Writer, you can also display the Navigation toolbar by clicking on the small Navigation icon near the lower right-hand corner of the window below the vertical scroll bar, as shown in Figure 56.

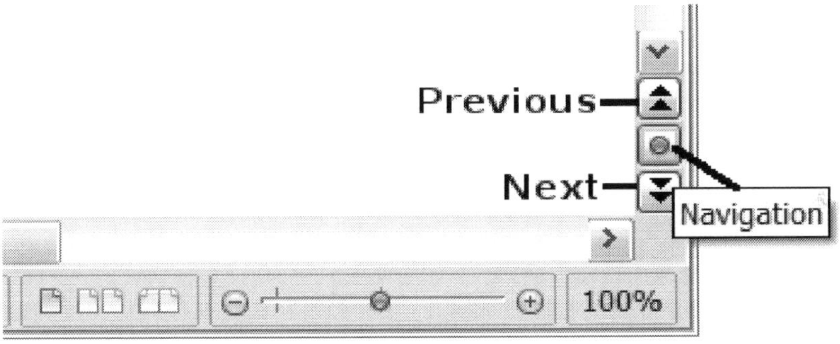

Previous

Next

Navigation

Figure 56: Navigation icons.

The Navigation toolbar (Figure 57) shows icons for all the object types shown in the Navigator, plus some extras (for example, the results of a **Find** command).

Navigation

Page

Figure 57: Navigation toolbar

Click an icon to select that object type. Now all the **Previous** and **Next** icons (in the Navigator itself, in the Navigation Toolbar, and on the scroll bar) will jump to the next object of the selected type. This is particularly helpful for finding items like index entries, which can be difficult to see in the text. The names of the icons (shown in the tooltips) change to match the selected category; for example, **Next Graphic**, **Next Bookmark**, or **Continue search forward**.

For more uses of the Navigator in Writer, see the *Writer Guide*.

Working with documents

Chapter 1 (Introducing OpenOffice.org) includes instructions on starting new documents, opening existing documents, and saving documents. Chapter 3 (Using Styles and Templates) covers how to create a document from a template.

Saving as a Microsoft Word file

To save a document as a Microsoft Word file:

1) First save your document in OOo's format (.odt). If you do not, any changes you made since the last time you saved will appear only in the Microsoft Word version of the document.

2) Then click **File > Save As**. The Save As window (Figure 58) appears.

3) In the **Save as type** drop-down menu, select the type of Word format you need.

4) Click **Save.**

From this point on, *all changes you make to the document will occur only in the Microsoft Word document.* You have actually changed the name of your document. If you want to go back to working with the OOo version of your document, you must open it again.

Tip	To have OOo save documents by default in the Microsoft Word file format, go to **Tools > Options > Load/Save**. See "Choosing options for loading and saving documents" in Chapter 2 (Setting up OpenOffice.org).

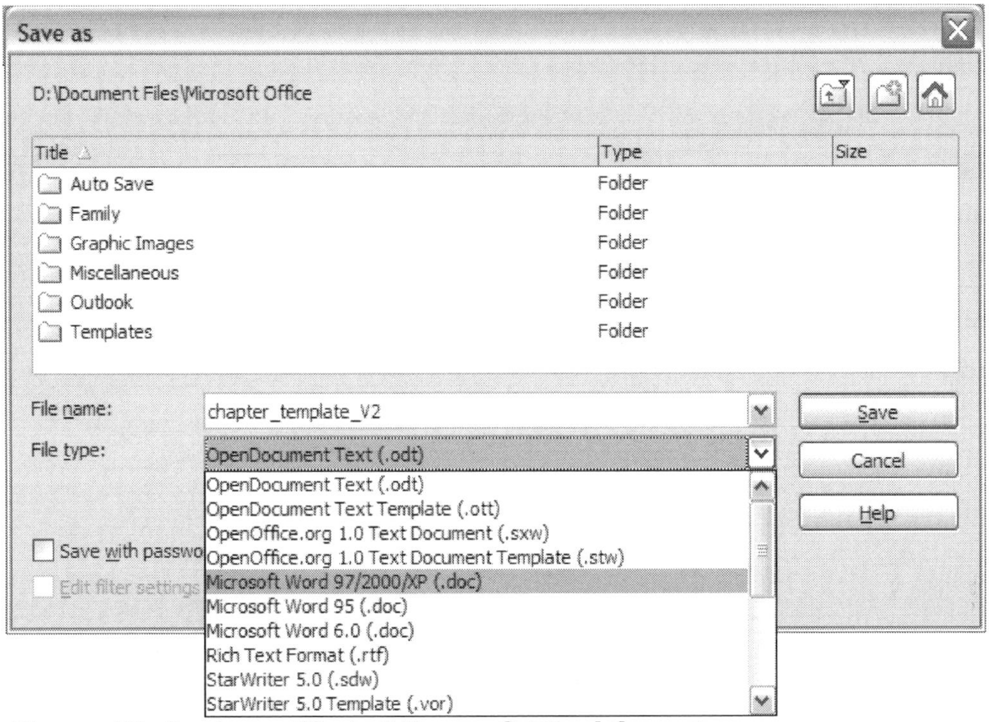

Figure 58. Saving a file in Microsoft Word format

Working with text

Working with text (selecting, copying, pasting, moving) in Writer is similar to working with text in any other program. OOo also has some convenient ways to select items that are not next to each other, select a vertical block of text, and paste unformatted text.

Selecting items that are not consecutive

To select nonconsecutive items (as shown in Figure 59) using the mouse:

1) Select the first piece of text.
2) Hold down the *Control* key and use the mouse to select the next piece of text.
3) Repeat as often as needed.

Now you can work with the selected text (copy it, delete it, change the style, or whatever).

Note   Macintosh users: substitute the *Command* key when instructions in this chapter say to use the *Control* key.

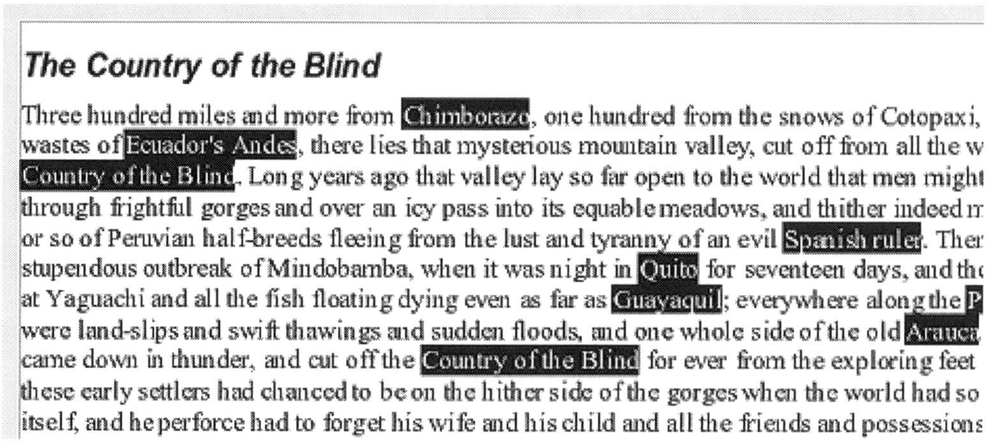

The Country of the Blind

Three hundred miles and more from Chimborazo, one hundred from the snows of Cotopaxi, wastes of Ecuador's Andes, there lies that mysterious mountain valley, cut off from all the w Country of the Blind. Long years ago that valley lay so far open to the world that men might through frightful gorges and over an icy pass into its equable meadows, and thither indeed m or so of Peruvian half-breeds fleeing from the lust and tyranny of an evil Spanish ruler. Ther stupendous outbreak of Mindobamba, when it was night in Quito for seventeen days, and the at Yaguachi and all the fish floating dying even as far as Guayaquil; everywhere along the P were land-slips and swift thawings and sudden floods, and one whole side of the old Arauca came down in thunder, and cut off the Country of the Blind for ever from the exploring feet these early settlers had chanced to be on the hither side of the gorges when the world had so itself, and he perforce had to forget his wife and his child and all the friends and possessions

Figure 59: Selecting items that are not next to each other

To select nonconsecutive items using the keyboard:

1) Select the first piece of text. (For more information about keyboard selection of text, see the topic "Navigating and selecting with the keyboard" in the Help.)

2) Press *Shift+F8*. This puts Writer in Add mode. The word ADD appears on the status bar.

3) Use the arrow keys to move to the start of the next piece of text to be selected. Hold down the *Shift* key and select the next piece of text.

4) Repeat as often as needed.

5) Now you can work with the selected text.

6) Press *Esc* to exit from this mode.

Selecting a vertical block of text

You can select a vertical block or "column" of text that is separated by spaces or tabs (as you might see in text pasted from e-mails, program listings, or other sources), using OOo's block selection mode. To change to block selection mode, use **Edit > Selection Mode > Block Area**, or click several times in the status bar on STD until it changes to BLK.

| Page 1 / 1 | Default | | English (USA) | | INSRT | STD | * | |

Now highlight the selection, using mouse or keyboard, as shown in Figure 60.

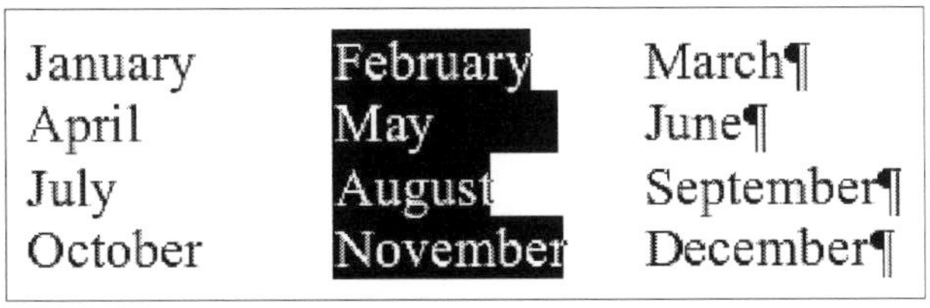

January February March¶
April May June¶
July August September¶
October November December¶

Figure 60: Selecting a vertical block of text

Cutting, copying, and pasting text

Cutting and copying text in Writer is similar to cutting and copying text in other applications. You can use the mouse or the keyboard for these operations.

Cut: Use **Edit > Cut** or *Control+X* or the **Cut** icon on the toolbar.

Copy: Use **Edit > Copy** or *Control+C* or the **Copy** icon.

Paste: Use **Edit > Paste** or *Control+V* or the **Paste** icon.

If you simply click on the **Paste** icon, any formatting the text has (such as bold or italics) is retained. To make the pasted text take on the formatting of the surrounding text where it is being pasted, click the triangle to the right of the **Paste** icon and select **Unformatted text** from the menu (Figure 61).

OpenOffice.org Writer
DDE link
HTML (HyperText Markup Language)
Formatted text [RTF]
Unformatted text

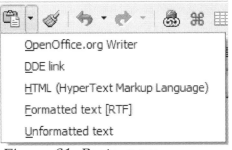

Figure 61: Paste menu

Finding and replacing text and formatting

Writer has a Find and Replace feature that automates the process of searching for text inside a document. In addition to finding and replacing words and phrases, you can:

- Use regular expressions (wildcards) to fine-tune a search (see the Help for details).

- Find and replace specific formatting (see the *Writer Guide*).
- Find and replace paragraph styles (see the *Writer Guide*).

To display the Find & Replace dialog (Figure 62), use the keyboard shortcut *Control+F* or select **Edit > Find & Replace**.

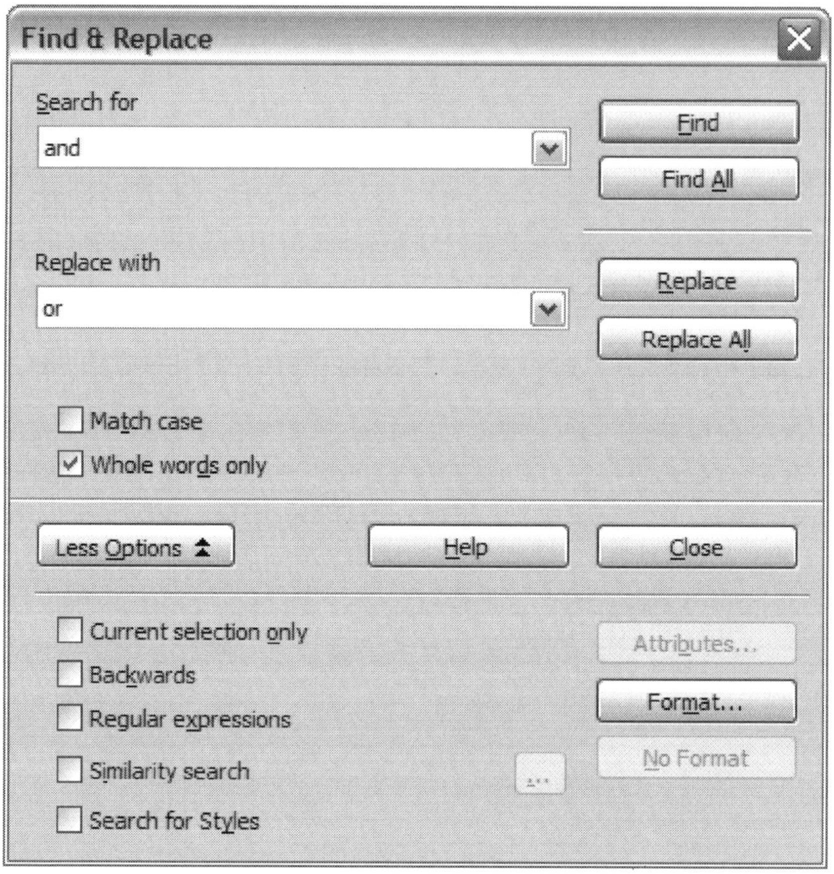

Figure 62: Expanded Find & Replace dialog

Type the text you want to find in the **Search for** box.

To replace the text with different text, type the new text in the **Replace with** box.

You can select various options such as matching the case, matching whole words only, or doing a search for similar words. (See below for some other choices.)

When you have set up your search, click **Find**. To replace text, click **Replace** instead.

Tip	If you click **Find All**, OOo selects all instances of the search text in the document. Similarly, if you click **Replace All**, OOo will replace all matches.

Caution	Use **Replace All** with caution; otherwise, you may end up with some hilarious (and highly embarrassing) mistakes. A mistake with **Replace All** might require a manual, word-by-word, search to fix.

Inserting special characters

A *special character* is one not found on a standard English keyboard. For example, © ¾ æ ç ñ ö ø ¢ are all special characters. To insert a special character:

1) Place the cursor where you want the character to appear.

2) Click **Insert > Special Character** to open the Special Characters window (Figure 63).

3) Select the characters you wish to insert, in order, then click **OK**. The selected characters are shown in the lower left of the dialog. As you select a character, it is shown on the lower right, along with its numerical code.

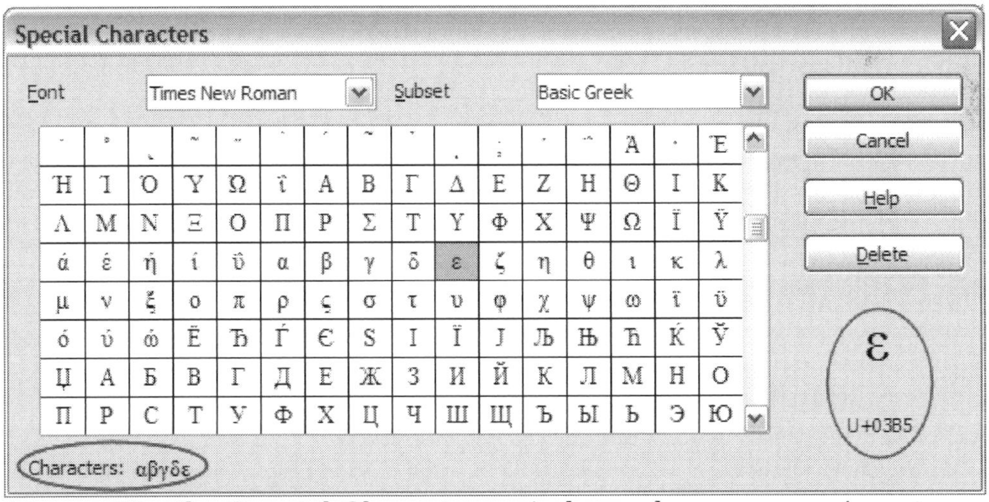

Figure 63: The Special Characters window, where you can insert special characters.

Note	Different fonts include different special characters. If you do not find a particular special character, try changing the *Font* selection.

Tip	Notice that the characters selected appear in the bottom-left corner of the window.

Setting tab stops and indents

The horizontal ruler shows both the default tab stops and any that you have defined. To set the measurement unit and the spacing of default tab stops, go to **Tools > Options > OpenOffice.org Writer > General**.

You can also set or change the measurement unit by right-clicking on the ruler to open a list of units, as shown in Figure 64. Click on one of them to change the ruler to that unit.

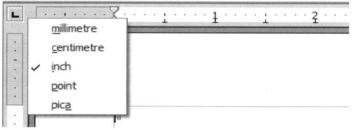

Figure 64: Ruler showing default tab stops

Double-click on a blank part of the ruler to open the Indents & Spacing page of the Paragraph dialog. Double-click on the ruler itself to open the Tabs page of the Paragraph dialog (Figure 65) and fine-tune tab stop settings.

Figure 65: The Tabs page of the Paragraph dialog

Checking spelling

Writer provides a spelling checker, which can be used in two ways.

 AutoSpellcheck checks each word as it is typed and displays a wavy red line under any misspelled words. When the word is corrected, the line disappears.

To perform a separate spelling check on the document (or a text selection) click the **Spellcheck** button. This checks the document or selection and opens the Spellcheck dialog if any misspelled words are found.

Here are some more features of the spelling checker:

*   Right-click on a word with a wavy underline to open a menu. If you select from the suggested words on the menu, the selection will replace the misspelled word in your text.

*   You can change the dictionary language (for example, to Spanish, French or German) on the Spellcheck dialog.

*   You can add a word to the dictionary. Click **Add** in the Spellcheck dialog and pick the dictionary to add it to.

*   The Options dialog of the Spellcheck tool has a number of different options such as whether to check uppercase words and words with numbers. It also allows you to manage custom dictionaries, that is, add or delete dictionaries, and add or delete words in a dictionary.

*   On the Font tab of the Paragraph Styles dialog, you can set paragraphs to be checked in a specific language (different from the rest of the document). See Chapter 7 (Working with Styles) in the *Writer Guide* for more information.

Using language tools

OOo provides some tools that make your work easier if you mix multiple languages within the same document or write documents in various languages.

You can set the language for the whole document, selected paragraphs, or even individual words or characters. In versions earlier than OOo 3.0 it was necessary to use styles in order to insert within a document paragraphs or individual groups of characters that use a different language, while now this can be conveniently done from the main menu.

Tip	Using character and paragraph styles is still the preferred method, as styles allow a greater level of control and make changing the language much faster. See Chapter 7 (Working with Styles) in the *Writer Guide* for information on how to manage the language settings of a style.

The main advantage of changing the language is that you can then use the correct dictionaries to check spelling and apply the localized versions of Autocorrect replacement tables, thesaurus, and hyphenation rules.

The language tools can be found in **Tools > Languages** on the main menu, as shown in Figure 66.

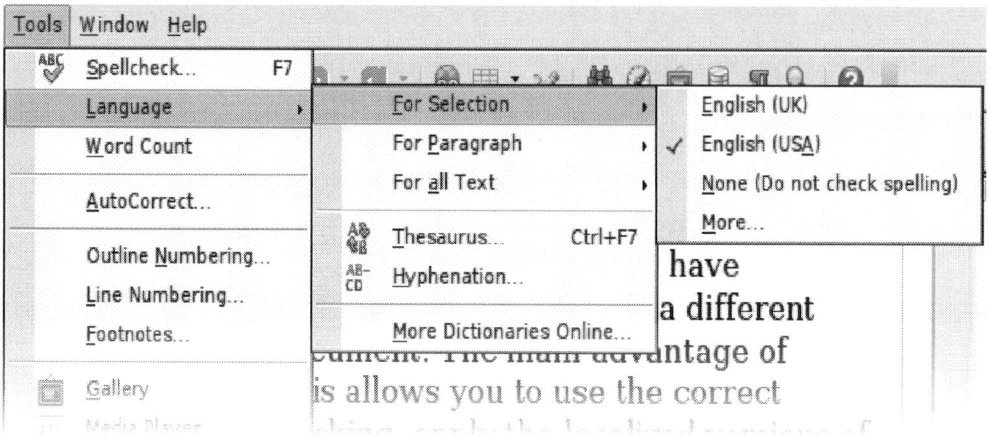

Figure 66: The Language menu

The following options are available:

- **For selection**: select this option to apply a specified language to the selected text (the selection can comprise only a few characters or several paragraphs).
- **For paragraph**: select this option to apply the specified language to the paragraph where the cursor is located.
- **For all text**: select this option to apply the specified language to all the document.

An alternative way to change the language of a whole document is to use **Tools > Options > Language Settings > Languages**. In the *Default languages for documents* section of the Options dialog (Figure 67), you can choose a different language for all the text.

<table>
<tr><td>

Caution

</td><td>

Unlike the menu tool that applies to the individual document, a change in the default language from the **Options** dialog is a general change of settings of OOo and will therefore apply to all the documents created in the future. If you want to change the language for the current document only, be sure to select the *For the current document only* option.

</td></tr>
</table>

Spell checking is available only for those languages in the list that have the symbol ![ABC] next to them. If you do not see the symbol next to your preferred language, you can install the additional dictionary using **Tools > Languages > More dictionaries online**.

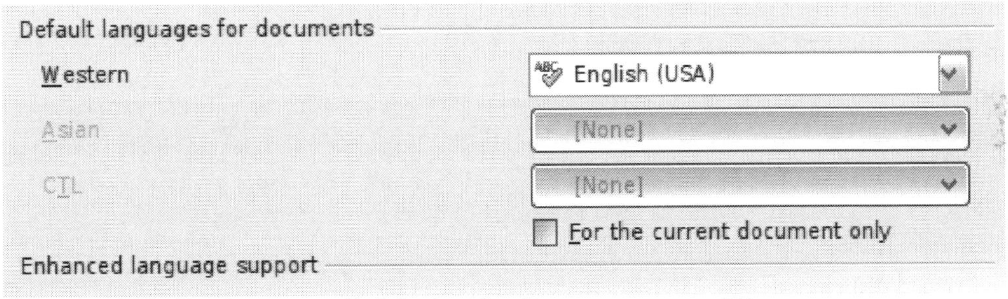

Default languages for documents

Western	ABC English (USA) ▼
Asian	[None] ▼
CTL	[None] ▼
	☐ For the current document only

Enhanced language support

Figure 67: Options available in the Languages settings

The language used for checking spelling is also shown in the status bar, next to the page style in use.

You can also configure the language for a paragraph or a group of characters as **None**. This option is particularly useful in the case where you insert in the document text that you do not want to spellcheck, such as web addresses or programming language snippets.

Using AutoCorrect

Writer's AutoCorrect function has a long list of common misspellings and typing errors, which it corrects automatically. For example, "hte" will be changed to "the". Select **Tools > AutoCorrect** to open the AutoCorrect dialog. There you can define which strings of text are corrected and how. In most cases, the defaults are fine.

<table>
<tr><td>

Tip

</td><td>

AutoCorrect is turned on by default. To turn it off, uncheck **Format > AutoFormat > While Typing**.

</td></tr>
</table>

To stop Writer from replacing a specific spelling, use **Tools > AutoCorrect > Replace**, highlight the word pair and click **Delete**.

To add a new spelling to correct, type it into the *Replace* and *With* boxes and click **New**.

See the different tabs of the dialog for the wide variety of other options available to fine-tune AutoCorrect.

Tip	AutoCorrect can be used as a quick way to insert special characters. For example, (c) will be autocorrected to ©. You can add your own special characters.

Using word completion

If Word Completion is enabled, Writer tries to guess which word you are typing and offers to complete the word for you. To accept the suggestion, press *Enter*. Otherwise continue typing.

Tip	Many people prefer not to use Word Completion. If you do not want to use it, select **Tools > AutoCorrect > Word Completion** and uncheck *Enable Word Completion*.

You can customize word completion from the **Tools > AutoCorrect > Word Completion** page:

- Add (append) a space automatically after an accepted word.
- Show the suggested word as a tip (hovering over the word) rather than completing the text as you type.
- Change the maximum number of words remembered for word completion and the length of the smallest words to be remembered.
- Delete specific entries from the word completion list.
- Change the key that accepts a suggested entry—the options are *Right arrow*, *End* key, *Return* (*Enter*), and *Space bar*.

Note	Automatic word completion only occurs after you type a word for the second time in a document.

Using AutoText

AutoText allows you to assign text, tables, graphics and other items to a key combination. For example, rather than typing "Senior Management" every time you use that phrase, you might just type "sm" and press *F3*. Or you can save a formatted Note (like the one on this page) as AutoText and then insert a copy by typing "note" and pressing *F3*.

To assign some text to an AutoText shortcut:

1) Type the text into your document.
2) Select the text so it is highlighted.
3) Select **Edit > AutoText** (or press *Control+F3*).
4) Enter a name for your shortcut. Writer will suggest a one-letter shortcut, which you can change.
5) Click the **AutoText** button on the right and select **New (text only)** from the menu.
6) Click **Close** to return to your document.

Tip	If the only option under the AutoText button is Import, either you have not entered a name for your AutoText or there is no text selected in the document.

AutoText is especially powerful when assigned to fields. See Chapter 14 (Working with Fields) in the *Writer Guide* for more information.

Inserting dashes and non-breaking spaces

You can insert a dash by using the Special Characters window or by using AutoCorrect. For more about AutoCorrect, see "Controlling OOO's AutoCorrect functions" in Chapter 2 (Setting up OpenOffice.org) and "Using AutoCorrect" on page 87 in this chapter.

– is an en-dash; that is, a dash the width of the letter "n" in the font you are using. It is U+2013 (scroll down to the *General Punctuation* section in the Special Characters window). To enter an en-dash using AutoCorrect, type at least one character, a space, one or two hyphens, another space, and at least one more letter, then a space. The one or two hyphens will be replaced by an en-dash.

— is an em-dash; that is, a dash the width of the letter "m" in the font you are using. It is U+2014. To enter it using AutoCorrect, type at least one character, two hyphens, and at least one more character, then a space. The two hyphens will be replaced by an em-dash.

To insert a non-breaking space (to keep characters together, for example in a telephone number), press *Control+Space* on the keyboard.

Formatting text

Using styles

Styles are central to using Writer. Styles enable you to easily format your document consistently, and to change the format with minimal effort. Often, when you format your document in Writer, you are using styles whether you realize it or not. A style is a named set of formatting options. Writer defines several types of styles, for different types of elements: characters, paragraphs, pages, frames, and lists. See Chapter 3 (Using Styles and Templates).

Formatting paragraphs

You can apply many formats to paragraphs using the buttons on the Formatting toolbar. Figure 68 shows the Formatting toolbar as a floating toolbar, customized to show only the buttons for paragraph formatting.

Tip	It is highly recommended that you use *paragraph styles* rather than manually formatting paragraphs, especially for long or standardized documents. For information on the advantages of styles, and how to use them, see Chapter 13 (Working with Styles) in this book and Chapters 6 and 7 in the *Writer Guide*.

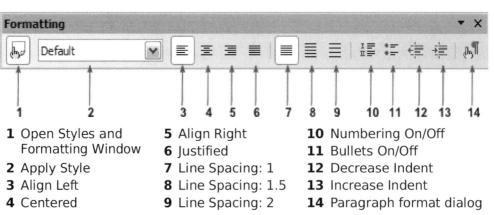

1 Open Styles and Formatting Window
2 Apply Style
3 Align Left
4 Centered

5 Align Right
6 Justified
7 Line Spacing: 1
8 Line Spacing: 1.5
9 Line Spacing: 2

10 Numbering On/Off
11 Bullets On/Off
12 Decrease Indent
13 Increase Indent
14 Paragraph format dialog

Figure 68: The Formatting toolbar, showing icons for paragraph formatting.

The appearance of the icons may vary with your operating system and the selection of icon size and style in **Tools > Options > OpenOffice.org > View**.

Figure 69 shows examples of the different alignment options.

Left aligned text

Centre aligned text

Right aligned text

Justified text inserts spacing between words to force the text to reach from margin to margin.

Figure 69: Different text alignment options.

Formatting characters

You can apply many formats to characters using the buttons on the Formatting toolbar. Figure 70 shows the Formatting toolbar as a floating toolbar, customized to show only the buttons for character formatting.

Tip	It is highly recommended that you use *character styles* rather than manually formatting characters. For information on the advantages of styles, and how to use them, see Chapter 6 (Introduction to Styles) in the *Writer Guide*.

The appearance of the icons may vary with your operating system and the selection of icon size and style in **Tools > Options > OpenOffice.org > View**.

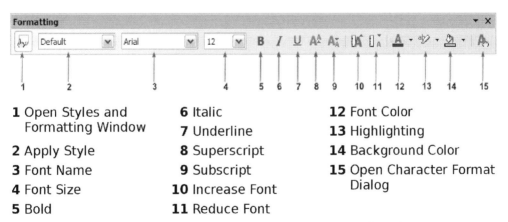

1 Open Styles and Formatting Window
2 Apply Style
3 Font Name
4 Font Size
5 Bold
6 Italic
7 Underline
8 Superscript
9 Subscript
10 Increase Font
11 Reduce Font
12 Font Color
13 Highlighting
14 Background Color
15 Open Character Format Dialog

Figure 70: The Formatting toolbar, showing icons for character formatting

Tip	To remove manual formatting, select the text and click **Format > Default Formatting**, or right-click and select **Default Formatting**.

Autoformatting

You can set Writer to automatically format parts of a document according to the choices made on the Options page of the AutoCorrect dialog (**Tools > AutoCorrect > Options**).

Tip	If you notice unexpected formatting changes occurring in your document, this is the first place to look for the cause.

Some common unwanted or unexpected formatting changes include:

- Horizontal lines. If you type three or more hyphens (---), underscores (___) or equal signs (===) on a line and then press *Enter*, the paragraph is replaced by a horizontal line as wide as the page. The line is actually the lower border of the preceding paragraph.

- Bulleted and numbered lists. A bulleted list is created when you type a hyphen (-), star (*), or plus sign (+), followed by a space or tab at the beginning of a paragraph. A numbered list is created when you type a number followed by a period (.), followed by a space or tab at the beginning of a paragraph. Automatic numbering is only applied to paragraphs formatted with the *Default*, *Text body* or Text body indent paragraph styles.

To turn autoformatting on or off, go to **Format > AutoFormat** and select or delete the items on the sub menu.

Creating numbered or bulleted lists

There are several ways to create numbered or bulleted lists:

- Use autoformatting, as described above.

- Use list (numbering) styles, as described in Chapters 6 (Introduction to Styles) and 7 (Working with Styles) in the *Writer Guide*.

- Use the Numbering and Bullets icons on the paragraph formatting toolbar (see Figure 68). This method is described here.

To produce a numbered or bulleted list, select the paragraphs in the list, and then click the appropriate icon on the toolbar.

Note	It is a matter of personal preference whether you type your information first, then apply Numbering/Bullets, or apply them as you type.

Using the Bullets and Numbering toolbar

You can create nested lists (where one or more list items has a sublist under it, as in an outline) by using the buttons on the Bullets and Numbering toolbar (Figure 71). You can move items up or down the list, or create subpoints, and even change the style of bullets. Use **View > Toolbars > Bullets and Numbering** to see the toolbar.

The appearance of the icons may vary with your operating system and the selection of icon size and style in **Tools > Options > OpenOffice.org > View**.

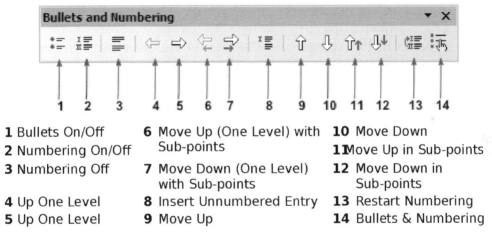

1 Bullets On/Off
2 Numbering On/Off
3 Numbering Off

4 Up One Level
5 Up One Level

6 Move Up (One Level) with Sub-points
7 Move Down (One Level) with Sub-points
8 Insert Unnumbered Entry
9 Move Up

10 Move Down
11 Move Up in Sub-points
12 Move Down in Sub-points
13 Restart Numbering
14 Bullets & Numbering

Figure 71: Bullets and Numbering toolbar

Hyphenating words

To turn automatic hyphenation of words on or off:

1) Press *F11* to open the Styles and Formatting window (Figure 72).

2) On the Paragraph Styles page of the Styles and Formatting window, right-click on **Default** in the list and select **Modify**.

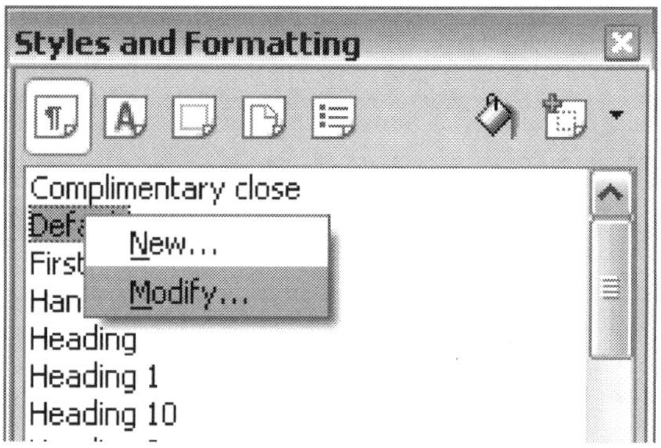

Figure 72: Modifying a style

3) On the Paragraph Style dialog, go to the **Text Flow** page (see Figure 73).

4) Under Hyphenation, select or deselect the **Automatically** option. Click **OK** to save.

| **Note** | Turning on hyphenation for the Default paragraph style affects all other paragraph styles that are based on Default. You can individually change other styles so that hyphenation is not active; for example, you might not want headings to be hyphenated. Any styles that are not based on Default are not affected. For more on paragraph styles, see Chapter 6 (Introduction to Styles) and Chapter 7 (Working with Styles) in the *Writer Guide*. |

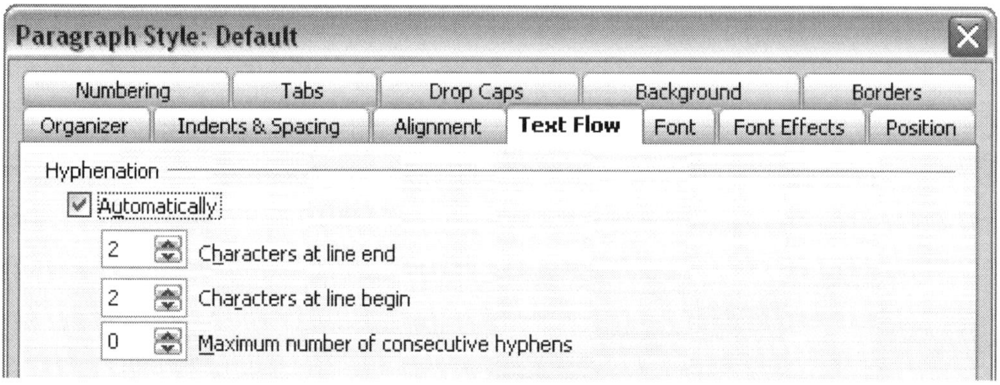

Figure 73: Turning on automatic hyphenation

You can also set hyphenation choices through **Tools > Options > Language Settings > Writing Aids**. In Options, near the bottom of the dialog, scroll down to the find the hyphenation settings (Figure 74).

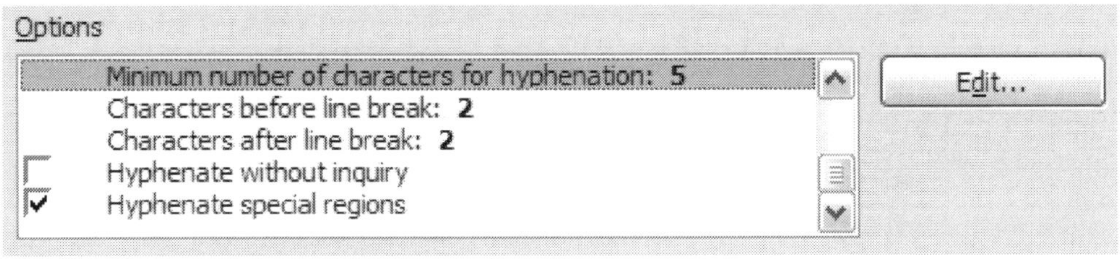

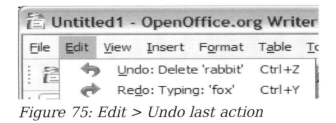

Figure 74: Setting hyphenation options

Note	Hyphenation options set on the Writing Aids dialog are effective only if hyphenation is turned on through paragraph styles. Choices on the Writing Aids dialog for "characters before line break" and "characters after line break" override settings in paragraphs styles for "characters at line end" and "characters at line begin".

To enter a conditional hyphen inside a word, press *Control+minus sign*. The word is hyphenated at this position when it is at the end of the line, even if automatic hyphenation for this paragraph is switched off.

To insert a non-breaking hyphen, press *Control+Shift+minus sign.*

Undoing and redoing changes

To undo the most recent change, press *Control+Z*, or click the Undo icon  on the Standard toolbar, or select **Edit > Undo** from the menu bar.

The Edit menu shows the latest change that can be undone, as shown in Figure 75.

Figure 75: Edit > Undo last action

Click the small triangle to the right of the **Undo** icon to get a list of all the changes that can be undone (Figure 76). You can select multiple changes and undo them at the same time.

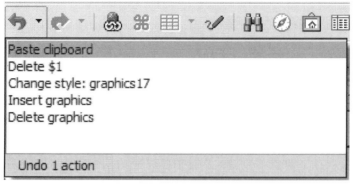

Figure 76: List of actions that can be undone

After changes have been undone, **Redo** becomes active. To redo a change, select **Edit > Redo**, or press *Control+Y* or click on the Redo icon . As with Undo, click on the triangle to the right of the arrow to get a list of the changes that can be reapplied.

To modify the number of changes OpenOffice.org remembers, select **Tools > Options > OpenOffice.org > Memory** and change **Undo number of steps**. Be aware that asking OOo to remember more changes consumes more computer memory.

Formatting pages

Writer provides several ways for you to control page layouts: page styles, columns, frames, tables, and sections.

For more information, see Chapter 4 (Formatting Pages) in the *Writer Guide*.

Tip	Page layout is usually easier if you show text, object, table, and section boundaries in **Tools > Options > OpenOffice.org > Appearance**, and paragraph ends, tabs, breaks, and other items in **Tools > Options > OpenOffice.org Writer > Formatting Aids**.

Which layout method to choose?

The best layout method varies depending on what the final document should look like and what sort of information will be in the document. Here are some examples.

For a book similar to this user guide, with one column of text, some figures without text beside them, and some other figures with descriptive text, use page styles for basic layout, and tables to place figures beside descriptive text when necessary.

For an index or other document with two columns of text, where the text continues from the left-hand column to the right-hand column and then to the next page, all in sequence (also known as "snaking columns" of text), use page styles (with two columns). If the title of the document (on the first page) is full-page width, put it in a single-column section.

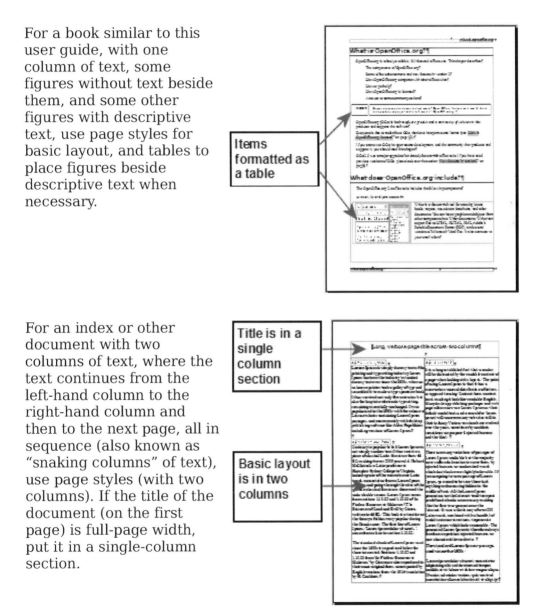

For a newsletter with complex layout, two or three columns on the page, and some articles that continue from one page to some place several pages later, use page styles for basic layout. Place articles in linked frames and anchor graphics to fixed positions on the page if necessary.

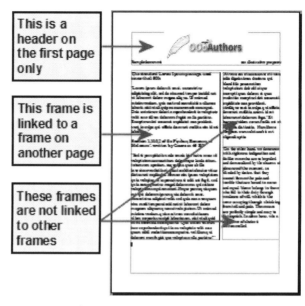

For a document with terms and translations to appear side-by-side in what appear to be columns, use a table to keep items lined up, and so you can type in both "columns".

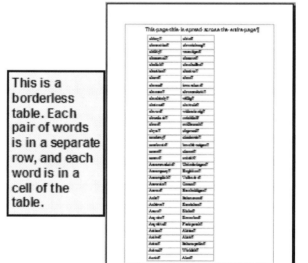

Creating headers and footers

A header is an area that appears at the top of a page. A footer appears at the bottom of the page. Information, such as page numbers inserted into a header or footer, displays on every page of the document with that page style.

To insert a header, click **Insert > Header > Default** (or the page style, if not Default) as shown in Figure 77.

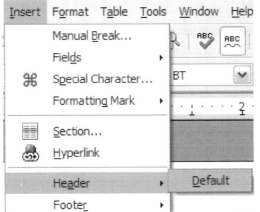

Figure 77: Inserting headers and footers

Other information such as document titles and chapter titles is often put into the header or footer. These items are best added as fields. That way, if something changes, the headers and footers are updated automatically. Here is one common example.

To insert the document title into the header:

1) Click **File > Properties > Description** and type a title for your document.

2) Add a header (**Insert > Header > Default**).

3) Place the cursor in the header part of the page.

4) Select **Insert > Fields > Title**. The title should appear on a gray background (which does not show when printed and can be turned off).

5) To change the title for the whole document, go back to **File > Properties > Description**.

Fields are covered in detail in Chapter 14 (Working with Fields) in the *Writer Guide*.

For more about headers and footers, see Chapter 4 (Formatting Pages) and Chapter 6 (Introduction to Styles) in the *Writer Guide*.

Numbering pages

To automatically number pages:

1) Insert a header or footer, as described in "Creating headers and footers" on page 98.

2) Place the cursor in the header or footer where you want the page number to appear and click **Insert > Fields > Page Number**.

Including the total number of pages

To include the total number of pages (as in "page 1 of 12"):

1) Type the word "page" and a space, then insert the page number as above.

2) Press the spacebar once, type the word "of" and a space, then click **Insert > Fields > Page Count**.

Note	The Page Count field inserts the total number of pages in the document, as shown on the Statistics tab of the document's Properties window (**File > Properties**). If you restart page numbering anywhere in the document, then the total page count may not be what you want. See Chapter 4 (Formatting Pages) in the *Writer Guide* for more information.

Restarting page numbering

Often you will want to restart the page numbering at 1, for example on the page following a title page or a table of contents. In addition, many documents have the "front matter" (such as the table of contents) numbered with Roman numerals and the main body of the document numbered in Arabic numerals, starting with 1.

You can restart page numbering in two ways.

Method 1:

1) Place the cursor in the first paragraph of the new page.

2) Click **Format > Paragraph**.

3) On the Text Flow tab of the Paragraph dialog (Figure 73 on page 94), select **Breaks**.

4) Select **Insert** and then **With Page Style** and specify the page style to use.

5) Specify the page number to start from, and then click **OK**.

Tip	Method 1 is also useful for numbering the first page of a document with a page number greater than 1. For example, you may be writing a book, with each chapter in a separate file. Chapter 1 may start with page 1, but Chapter 2 could begin with page 25 and Chapter 3 with page 51.

Method 2:

1) **Insert > Manual break.**
2) By default, **Page break** is selected on the Insert Break dialog (Figure 78).
3) Choose the required page **Style**.
4) Select **Change page number.**
5) Specify the page number to start from, and then click **OK**.

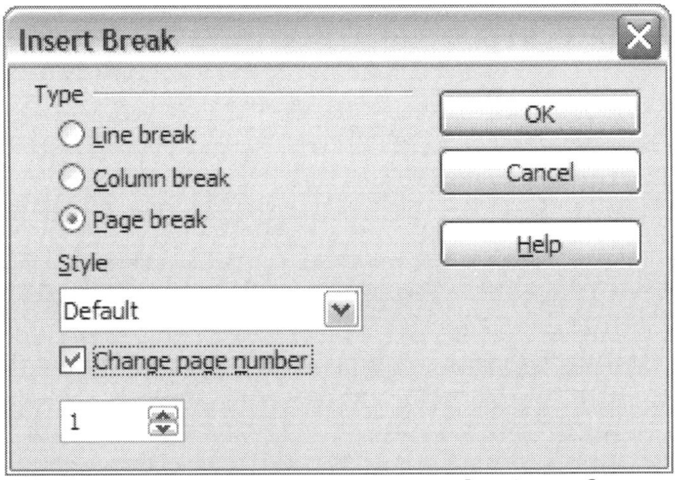

Figure 78: Restarting page numbering after a manual page break

Changing page margins

You can change page margins in two ways:

- Using the page rulers—quick and easy, but does not have fine control.
- Using the Page Style dialog—can specify margins to two decimal places.

Note	If you change the margins using the rulers, the new margins affect the page style and will be shown in the Page Style dialog the next time you open it.

To change margins using the rulers:

1) The gray sections of the rulers are the margins (see Figure 79). Put the mouse cursor over the line between the gray and white sections. The pointer turns into a double-headed arrow.

2) Hold down the left mouse button and drag the mouse to move the margin.

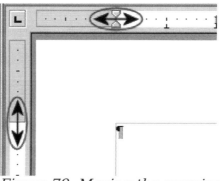

Figure 79: Moving the margins

Tip	The small arrows on the ruler are used for indenting paragraphs. They are often in the same place as the page margins, so you need to be careful to move the margin marker, not the arrows. Place the mouse pointer between the arrows and, when the pointer turns into a double-headed arrow, you can move the margin (the indent arrows will move with it).

To change margins using the Page Style dialog:

1) Right-click anywhere on the page and select **Page** from the pop-up menu.

2) On the **Page** tab of the dialog, type the required distances in the Margins boxes.

Adding notes to a document

The use of notes in a Writer document has been improved in OOo3. Notes are now displayed at the side of the page and color-coded according to the user who created them.

To insert a note in the text, place the cursor in the text and select **Insert > Note** or press *Ctrl+Alt+N*. The anchor point of the note is connected by a dotted line to a box on the right-hand side of the page where you can type the text of the note. OOo automatically adds at the bottom of the note the name or initials of the author and a time stamp. Figure 80 shows an example of text with notes from two different authors.

Select **Tools > Options > User Data** to configure the name you want to appear in the Author field of the note, or to change it.

If more than one person edits the document, each author is automatically allocated a different background color.

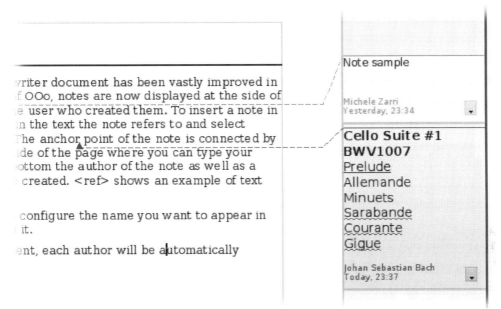

Figure 80: Notes in OOo3

Right-clicking on any note pops up a menu where you can delete the current note, all the notes from the same author, or all the notes in the document. From this menu, you can also apply some basic formatting to the text of the notes. You can also change the font type, size, and alignment from the main menu.

To navigate from one note to the other, open the Navigator (*F5*), expand the Notes section, and click on the note text to move the cursor to the anchor point of the note in the document. Right-click on the note to quickly edit or delete it.

You can also navigate the notes using the keyboard. Use *Ctrl+Alt+Page Down* to move to the next note and *Ctrl+Alt+Page Up* to move to the previous note.

Creating a table of contents

Writer's table of contents feature lets you build an automated table of contents from the headings in your document. Before you start, make sure that the headings are styled consistently. For example, you can use the *Heading 1* style for chapter titles and the *Heading 2* and *Heading 3* styles for chapter subheadings.

Although tables of contents can be customized extensively in Writer, often the default settings are all you need. Creating a quick table of contents is simple:

1) When you create your document, use the following paragraph styles for different heading levels (such as chapter and section headings): *Heading 1*, *Heading 2*, and *Heading 3*. These are what will appear in your table of contents. You can use more levels of headings, but the default setting is to use only the first three levels in the table of contents.

2) Place the cursor where you want the table of contents to be inserted.

3) Select **Insert > Indexes and Tables > Indexes and Tables**.

4) Change nothing in the Insert Index/Table dialog. Click **OK**.

If you add or delete text (so that headings move to different pages) or you add, delete, or change headings, you need to update the table of contents. To do this:

1) Place the cursor within the table of contents.

2) Right-click and select **Update Index/Table** from the pop-up menu.

Note	If you cannot place your cursor in the table of contents, choose **Tools > Options > OpenOffice.org Writer > Formatting Aids**, and then select **Enable** in the **Cursor in protected areas** section.

You can customize an existing table of contents at any time. Right-click anywhere in it and select **Edit Index/Table** from the pop-up menu. Chapter 12 (Creating Tables of Contents, Indexes and Bibliographies) of the *Writer Guide* describes in detail all the customizations you can choose.

Creating indexes and bibliographies

Indexes and bibliographies work in a similar way to tables of contents. Chapter 12 (Creating Tables of Contents, Indexes and Bibliographies) in the *Writer Guide* describes the process in detail.

In addition to alphabetical indexes, other types of indexes supplied with Writer include those for illustrations, tables, and objects, and you can even create a user-defined index. For example, you might want an index containing only the scientific names of species mentioned in the text, and a separate index containing only the common names of species. Before creating some types of indexes, you first need to create index entries embedded in your Writer document.

Working with graphics

Graphics in Writer are of three basic types:

* Image files, including photos, drawings, scanned images, and others
* Diagrams created using OOo's drawing tools
* Charts created using OOo's Chart facility.

See Chapter 11 (Graphics, the Gallery, and Fontwork).

Printing from Writer

Writer provides a range of choices when printing.

Quick printing

Click the **Print File Directly** icon 🖨 to send the entire document to the default printer defined for your computer.

Note	You can change the action of the **Print File Directly** icon to send the document to the printer defined for the document instead of the default printer for the computer. Go to **Tools > Options > Load/Save > General** and select the **Load printer settings with the document** option.

Controlling printing

For more control over printing, use **File > Print** to display the Print dialog (Figure 81).

On the Print dialog, you can choose:

* Which printer to use (if more than one are installed on your system) and the properties of the printer—for example, orientation (portrait or landscape), which paper tray to use, and what paper size to print on. The properties available depend on the selected printer; consult the printer's documentation for details.

- What pages to print, how many copies to print, and in what order to print them. Use dashes to specify page ranges and commas or semicolons to separate ranges; for example: 1, 5, 11–14, 34–40. *Selection* is the highlighted part of a page or pages.

- What items to print. Click the **Options** button to display the Printer Options dialog (Figure 82).

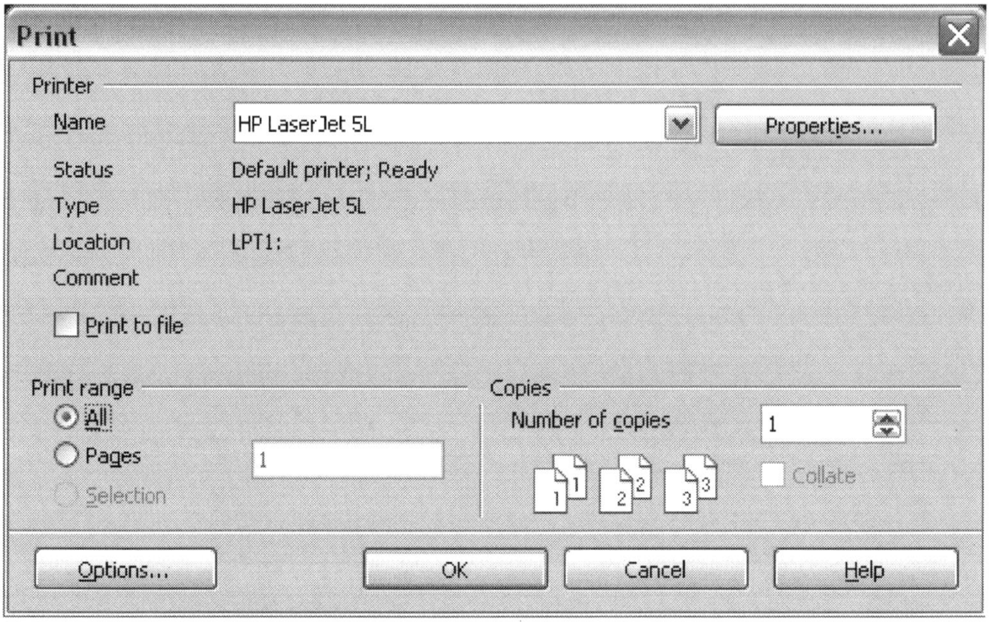

Figure 81. The Print dialog

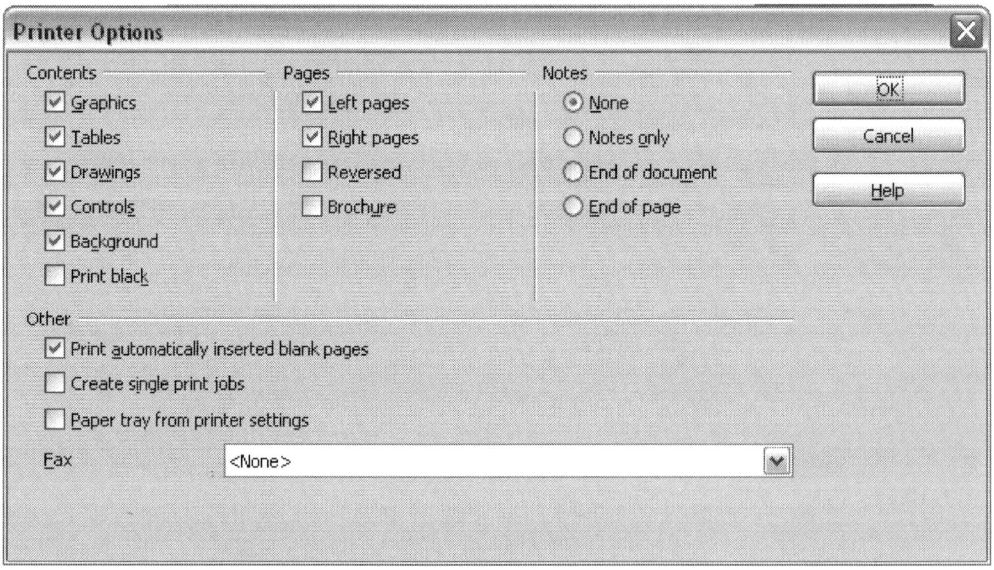

Figure 82. Printer Options dialog for Writer

Selecting print options for a document

Selections on the Printer Options dialog apply to this printing of this document only.

To specify default printing options, you need to use two pages in **Tools > Options**: **OpenOffice.org – Print** (see Chapter 2) and **OpenOffice.org Writer – Print** (which looks very similar to the Printer Options dialog.

Some items of interest on the Printer Options dialog include:

- In the *Contents* section, you might choose not to print graphics or page background in drafts, for example (to save toner or ink).
- In the *Pages* section, you can choose:
  - Print only left (even-numbered) pages or only right (odd-numbered) pages. These settings are useful when you want to print on both sides of the page, but do not have a printer that handles this automatically.
  - Print in reversed page order.
  - *Brochure*—the results of this selection are discussed in "Printing a brochure" on page 109.
- In the *Notes* section, you can choose whether to print any notes that have been added to your document (using **Insert > Note**), and where to print the notes.

Printing in black and white on a color printer

You may wish to print documents in black and white on a color printer, to save expensive color ink or toner. Common uses are for drafts or documents to be photocopied in black and white. Several choices are available.

To print the current document in black and white or grayscale:

1) Click **File > Print** to open the Print dialog.
2) Click **Properties** to open the properties dialog for the printer. The available choices vary from one printer to another, but you should find an option for Color. See your printer's help or user manual for more information.
3) The choices for color may include *black and white* or *grayscale*. Choose one of these. Grayscale is best if you have any graphics in the document. Click **OK** to confirm your choice and return to the Print dialog, then click **OK** again to print the document.

To set up OOo to print all color text and graphics as grayscale:

1) Click **Tools > Options > OpenOffice.org > Print**.

2) Select the **Convert colors to grayscale** option. Click **OK** to save the change.

To set up OOo Writer to print all color text as black, and all graphics as grayscale:

1) Click **Tools > Options > OpenOffice.org Writer > Print**.

2) Under *Contents*, select the **Print black** option. Click **OK** to save the change.

Previewing pages before printing

The normal page view in Writer shows you what each page will look like when printed, but it shows only one page at a time. If you are designing a document to be printed double-sided, you may want to see what facing pages look like. OOo provides two ways to do this:

- View Layout (editable view) —see "View layout" on page 75.

- Page Preview (read-only view) —from which you can print multiple pages onto one sheet of paper.

To use Page Preview:

1) Click **File > Page Preview**, or click the **Page Preview** button  .

   The Writer window changes to display the current page and the following page, and shows the **Page Preview** toolbar in place of the Formatting toolbar.

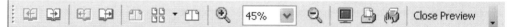

Figure 83. Page Preview toolbar

2) Click the **Book Preview** icon  to display left and right pages in their correct orientation.

3) To print the document from this page view, click the **Print page view** icon  to open the Print dialog. Choose your options and click **OK** to print as usual.

4) To choose margins and other options for the printout, click the **Print options page view** icon  to display the Print Options dialog.

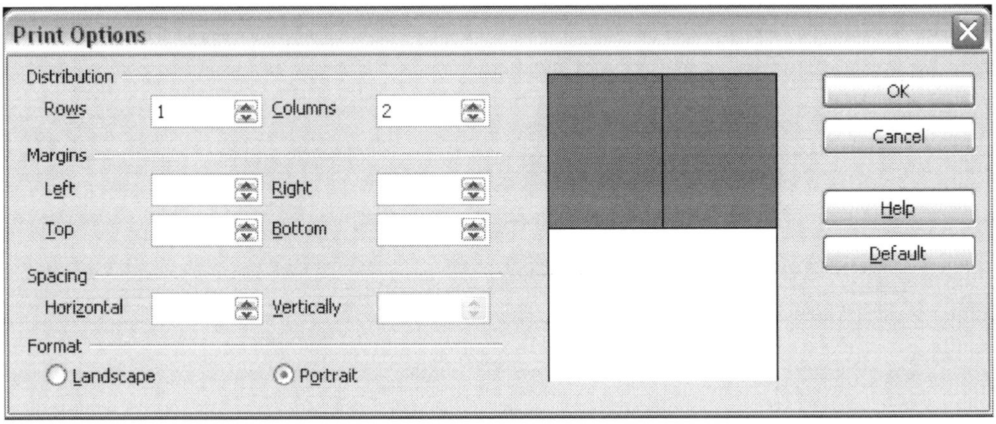

Figure 84. Print Options dialog

Printing a brochure

You can print a document with two pages on each side of a sheet of paper, arranged so that when the printed pages are folded in half, the pages are in the correct order to form a booklet or brochure.

To print a brochure on a single-sided printer:

1) Plan your document so it will look good when printed half size (choose appropriate margins, font sizes, and so on). Click **File > Print**. In the Print dialog, click **Properties** and be sure the printer is set to the same orientation (portrait or landscape) as specified in the page setup for your document. (Usually the orientation does not matter, but it does for brochures.)

2) Click **Options**. In the Pages section of the Printer Options dialog, choose **Brochure** and **Right pages**. Click **OK** twice to print the first side of each page.

3) Flip the pages and put them back into the printer, in the correct orientation to print on the blank side. You may need to experiment a bit to find out what the correct arrangement is for your printer.

4) Click **File > Print** and check **Properties** to make sure the printer setup is still correct.

5) Click **Options** again. In the Pages section of the Printer Options dialog, choose **Brochure** and **Left page**. Click **OK** twice to print the second sides.

6) If your printer can do double-sided, then click on the options for **Left pages**, **Right pages**, and **Brochure**, and it should not only do those but collate too.

Printing envelopes

Printing envelopes involves two steps: setup and printing.

To set up an envelope to be printed by itself or with your document:

1) Click **Insert > Envelope** from the menu bar.

2) In the Envelope dialog, start with the *Envelope* tab (Figure 85). Verify, add, or edit the information in the Addressee and Sender boxes (the "from" on the envelope).

   You can type information directly into the Addressee and Sender boxes, or use the right-hand drop-down lists to select the database or table from which to draw the envelope information, if desired. See Chapter 11 (Using Mail Merge) in the *Writer Guide* for details on how to print envelopes from a database.

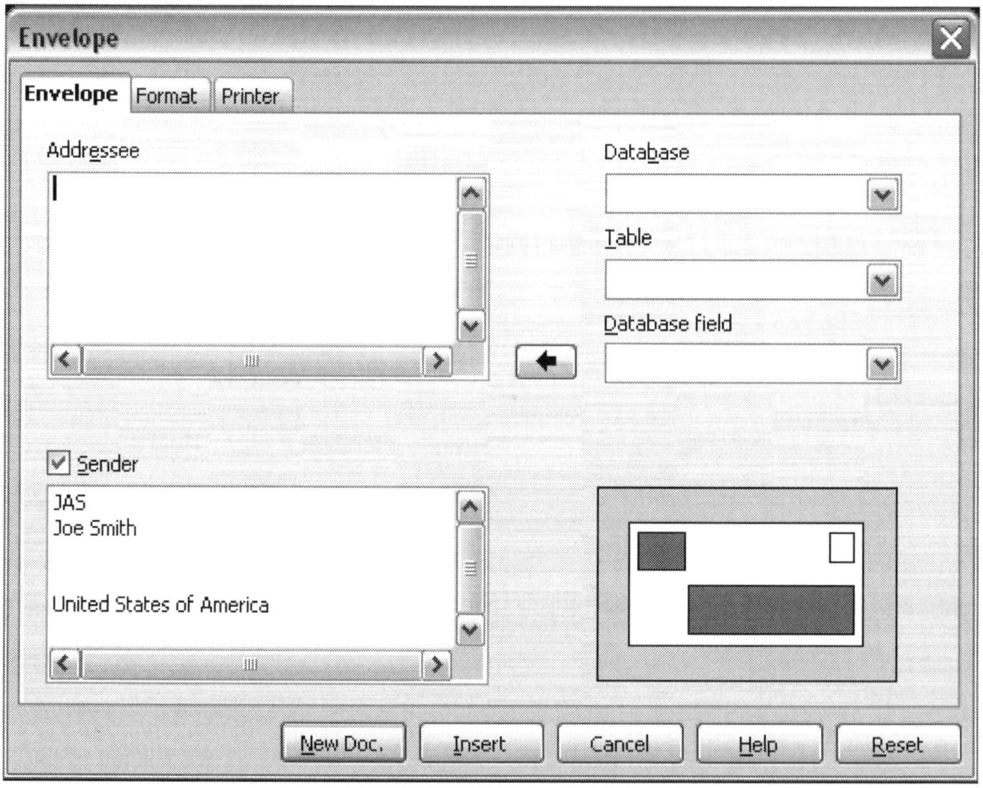

Figure 85. Choosing addressee and sender information

3) On the *Format* page (Figure 86), verify or edit the positioning of the addressee and the sender information. The preview area on the lower right shows the effect of your positioning choices.

   To format the text of these blocks, click the **Edit** buttons to the right. In the drop-down list you have two choices: Character and Paragraph.

- In Character, you can choose Fonts (Sizes...), Fonts Effects (Underlining, Color...), Position (Rotating/scaling...), Hyperlink, Background and more.

- In Paragraph, you can choose Indents & Spacing, Alignment, Text Flow, Tabs, Drop Caps, Borders and Backgrounds.

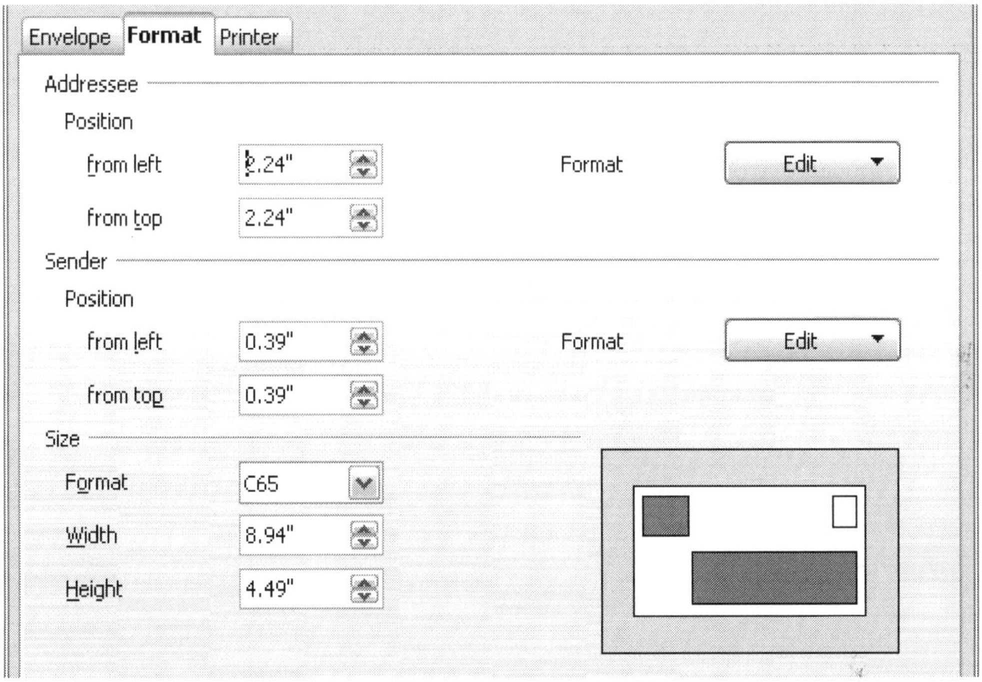

Figure 86. Choosing positioning and size of elements

4) In the lower left of this page, choose the envelope format from the drop-down list. The width and height of the selected envelope then show in the boxes below the selected format. If you chose a pre-existing format, just verify these sizes. If you chose *User defined* in the Format list, then you can edit the sizes.

5) After formatting, go to the *Printer* page (Figure 87) to choose printer options such as envelope orientation and shifting. You may need to experiment a bit to see what works best for your printer.

   You can also choose a different printer or alter printer setup (for example, specify the tray that holds envelopes) for this print job.

6) When you have finished formatting and are ready to print, click either the **New Doc** or **Insert** button to finish. **New Doc** makes only an envelope or starts a new document with the envelope. **Insert** inserts the envelope into an existing document as page 1.

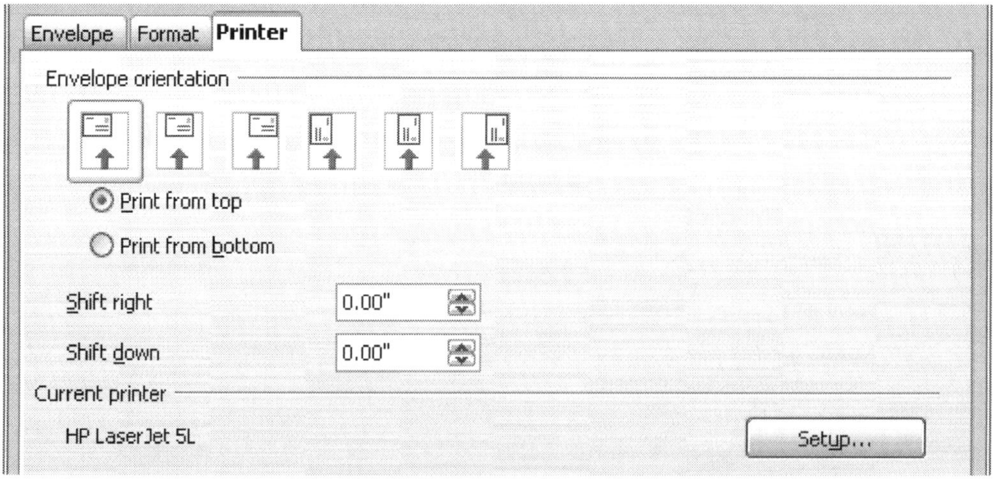

Figure 87. Choosing printer options for an envelope

> To not proceed with this envelope, click **Cancel** or press the *Esc* key. You can also click **Reset** to remove your changes and return to the original settings when the dialog opened.

7) When the Envelope dialog closes, you are returned to your document, which now has the envelope in the same file as the document. Save this file before you do anything else.

To print the envelope:

1) Choose **File > Print** from the menu bar.
2) On the Print dialog, under *Print range*, choose **Pages** and type 1 in the box. Click **OK** to print.

Printing labels

Labels are commonly used for printing address lists (where each label shows a different address), but they can also be used for making multiple copies of one label only, for example return-address stickers.

To print labels:

1) Choose **File > New > Labels** on the menu bar. The Labels dialog opens.
2) On the *Labels* page (Figure 88), fill in your own label text in the **Inscription** box, or use the **Database** and **Table** drop-down lists to choose the required information, as described in Chapter 11 (Using Mail Merge) in the *Writer Guide*.
3) Select the label stock in the **Brand** drop-down list. The types for that brand then appear in the **Type** drop-down list. Select the size and type of labels required. You can also select User in the **Type** drop-down list and then make specific selections on the *Format* page.

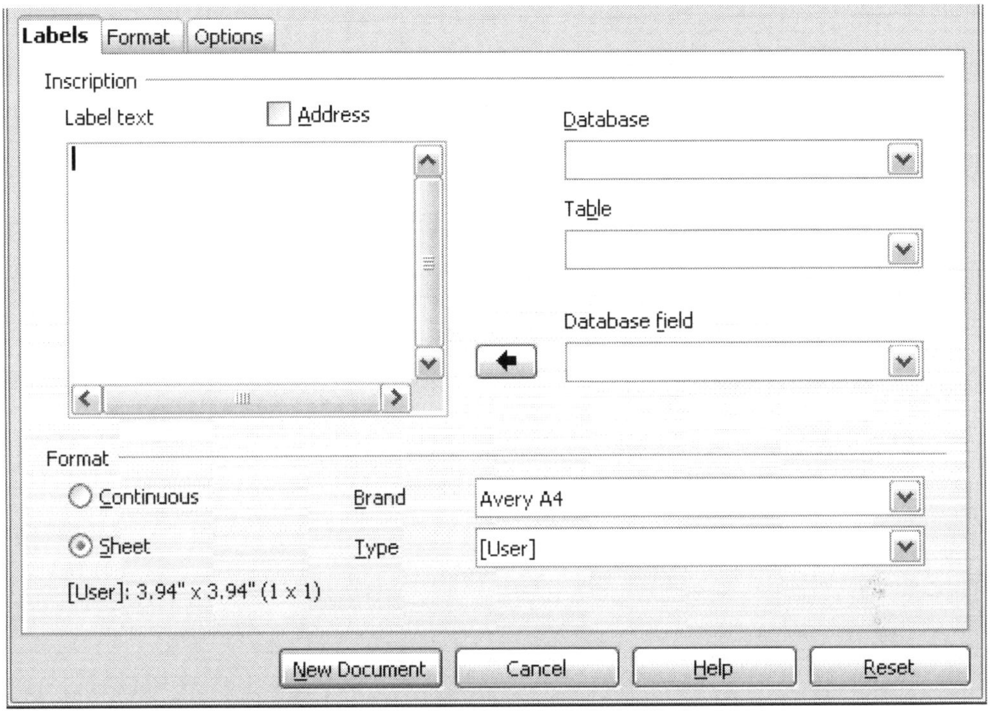

Figure 88. Labels dialog, Labels page

4) On the *Format* page (Figure 89), choose the pitch, sizes, margins, columns and rows for user-defined labels, or just verify with a brand of label stock you have loaded into the printer.

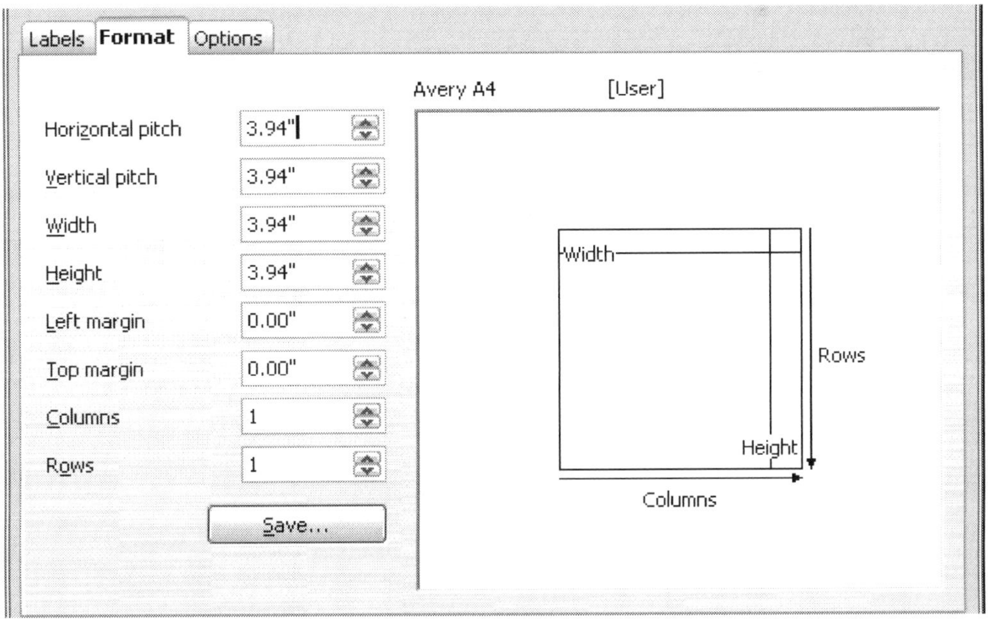

Figure 89. Labels dialog, Format page

5) Click **Save** to save your new format.

6) When you have finished formatting, click **New Document** to make your sheet of labels or click **Cancel** (or press the *Esc* key). You can also click **Reset** to remove your changes and return to the original settings when the dialog opened. On the *Options* page, choose to print the entire page of labels or one single label, then select which one by the column and row. You can also change printer setup.

7) You can print right away using the **Print File Directly** icon on the toolbar or by choosing **File > Print** from the menu bar, or you can save the file to print later.

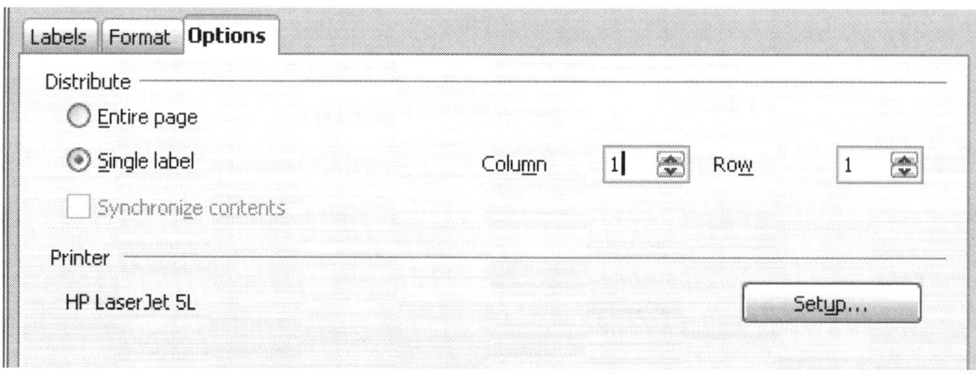

Figure 90. Labels dialog, Options page

Sending a fax using Writer

To send a fax directly from OpenOffice.org, you need a fax modem and a fax driver that allows applications to communicate with the fax modem.

Sending a fax through the Print dialog

1) Open the Print dialog by choosing **File > Print** and select the fax driver in the **Name** list.

2) Click **OK** to open the dialog for your fax driver, where you can select the fax recipient.

Adding a Fax icon to the toolbar

You can configure OpenOffice.org so that a single click on an icon automatically sends the current document as a fax. See Chapter 14 (Customizing OpenOffice.org) for instructions.

Tracking changes to a document

You can use several methods to keep track of changes made to a document.

1) Make your changes to a copy of the document (stored in a different folder, or under a different name, or both), then use Writer to combine the two files and show the differences. Click **Edit > Compare Document**. This technique is particularly useful if you are the only person working on the document, as it avoids the increase in file size and complexity caused by the other methods.

2) Save versions that are stored as part of the original file. However, this method can cause problems with documents of non-trivial size or complexity, especially if you save a lot of versions. Avoid this method if you can.

3) Use Writer's change marks (often called "redlines" or "revision marks") to show where you have added or deleted material, or changed formatting. Later, you or another person can review and accept or reject each change. Click **Edit > Changes > Record**. Details are in the *Writer Guide*.

Tip	Not all changes are recorded. For example, changing a tab stop from align left to align right, and changes in formulas (equations) or linked graphics are not recorded.

Using mail merge

Writer provides very useful features to create and print:

- Multiple copies of a document to send to a list of different recipients (form letters)
- Mailing labels
- Envelopes

All these facilities, though different in application, are based around the concept of a registered data source (a spreadsheet or database containing the name and address records and other information), from which is derived the variable information necessary to their function.

Chapter 11 (Using Mail Merge) in the *Writer Guide* describes the process.

Using master documents

Master documents are typically used for producing long documents such as a book, a thesis, or a long report; or when different people are writing different chapters or other parts of the full document, so you don't need to share files. A master document joins separate text documents into one larger document, and unifies the formatting, table of contents (ToC), bibliography, index, and other tables or lists.

Yes, master documents do work in Writer. However, until you become familiar with them, you may think that master documents are unreliable or difficult to use. See Chapter 13 (Working with Master Documents) in the *Writer Guide*.

Creating fill-in forms

A standard text document displays information: a letter, report, or brochure, for example. Typically the reader may edit everything or nothing in any way. A form has sections that are not to be edited, and other sections that are designed for the reader to make changes. For example, a questionnaire has an introduction and questions (which do not change) and spaces for the reader to enter answers.

Forms are used in three ways:

- To create a simple document for the recipient to complete, such as a questionnaire sent out to a group of people who fill it in and return it.

- To link into a database or data source and allow the user to enter information. Someone taking orders might enter the information for each order into a database using a form.

- To view information held in a database or data source. A librarian might call up information about books.

Writer offers several ways to fill information into a form, including check boxes, option buttons, text boxes, pull-down lists and spinners. See Chapter 15 (Using Forms in Writer) in the *Writer Guide*.

Using fields

Fields are extremely useful features of Writer. They are used for data that changes in a document (such as the current date or the total number of pages) and for inserting document properties such as name, author, and date of last update. Fields are the basis of cross-referencing (see below); automatic numbering of figures, tables, headings, and other elements; and a wide range of other functions—

far too many to describe here. See Chapter 14 (Working with Fields) in the *Writer Guide* for details.

Using cross-references

If you type in references to other parts of the document, those references can easily get out of date if you reword a heading, add or remove figures, or reorganize topics. Replace any typed cross-references with automatic ones and, when you update fields, all the references will update automatically to show the current wording or page numbers. The *Cross-references* tab of the Fields dialog lists some items, such as headings, bookmarks, figures, tables, and numbered items such as steps in a procedure.

To insert a cross-reference to a heading or other text:

1) In your document, place the cursor where you want the cross-reference to appear.

2) If the Fields dialog is not open, click **Insert > Cross-reference**. On the *Cross-references* tab, in the *Type* list, select the type of item to be referenced (for example, *Heading* or *Figure*).

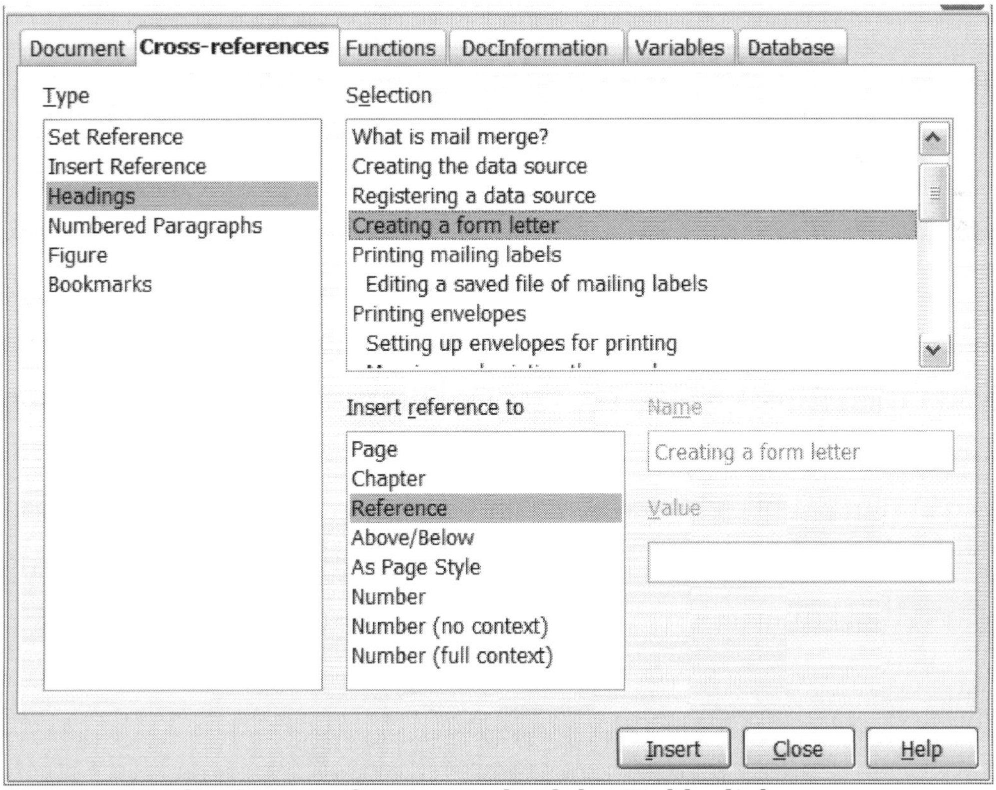

Figure 91: The Cross-references tab of the Fields dialog

You can leave this page open while you insert many cross-references.

3) Click on the required item in the *Selection* list, which shows all the items of the selected type. In the *Format* list, choose the format required. Usually this will be **Reference** (to insert the full text of the heading or caption), **Category and Number** (to insert the word "Figure" or "Table" and its number, but without the caption text), Numbering (to insert only the figure or table number, without the word "Figure" or "Table"), or **Page** (to insert the number of the page the referenced text is on). Click **Insert**.

Using bookmarks

Bookmarks are listed in the Navigator and can be accessed directly from there with a single mouse click. You can cross-reference to bookmarks, as described above. In HTML documents, bookmarks are converted to anchors that you can jump to using a hyperlink.

1) Select the text you want to bookmark. Click **Insert > Bookmark**.

2) On the Insert Bookmark dialog, the larger box lists any previously defined bookmarks. Type a name for this bookmark in the top box, and then click **OK** to save.

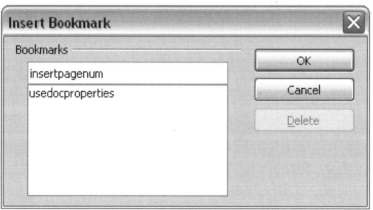

Figure 92: Inserting a bookmark

Chapter *5*
Getting Started with Calc

Using spreadsheets in OpenOffice.org

What is Calc?

Calc is the spreadsheet component of OpenOffice.org (OOo). A spreadsheet simulates a worksheet on your computer: you can fill the worksheet with data—usually numerical data—and then manipulate the data to produce certain results, organize the data, or display the data in diagrams.

Alternatively you can enter data and then use Calc in a 'What If...' manner by changing some of the data and observing the results without having to retype the entire spreadsheet or sheet.

Spreadsheets, sheets and cells

Calc works with elements called *spreadsheets*. Spreadsheets consist of a number of individual *sheets*, each containing a block of cells arranged in rows and columns.

These cells hold the individual elements—text, numbers, formulas etc.—which make up the data to be displayed and manipulated.

Each spreadsheet can have many sheets and each sheet can have many individual cells. In version 3.0 of OOo, each sheet can have a maximum of 65,536 rows and a maximum of 1024 columns.

Parts of the main Calc window

When Calc is started, the main window looks similar to Figure 93.

Title bar and Menu bar

The Title bar, at the top, shows the name of the current spreadsheet. If the spreadsheet is new, then its name is *Untitled X*, with *X* being a number. When you save a new spreadsheet for the first time, you will be prompted to enter a name.

Under the Title bar is the Menu bar. When you choose one of the menus, a submenu appears with other options. The Menu bar can be modified, as discussed in Chapter 14 (Customizing OpenOffice.org).

Toolbars

Under the Menu bar by default are three toolbars: the Standard toolbar, the Formatting toolbar, and the Formula bar.

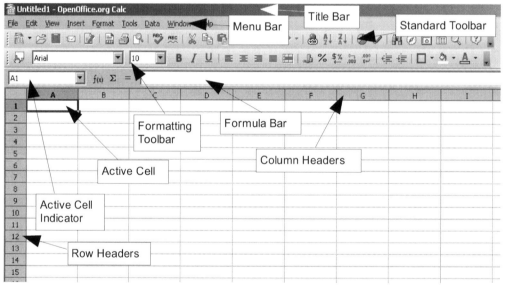

Figure 93. Parts of the Calc window

The icons on these toolbars provide a wide range of common commands and functions. The toolbars can be modified, as discussed in Chapter 14 (Customizing OpenOffice.org).

Placing the mouse pointer over any of the icons displays a small box, called a tooltip. It gives a brief explanation of the icon's function. For a more detailed explanation, select **Help > What's This?** and hover the mouse pointer over the icon. Tips and extended tips can now be turned on or off from **Tools > Options > OpenOffice.org > General**.

In the Formatting toolbar, the two rectangular areas on the left are the **Font Name** and **Font Size** menus (see Figure 94). If there is something in these boxes, they show the current setting for the selected area.

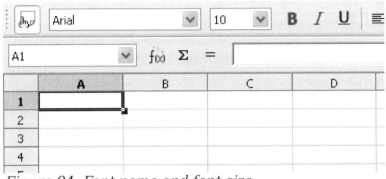

Figure 94. Font name and font size

Click the little button with an inverted triangle to the right of the box to open a menu. From the **Font Name** and **Font Size** menus, you can change the font and its size in selected cells.

Formula bar

On the left of the Formula bar (see Figure 95) is a small text box, called the **Name** box, with a letter and number combination in it, such as *D7*. This is the column letter and row number, called the cell reference, of the current cell.

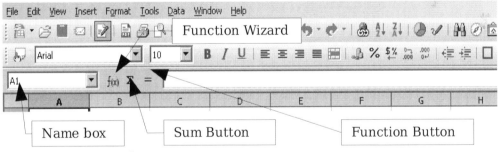

Figure 95. Formula Bar

To the right of the Name box are the the Function Wizard, Sum, and Function buttons.

Clicking the **Function Wizard** button opens a dialog from which you can search through a list of available functions, what variables each function takes and the result of the function with the given input .

The **Sum** button inserts a formula into the current cell that totals the numbers in the cells above, or to the left if there are no numbers above, the current cell.

The **Function** button inserts an equals sign into the selected cell and the Input Line, thereby setting the cell ready to accept a formula.

When you enter new data into a cell, the Sum and Equals buttons change to **Cancel** and **Accept** buttons ✖ ✔ .

The contents of the current cell (data, formula, or function) are displayed in the Input Line, the remainder of the Formula bar. You can edit the cell contents of the current cell here, or you can do that in the current cell. To edit inside the Input Line area, click the appropriate part of the Input Line area, then type your changes. To edit within the current cell, just double-click the cell.

Individual cells

The main section of the screen displays the individual cells in the form of a grid, with each cell being at the intersection of a particular column and row.

At the top of the columns and at the left-hand end of the rows are a series of gray boxes containing letters and numbers. These are the column and row headers. The columns start at A and go on to the right and the rows start at 1 and go on down.

These column and row headers form the cell references that appear in the *Sheet Area* box on the Formula Bar (Figure 101). These headers can also be turned off by selecting **View > Column & Row Headers**.

Sheet tabs

At the bottom of the grid of cells are the sheet tabs (see Figure 96). These tabs enable access to each individual sheet, with the visible, or active, sheet having a white tab.

Clicking on another sheet tab displays that sheet and its tab turns white. You can also select multiple sheet tabs at once by holding down the *Control* key while you click the names.

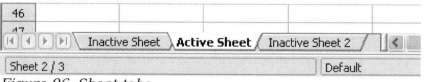

Figure 96. Sheet tabs

Status bar

At the very bottom of the Calc window you will find the status bar (shown in Figure 97) where you can quickly obtain some information on the current spreadsheet.

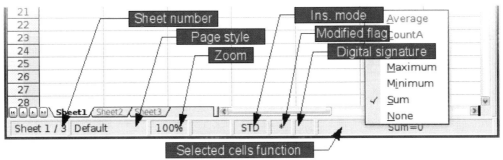

Figure 97: Status bar information

From left to right the status bar displays:

- The current sheet and the total number of sheets in the spreadsheet.

- The page style in use for the current sheet. Double-click to open the dialog and modify the page style.

- The zoom level. Double-click to modify the zoom level.

- Selection mode. Click to toggle between default mode (STD), extended mode (EXT) and incremental mode (ADD).

- Modified flag. When the document has been modified, a star is displayed in this area of the status bar.

- Digital signature flag. If you have added a digital signature to the spreadsheet, a small padlock icon is displayed in this area. Double-click to digitally sign the spreadsheet.

- Selected cells functions. By default, this area shows the sum of the values contained in the selected cells. You can, however, change the function used by right-clicking on the area. The available functions are:
  - *Average* (averages the values of the selection)
  - *CountA* (counts the cells in the selection which are not empty)
  - *Count* (counts the cells in the selection with a numeric value)
  - *Maximum* (displays the maximum value in the selection)
  - *Minimum* (displays the minimum value in the selection)
  - *Sum* (the sum of the values in the selection)
  - *None*.

Starting new spreadsheets

A new spreadsheet can be opened from any component of OOo, for example from Writer or Draw.

From the menu bar
Click **File** and then select **New > Spreadsheet**.

From the toolbar
Use the **New Document** [icon] ▾ button on the Standard toolbar. (This button is always a page of text from the current component with a black arrow to the right.) Click the drop-down arrow for a choice of what type of document to open (text document, spreadsheet, and so on). Click the button itself to create a new document of the type that is currently open (if a spreadsheet is open, a new spreadsheet document will be created).

From the keyboard
If you already have a spreadsheet open, you can press *Control+N* to open a new spreadsheet.

From a template
Calc documents can also be created from templates, if you have any spreadsheet templates available. Follow the above procedures, but instead of selecting Spreadsheet from the File menu, select **Templates and Documents**. On the Templates and Documents window, navigate to the appropriate folder and double-click on the required template. A new spreadsheet, based on the selected template, opens.

Opening existing spreadsheets

An existing spreadsheet can also be opened from any component of OOo.

From the menu bar
Click **File** and then select **Open**.

From the toolbar
Click the **Open** button [icon] on the Standard toolbar.

From the keyboard
Use the key combination *Control+O*.

Each of these options displays the Open dialog, where you can locate the spreadsheet that you want to open.

Saving spreadsheets

Spreadsheets can be saved in three ways.

From the menu bar
Click **File** and then select **Save**.

From the toolbar
Click on the **Save** button 🖫 on the Function bar. If the file has been saved and no subsequent changes have been made, this button is grayed-out and unselectable.

From the keyboard
Use the key combination *Control+S*.

If the spreadsheet has not been saved previously, then each of these actions will open the Save As dialog. Here you can specify the spreadsheet name and the location in which to save it.

Note	If the spreadsheet has been previously saved, then saving will overwrite the existing copy without opening the Save As dialog. If you want to save the spreadsheet in a different location or with a different name, then select **File > Save As**.

Navigating within spreadsheets

Going to a particular cell

Using the mouse
Place the mouse pointer over the cell and click.

Using a cell reference
Click on the little inverted black triangle just to the right of the Name box (Figure 101). The existing cell reference will be highlighted. Type

the cell reference of the cell you want to go to and press *Enter.* Or just click into the Name box, backspace over the existing cell reference and type in the cell reference you want.

Using the Navigator

Click on the Navigator button in the Standard toolbar (or press *F5*) to display the Navigator. Type the cell reference into the top two fields, labeled Column and Row, and press *Enter.* In Figure 98 the Navigator would select cell G28.

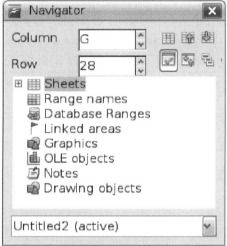

Moving from cell to cell

In the spreadsheet, one cell, or a group of cells, normally has a darker black border. This black border indicates where the *focus* is (see Figure 99).

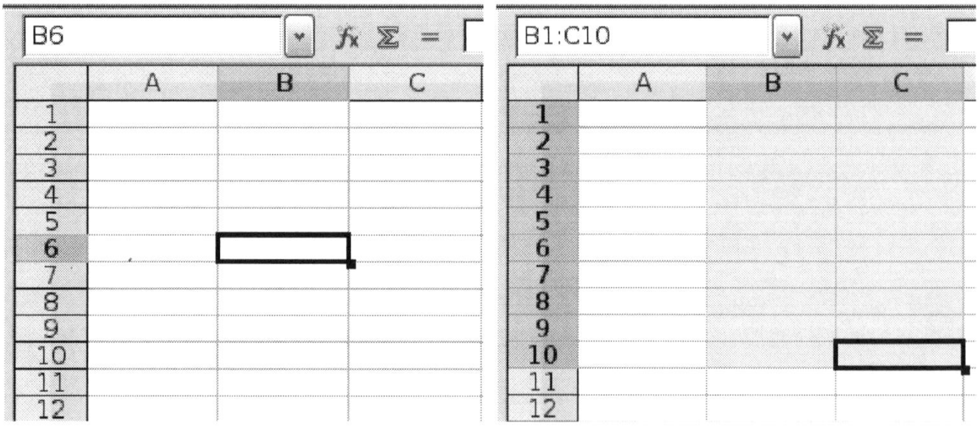

Figure 98. Calc Navigator

Figure 99. (Left) One selected cell and (right) a group of selected cells

Using the mouse

To move the focus using the mouse, simply move the mouse pointer to the cell where the focus should be and click the left mouse button. This changes the focus to the new cell. This method is most useful when the two cells are a large distance apart.

Using the Tab and Enter keys

- Pressing *Enter* or *Shift+Enter* moves the focus down or up, respectively.
- Pressing *Tab* or *Shift+Tab* moves the focus right or left, respectively.

Customizing the Enter key

You can customize the direction in which the *Enter* key moves the focus, by selecting **Tools > Options > OpenOffice.org Calc > General**.

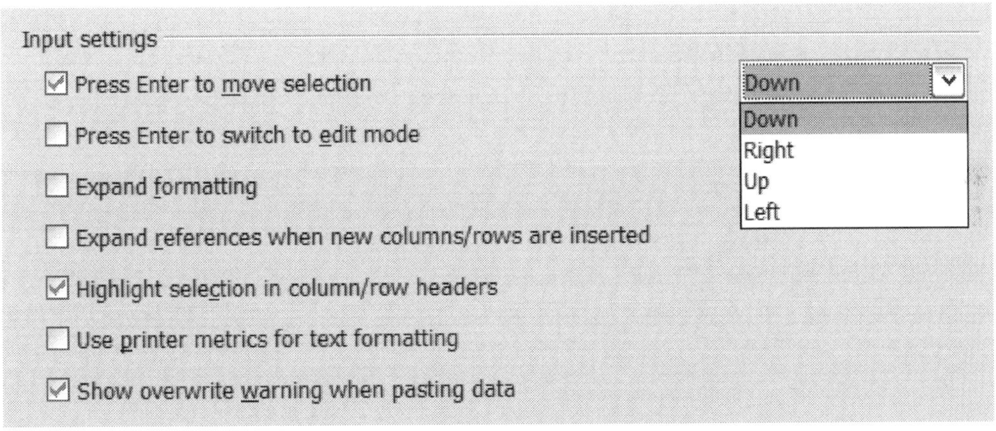

Figure 100: Customizing the effect of the Enter key

The four choices for the direction of the *Enter* key are shown on the right side of Figure 100. Depending on the file being used or on the type of data being entered, different directions can be useful.

The *Enter* key can also be used to switch into and out of editing mode. Use the options under *Input settings* in Figure 100 to change the *Enter* key settings.

Using the arrow keys

Pressing the arrow keys on the keyboard moves the focus in the direction of the arrows.

Using Home, End, Page Up and Page Down

- *Home* moves the focus to the start of a row.
- *End* moves the focus to the column furthest to the right that contains data.
- *Page Down* moves the display down one complete screen and *Page Up* moves the display up one complete screen.

- Combinations of *Control* and *Alt* with *Home, End, Page Down, Page Up,* and the cursor keys move the focus of the current cell in other ways.

Tip   Holding down *Alt+Cursor key* resizes a cell.

Moving from sheet to sheet

Each sheet in a spreadsheet is independent of the others though they can be linked with references from one sheet to another. There are three ways to navigate between different sheets in a spreadsheet.

Using the keyboard

Pressing *Control+PgDn* moves one sheet to the right and pressing *Control+PgUp* moves one sheet to the left.

Using the mouse

Clicking one of the Sheet Tabs at the bottom of the spreadsheet selects that sheet.

If you have a lot of sheets, then some of the sheet tabs may be hidden behind the horizontal scroll bar at the bottom of the screen. If this is the case, then the four buttons at the left of the sheet tabs can move the tabs into view. Figure 101 shows how to do this.

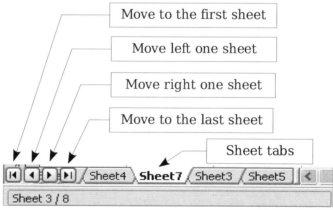

Figure 101. Sheet tab arrows

Notice that the sheets here are not numbered in order. Sheet numbering is arbitrary—you can name a sheet as you wish.

Note   The sheet tab arrows that appear in Figure 101 only appear if you have some sheet tabs that can not be seen. Otherwise they will appear faded as in Figure 96.

Selecting items in a sheet or spreadsheet

Selecting cells

Cells can be selected in a variety of combinations and quantities.

Single cell

Left-click in the cell. The result will look like the left side of Figure 99. You can verify your selection by looking in the Name box.

Range of contiguous cells

A range of cells can be selected using the keyboard or the mouse.

To select a range of cells by dragging the mouse:

1) Click in a cell.
2) Press and hold down the left mouse button.
3) Move the mouse around the screen.
4) Once the desired block of cells is highlighted, release the left mouse button.

To select a range of cells without dragging the mouse:

1) Click in the cell which is to be one corner of the range of cells.
2) Move the mouse to the opposite corner of the range of cells.
3) Hold down the *Shift* key and click.

To select a range of cells without using the mouse:

1) Select the cell that will be one of the corners in the range of cells.
2) While holding down the *Shift* key, use the cursor arrows to select the rest of the range.

The result of any of these methods looks like the right side of Figure 99.

Tip	You can also directly select a range of cells using the Name box. Click into the Name box as described in "Using a cell reference" on page 125. To select a range of cells, enter the cell reference for the upper left hand cell, followed by a colon (:), and then the lower right hand cell reference. For example, to select the range that would go from A3 to C6, you would enter *A3:C6*.

Range of non-contiguous cells

1) Select the cell or range of cells using one of the methods above.
2) Move the mouse pointer to the start of the next range or single cell.
3) Hold down the *Control* key and click or click-and-drag to select a range.
4) Repeat as necessary.

Selecting columns and rows

Entire columns and rows can be selected very quickly in OOo.

Single column or row

To select a single column, click on the column identifier letter (see Figure 95).

To select a single row, click on the row identifier number.

Multiple columns or rows

To select multiple columns or rows that are contiguous:

1) Click on the first column or row in the group.
2) Hold down the *Shift* key.
3) Click the last column or row in the group.

To select multiple columns or rows that are not contiguous:

1) Click on the first column or row in the group.
2) Hold down the *Control* key.
3) Click on all of the subsequent columns or rows while holding down the *Control* key.

Entire sheet

To select the entire sheet, click on the small box between the A column header and the 1 row header (see Figure 102).

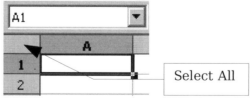

Figure 102. Select All box

You can also use the keyboard to select the entire sheet by pressing *Control+A.*

Selecting sheets

You can select either one or multiple sheets. It can be advantageous to select multiple sheets at times when you want to make changes to many sheets at once.

Single sheet

Click on the sheet tab for the sheet you want to select. The active sheet becomes white (see Figure 96).

Multiple contiguous sheets

To select multiple contiguous sheets:
  1) Click on the sheet tab for the first sheet.
  2) Move the mouse pointer over the last sheet tab.
  3) Hold down the *Shift* key and click on the sheet tab.

All the tabs between these two sheets will turn white. Any actions that you perform will now affect all highlighted sheets.

Multiple non contiguous sheets

To select multiple non contiguous sheets:
  1) Click on the sheet tab for the first sheet.
  2) Move the mouse pointer over the second sheet tab.
  3) Hold down the *Control* key and click on the sheet tab.
  4) Repeat as necessary.

The selected tabs will turn white. Any actions that you perform will now affect all highlighted sheets.

All sheets

Right-click over any one of the sheet tabs and select **Select All Sheets** from the pop-up menu.

Working with columns and rows

Inserting columns and rows

Columns and rows can be inserted in several different way and quantities.

Single column or row

A single column or row can be added using the **Insert** menu:

1) Select the column or rows where you want the new column or row inserted.

2) Select either **Insert > Columns** or **Insert > Rows**.

Note	When you insert a single new column, it is inserted to the left of the highlighted column. When you insert a single new row, it is inserted above the highlighted row.

A single column or row can also be added using the mouse:

1) Select the column or rows where you want the new column or row inserted. Right-click the header.

2) Select **Insert Rows** or **Insert Columns**.

Multiple columns or rows

Multiple columns or rows can be inserted at once rather than inserting them one at a time.

1) Highlight the required number of columns or rows by holding down the left mouse button on the first one and then dragging across the required number of identifiers.

2) Proceed as for inserting a single column or row above.

Deleting columns and rows

Columns and rows can be deleted individually or in groups.

Single column or row

A single column or row can only be deleted by using the mouse:

1) Select the column or row to be deleted.

2) Right-click on the column or row header.

3) Select **Delete Columns** or **Delete Rows** from the pop-up menu.

Multiple columns or rows

Multiple columns or rows can be deleted at once rather than deleting them one at a time.

1) Highlight the required number of columns or rows by holding down the left mouse button on the first one and then dragging across the required number of identifiers.

2) Proceed as for deleting a single column or row above.

Working with sheets

Like any other Calc element, sheets can be inserted, deleted and renamed.

Inserting new sheets

There are many ways to insert a new sheet. The first step for all of the methods is to select the sheets that the new sheet will be inserted next to. Then any of the following options can be used.

- Click on the **Insert** menu and select **Sheet**, or
- Right-click on its tab and select **Insert Sheet**, or
- Click into an empty space at the end of the line of sheet tabs (see Figure 103).

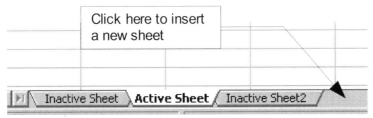

Figure 103. Creating a new sheet

Each method will open the Insert Sheet dialog (Figure 104). Here you can select whether the new sheet is to go before or after the selected sheet and how many sheets you want to insert. If you are inserting only one sheet, there is the opportunity to give the sheet a name.

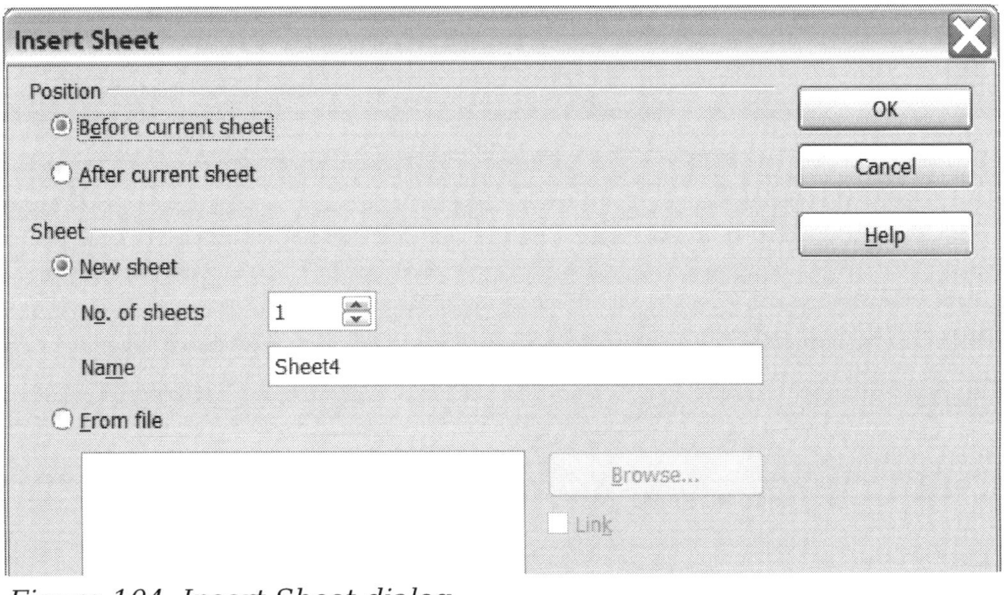

Figure 104. Insert Sheet dialog

Deleting sheets

Sheets can be deleted individually or in groups.

Single sheet
Right-click on the tab of the sheet you want to delete and select **Delete Sheet** from the pop-up menu, or click **Edit > Sheet > Delete.**

Multiple sheets
To delete multiple sheets, select them as described earlier, then either right-click over one of the tabs and select **Delete Sheet** from the popup menu, or click **Edit > Sheet > Delete** from the menu bar.

Renaming sheets

The default name for the a new sheet is "*SheetX*", where *X* is a number. While this works for a small spreadsheet with only a few sheets, it becomes awkward when there are many sheets.

To give a sheet a more meaningful name, you can:

* Enter the name in the name box when you create the sheet, or

* Right-click on a sheet tab and select **Rename Sheet** from the pop-up menu and replace the existing name with a better one.

Note	Sheet names can contain almost any characters with the exception of those characters not allowed in MS Excel. This restriction has been artificially created for compatibility reasons. Attempting to rename a sheet with an invalid name will produce an error message.

Viewing Calc

Using zoom

Use the zoom function to change the view to show more or fewer cells in the window. For more about zoom, see Chapter 1 (Introducing OOo).

Freezing rows and columns

Freezing locks a number of rows at the top of a spreadsheet or a number of columns on the left of a spreadsheet or both. Then when scrolling around within the sheet, any frozen columns and rows remain in view.

Figure 105 shows some frozen rows and columns. The heavier horizontal line between rows 3 and 14 and the heavier vertical line between columns C and H denote the frozen areas.. Rows 4 through 13 and columns D through G have been scrolled off the page. Because the first three rows and columns are frozen into place, they remained.

	A	B	C	H	I	J	K	L	M	N	O	P
1				Safety Poster	Safety Contract	Safety Quiz 2	Unit Conv. Pop Qu	Element Quiz 1	Element Quiz 2	p. 36 15 & 16	Article Quiz	Lab #1
2		Total	Date	10-02	10-03	10-04	10-05	10-06	10-07	10-08	10-09	10-10
3	Average	267.5	Possible	28.0	1.0	3.0	12.0	18.0	28.0	4.0	6.0	6.0
14	78.6%	200.0	Smith, John	28.00	1.00	X	0.00	8.00	26.00	0.00	6.00	0.00
15	67.9%	181.5	Klein, Mike	28.00	1.00	1.00	11.50	8.00	6.00	0.00	5.00	6.00
16	72.7%	186.5	Johnson, Tom	27.00	1.00	3.00	0.00	13.00	6.00	0.00	6.00	6.00
17	82.6%	213.0	Doe, John	27.00	1.00	1.00	2.00	17.00	17.00	4.00	6.00	6.00
18	96.4%	258.0	Doe, Jane	28.00	1.00	3.00	9.00	16.00	28.00	4.00	6.00	6.00
19	67.3%	172.0	Kupfer, Peter	26.00	1.00	3.00	X	16.00	20.00	0.00	6.00	6.00
20	83.9%	224.5	Newton, Issac	28.00	1.00	3.00	6.00	15.00	23.00	4.00	6.00	6.00
21	80.6%	207.5	Lunak, Robert	26.00	0.00	2.00	5.00	15.00	17.00	4.00	6.00	6.00
22	78.1%	209.0	Matteson, Brittany	28.00	0.00	3.00	3.00	17.00	22.00	4.00	6.00	6.00
23	79.4%	212.5	Murphy, Kathleen	26.00	1.00	3.00	6.00	16.00	11.00	4.00	6.00	6.00

Figure 105. Frozen rows and columns

You can set the freeze point at one row, one column, or both a row and a column as in Figure 105.

Freezing single rows or columns

1) Click on the header for the row below where you want the freeze or for the column to the right of where you want the freeze.

2) Select **Window > Freeze**.

   A dark line appears, indicating where the freeze is put.

Freezing a row and a column

1) Click into the cell that is immediately below the row you want frozen and immediately to the right of the column you want frozen.

2) Select **Window > Freeze**.

Two lines appear on the screen, a horizontal line above this cell and a vertical line to the left of this cell. Now as you scroll around the screen, everything above and to the left of these lines will remain in view.

Unfreezing

To unfreeze rows or columns, select **Window > Freeze**. The check mark by **Freeze** will vanish.

Splitting the window

Another way to change the view is by splitting the window—also known as splitting the screen. The screen can be split either horizontally or vertically or both. This allows you to have up to four portions of the spreadsheet in view at any one time.

Why would you want to do this? Imagine you have a large spreadsheet and one of the cells has a number in it which is used by three formulas in other cells. Using the split screen technique, you can position the cell containing the number in one section and each of the cells with formulas in the other sections. Then you can change the number in the cell and watch how it affects each of the formulas.

E9			fx Σ =	
	A	**B**	**C**	
1		Beta =	3.2000	
2		A0 =	0.1000	
5	A1=	Beta*A0*(1-A0)	0.2880	
6	A2=	Beta*A1*(1-A1)	0.6562	
7	A3=	Beta*A2*(1-A2)	0.7219	
8	A4=	Beta*A3*(1-A3)	0.6424	
9	A5=	Beta*A4*(1-A4)	0.7351	
10	A6=	Beta*A5*(1-A5)	0.6231	
11	A7=	Beta*A6*(1-A6)	0.7515	
12	A8=	Beta*A7*(1-A7)	0.5975	
13	A9=	Beta*A8*(1-A8)	0.7696	
14	A10=	Beta*A9*(1-A9)	0.5675	
15	A11=	Beta*A10*(1-A10)	0.7854	
16	A12=	Beta*A11*(1-A11)	0.5393	
17	A13=	Beta*A12*(1-A12)	0.7951	

Figure 106. Split screen example

Splitting the screen horizontally

To split the screen horizontally:

1) Move the mouse pointer into the vertical scroll bar, on the right-hand side of the screen, and place it over the small button at the top with the black triangle.

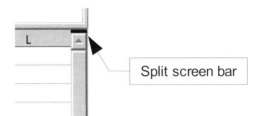

Figure 107. Split screen bar on vertical scroll bar

2) Immediately above this button you will see a thick black line (Figure 107). Move the mouse pointer over this line and it turns into a line with two arrows (Figure 108).

Figure 108. Split screen bar on
vertical scroll bar with cursor

3) Hold down the left mouse button and a gray line appears, running across the page. Drag the mouse downwards and this line follows.

4) Release the mouse button and the screen splits into two views, each with its own vertical scroll bar.

Notice in Figure 106, the 'Beta' and the 'A0' values are in the upper part of the window and other calculations are in the lower part. You may scroll the upper and lower parts independently. Thus you can make changes to the Beta and A0 values and watch their affects on the calculations in the lower half of the window.

You can also split the window vertically as described below—with the same results, being able to scroll both parts of the window independently. With both horizontal and vertical splits, you have four independent windows to scroll.

Splitting the screen vertically

To split the screen vertically:

1) Move the mouse pointer into the horizontal scroll bar at the bottom of the screen and place it over the small button on the right with the black triangle.

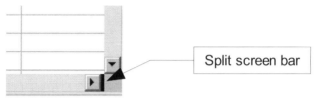

Figure 109: Split bar on horizontal scroll bar

2) Immediately to the right of this button is a thick black line (Figure 109). Move the mouse pointer over this line and it turns into a line with two arrows.

3) Hold down the left mouse button and a gray line appears, running up the page. Drag the mouse to the left and this line follows.

4) Release the mouse button and the screen is split into two views, each with its own horizontal scroll bar.

Note	Splitting the screen horizontally and vertically at the same time gives four views, each with its own vertical and horizontal scroll bars.

Removing split views

To remove a split view, do any of the following:

* Double-click on each split line.

* Click on and drag the split lines back to their places at the ends of the scroll bars.

* Select **Window > Split** to remove all split lines at the same time.

Tip	You can also split the screen using a menu command. Click in a cell that is immediately below and immediately to the right of where you wish the screen to be split, and choose **Window > Split**.

Entering data using the keyboard

Most data entry in Calc can be accomplished using the keyboard.

Entering numbers

Click in the cell and type in the number using the number keys on either the main keyboard or the numeric keypad.

To enter a negative number, either type a minus (–) sign in front of it or enclose it in parentheses (brackets), like this: (1234).

By default, numbers are right-aligned and negative numbers have a leading minus symbol.

Entering text

Click in the cell and type the text. Text is left-aligned by default.

Entering numbers as text

If a number is entered in the format *01481*, Calc will drop the leading 0. (Exception: see Tip below.) To preserve the leading zero, for example for telephone area codes, type an apostrophe before the number, like this: '01481.

The data is now regarded as text by Calc. Formulas and functions will treat the entry like any other text entry, which typically results in it being a zero in a formula, and being ignored in a function.

Tip	Numbers can have leading zeros and be regarded as numbers (as opposed to text) if the cell is formated appropriately. Right-click on the cell and chose **Format Cells > Numbers**. Adjust the leading zeros setting to add leading zeros to numbers.

Note	When using an apostrophe to allow a leading 0 to be displayed, the apostrophe is not visible in the cell after the *Enter* key is pressed—*if* the apostrophe is a plain apostrophe (not a "smart quote" apostrophe). If "smart quotes" are selected for apostrophes, the apostrophe remains visible in the cell. To choose the type of apostrophe, use **Tools > AutoCorrect > Custom Quotes**. The selection of the apostrophe type affects both Calc and Writer.

Caution	When a number is formatted as text care must be taken that the cell containing the number is not used in a formula since Calc will ignore the value.

Entering dates and times

Select the cell and type the date or time. You can separate the date elements with a slant (/) or a hyphen (–) or use text such as 10 Oct 03. Calc recognizes a variety of date formats. You can separate time elements with colons such as 10:43:45.

Speeding up data entry

Entering data into a spreadsheet can be very labor-intensive, but Calc provides several tools for removing some of the drudgery from input.

The most basic ability is to drop and drag the contents of one cell to another with a mouse. However, Calc also includes several other tools for automating input, especially of repetitive material. They include the Fill tool, selection lists, and the ability to input information into multiple sheets of the same document.

Using the Fill tool on cells

At its simplest, the Fill tool is a way to duplicate existing content. Start by selecting the cell to copy, then drag the mouse in any direction (or hold down the Shift key and click in the last cell you want to fill), and then choose **Edit > Fill** and the direction in which you want to copy: Up, Down, Left or Right.

Caution	Choices that are not available are grayed out, but you can still choose the opposite direction from what you intend, which could cause you to overwrite cells accidentally unless you are careful.

Tip	A shortcut way to fill cells is to grab the "handle" in the lower right-hand corner of the cell and drag it in the direction you want to fill.

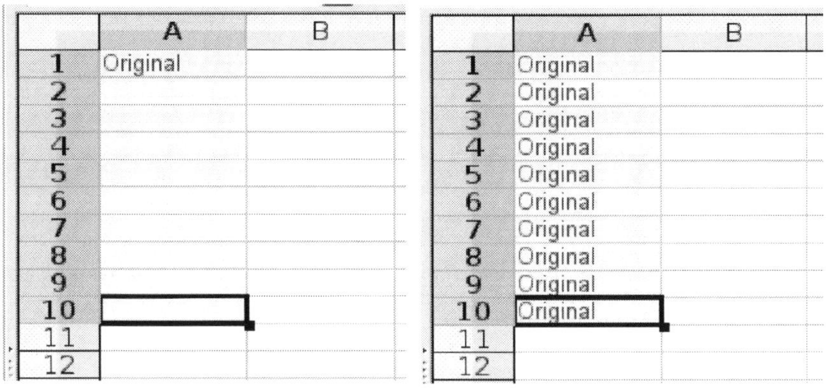

Figure 110: Using the Fill tool

You can also use the fill tool selecting some existing series of data that you want to extend. If the interval between the values in the selected cells is constant, Calc will try to guess and fill the selection with values that continue the sequence. For example, if you select three cells containing the values 1, 2 and 3 and fill the subsequent cell Calc will insert the value 4.

Using a fill series

A more complex use of the Fill tool is to use a fill series. The default lists are for the full and abbreviated days of the week and the months of the year, but you can create your own lists as well.

To add a fill series to a spreadsheet, select the cells to fill, choose **Edit > Fill > Series**. In the Fill Series dialog, select **AutoFill** as the *Series type*, and enter as the *Start value* an item from any defined series. The selected cells then fill in the other items on the list sequentially, repeating from the top of the list when they reach the end of the list.

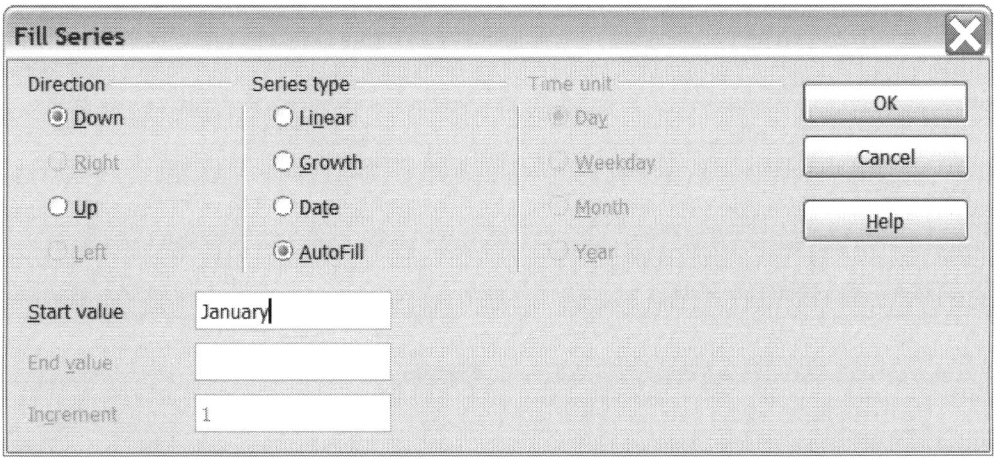

Figure 111: Specifying the start of a fill series (result is in Fig. 112)

You can also use **Edit > Fill > Series** to create a one-time fill series for numbers by entering the start and end values and the increment. For example, if you entered start and end values of 1 and 7 with an increment of 2, you would get the sequence of 1, 3, 5, 7.

In all these cases, the Fill tool creates only a momentary connection between the cells. Once they are filled, the cells have no further connection with one another.

	A	B
1	January	
2	February	
3	March	
4	April	
5	May	
6	June	
7	July	
8	August	
9	September	
10	October	
11	November	
12	December	
13		

Figure 112: Result of fill series selection shown in Figure 111.

Defining a fill series

To define a fill series, go to **Tools > Options > OpenOffice.org Calc > Sort Lists**. This dialog shows the previously-defined series in the *Lists* box on the left, and the contents of the highlighted list in the *Entries* box.

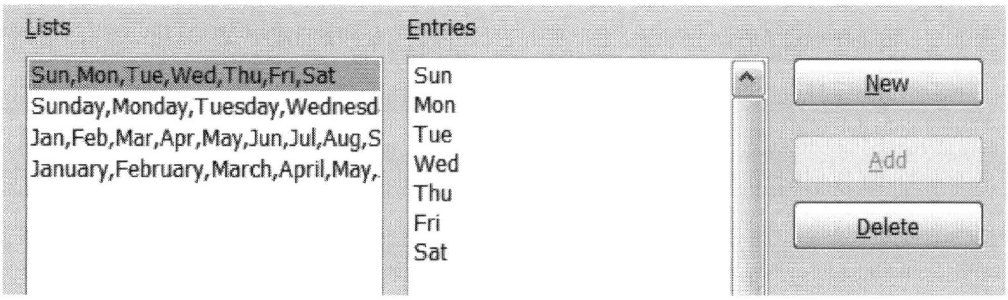

Figure 113: Predefined fill series

Click **New**. The *Entries* box is cleared. Type the series for the new list in the *Entries* box (one entry per line), and then click **Add**.

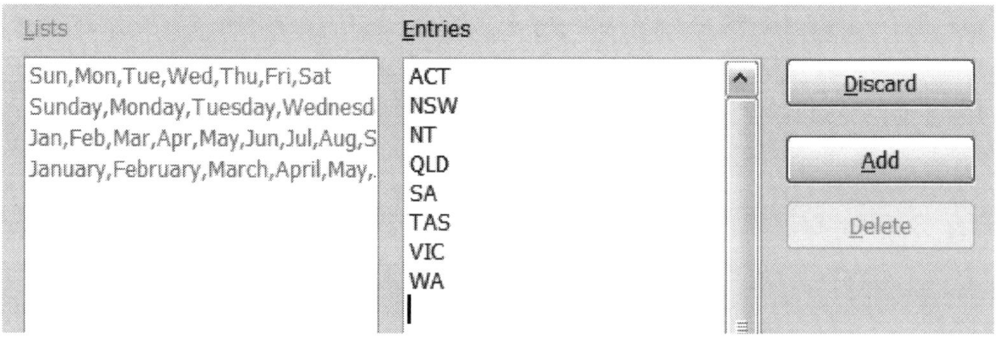

Figure 114: Defining a new fill series

Using selection lists

Selection lists are available only for text, and are limited to using only text that has already been entered in the same column.

To use a selection list, select a blank cell and press *Ctrl+D*. A drop-down list appears of any cell in the same column that either has at least one text character or whose format is defined as Text. Click on the entry you require.

Sharing content between sheets

You might want to enter the same information in the same cell on multiple sheets, for example to set up standard listings for a group of individuals or organizations. Instead of entering the list on each sheet individually, you can enter it in all the sheets at once. To do this, select all the sheets, then enter the information in the current one.

Caution ⚠️	This technique overwrites any information that is already in the cells on the other sheets—without any warning. For this reason, when you are finished, be sure to deselect all the tabs, so that each sheet can be edited without affecting any others.

Editing data

Editing data is done is in much the same way as it is entered. The first step is selecting the cell containing the data to be edited.

Removing data from a cell

Data can be removed (deleted) from a cell in several ways.

Removing data only

The data alone can be removed from a cell without removing any of the formatting of the cell. Click in the cell to select it, and then press the *Backspace* key.

Removing data and formatting

The data and the formatting can be removed from a cell at the same time. Press the *Delete* key (or right-click and choose **Delete Contents**, or use **Edit > Delete Contents**) to open the **Delete Contents** dialog (Figure 115). From this dialog, the different aspects of the cell can be deleted. To delete everything in a cell (contents and format), check **Delete all**.

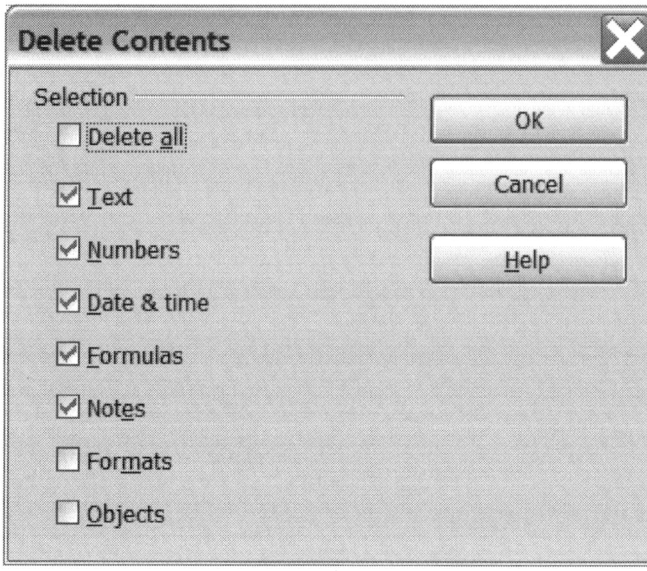

Figure 115: Delete Contents dialog

Replacing all the data in a cell

To remove data and insert new data, simply type over the old data. The new data will retain the original formatting.

Changing part of the data in a cell

Sometimes it is necessary to change the contents of cell without removing all of the contents, for example if the phrase "See Dick run" is in a cell and it needs to be changed to "See Dick run fast." It is often useful to do this without deleting the old cell contents first.

The process is the similar to the one described above, but you need to place the cursor inside the cell. You can do this in two ways.

Using the keyboard

After selecting the appropriate cell, press the *F2* key and the cursor is placed at the end of the cell. Then use the keyboard arrow keys to move the cursor through the text in the cell.

Using the mouse

Using the mouse, either double-click on the appropriate cell (to select it and place the cursor in it for editing), or single-click to select the cell and then move the mouse pointer up to the input line and click into it to place the cursor for editing.

Formatting data

The data in Calc can be formatting in several ways. It can either be edited as part of a cell style so that it is automatically applied, or it can be applied manually to the cell. Some manual formatting can be applied using toolbar icons. For more control and extra options, select the appropriate cell or cells, right-click on it, and select **Format Cells**. All of the format options are discussed below.

Note	All the settings discussed in this section can also be set as a part of the style using the Styles and Formatting window. See Chapter 10 (Using Styles in Calc) in the *Calc Guide* for more information.

Formatting multiple lines of text

Multiple lines of text can be entered into a single cell using automatic wrapping or manual line breaks. Each method is useful for different situations.

Using automatic wrapping

To set text to wrap at the end of the cell, right-click on the cell and select **Format Cells** (or choose **Format > Cells** from the menu bar, or press *Ctrl+1*). On the *Alignment* tab (Figure 117), under Properties, select **Wrap text automatically**. The results are shown in Figure 116.

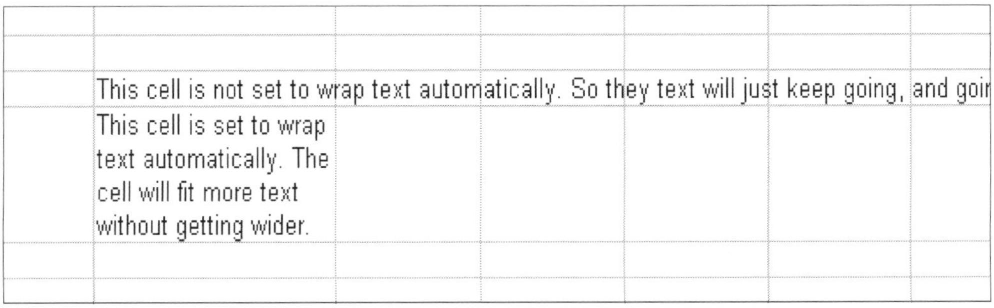

Figure 116: Automatic text wrap

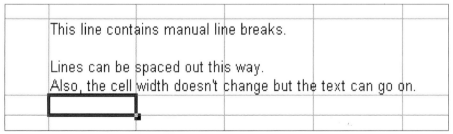

Figure 117: Format Cells > Alignment dialog

Using manual line breaks

To insert a manual line break while typing in a cell, press *Ctrl+Enter*. This method does not work with the cursor in the input line. When editing text, first double-click the cell, then single-click at the position where you want the line break.

When a manual line break is entered, the cell width does not change. Figure 118 shows the results of using two manual line breaks after the first line of text.

This line contains manual line breaks.				
Lines can be spaced out this way. Also, the cell width doesn't change but the text can go on.				

Figure 118: Cell with manual line breaks

Shrinking text to fit the cell

The font size of the data in a cell can automatically adjust to fit in a cell. To do this, select the **Shrink to fit cell size** option in the Format Cells dialog (Figure 117). Figure Figure 119 shows the results.

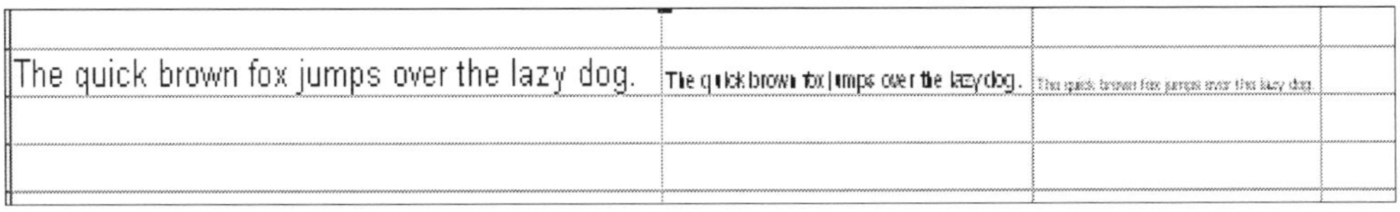

The quick brown fox jumps over the lazy dog.	The quick brown fox jumps over the lazy dog.	The quick brown fox jumps over the lazy dog

Figure 119: Shrinking font size to fit cells

Formatting numbers

Several number formats can be applied to cells by using icons on the Formatting toolbar. Select the cell, then click the relevant icon.

Figure 120: Number format icons. L to R: currency, percentage, date, exponential, standard, add decimal place, delete decimal place.

For more control or to select other number formats, use the *Numbers* tab (Figure 121).

• Apply any of the data types in the Category list to the data.

• Control the number of decimal places and leading zeros.

• Enter a custom format code.

The Language setting controls the local settings for the different formats such as the date order and the currency marker.

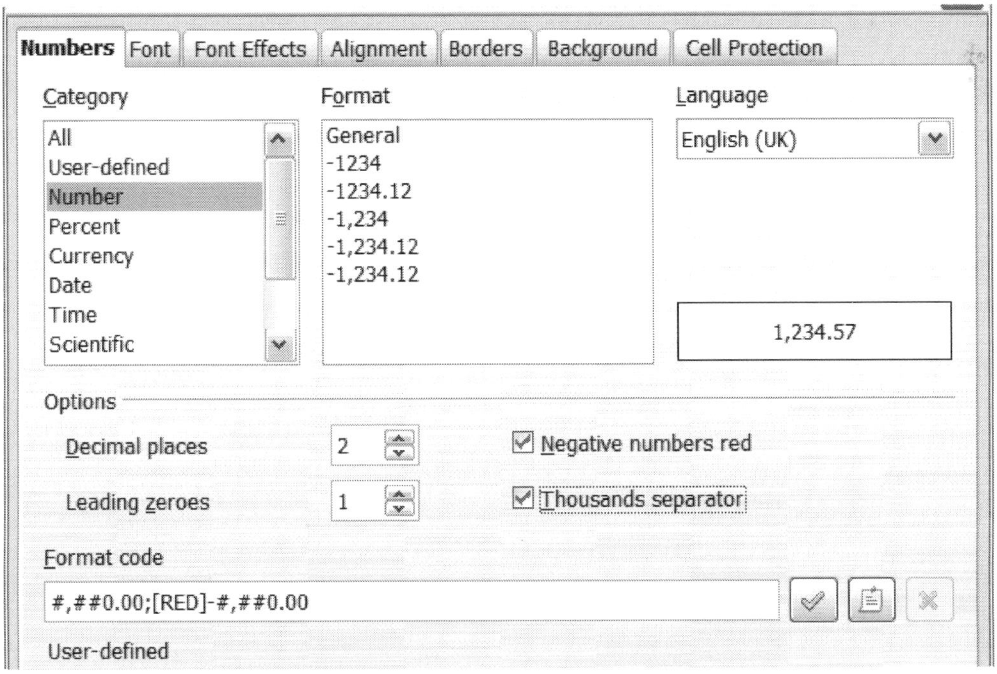

| **Numbers** | Font | Font Effects | Alignment | Borders | Background | Cell Protection |

Category
- All
- User-defined
- **Number**
- Percent
- Currency
- Date
- Time
- Scientific

Format
- General
- -1234
- -1234.12
- -1,234
- -1,234.12
- -1,234.12

Language
- English (UK)

1,234.57

Options

Decimal places   2

Leading zeroes   1

☑ Negative numbers red

☑ Thousands separator

Format code

`#,##0.00;[RED]-#,##0.00`

User-defined

Figure 121: Format Cells > Numbers

Formatting the font

To quickly choose the font used in a cell, select the cell, then click the arrow next to the Font Name box on the Formatting toolbar and choose a font from the list.

Tip	To choose whether to show the font names in their font or in plain text, go to **Tools > Options > OpenOffice.org > View** and select or deselect the Show preview of fonts option in the Font Lists section. For more information, see Appendix D (Setting Up and Customizing Calc) of the *Calc Guide*.

To choose the size of the font, click the arrow next to the Font Size box on the Formatting toolbar. For other formatting, you can use the Bold, Italic, or Underline icons.

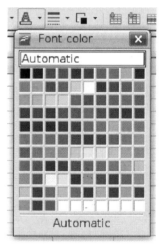

To choose a font color, click the arrow next to the Font Color icon to display a color palette. Click on the required color.

(To define custom colors, use **Tools > Options > OpenOffice.org > Colors**. Ssee Appendix D of the *Calc Guide*.)

To specify the language of the cell (useful because it allows different languages to exist in the same document and be spell checked correctly), use the *Font* tab of the Format Cells dialog. Use the *Font Effects* tab to set other font characteristics. See Chapter 10 of the *Calc Guide* for more information.

Formatting the cell borders

To quickly choose a line style and color for the borders of a cell, click the small arrows next to the Line Style and Line Color icons on the Formatting toolbar. In each case, a palette of choices is displayed.

Note	The cell border properties apply to a cell, and can only be changed if you are editing that cell. For example, if cell C3 has a top border (which would be equivalent visually to a bottom border on C2), that border can only be removed by selecting C3. It cannot be removed in C2.

For more control, including the spacing between the cell borders and the text, use the *Borders* tab of the Format Cells dialog. There you can also define a shadow. See Chapter 10 of the *Calc Guide* for details.

Formatting the cell background

To quickly choose a background color for a cell, click the small arrow next to the Background Color icon on the Formatting toolbar. A palette of color choices, similar to the Font Color palette, is displayed.

(To define custom colors, use **Tools > Options > OpenOffice.org > Colors**. See Appendix D for more information.)

You can also use the *Background* tab of the Format Cells dialog. See Chapter 10 of the *Calc Guide* for details.

Autoformatting cells and sheets

You can use the AutoFormat feature to quickly apply a set of cell formats to a sheet or a selected cell range.

1) Select the cells, including the column and row headers, that you want to format.
2) Choose **Format > AutoFormat**.

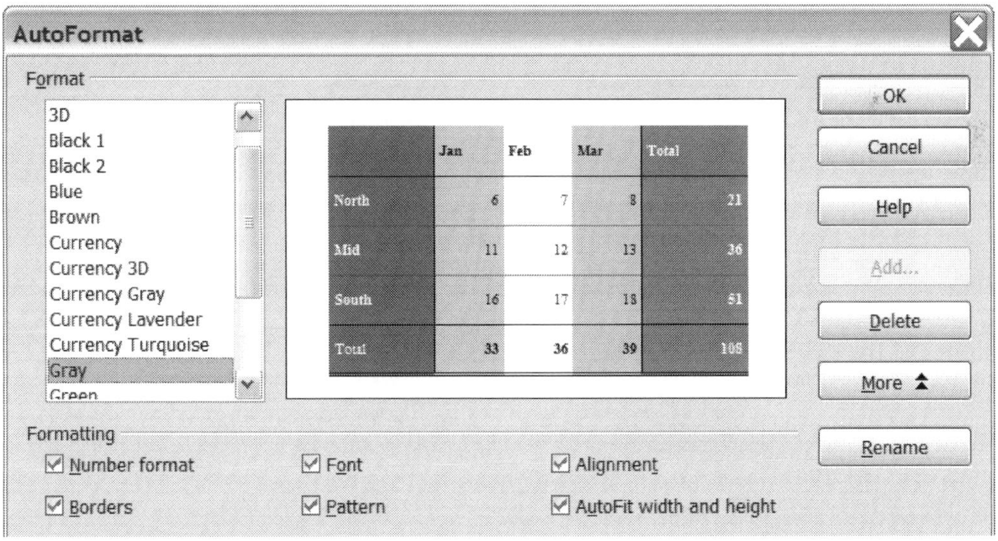

Figure 122: Choosing an AutoFormat

3) To select which properties (number format, font, alignment, borders, pattern, autofit width and height) to include in an AutoFormat, click **More**. Select or deselect the required options.
4) Click **OK**.

If you do not see any change in color of the cell contents, choose **View > Value Highlighting** from the menu bar.

Defining a new AutoFormat

You can define a new AutoFormat that is available to all spreadsheets.

1) Format a sheet.

2) Choose **Edit > Select All**.

3) Choose **Format > AutoFormat**. The **Add** button is now active.

4) Click **Add**.

5) In the *Name* box of the Add AutoFormat dialog, type a meaningful name for the new format.

6) Click **OK** to save. The new format is now available in the *Format* list in the AutoFormat dialog.

Formatting spreadsheets using themes

Calc comes with a predefined set of formatting themes that you can apply to your spreadsheets.

It is not possible to add themes to Calc, and they cannot be modified. However, you can modify their styles after you apply them to a spreadsheet.

To apply a theme to a spreadsheet:

1) Click the **Choose Themes** icon in the Tools toolbar. If this toolbar is not visible, you can show it using **View > Toolbars > Tools**.

The Theme Selection dialog appears. This dialog lists the available themes for the whole spreadsheet, and the Styles and Formatting window lists the custom styles for specific cells.

2) In the Theme Selection dialog, select the theme that you want to apply to the spreadsheet.

As soon as you select a theme, some of the properties of the custom styles are applied to the open spreadsheet and are immediately visible.

3) Click **OK**.

Hiding and showing data

When elements are hidden, they are neither visible nor printed, but can still be selected for copying if you select the elements around them. For example, if column B is hidden, it is copied when you select columns A and C. When you need a hidden element again, you can reverse the process, and show the element.

To hide or show sheets, rows, and columns, use the options on the Format menu or the right-click (context) menu. For example, to hide a row, first select the row, and then choose **Format > Row > Hide** (or right-click and choose **Hide**).

To hide or show selected cells, choose **Format > Cells** from the menu bar (or right-click and choose **Format Cells**). On the Format Cells dialog, go to the *Cell Protection* tab.

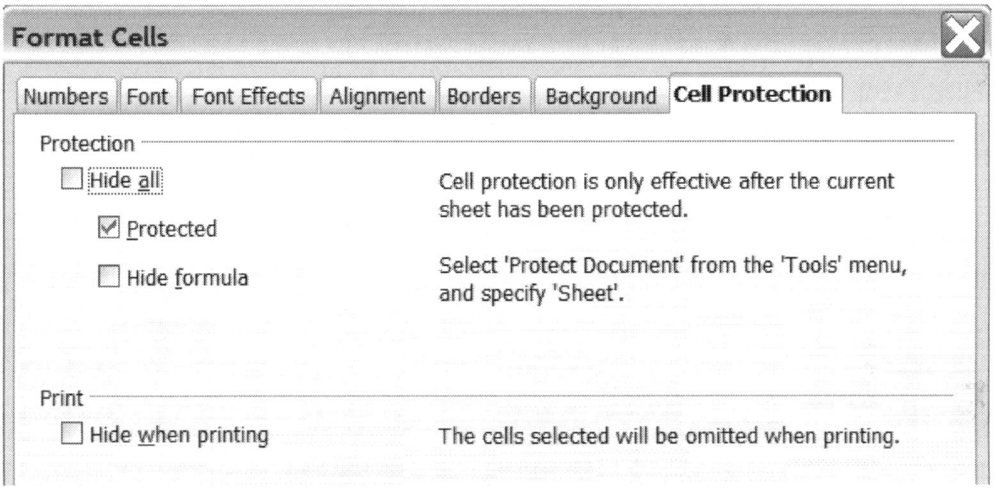

Figure 123: Hiding or showing cells

Outline group controls

If you are continually hiding and showing the same cells, you can simplify the process by creating *outline groups*, which add a set of controls for hiding and showing the cells in the group that are quick to use and always available.

If the contents of cells falls into a regular pattern, such as four cells followed by a total, then you can use **Data > Group and Outline > AutoOutline** to have Calc add outline controls based on the pattern. Otherwise, you can set outline groups manually by selecting the cells for grouping, then choosing **Data > Group and Outline > Group**. On the Group dialog, you can choose whether to group the selected cells by rows or columns.

When you close the dialog, the outline group controls are visible between either the row or column headers and the edges of the editing window. The controls resemble the tree-structure of a file-manager in appearance, and can be hidden by selecting **Data > Outline > Hide Details**. They are strictly for on screen use, and do not print.

The basic outline controls have plus or minus signs at the start of the group to show or hide hidden cells. However, if one or more outline group is nested in another, the controls have numbered buttons for hiding different levels of group.

If you no longer need a group, place the mouse cursor in any cell in it and select **Data > Group and Outline > Ungroup**. To remove all groups on a sheet, select **Data > Group and Outline > Remove**.

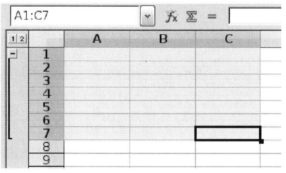

Figure 124: Outline group controls

Filtering which cells are visible

A filter is a list of conditions that each entry has to meet in order to be displayed. You can set three types of filters from the **Data > Filter** sub-menu.

Automatic filters add a drop-down list to the top row of a column that contains commonly used filters. They are quick and convenient, and, because the condition includes every unique entry in the selected cells, are almost as useful with text as with numbers.

In addition to each unique entry, automatic filters include the option to display all entries, the ten highest numerical values, and all cells that are empty or not-empty, as well as a standard filter. Their drawback is that they are somewhat limited. In particular, they do not allow regular expressions, so you cannot display contents that are similar, but not identical, by using automatic filters.

Standard filters are more complex than automatic filters. You can set as many as three conditions as a filter, combining them with the operators AND and OR. Standard filters are mostly useful for numbers, although a few of the conditional operators, such as = and < > can also be useful for text.

Other conditional operators for standard filters include options to display the largest or smallest values, or a percentage of them. Useful in themselves, standard filters take on added value when used to further refine automatic filters.

Advanced filters are structured similarly to standard filters. The differences are that advanced filters are not limited to three conditions, and their criteria are not entered in a dialog. Instead, advanced filters are entered in a blank area of a sheet, then referenced by the advanced filter tool to apply them.

Sorting records

Sorting arranges the visible cells on the sheet. In Calc, you can sort by up to three criteria, with each criterion applied one after the other. Sorts are handy when you are searching for a particular item, and become even more powerful after you have filtered data.

In addition, sorting is often useful when you add new information. When a list is long, it is usually easier to add new information at the bottom of the sheet, rather than adding rows in the proper places. After you have added information, you can then sort it to update the sheet.

You can sort by highlighting the cells to be sorted, then selecting **Data > Sort**. The selected cells can be sorted by the order of information in up to three columns or rows, in either ascending (A-Z, 1-9) or descending (Z-A, 9-1) order.

On the *Options* tab of the Sort dialog, you can choose the following options:

Case sensitive
If two entries are otherwise identical, one with an upper case letter is placed before one with a lower case letter in the same position.

Range contains column labels
Does not include the column heading in the sort.

Include formats
A cell's formatting is moved with its contents. If formatting is used to distinguish different types of cells, then use this option.

Copy sort results to
Sets a spreadsheet address to which to copy the sort results. If a range is specified that does not have the necessary number of

cells, then cells are added. If a range contains cells that already have content, then the sort fails.

Custom sort order

Select the box, then choose one of the sort orders defined in **Tools > Options > Spreadsheet > Sort Lists** from the drop-down list.

Direction

Sets whether rows or columns are sorted. The default is to sort by columns unless the selected cells are in a single column.

Printing

Printing from Calc is the same as printing from other OOo components (see Chapter 10), but some details are different, especially regarding preparation for printing.

The Print dialog (Figure 125), reached from **File > Print**, has some Calc-specific options: which sheets to print.

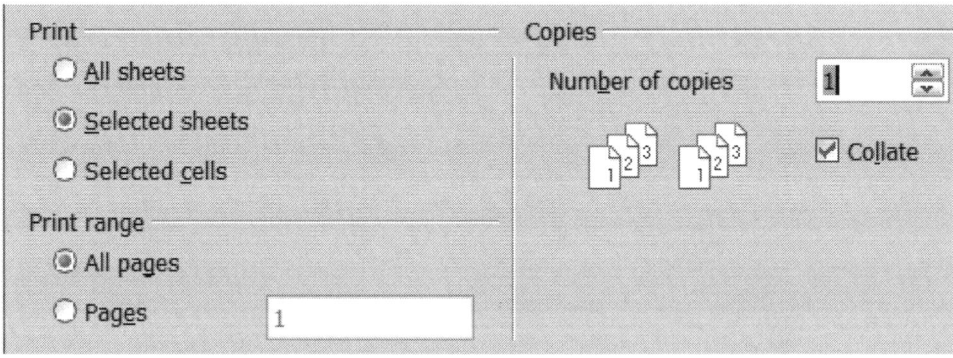

Figure 125. Part of the Print dialog

The Printer Options dialog (reached by clicking the **Options** button on the bottom left of the **Print** dialog) has only two choices, as shown in Figure 126: **Suppress output of empty pages** and **Print only selected sheets**.

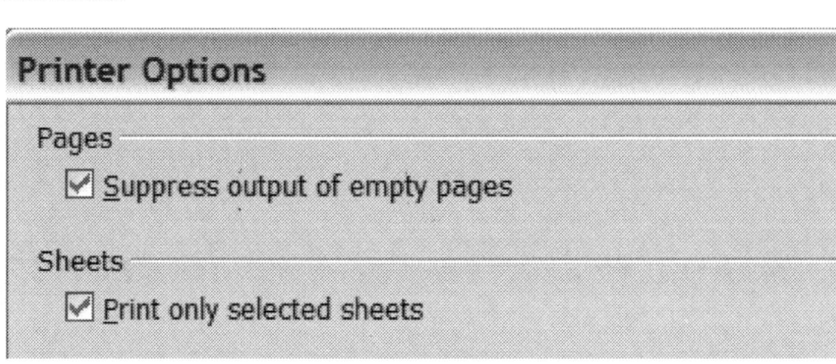

Figure 126. Top of the Printer Options dialog

Selecting sheets to print

You can select one or more sheets for printing. This can be useful if you have a large spreadsheet with multiple sheets and only want to print certain sheets. For example, an accountant might record costs over time with one sheet for each month. To print the November and December sheets, follow this procedure:

1) Go to the November sheet. Hold down the *Control* key and click on the tab of the December sheet.

2) To print all of the sheets, go to **File > Print** and select **Options.**

Note	The *Options* button is different from the *Properties* button. *Properties* deals with the settings of the printer, whereas *Options* deals with OOo's settings.

3) Select **Print only selected sheets**. This choice affects the print preview, export, and printing of your spreadsheet. Click **OK**.

Caution	If you keep the selected sheets selected, when you enter data on one sheet, you enter data on all sheets at the same time. This might not be what you want.

Selecting the page order, details, and scale

To select the page order, details, and scale to be printed:

1) Select **Format > Page** from the main menu.

2) Select the **Sheet** tab (Figure 127).

3) Make your selections, and then click **OK.**

Page Order

You can set the order in which pages print. This is especially useful in a large document; for example, controlling the print order can save time if you have to collate the document a certain way. Where a sheet prints on more than one page of paper, it can be printed either by column, where the first column of pages prints, and then the second column and so on, or by row as shown in the graphic on the top right of the page order dialog in Figure 127.

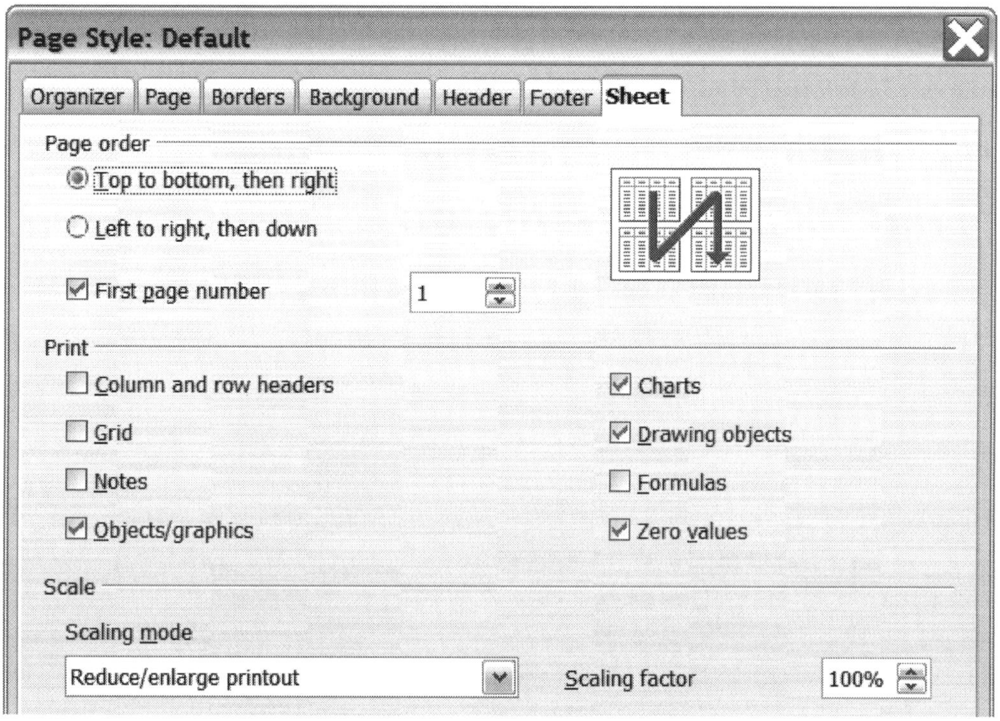

Figure 127. The Sheet tab of the Page Style dialog

Print

You can specify which details to print. Those details include:

- Row and column headers
- Sheet grid—prints the borders of the cells as a grid
- Notes—prints the notes defined in your spreadsheet on a separate page, along with the corresponding cell reference
- Objects and graphics
- Charts
- Drawing objects
- Formulas—prints the formulas contained in the cells, instead of the results
- Zero Values—prints cells with a zero value

Note	Remember that since the print detail options are a part of the page's properties, they are also a part of the page style's properties. Therefore, different page styles can be set up to quickly change the print properties of the sheets in the spreadsheet.

Scale

Use the scale features to control the number of pages the data will print on. This can be useful if a large amount of data needs to be printed more compactly or, if the reader has poor eyesight, text can be enlarged when it prints.

- Reduce/Enlarge printout—scales the data in the printout either larger or smaller. For example if a sheet would normally print out as four pages (two high and two wide), a scaling of 50% would print as one page (both width and height are halved).

- Fit print range(s) on number of pages—defines exactly how many pages the printout will take up. This option will only reduce a printout, it will not enlarge it. To enlarge a printout, the reduce/enlarge option must be used.

- Fit print range(s) to width/height—defines how high and wide the printout will be, in pages.

Using print ranges

Print ranges have several uses, including printing only a specific part of the data or printing selected rows or columns on every page. For more about using print ranges, see Chapter 5 (Printing, Exporting, and E-mailing) in the *Calc Guide*.

Defining a print range

To define a new print range or modify an existing print range:

1) Highlight the range of cells that comprise the print range.

2) Choose **Format > Print Ranges > Define**.

The page break lines display on the screen.

Tip   You can check the print range by using **File > Page Preview**. OOo will only display the cells in the print range.

Removing a print range

It may become necessary to remove a defined print range, for example if the whole sheet needs to be printed later.

Choose **Format > Print Ranges > Remove**. This removes *all* defined print ranges on the sheet. After the print range is removed, the default page break lines will appear on the screen.

Printing rows or columns on every page

If a sheet is printed on multiple pages, you can set up certain rows or columns to repeat on each printed page.

For example, if the top two rows of the sheet as well as column A need to be printed on all pages, do the following:

1) Choose **Format > Print Ranges > Edit**. On the Edit Print Ranges dialog, type the rows in the text entry box under *Rows to repeat*. For example, to repeat rows 1 and 2, type **$1:$2**. In the *Rows to repeat* list, **- none -** changes to **- user defined -**.

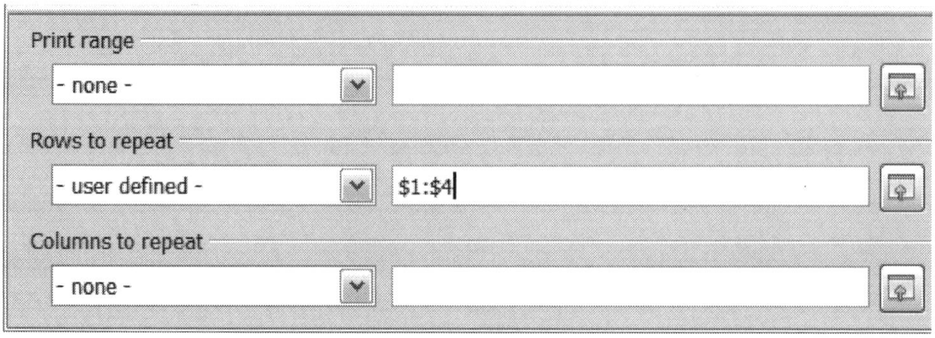

Figure 128: Specifying repeating rows

2) Columns can also repeat; type the columns in the text entry box under *Columns to repeat*. For example, to repeat column A, type **$A**. In the *Columns to repeat* list, **- none -** changes to **- user defined -**.

3) Click **OK**.

Note   You do not need to select the entire range of the rows to be repeated; selecting one cell in each row works.

Page breaks

While defining a print range can be a powerful tool, it may sometimes be necessary to manually tweak Calc's printout. To do this, you can use a *manual break*. A manual break helps to ensure that your data prints properly. You can insert a horizontal page break above, or a vertical page break to the left of, the active cell.

Inserting a page break

To insert a page break:

1) Navigate to the cell where the page break will begin.

2) Select **Insert > Manual Break**.

3) Select **Row Break** or **Column Break** depending on your need.

The break is now set.

Row break

Selecting *Row Break* creates a page break above the selected cell. For example, if the active cell is H15, then the break is created between rows 14 and 15.

Column break

Selecting *Column Break* creates a page break to the left of the selected cell. For example, if the active cell is H15, then the break is created between columns G and H.

Tip	To see page break lines more easily on screen, you can change their color. Choose **Tools > Options > OpenOffice.org > Appearance** and scroll down to the Spreadsheet section.

Deleting a page break

To remove a page break:

1) Navigate to a cell that is next to the break you want to remove.
2) Select **Edit > Delete Manual Break**.
3) Select **Row Break** or **Column Break** depending on your need.

The break is now removed.

Note	Multiple manual row and column breaks can exist on the same page. When you want to remove them, you have to remove each one individually. This may be confusing at times, because although there may be a column break set on the page, when you go to **Edit > Manual Break**, Column break may be grayed out.
	In order to remove the break, you have to be in the cell next to the break. So, for example, if you set the column break while you are in H15, you can not remove it if you are in cell D15. However, you can remove it from any cell in column H.

Headers and footers

Headers and footers are predefined pieces of text that are printed at the top or bottom of a sheet outside of the sheet area. They are set the same way.

Headers and footers are assigned to a page style. You can define more than one page style for a spreadsheet and assign different page styles to different sheets. For more about page styles, see Chapter 10 of the *Calc Guide*.

To set a header or footer:

1) Navigate to the sheet that you want to set the header or footer for. Select **Format > Page**.

2) Select the Header (or Footer) tab. See Figure 129.

3) Select the **Header on** option.

From here you can also set the margins, the spacing, and height for the header or footer. You can check the **AutoFit height** box to have the height of the header or footer automatically adjust.

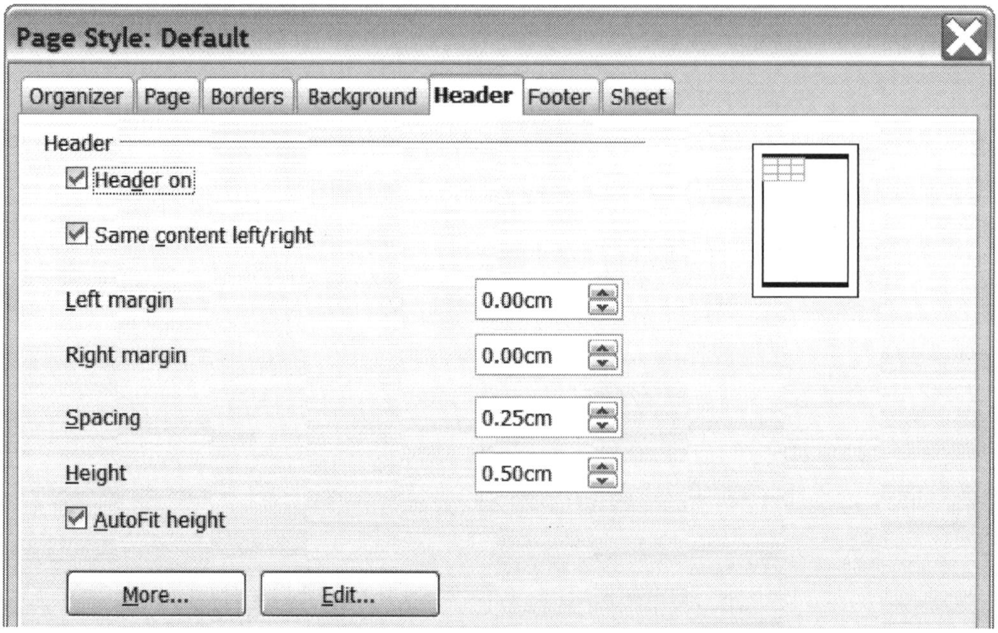

Figure 129: Header dialog

Margin
Changing the size of the left or right margin adjusts how far the header or footer is from the side of the page.

Spacing
Spacing affects how far above or below the sheet the header or footer will print. So, if spacing is set to 1.00", then there will be 1 inch between the header or footer and the sheet.

Height
Height affects how big the header or footer will be.

Header or footer appearance

To change the appearance of the header or footer, click **More**.

From this dialog (Figure 130) you can set the background and border of the header or footer. See Chapter 10 (Using Styles in Calc) in the *Calc Guide* for more information.

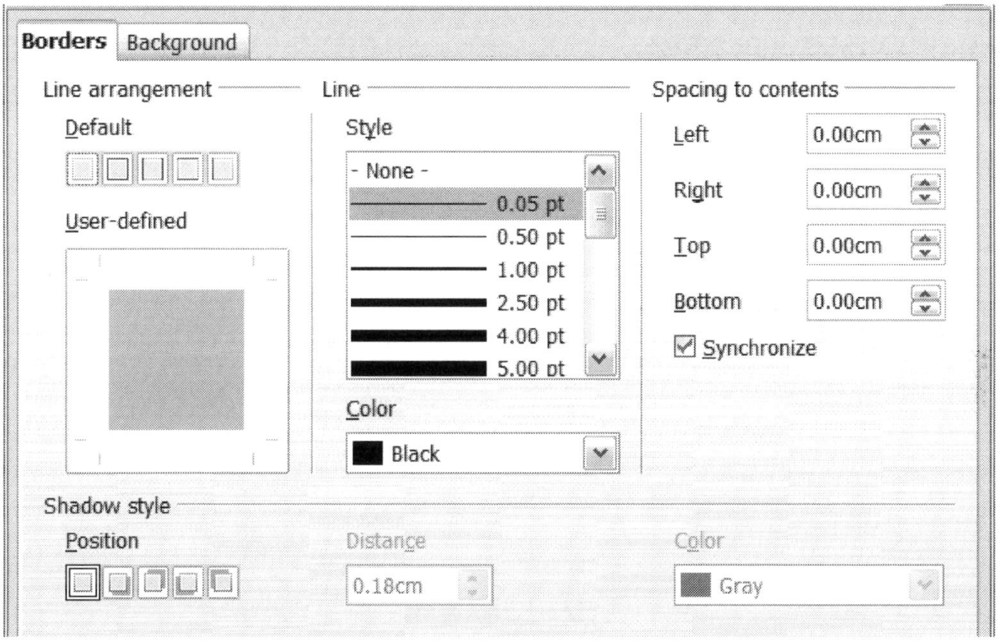

Figure 130: Header/Footer Border/Background

Contents of the header or footer

The header or footer of a Calc spreadsheet has three columns for text. Each column can have different contents.

To set the contents of the header or footer, click the **Edit** button in the header or footer dialog shown in Figure 129 to display the dialog shown in Figure 131.

Areas

Each area is independent and can have different information in it.

Header

You can select from several preset choices in the Header drop-down list, or specify a custom header using the buttons below. (If you are formatting a footer, the choices are the same.)

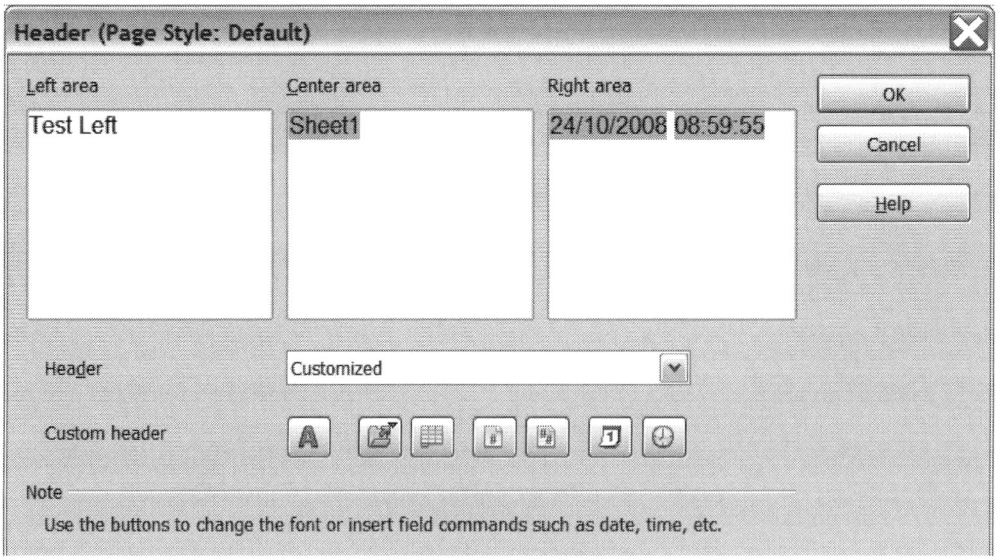

Figure 131: Edit contents of header or footer

Custom header

Click in the area (Left, Center, Right) that you want to customize, then use the buttons to add elements or change text attributes.

A Opens the Text Attributes dialog.

Inserts the total number of pages.

Inserts the File Name field.

Inserts the Date field.

Inserts the Sheet Name field.

Inserts the Time field.

Inserts the current page number.

Chapter *6*
Getting Started with Impress

Presentations in OpenOffice.org

What is Impress?

Impress is OpenOffice.org's slide show (presentations) program. You can create slides that contain many different elements, including text, bulleted and numbered lists, tables, charts, clip art, and a wide range of graphic objects. Impress also includes a spelling checker, a thesaurus, prepackaged text styles, and attractive background styles.

This chapter includes instructions, screenshots, and hints to guide you through the Impress environment while designing the easier presentations. Although more difficult designs are mentioned throughout this chapter, explanations for creating them are in the *Impress Guide*. If you have a working knowledge of how to create slide shows, we recommend you use the *Impress Guide* for your source of information.

To use Impress for more than very simple slide shows requires some knowledge of the elements which the slides contain. Slides containing text use styles to determine the appearance of that text. Slides containing objects are created the same way that drawings are created in Draw. For this reason, we recommend that you also study Chapter 3 (Working with Styles and Templates) and Chapter 7 (Getting Started with Draw).

Parts of the main Impress window

The main Impress window (Figure 132) has three parts: the *Slides pane*, *Workspace*, and *Tasks pane*. Additionally, several toolbars can be displayed or hidden during the creation of a presentation.

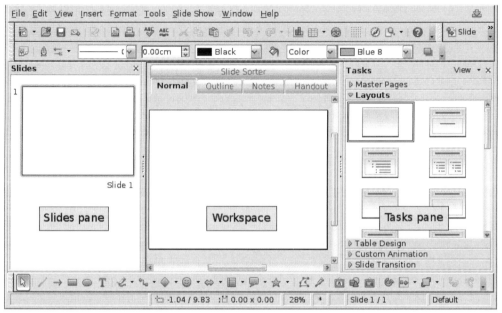

Figure 132: Main window of Impress

Tip	You can remove the *Slides pane* or *Tasks pane* from view by clicking the *X* in the upper right corner. You can also show or hide these panes using **View > Slide Pane** or **View > Tasks Pane**.

Slides pane

The *Slides pane* contains thumbnail pictures of the slides in your presentation, in the order they will be shown (unless you change the order). Clicking a slide selects it and places it in the *Workspace*. While it is there, you can apply any changes desired to that particular slide.

Several additional operations can be performed on one or more slides in the Slides pane:

* Add new slides at any place within the presentation after the first slide.

* Mark a slide as hidden so that it will not be shown as part of the slide show.

- Delete a slide from the presentation if it is no longer needed.

- Rename a slide.

- Copy or move the contents of one slide to another (copy and paste, or cut and paste, respectively).

It is also possible to perform the following operations, although there are more efficient methods than using the Slides pane:

- Change the slide transition following the selected slide or after each slide in a group of slides.

- Change the sequence of slides in the presentation.

- Change the slide design. (A window opens allowing you to load your own design.)

- Change slide layout for a group of slides simultaneously. (This requires using the *Layouts* section of the Tasks pane.)

Tasks pane

The Tasks pane has five sections.

Master Pages

Here you define the page style for your presentation. Impress contains 28 prepackaged Master Pages (slide masters). One of them—Default—is blank, and the rest have a background.

Tip	Press *F11* to open the Styles and Formating window, where you can modify the styles used in any slide master to suit your purpose. This can be done at any time.

Layout

Twenty prepackaged layouts are shown. You can choose the one you want, use it as it is or modify it to your own requirements. At present it is not possible to create custom layouts.

Table Design

Eleven standard table styles are provided in this pane. You can further modify the appearance of a table with the selections to show or hide specific rows and columns, or to apply a banded appearance to the rows and columns.

Custom Animation

A variety of animations for selected elements of a slide are listed. Animation can be added to a slide, and it can also be changed or removed later.

Slide Transition

Fifty-six transitions are available, including *No Transition*. You can select the transition speed (slow, medium, fast). You can also choose between an automatic or manual transition, and how long you want the selected slide to be shown (automatic transition only).

Workspace

The *Workspace* has five tabs: **Normal**, **Outline**, **Notes**, **Handout**, and **Slide Sorter**. These five tabs are called **View buttons**. There are also many toolbars that can be used during slide creation; they are revealed by selecting them with **View > Toolbars**. The *Workspace* is below the View buttons. This is where you assemble the various parts of your selected slide.

Each view is designed to make completing certain tasks easier. In summary:

- *Normal view* is the main view for creating individual slides. Use this view to format and design slides and to add text, graphics, and animation effects.

- *Outline view* shows topic titles, bulleted lists, and numbered lists for each slide in outline format. Use this view to rearrange the order of slides, edit titles and headings, rearrange the order of items in a list, and add new slides.

- *Notes view* lets you add notes to each slide that are not seen when the presentation is shown.

- *Slide Sorter view* shows a thumbnail of each slide in order. Use this view to rearrange the order of slides, produce a timed slide show, or add transitions between selected slides.

- *Handout view* lets you print your slides for a handout. You can choose one, two, three, four, or six slides per page from **Tasks pane > Layouts**. Thumbnails can be re-arranged in this view by dragging and dropping them.

Toolbars

The various Impress toolbars can be displayed or hidden by clicking **View > Toolbars** and selecting from the menu. You can also select the icons that you wish to appear on each toolbar. For more information, refer to Chapter 1 (Introducing OpenOffice.org).

Many of the toolbars in Impress are similar to the toolbars in OOo Draw. Refer to the *Draw Guide* for details on the functions available and how to use them.

Navigator

The Navigator (Figure 133) displays all objects contained in a document. It provides another convenient way to move around a document and find items in it. The Navigator icon 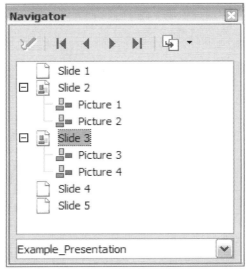 is located on the Standard toolbar. You can also display the Navigator by choosing **Edit > Navigator** on the menu bar or pressing *Ctrl+Shift+F5*.

The Navigator is more useful if you give your slides and objects (pictures, spreadsheets, and so on) meaningful names, instead of leaving them as the default "Slide 1" and "Picture 1" shown in Figure 133.

Figure 133: Navigator in Impress

Working with views

This section describes the use of the five views.

Normal view

Normal view is the main view for working with individual slides. Use this view to format and design and to add text, graphics, and animation effects.

To place a slide in the Slide Design area of the Normal view, click the slide thumbnail in the Slides pane or use the Navigator.

To select a slide in the Navigator, scroll down the list until you find it and then double-click it.

Outline view

Outline view (Figure 134) contains all the slides of the presentation in their numbered sequence. It shows topic titles, bulleted lists, and numbered lists for each slide in outline format. Only the text contained in the default text boxes in each slide is shown, so if your slide includes other text boxes or drawing objects, the text in these objects is not displayed. Slide names are also not included.

Figure 134: Outline view

Outline view serves at least two purposes.

1) Making changes in the text of a slide:

- You can add and delete the text in a slide just as you would in the Normal view.

- You can move the paragraphs of text in the selected slide up or down by using the up and down arrow buttons (Move Up or Move Down) on the Text Formatting toolbar.

- You can change the Outline Level for any of the paragraphs in a slide using the left and right arrow buttons (Promote or Demote).

- You can both move a paragraph and change its outline level using a combination of these four arrow buttons.

2) Comparing the slides with your outline (if you have prepared one in advance). If you notice from your outline that another

slide is needed, you can create it directly in the Outline view (pressing *Enter* when the cursor is on the first line of the slide) or you can change to the Normal view to create it, then return to Outline view to continue reviewing the slides against your outline.

If a slide is not in the correct sequence, you can move it to its proper place.

a) In the slide pane, click the slide icon of the slide you are moving.

b) Drag and drop it where you want it.

Notes view

Use the Notes view to add notes to a slide.

1) Click the **Notes** tab in the Workspace (Figure 135).

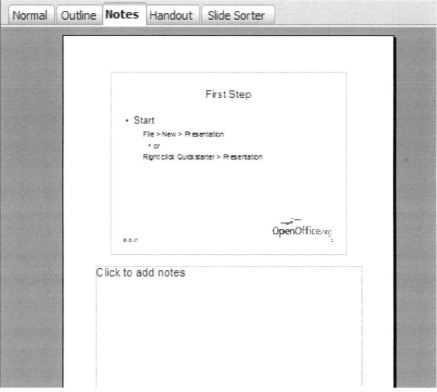

Figure 135: Notes view

2) Select the slide to which you want to add notes.

- Click the slide in the Slide pane, or

- Use the **Previous Slide** and **Next Slide** buttons to move to the desired slide in the Navigator.

3) In the text box below the slide, click on the words *Click to add notes* and begin typing.

You can resize the Notes text box using the green resizing handles and move it by placing the pointer on the border, then clicking and dragging. To make changes in the text style, press the *F11* key to open the Styles and Formatting window.

Slide Sorter view

Slide Sorter view contains all the slide thumbnails (Figure 136). Use this view to work with a group of slides or with only one slide.

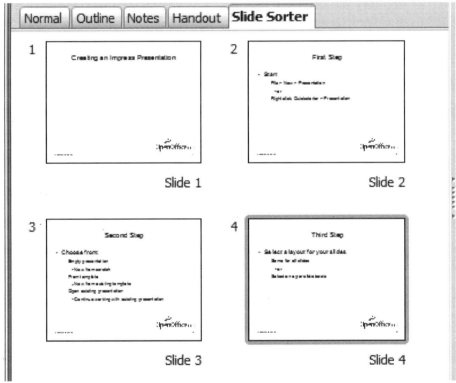

Figure 136: Slide Sorter view

Change the number of slides per row if desired.

1) Check **View > Toolbars > Slide View** to make the Slide View toolbar (Figure 137) visible.

Figure 137: Slide Sorter and Slide View toolbars

2) Adjust the number of slides (up to a maximum of 15).

3) When you have adjusted the number of slide per row, click **View > Toolbars > Slide View** to remove this toolbar from view.

To move a slide in a presentation in the Slide Sorter:

1) Click the slide. A thick black border is drawn around it.
2) Drag and drop it to the location you want.

   - As you move the slide, a black vertical line appears to one side of the slide.
   - Drag the slide until this black vertical line is located where you want the slide to be moved.

To select a group of slides, use one of these methods:

- Use the *Control* (*Ctrl*) key: Click on the first slide and, while pressing Control, select the other desired slides.

- Use the *Shift* key: Click on the first slide, and while pressing the *Shift* key, click on the final slide in the group. This selects all of the other slides in between the first and the last.

- Use the mouse cursor: Click on the first slide to be selected. Hold down the left mouse button. Drag the cursor to the last slide thumbnail. A dashed outline of a rectangle forms as you drag the cursor through the slide thumbnails and a thick black border is drawn around the selected slides. Make sure the rectangle includes all the slides you want to select.

To move a group of slides:

1) Select the group.
2) Drag and drop the group to their new location. The same vertical black line appears to show you where the group of slides will go.

Note	Selection of a group of slides works in a rectangular fashion. Slides that do not fall within a rectangular area cannot be grouped.

You can work with slides in the Slide Sorter view just as you can in the Slide pane. To make changes, right-click a slide and do any of the following using the pop-up menu:

- Add a new slide after the selected slide.

- Delete the selected slide.

- Change the slide layout.

- Change the slide transition.

– For one slide, click the slide to select it. Then add the desired transition.

– For more than one slide, select the group of slides and add the desired transition.

- Mark a slide as hidden. Hidden slides are not shown in the slide show.

- Copy or cut and paste a slide.

Handout view

Handout view is for setting up the layout of your slide for a printed handout. Click the *Handout* tab in the workspace, then choose **Layouts** in the Tasks pane. Layout contains five choices: 1, 2, 3, 4, 6, or 9 slides per page (Figure 138).

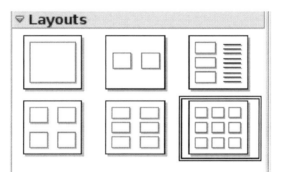

Figure 138: Handout layouts

To print a handout:
1) Select the slides using the Slide Sorter. (Use the steps listed in selecting a group of slides on page 171.)
2) Select **File > Print** or press *Control+P* to open the Print dialog.
3) Select **Options** in the bottom left corner. of the Print dialog.
4) Check **Handouts** in the *Contents* section, and then click **OK**.
5) Click **OK** to close the Print dialog.

Creating a new presentation

This section describes how to set up a new presentation. The settings selected here are general: they apply to all the slides.

Planning a presentation

The first thing to do is to decide what you are going to do with the presentation. For example, putting a group of digital photos together in a presentation requires very little planning. However, using a presentation to increase the knowledge of others about your topic requires much more planning.

You need to ask and answer many questions before you begin creating a presentation. If you are not acquainted with creating presentations, the answers will be more general. Those who have created a variety of presentations in the past will want to have more specific answers.

Who is to see the presentation? How will it be used? What is the subject matter? What should be in its outline? How detailed should the outline be? Will an audio file be played? Is animation desirable? How should the transition between slides be handled? These are some of the many questions that should be asked, answered, and written down before creating the presentation. Sound and animation are more advanced topics and are explained in the *Impress Guide*.

Again, it is not always necessary at this point to have specific answers to every question. Making an outline is extremely important. You may already know exactly what some of the slides will contain. You may only have a general idea of what you want on some of the slides. That is alright. You can make some changes as you go. Change your outline to match the changes you make in your slides.

The important part is that you have a general idea of what you want and how to get it. Put that information on paper. That makes it much easier to create the presentation.

Using the Presentation Wizard

You can start Impress in several ways:

*   From the OOo Welcome screen, if no component is open.

*   From the system menu or the OOo Quickstarter. Details vary with your operating system; see Chapter 1 for more information.

*   From any open component of OOo. Click the triangle to the right of the **New** icon on the main toolbar and select *Presentation* from the drop-down menu or choose **File > New > Presentation** from the menu bar.

When you start Impress, the Presentation Wizard appears (Figure 139).

Tip	If you do not want the wizard to start every time you launch Impress, select the **Do not show this wizard again** checkbox. You can enable it again later if you need under **Tools > Options > OpenOffice.org Impress > General > Wizard**, and select the **Start with wizard** checkbox. Leave the **Preview** checkbox selected, so templates, slide designs, and slide transitions appear in the preview box as you choose them.

Figure 139. Choosing the type of presentation

1) Select *Empty Presentation* under **Type.** It creates a presentation from scratch.

Note	*From Template* uses a template design already created as the basis for a new presentation. The wizard changes to show a list of available templates. Choose the template you want. *Open Existing Presentation* continues work on a previously created presentation. The wizard changes to show a list of existing presentations. Choose the presentation you want. Both of these options are covered in the *Impress Guide*.

2) Click **Next.** Figure 140 shows the Presentation Wizard step 2 as it appears if you selected *Empty Presentation* at step 1. If you selected *From Template*, an example slide is shown in the Preview box.

Figure 140. Selecting a slide design

3) Choose a design under **Select a slide design**. The slide design section gives you two main choices: *Presentation Backgrounds* and *Presentations*. Each one has a list of choices for slide designs. If you want to use one of these other than <Original>, click it to select it.

- The types of *Presentation Backgrounds* are shown in Figure 140. By clicking an item, you will see a preview of the slide design in the Preview window. Impress contains three choices under *Presentations*: *<Original>*, *Introducing a New Product*, and *Recommendation of a Strategy*.

- <Original> is for a blank presentation slide design.

- Both *Introducing a New Product* and *Recommendation of a Strategy* have their own prepackaged slide designs. Each design appears in the Preview window when its name is clicked.

Note	*Introducing a New Product* and *Recommendation of a Strategy* are prepackaged presentation templates. They can be used to create a presentation by choosing **From template** in the first step (Figure 139).

4) Select how the presentation will be used under **Select an output medium.** Most often, presentations are created for computer screen display. Select *Screen*.

5) Click **Next**. The **Presentation** Wizard step 3 appears.

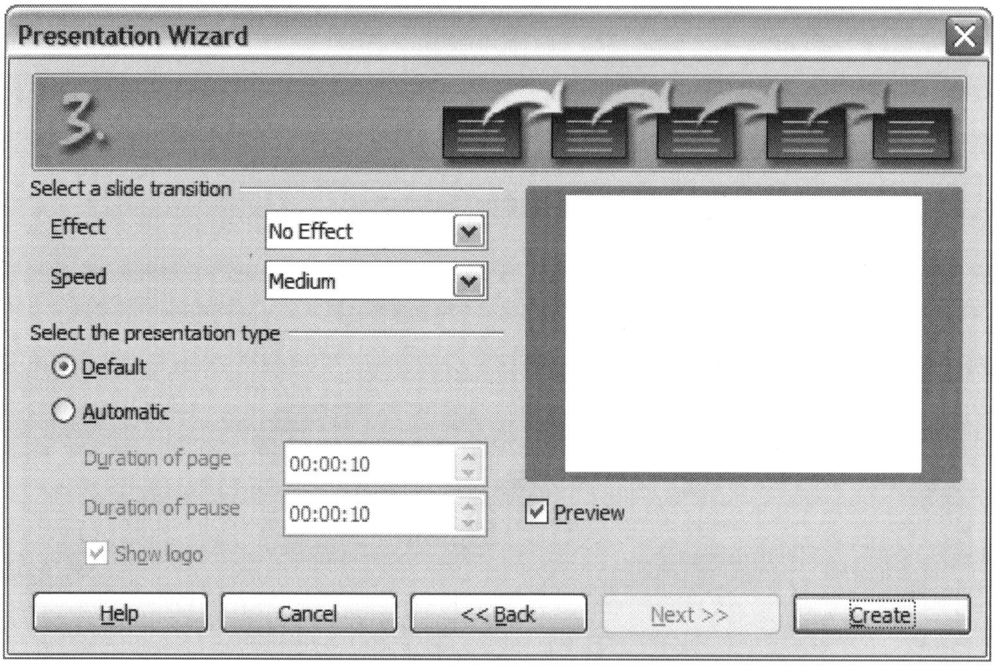

Figure 141. Selecting a slide design

6) Choose the desired slide transition from the *Effect* drop-down menu.

7) Select the desired speed for the transition between the different slides in the presentation from the **Speed** drop-down menu. *Medium* is a good choice for now.

8) Click **Create.** A new presentation is created.

Tip	You might want to accept the default values for both *Effect* and *Speed* unless you are skilled at doing this. Both of these values can be changed later while working with **Slide transitions** and **animations**. These two are explained in more detail in Chapter 9 of the *Impress Guide*.

Note	If you selected *From template* on step 1 of the Wizard, the **Next** button will be active on step 3 and other pages will be available. These pages are not described here.

Formatting a presentation

Now put your presentation together based on your outline.

Caution	Remember to save frequently while working on the presentation, to prevent any loss of information should something unexpected occur. You might also want to activate the AutoRecovery function (**Tools > Options > Load/Save > General**). Make sure **Save AutoRecovery information every** is selected and that you have entered a recovery frequency.

Creating the first slide

The first slide is normally a title slide. Decide which of the layouts will best suit your purposes for this first slide: simplicity would be appropriate in this instance. You can use the prepackaged layouts available in the Layout section of the Tasks pane. Suitable layouts are *Title Slide* (which also contains a section for a subtitle) or *Title Only*, however all but one layout (the blank one) contains a title section, so you are not restricted to the two layouts described here.

| Tip | If you do not know the names for the prepackaged layouts, you can use the tooltip feature. Position the cursor on an icon in the Layout section (or on any toolbar icon) and its name will be displayed in a small rectangle.
If the tooltips are not enabled, you can enable them. From the main menu, select **Tools > Options > OpenOffice.org > General > Help** and mark the **Tips** checkbox. If the **Extended tips** checkbox is also marked, you will get more detailed tooltip information, but the tooltip names themselves will not be provided. |
| --- | --- |

Select a layout in the Layout section of the Tasks pane by clicking on it: it appears in the Workspace. To create the title, click on *"Click to add title"* (assuming the *Blank Slide* layout was not used) and then type the title text. Adjustments to the formatting of the title can be done by pressing the *F11* key, right-clicking the *Title* presentation style entry, and selecting **Modify** from the pop-up menu.

If you are using the *Title Slide* layout, click on *Click to add text* to add a *subtitle*. Proceed as above to make adjustments to the formatting if required.

Inserting additional slides

The steps for inserting additional slides are basically the same as for selecting the title page. It is a process that has to be repeated for each slide. Unless you are using more than one slide master, your only concern is the *Layouts* section of the Tasks pane (Figure 142).

Figure 142: Choosing a slide layout

First insert all the slides your outline indicates you will need. Only after this should you begin adding special effects such as custom animation and slide transitions.

Step 1: Insert a new slide. This can be done in a variety of ways—take your pick.

- **Insert > Slide**.

- Right-click on the present slide, and select **Slide > New Slide** from the pop-up menu.

- Click the **Slide** icon in the *Presentation* toolbar (Figure 143).

Figure 143: Presentation toolbar

Step 2: Select the layout slide that bests fits your needs.

Step 3: Modify the elements of the slide. At this stage, the slide consists of everything contained in the slide master, as well as the chosen layout slide, so this includes removing unneeded elements, adding needed elements (such as pictures), and inserting text.

Caution	Changes to any of the pre-packaged layouts can only be made using **View > Normal**, which is the default. Attempting to do this by modifying a slide master may result in unpredictable results and requires extra care as well as some trials and errors.

---

1) Remove any element on the slide that is not required.

   - Click the element to highlight it. (The green squares show it is highlighted.)

   - Press the *Delete* key to remove it.

Tip	Sometimes you will accidentally select the wrong layout slide or decide to change it. This is safe and does not cause loss of the contents already on the slide.

---

2) Add any elements to the slide that you do need.

   a) Adding pictures to the clipart frame, if your chosen layout includes one:

      - Double-click the picture within the frame. The Insert picture dialog opens.

      - Browse to the location of the picture you want to include. To see a preview of the picture, check **Preview** at the bottom of the Insert picture dialog.

- Select the picture and click **Open**.

- Resize the picture as necessary. Follow the directions in the Caution note below.

b) Adding pictures from graphic files to places other than the clipart frame:

- **Insert > Picture > From File**. The Insert picture dialog opens.

- Browse to the graphic file. To see a preview of the picture, check **Preview** at the bottom of the Insert picture dialog. Select a picture and click **Open**.

- Move the picture to its location.

- Resize the picture, if necessary.

c) Adding OLE Objects is an advanced technique covered in Chapter 7 of the *Impress Guide*.

Caution	When resizing a graphic, right-click the picture. Select **Position and Size** from the context menu and make sure that **Keep ratio** is selected. Then adjust the height or width to the size you need. (As you adjust one dimension both dimensions will change.) Failure to do so will cause the picture to become distorted. Remember also that resizing a bitmap image will reduce its quality; better by far to create an image of the desired size outside of Impress.

3) Adding text to a slide: If the slide contains text, click on *Click to add an outline* in the text frame and then type your text. The Outline styles from 1 to 10 are automatically applied to the text as you insert it. You can change the outline level of each paragraph as well as its position within the text using the arrow buttons on the *Text Formatting* toolbar.

Step 4: To create additional slides, repeat steps 1–3.

Modifying the appearance of slides

To change the background and other characteristics of all slides in the presentation, you need to modify the slide master or choose a different slide master.

A *Slide Master* is a slide with a specified set of characteristics which is used as the beginning point for creating other slides. These characteristics include the background, objects in the background, formatting of any text used, and any background graphics.

Note	OOo uses three interchangeable terms for this one concept. *Master slide*, *slide master*, and *master page* all refer to a slide that is used to create other slides. This book, however, will use only the term *slide master,* except when describing the user interface.

Impress has 28 prepackaged slide masters, found in the Master Pages section of the Tasks pane. You can also create and save additional slide masters.

Modifying the slide show

Now review the entire presentation and answer some questions. Run the slide show at least once before answering them. You might want to add some questions of your own.

1) Are the slides in the correct order? If not, some of them will need to be moved.
2) Would an additional slide make a particular point clearer? If so, another slide needs to be created.
3) Would some custom animations help some of the slides? (Advanced technique.)
4) Should some of the slides have a different slide transition than others? The transition of those slides should be changed.
5) Do some of the slides seem unnecessary? Delete the affected slide or slides after checking if they are indeed unnecessary.

Tip	If one or more slides seems to be unnecessary, hide the slide or slides, and view the slide show a few more times to make sure. To hide a slide, right-click the slide in the Slides pane and select **Hide Slide** in the pop-up menu. Do not delete a slide until you have done this, otherwise you may have to create that slide again.

Once you have answered these and your own questions, you should make the necessary changes. This is done most easily in the Slide Sorter view. If you need one or more new slides, create them using the steps listed in "Inserting additional slides" on page 178.

Slide masters and styles

A *slide master* is a slide that is used as the starting point for other slides. It is similar to a page style in Writer: it controls the basic formatting of all slides based on it. A slide show can have more than one slide master.

Note	OOo uses three terms for this one concept. *Master slide*, *slide master*, and *master page* all refer to a slide which is used to create other slides. This book uses the term *slide master*, except when describing the user interface.

A slide master has a defined set of characteristics, including the background color, graphic, or gradient; objects (such as logos, decorative lines, and other graphics) in the background; headers and footers; placement and size of text frames; and the formatting of text.

All of the characteristics of slide masters are controlled by *styles*. The styles of any new slide you create are inherited from the slide master from which it was created. In other words, the styles of the slide master are available and applied to all slides created from that slide master. Changing a style in a slide master results in changes to all the slides based on that slide master; it is, however, possible to modify each individual slide without affecting the slide master.

Slide masters have two types of styles associated with them: *presentation styles* and *graphic styles*. The pre-packaged presentation styles can be modified, but new presentation styles cannot be created. However, not only can the prepackaged graphic styles be modified, but new graphic styles can also be created. What styles to use and when to use them is described later in this chapter.

Presentation styles affect three elements of a slide master: the background, background objects (such as icons, decorative lines, and text frames), and the text placed on the slide. Text styles are further divided into *Notes*, *Outline 1* through *Outline 9*, *Subtitle*, and *Title*. The outline styles are used for the different levels of the outline to which they belong. For example, Outline 2 is used for the subpoints of Outline 1, and Outline 3 is used for the subpoints of Outline 2.

Graphic styles affect many of the elements of a slide. Notice that text styles exist in both the presentation and graphic style selections.

Working with slide masters

Impress comes with 28 prepackaged slide masters. They are shown in the Master Pages section of the Tasks pane (Figure 144). This section has three subsections: *Used in This Presentation*, *Recently Used*, and *Available for Use*. Click the + sign next to the name of a subsection to expand it to show thumbnails of the slides, or click the – sign to collapse the subsection to hide the thumbnails.

Each of the slide masters shown in the *Available for Use* list is from a template of the same name. If you have created your own templates, or added templates from other sources, slide masters from those templates will also appear in this list.

Figure 144: Available master pages (slides)

Creating slide masters

You can create a new slide master in a similar way to modifying the default slide master.

To start, enable editing of slide masters by **View > Master > Slide Master**.

On the Master View toolbar, click the **New Master** icon.

A second slide master appears in the Slides pane. Modify this slide master to suit your requirements. It is also recommended that you rename this new slide master: right-click on the slide in the Slides pane and select **Rename master** from the popup menu.

When you are done, close the Master View toolbar to return to normal slide editing mode.

Applying a slide master

In the Tasks Pane, be sure the Master Pages section is showing.

To apply one of the slide masters to *all slides* in your presentation, click on it in the list.

To apply a different slide master to one or more *selected slides*:

1) In the Slide Pane, select the slides you want to change.
2) In the Tasks Pane, right-click on the slide master you want to apply to the selected slides, and click **Apply to Selected Slides** on the pop-up menu.

Loading additional slide masters

Sometimes, in the same set of slides, you may need to mix multiple slide masters that may belong to different templates. For example, you may need a completely different layout for the first slide of the presentation, or you may want to add to your presentation a slide from a different presentation (based on a template available on the hard disk).

The Slide Design dialog makes this possible. Access this dialog either from the menu bar (**Format > Slide design**) or by right-clicking on a slide in the Slides pane.

The main window in the dialog shows the slide masters already available for use. To add more:

1) Click the **Load** button.
2) Select in the new dialog the template from which to load the slide master. Click **OK.**
3) Click **OK** again to close the slide design dialog.

The slide masters in the template you selected are now shown also in the Master Pages section of the Tasks pane in the *Available for use* subsection.

Note	The slide masters you have loaded will also be available the next time you load the presentation. If you want to delete the unused slide masters, click the corresponding checkbox in the Slide Design dialog. Due to a bug, if the slide master was not used in the presentation, it is removed from the list of available slide masters anyway.

Tip	To limit the size of the presentation file, you may want to minimize the number of slide masters used.

Modifying a slide master

The following items can be changed on a slide master:

* Background (color, gradient, hatching, or bitmap)
* Background objects (for example, add a logo or decorative graphics)
* Size, placement, and contents of header and footer elements to appear on every slide
* Size and placement of default frames for slide titles and content

Before working on the slide master, make sure that the Styles and Formatting window is open.

To select the slide master for modification:

1) Select **View > Master > Slide Master** from the menu bar. This unlocks the properties of the slide master so you can edit it.
2) Click *Master Pages* in the Tasks pane. This gives you access to the pre-packaged slide masters.
3) Click on the slide master you want to modify among the ones available (Figure 144).
4) Make changes as required, then click the **Close Master View** icon on the Master View toolbar. For details, see Chapter 2 of the *Impress Guide*
5) Save the file before continuing.

Caution	Any changes made to one slide when in Master View mode will appear on *all* slides using this slide master. Always make sure you close Master View and return to Normal view before working on any of the presentation slides. Select **View > Normal** from the menu bar, or click **Close Master View** in the Master View toolbar to return to the normal slide view.

The changes made to one of the slides in Normal view (for example changes to the bullet point style or the color of the title area and so on...) will not be overridden by subsequent changes to the slide master. There are cases, however, where it is desirable to revert a manually modified element of the slide to the style defined in the slide master: to do that, select that element and choose **Format > Default Formatting** from the menu bar.

Sometimes you may want to try several of the available layouts to see which one is more suitable for your contents. Applying a layout only requires that you open the Layouts section of the Tasks pane and double-click on the new layout. Alternatively you can right-click on the desired layout thumbnail and select **Apply to selected slide** from the pop-up menu.

Adding text to all slides

Some of the supplied slide masters have text objects in the footer. You can add other text objects to the master page for your slides to act as a header or a footer.

1) Choose **View > Master > Slide Master** from the menu bar.
2) On the **Drawing** toolbar (see Figure 140), select the **Text** icon.
3) Click once and drag in the master page to draw a text object, and then type or paste your text into the object or add fields as described below.
4) Choose **View > Normal** when you are finished.

To add a field, such as the date or page number, to a text object in the header or footer, choose **Insert > Fields**. and select the required field from the submenu. If you want to edit a field in your slide, select it and choose **Edit > Fields**.

The fields you can use in Impress are:

- Date (fixed)
- Date (variable)—updates automatically when you reload the file
- Time (fixed)
- Time (variable)—updates automatically when you reload the file
- Author—First and last names listed in the OpenOffice.org user data
- Page number (slide number)
- File name

| Tip | To change the number format (1,2,3 or a,b,c or i,ii,iii, etc.) for the page number field, choose **Format > Page** and then select a format from the list in the **Layout Settings** area. |
| | To change the author information, go to **Tools > Options > OpenOffice.org > User Data**. |

Adding and formatting text

Text in slides is contained in *text boxes*. There are two ways to add text boxes to a slide:

- Choose a predefined layout from the *Layouts* section of the Tasks pane. These text boxes are called **AutoLayout** text boxes.
- Create a text box using the text tool.

Using text boxes created from the Layout pane

In Normal view:

1) Click in the text box that reads **Click to add text**, **Click to add an outline**, or a similar notation.
2) Type or paste your text in the text box.

Using text boxes created from the text box tool

In Normal View:

1) Click on the **Text** icon **T** on the Drawing toolbar. If the toolbar with the text icon is not visible, choose **View > Toolbars > Drawing**.
2) Click and drag to draw a box for the text on the slide. Do not worry about the vertical size and position—the text box will expand if needed as you type.
3) Release the mouse button when finished. The cursor appears in the text box, which is now in edit mode (gray hashed border with green resizing handles shown in Figure 145).
4) Type or paste your text in the text box.
5) Click outside the text box to deselect it.

You can move, resize, and delete text boxes. For more information, see Chapter 3 in the *Impress Guide*.

Note

In addition to the normal text boxes where text is horizontally aligned, it is possible to insert text boxes where the text is aligned vertically. This choice is available only when Asian languages are enabled in **Tools > Options > Language Settings > Languages**.

Click on the ⊣ button in the drawing toolbar to create a vertical text box. Note that when editing the contents, the text is displayed horizontally.

1)Click and drag to draw a box for the text on the slide. Do not worry about the vertical size and position—the text box will expand if needed as you type. To change the horizontal size see "Resizing a text box"; to reposition the text box to a different part of the slide see "Moving a text box".

2)Release the mouse button when finished. The cursor appears in the text box, which is now in edit mode (gray hashed border with green resizing handles).

3)Type or paste your text in the text box.

4)Click outside the text box to de-select it.

Figure 145: Selected text box showing the green resizing handles and text toolbar

Pasting text

You can insert text into a text box by copying it from another document and pasting it into Impress. However, the pasted text will probably not match the formatting of the surrounding text or that of the other slides in the presentation. This may be what you want on some occasions, however in most cases you want to make sure that the presentation does not become a patchwork of different paragraph styles, font types, bullet points and so on. There are several ways to ensure consistency; these methods are explained below.

Pasting unformatted text

It is normally good practice to paste text without formatting and apply the formatting later. To paste without formatting, either press *Control+Shift+V* and then select **Unformatted text** from the dialog that appears, or click on the small black triangle next to the paste symbol in the standard toolbar and select **Unformatted text**. The unformatted text will be formatted with the outline style at the cursor position in an AutoLayout text box or with the default graphic style in a normal text box.

Formatting pasted text

If pasting the text into an **AutoLayout** area, then to give the pasted text the same look and feel of the rest of the presentation. you need to apply the appropriate *outline style* to the text.

1) Paste the text in the desired position. Do not worry if it does not look right: it will in a minute.
2) Select the text you have just pasted.
3) Select **Format > Default formatting** from the menu bar.
4) Use the four arrow buttons in the Text Formatting toolbar

   ⇐ ⇒ ⇧ ⇩   to move the text to the appropriate position and give it the appropriate outline level. The button with the arrow pointing left promotes the list entry by one level (for example from Outline 3 to Outline 2), the right arrow button demotes the list entry by one level, the up and down arrow buttons move the list entry.
5) Apply manual formatting as required to sections of the text (to change font attributes, tabs, and so on).

If you are pasting text in a **text box**, you can still use styles to quickly format the text. Note that *one and only one* graphic style can be applied to the copied text. To do that:

1) Paste the text in the desired position.
2) Select the text you have just pasted.
3) Select the desired graphic style.
4) Apply manual formatting as required to sections of the text.

Tip	Presentation styles are very different from Writer styles and are applied in quite a different way.

Creating bulleted and numbered lists

The procedure to create a bulleted or numbered list is quite different depending on the type of text box used, although the tools to manage the list and customize the appearance are the same.

In text boxes created automatically by Impress (called AutoLayout), the outline styles available are by default bulleted lists, while for normal text boxes an additional step is required to create a bulleted list.

Creating lists in AutoLayout text boxes

Every text box included in the available layouts is already formatted as a bulleted list, therefore to create a bulleted list the only necessary steps are:

1) From the Layout pane, choose a slide design that contains a text box. Those are easily recognizable from the thumbnail.
2) Click in the text box that reads **Click to add an outline.**
3) Type the text, then press *Enter* to start a new bulleted line.
4) The default list type is a bulleted list. The mechanisms to change the list from bulleted to numbered and vice versa are explained in "Changing the appearance of the list" on page 191.

Tip	Press *Shift + Enter* to start a new line without creating a new bullet or number. The new line will have the same indentation of the previous line. Press instead the button bullets on/off on the text formatting toolbar for a line without bullet. If the text formatting toolbar is not showing, enable it selecting **View > Toolbar > Formatting** in the menu bar.

Creating lists in other text boxes

To create a list in a text box, follow these steps:

1) Place the cursor in the text box.
2) Click the **Bullets On/Off** button on the text formatting toolbar. If the text formatting toolbar is not showing, enable it by selecting **View > Toolbar > Formatting** from the menu bar.
3) Type the text and press *Enter* to start a new bulleted line.
4) The default list type is a bulleted list. The mechanisms to change the appearance of the list are explained on page 191.

Creating a new outline level

1) If necessary, press *Enter* to begin a new line.
2) Press *Tab*. Each time you press *Tab* the line indents to the next outline level. Pressing *Enter* creates a new line at the same level as the previous one. To return to the previous level, press *Shift+Tab*.

In the AutoLayout text boxes, promoting or demoting an item in the list corresponds to applying a different outline style, so the second outline level corresponds to Outline 2 style, the third to Outline 3 style, and so on.

Note	Unlike styles in Writer, do not try to change the outline level by selecting the text and then clicking the desired outline style. Due to the way the presentation styles work, it is not possible to apply them in this way.

Changing the appearance of the list

You can fully customize the appearance of a list, changing the bullet type or numbering for the entire list or for single entry. All of the changes can be made using the Bullets and Numbering dialog, which is accessed by selecting **Format > Bullets and Numbering** or by clicking on the **Bullets and Numbering** icon on the text formatting toolbar.

For the entire list:

1) Select the entire list or click on the gray border of the text box so that just the green resizing handles are displayed.

2) Select **Format > Bullets and Numbering** or click on the **Bullets and Numbering** icon.

3) The Bullets and Numbering dialog contains five tabs: Bullets, Numbering type, Graphics, Position, and Customize.

- If a bullet list is needed, select the desired bullet style from the six default styles available on the *Bullets* page.

- If a graphics style is needed, select one from those available on the *Graphics* page.

- If a numbered list is needed, select one of the 6 default numbering styles on the *Numbering type* page.

For a single line in the list:

1) Click anywhere in the line to place the cursor in it.

2) Follow steps 2–4 of the previous instruction set.

If the list was created in an AutoLayout text box, then an alternative way to change the entire list is to modify the Outline styles. Changes made to the outline style will apply to all the slides using them. Sometimes this is what you want; sometimes it is not, so some care must be taken.

Creating tables

For displaying tabular data, you can insert basic tables directly into your slides in a number of ways:

- Use the **Insert > Table** menu option.
- With the Table button on the main toolbar. ⊞ ▾ 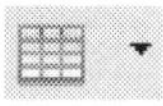
- With the *Table Design* button on the table toolbar.
- By selecting a Style option from the Table Design section of the Tasks pane.

Each method opens the Insert Table dialog, shown in Figure 146. Alternatively, clicking on the black arrow next to the Table button displays a graphic that you can drag and select the number of rows and columns for your table.

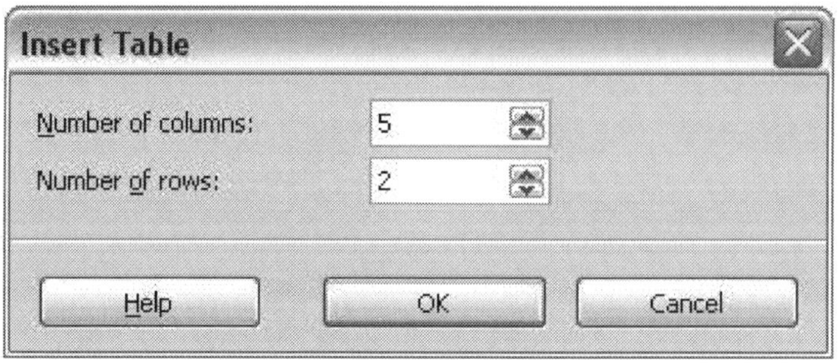

Insert Table

Number of columns: 5

Number of rows: 2

Help   OK   Cancel

Figure 146. Creating a table with the Insert Table dialog.

Note	Selecting from any of the styles in the Table Design section of the Tasks pane creates a table based on that style. If you create a table by another method, you can still apply a style of your choice later.

With the table selected, the Table toolbar should appear. If it does not, you can access it by selecting **View > Toolbars > Table**. The Table toolbar offers many of the same buttons as the table toolbar in Writer, with the exception of functions like Sort and Sum for performing calculations. For those functions, you need to use a spreadsheet inserted from Calc (discussed below).

After the table is created, you can modify it in much the same ways as you would modify a table in Writer: adding and deleting rows and columns, adjusting width and spacing, adding borders, background colors and so on. Detailed information on working with tables and the Table Properties dialog can be found in Chapter 9 of the *Writer Guide*.

By modifying the style of the table from the Table Design section of the Tasks pane, you can quickly change the appearance of the table or any newly created tables based on the Style options you select. You can choose to add emphasis to a header and total row as well as the first and last columns of the table, and apply a banded appearance to the rows and columns.

Having completed the table design, entering data into the cells is similar to working with text box objects. Click in the cell you wish to add data to, and begin typing. To move around cells quickly, use the following key options:

- The *arrow keys* move the cursor to the next table cell if the cell is empty, otherwise they move the cursor to the next character in the cell.

- The *Tab* key moves to the next cell, skipping over the contents of the cell; *Shift+Tab* move backwards in this manner.

Adding graphics, spreadsheets, charts, and other objects

Graphics in Impress are handled much the same as graphics in Draw. For more information, see Chapter 7 (Getting Started with Draw), the *Draw Guide*, or Chapters 4, 5, and 6 in the *Impress Guide*.

Spreadsheets embedded in Impress include most of the functionality of spreadsheets in Calc and are therefore capable of performing extremely complex calculations and data analysis. If you need to analyze your data or apply formulas, these operations are best performed in a Calc spreadsheet and the results displayed in an embedded Impress spreadsheet.

To add a spreadsheet to a slide, select the corresponding layout in the list of predefined layouts in the Tasks pane. This inserts a placeholder for a spreadsheet in the center of a slide. To insert data and modify the formatting of the spreadsheet, it is necessary to *activate* it and enter the edit mode. To do so, double-click inside the frame with the green handles.

Alternatively, select **Insert > Spreadsheet** from the main menu bar. This opens a small spreadsheet in the middle of the slide. When a spreadsheet is inserted using this method, it is already in edit mode. It is also possible to insert a spreadsheet as an OLE object.

To add a chart to a slide, select the corresponding layout in the list of predefined layouts in the task pane or use the **Insert Chart** feature.

Impress offers the capability of inserting in a slide various other types of objects such as music or video clips, Writer documents, Math formulas, generic OLE objects and so on. A typical presentation may contain movie clips, sound clips, OLE objects and formulas; other objects are less frequently used since they do not appear during a slide show.

For details on using spreadsheets, charts, and other objects in Impress, refer to Chapter 7 of the *Impress Guide*.

Setting up the slide show

Impress gives you the tools to organize and display a slide show, including:

- Which slides to show and in what order
- Whether to run the show automatically or manually
- Transitions between slides
- Animations on individual slides
- Interactions: what happens when you click a button or link

Chapter 9 of the Impress Guide describes these tools.

Most tasks associated with putting together a show from your slides are best done in Slide Sorter view. Choose **View > Slide Sorter** from the menu bar or click the Slide Sorter tab at the top of the workspace. All of your slides appear in the workspace; you may need to scroll to see them all.

Custom animations are found on the Tasks pane. This is an advanced technique and is explained in Chapter 9 (Slide Shows) in the *Impress Guide*.

Your first slide show should probably have the same slide transition for all slides. Setting *Advance slide* to **On mouse click** is the default and a simple setting. If you want each slide to be shown for a specific amount of time, click **Automatically after** and enter the number of seconds. Click **Apply to all slides**.

Slide transition choices are also found on the Tasks pane. For more information about slide transitions, see Chapter 9 in the *Impress Guide*.

Tip	The Slide transition section has a very useful choice: *Automatic preview*. Select its checkbox. Then when you make any changes in a slide transition, the new slide is previewed in the Slide Design area, including its transition effect.

Running the slide show

To run the slide show, do one of the following:

- Click **Slide Show > Slide Show.**
- Click the Slide Show button on the Presentation toolbar.

Figure 147: Presentation Toolbar

- Press *F5* or *F9*.

If the slide transition is *Automatic after x seconds*, let the slide show run by itself.

If the slide transition is *On mouse click*, do one of the following to move from one slide to the next:

- Use the arrow keys on the keyboard to go to the next slide or to go back to the previous one.
- Click the mouse to move to the next slide.
- Press the spacebar on the keyboard to advance to the next slide.

Right-click anywhere on the screen to open a menu from which you can navigate the slides and set other options.

To exit the slide show at any time including at the end, press the *Esc* key.

Chapter *7*
Getting Started with Draw

Vector drawing in OpenOffice.org

What is Draw?

Draw is a vector graphics drawing program. It offers a series of powerful tools that enable you to quickly create all sorts of graphics. Vector graphics store and display an image as vectors (two points and a line) rather than a collections of pixels (dots on the screen). Vector graphics allow for easier storage and scaling of the image.

Draw is perfectly integrated into the OpenOffice.org suite, and this makes exchanging graphics with all components of the suite very easy. For example, if you create an image in Draw, reusing it in a Writer document is as simple as copying and pasting. You can also work with drawings directly from within Writer and Impress, using a subset of the functions and tools from Draw.

Draw's functionality is very extensive and complete. Although it was not designed to rival high-end graphics applications, Draw possesses more functions than the majority of drawing tools that are integrated into office productivity suites.

A few examples of drawing functions might whet your appetite: layer management, magnetic grid point system, dimensions and measurement display, connectors for making organization charts, 3D functions enabling small three-dimensional drawings to be created (with texture and lighting effects), drawing and page style integration, and Bézier curves, to name a few.

This chapter introduces some of Draw's features, but it does not attempt to cover all of the them. See the *Draw Guide* and the application Help for more information.

The Draw workspace

The main components of the Draw workspace are shown in Figure 148.

You can surround the drawing area with toolbars and information areas. The number and position of the visible tools vary with the task at hand or user preferences. Therefore, your setup may appear a little different. For example, many people put the main Drawing toolbar on the left-hand side of the workspace, not at the bottom as shown here.

You can split drawings in Draw over several pages. Multipage drawings are used mainly for presentations. The *Pages* pane, on the left side of the Draw window in Figure 148 gives an overview of the pages that you create. If the Pages pane is not visible on your setup,you can enable it from the View menu (**View > Page Pane**).

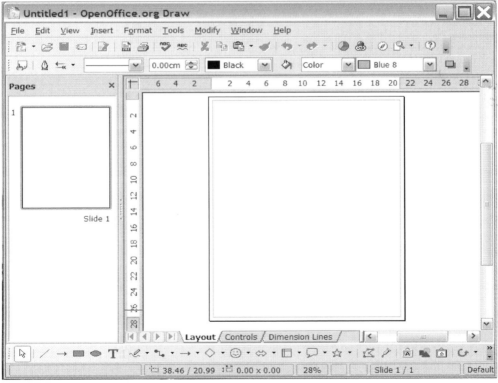

Figure 148. Initial Draw window

Rulers

You should see rulers (bars with numbers) on the upper and left-hand side of the workspace. These show the size of a selected object on the page (see the gray double lines, highlighted in Figure 149). When no object is selected, they show the location of the mouse pointer, which helps to accurately position drawing objects. You can also use the rulers to manage object handles and guide lines, making it easier to position objects. The page margins in the drawing area are also represented on the rulers. You can change the margins directly on the rulers by dragging them with the mouse.

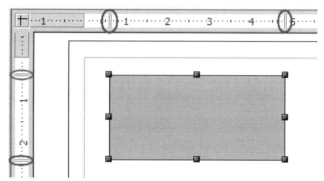

Figure 149: Rulers show the size of the selected object

To modify the units of measurement of the rulers, right-click on one of the rulers. The two rulers can have different units.

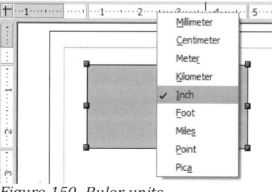

Figure 150. Ruler units

Status bar

The Status bar is located at the bottom of the workspace. The middle part of the Status bar shows Draw-specific fields, as identified in Figure 151.

For details on the contents and use of these fields, please refer to the *Draw Guide*.

Note	The sizes are given in the current measurement unit (not to be confused with the ruler units). This unit is defined in **Tools > Options > OpenOffice.org Draw > General**, where you can also change the scale of the page. Another way to change the scale is to double-click on the number shown in the status bar.

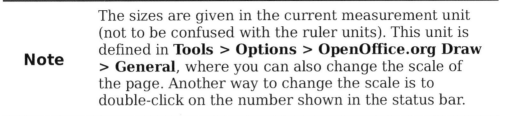

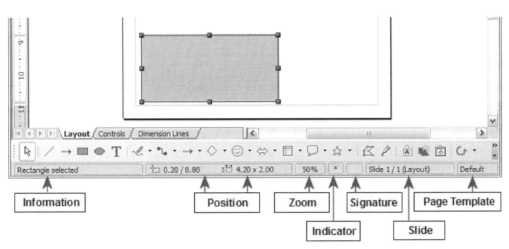

Figure 151: Items on the Draw status bar

Toolbars

The various Draw toolbars can be displayed or hidden according to your needs.

To display or hide the toolbars, click **View > Toolbars**. On the menu that appears, choose which toolbars you want to display.

You can also select the buttons that you wish to appear on the corresponding toolbar. On the **View > Toolbars** menu, select **Customize**, click on the **Toolbars** tab, select the toolbar you want to change, and then select the desired buttons for that toolbar.

Many toolbar buttons are marked with a small arrow beside the button. The arrow indicates that this button has additional functions. Click the arrow and a submenu or toolbar appears, showing its additional functions (see Figure 152). Most buttons marked with the small arrow can become *floating toolbars*.

To make a submenu into a floating toolbar, click the area at the top of the submenu, drag it across the screen, and then release the mouse button. Floating toolbars can be docked on an edge of the screen or within one of the existing toolbar areas at the top of the screen, as described in Chapter 1.

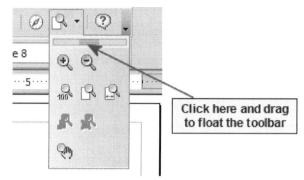

Figure 152. An arrow next to a button indicates additional functions

Click the arrow on the title bar of a floating toolbar to display additional functions (see Figure 153).

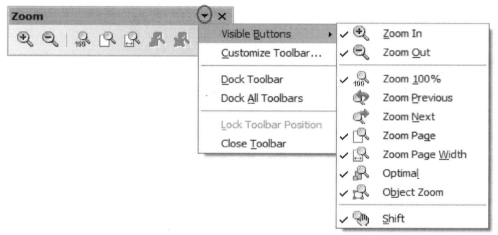

Figure 153. An arrow on a floating toolbar indicates additional functions

The tools available in the various toolbars are explained in the following sections. The appearance of the toolbar icons may vary with your operating system and the selection of icon size and style in **Tools > Options > OpenOffice.org > View**.

Standard toolbar

The Standard toolbar looks like this:

It is the same for all parts of OpenOffice.org.

Line and Filling toolbar

The Line and Filling toolbar lets you modify the main properties of a drawing object. See page 221 for details.

If the selected object is text, the toolbar changes to the one shown below, which is similar to the Formatting toolbar in Writer.

Drawing toolbar

The Drawing toolbar is the most important toolbar in Draw. It contains all the necessary functions for drawing various geometric and freehand shapes and organizing them on the page.

Color Bar

To display the Color Bar, use **View > Toolbars > Color Bar**. The toolbar then appears at the bottom of the workspace.

This toolbar lets you rapidly choose the color of the objects in your drawing. The first box in the panel corresponds to transparency (no color).

You can access several specialized color palettes in Draw, as well as change individual colors to your own taste. This is done using the Area dialog, reached by choosing **Format > Area** or the *pouring can* icon on the Line and Filling toolbar.

On the Area dialog (Figure 154), choose the tab marked **Colors**.

To load another palette, click on the **Load Color List** button (circled). The file selector dialog asks you to choose one of the standard OOo palettes (files bearing the file extension *.soc). For example, web.soc is a color palette that is adapted to creating drawings that are going to appear in Web pages. The colors will correctly display on workstations with screens displaying at least 256 colors.

The color selection box also lets you individually change any color by modifying the numerical values in the fields provided to the right of the color palette. You can use the color schemes known as CMYK (Cyan, Magenta, Yellow, Black), RGB (Red, Green, Blue) or HSB (Hue, Saturation, Brightness).

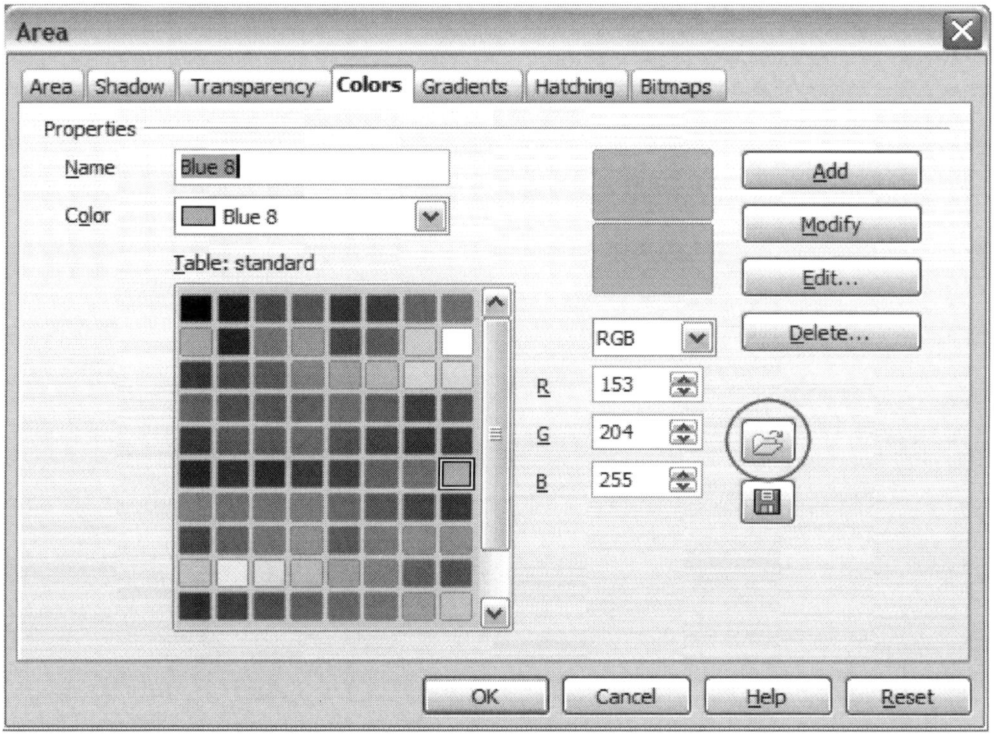

Figure 154. Changing the color palette

Clicking on the **Edit** button opens a special dialog to allow setting individual colors (see Figure 155). Many more input possibilities are available in this dialog.

In the lower area you can enter values in the RGB and CMYK models as well as the HSB (Hue, Saturation and Brightness) model.

The two color fields at lower right show the value of the color as selected (left) and the currently set value from the color value fields (right).

For a more detailed description of color palettes and their options, see Chapter 8 (Tips and Tricks) in the *Draw Guide*.

Options toolbar

The Options toolbar (Figure 156) lets you activate or deactivate various drawing aids. The Options toolbar is not displayed by default. To display it, select **View > Toolbars > Options**. The most important options to learn when starting to work in Draw are enclosed in red. The functions of the various icons are described in Table 2.

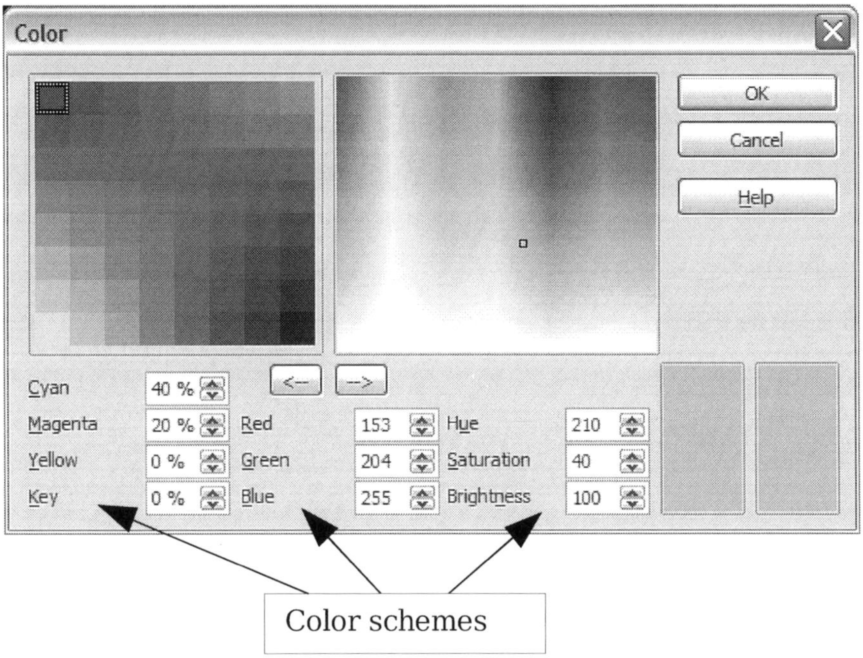

Figure 155. Defining color schemes

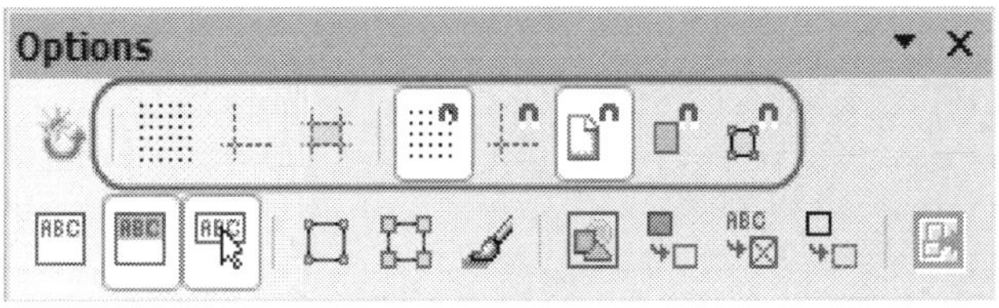

Figure 156: Options toolbar

Table 2: Functions on the Options toolbar

Icon	Function
	Rotation mode after clicking object
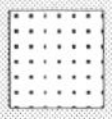	Display (or hide) the grid
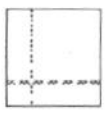	Display (or hide) the guides
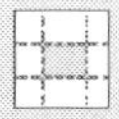	Display (or hide) guides when moving
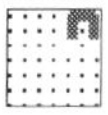	Snap to grid
	Snap to guides

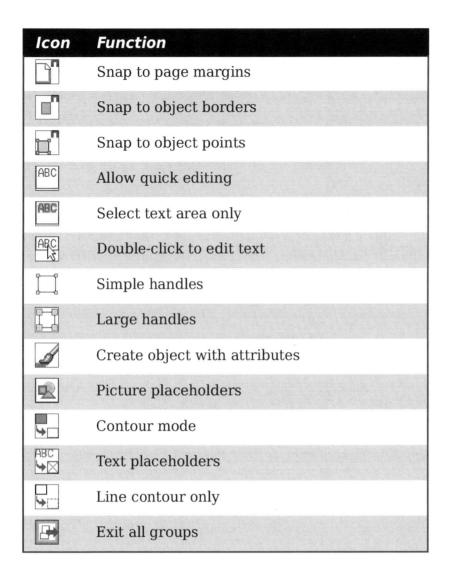

Icon	Function
	Snap to page margins
	Snap to object borders
	Snap to object points
	Allow quick editing
	Select text area only
	Double-click to edit text
	Simple handles
	Large handles
	Create object with attributes
	Picture placeholders
	Contour mode
	Text placeholders
	Line contour only
	Exit all groups

Positioning objects with snap functions

In Draw, objects can be positioned to grid points, to special snap points and lines, to object frames, to single object points, or to page edges. This function is known as *Snap*. In this manner objects can be very accurately positioned in a drawing.

If you want to use the snap function, it is much easier to work with the highest practical zoom value. It is possible to use two different snap functions at the same time, for example snap to a guide line and to the page edge. It is best, however, to activate only those functions that you really need.

This section describes the snap-to-grid function. For more information about this and the other snap functions, see Chapter 8 (Tips and Tricks) and Chapter 10 (Advanced Draw Techniques) in the *Draw Guide*.

Snap to grid

Use this function to move an object exactly to a grid point (see Figure 157). This function can be switched on and off with **View > Grid > Snap to Grid** and on the Options toolbar with the icon .

Figure 157: With snap to grid, objects align to the grid precisely.

Showing the grid

Make the grid visible under **View > Grid > Display Grid**. Alternatively turn the grid on and off with the icon on the Options toolbar.

Configuring the grid

The color, spacing, and resolution of the grid points can be individually chosen for each axis.The spacing between the lines is defined in the Grid options dialog under the Drawing area of the OOo options (**Tools > Options > OpenOffice.org Draw > Grid**). In the dialog shown in Figure 158, you can set the following parameters:

- Vertical and horizontal spacing of the dots in the grid. You can also change the unit of measurement used in the general Draw options (**Tools > Options > OpenOffice.org Draw > General**).

- The resolution is the size of the squares or rectangles in the grid. If the resolution is Horizontal 1 cm, Vertical 2 cm, the grid consists of rectangles 2 cm high and 1 cm wide.

- Subdivisions are additional points that appear along the sides of each rectangle or square in the grid. Objects snap to subdivisions as well as to the corners of the grid.

- The pixel (pix element) size of the snap area defines how close you need to bring an object to a snap point or line before it will snap to it.

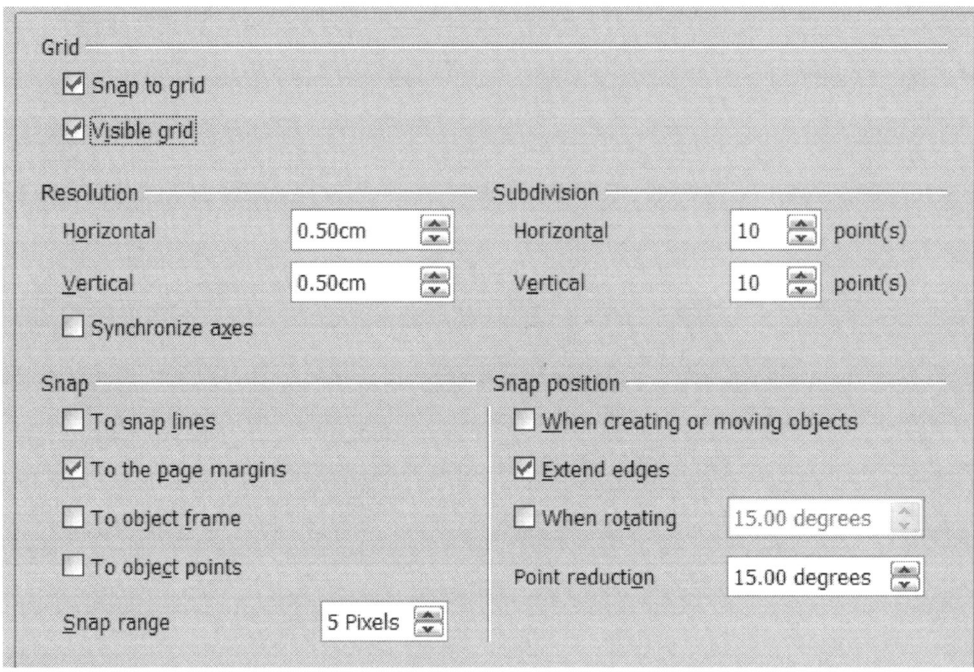

Figure 158. Setting grid options

Changing the color of the grid points

The default grid dots are light gray, which can be hard to see. To improve visibility, go to **Tools > Options**, then **OpenOffice.org > Appearance** (Figure 159).

In the *Drawing / Presentation* section, you can change the color of the grid points. On the *Color Settings* pulldown menu, select a more suitable/visible color, for example black.

Positioning objects with helper lines

To simplify the positioning of objects it is possible to make visible guiding lines—extensions of the edges of the object—while it is being moved. These guiding lines have no snap function.

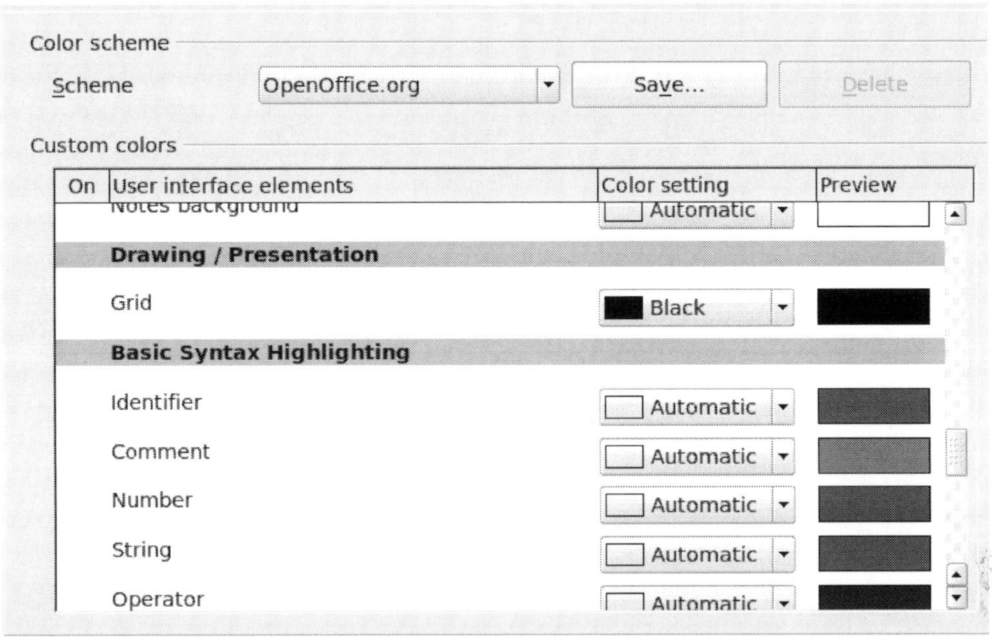

Color scheme

| Scheme | OpenOffice.org | ▾ | | Save... | | | Delete | |

Custom colors

On	User interface elements	Color setting		Preview	
	Notes background	☐ Automatic ▾			▲
	Drawing / Presentation				
	Grid	■ Black ▾		⬛	
	Basic Syntax Highlighting				
	Identifier	☐ Automatic ▾		⬛	
	Comment	☐ Automatic ▾		⬛	
	Number	☐ Automatic ▾		⬛	
	String	☐ Automatic ▾		⬛	▲
	Operator	☐ Automatic ▾		⬛	▼

Figure 159: Changing the grid color

The guiding lines can be (de-)activated under **Tools > Options > OpenOffice.org Draw > View > Guides when moving**, or by

clicking on the ⊞ icon on the *Options* toolbar.

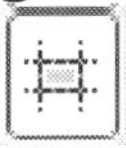

The basic drawing shapes

Draw provides a wide range of shapes, located in palettes accessed from the Drawing Toolbar. This chapter describes only a few of the basic shapes; see the *Draw Guide* for a complete description of the shapes available. These shapes include rectangles and squares; circles, ellipses, and arcs; 3D objects; curves; lines and arrows; text; and connectors.

When you draw a basic shape or select one for editing, the *Info* field in the status bar changes to reflect the action taken: *Line created*, *Text frame xxyy selected*, and so on.

Figure 160 shows part of the Drawing toolbar with the icons needed in the following sections. The *Text* icon is also included.

Figure 160: Part of the Drawing toolbar

Drawing a straight line

Let's start by drawing the simplest of shapes: a straight line. Click on the **Line** icon 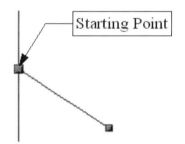 on the Drawing Toolbar and place the mouse pointer where you want to start the line. Drag the mouse while keeping the button pressed. Release the mouse button when you want to end the line.

A blue or green selection handle appears at each end of the line, showing that this is the currently selected object. The colors depend on the selection mode (green for simple selection and blue when in point edit mode). This effect is easily apparent if on the Options toolbar both **Simple Handles** and **Large Handles** are switched on.

Starting Point

Figure 161: Drawing a straight line

Hold down the *Shift* key while drawing the line to restrict the angle of the line to a multiple of 45 degrees (0, 45, 90, 135, and so on.

Hold down the *Control* key (*Ctrl* in PCs) to snap the end of the line to the nearest grid point.

Note	The effect of the *Ctrl* key depends on the settings of the **Snap to Grid** option on the **View->Grid** menu: **Snap to Grid on**: *Ctrl* deactivates the snap option for this activity. **Snap to Grid off**: *Ctrl* activates the snap option for this activity.

The spacing (resolution) of the grid points can be adjusted under **Tools > Options > OpenOffice.org-Draw > Grid**. See also Chapter 8 (Tips and Tricks) in the *Draw Guide*.

Hold down the *Alt* key to extend the line symmetrically outward from the start point (the line extends to each side of the start point equally). This lets you draw straight lines by starting from the middle of the line.

The line just drawn has all the default attributes, such as color and line type. To change the line attributes, click on the line to select it and then use the tools in the Line and Filling toolbar; or for more control, right-click on the line and choose **Line** to open the Line dialog.

Drawing an arrow

Arrows are drawn like lines. Draw classifies arrows as a subgroup of lines: Lines with arrowheads. They are shown in the information field on the status bar only as lines. Click on the **Line Ends with Arrow** icon → to draw an arrow.

Drawing lines and arrows

Click on the small black triangle on the **Lines and Arrows** →˅ icon to open a floating toolbar with ten tools for drawing lines and arrows (Figure 162). Alternatively, you can click directly on the symbol to repeat the last-used command chosen from this toolbar. In both cases, the last-used command will be stored on the toolbar to make it quicker to call it up again.

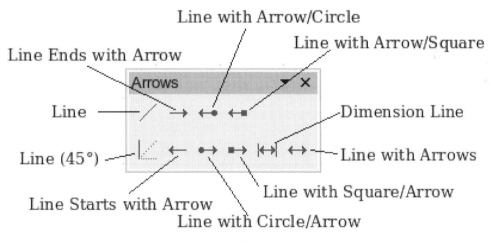

Figure 162: Lines and Arrows toolbar

Drawing a rectangle or square

Drawing rectangles is similar to drawing straight lines, except that you use the **Rectangle** icon 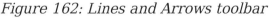 from the Drawing Toolbar. The (imaginary) line drawn with the mouse corresponds to the diagonal of the rectangle. In addition, the outline of the future rectangle changes shape as you drag the mouse around. The outline is shown as a dashed line until you release the mouse button, when the rectangle is drawn.

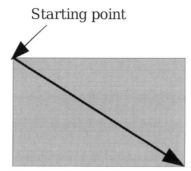

Figure 163: Drawing a rectangle

Hold down the *Shift* key to draw a square. Hold down the *Alt* key to draw a rectangle starting from its center. To combine the effects, hold down both the *Shift* and *Alt* keys simultaneously.

Drawing a circle or ellipse

To draw an ellipse (also called an oval) or a circle, use the Ellipse icon from the Drawing Toolbar. (A circle is simply an ellipse where the two axes are the same length.) The ellipse drawn is the largest ellipse that would fit inside the (imaginary) rectangle drawn with the mouse.

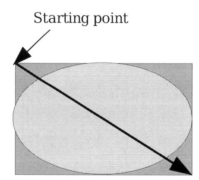

Figure 164: Drawing an ellipse

There are three other ways to draw an ellipse or circle:

* Hold down the *Shift* key while drawing to force the ellipse to be a circle.

* Hold down the *Alt* key to draw a symmetrical ellipse or circle from the center instead of dragging corner to corner.

- Hold down the *Control* key while drawing to snap the ellipse or circle to grid lines.

Note	If you first press and hold the *Control* key and then click on one of the icons (Line, Rectangle, Ellipse, or Text), an object is drawn automatically in the work area—the size, shape, and color are all standard values. These attributes can be changed later, if desired.

Drawing curves

The tools for drawing curves or polygons are on the toolbar that appears when you click the **Curve** icon ✎▾ on the Drawing toolbar. This toolbar contains eight tools (Figure 165).

Note	Hovering the mouse over this icon gives a tooltip of *Curve*. If you convert the icon to a floating toolbar, however, the title is *Lines*, as shown in Figure 165.

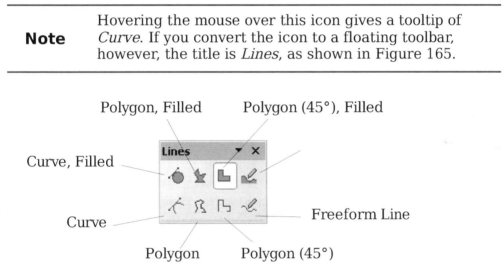

Figure 165: Floating Curves toolbar (incorrectly titled "Lines")

If you move the mouse cursor over one of the icons, a tooltip pops up with a description of the function. For a more detailed description of the handling of Bézier curves (curves and filled curves), see Chapter 10 (Advanced Draw Techniques) in the *Draw Guide*.

Polygons

Draw the first line from the start point with the left mouse button held down. As soon as you release the mouse button, a first corner point is drawn, and you can move the mouse to see how the second line will look. Every mouse click sets another corner point.

A double-click ends the drawing. A filled polygon automatically joins the last point to the first point to close off the figure and fills it with the current standard fill color. A polygon without filling will not be closed at the end of the drawing.

Polygon 45°

Just as with ordinary polygons, these will be formed from lines but with angles of 45 or 90 degrees between them.

Freeform Line

With this tool you can draw just like with a pencil. Press and hold the left mouse button and move the mouse. It is not necessary to end the drawing with a double-click. Just release the mouse button and the drawing is completed. If you have selected *Freeform Line, Filled*, the end point is joined automatically to the start point and the object is filled with the appropriate color.

Writing text

Use the Text tool T to write text and select the font, color, size, and other attributes. Click on an empty space in the workspace to write the text at that spot or drag an area to write inside the dragged frame. Press *Enter* to drop to the next line.

When you have finished typing text, click outside the text frame. Double-click on the text at any time to edit it.

When you type text, the upper toolbar includes the usual paragraph attributes: indents, first line, and tab stops.

You can change the style of all or part of the text. The Styles and Formatting window also works here (select **Format > Styles and Formatting** or press *F11* to launch), so you can create Graphics styles that you can reuse for other text frames. Graphics styles affect all of the text within a text frame. To style parts of the text, use direct formating with the toolbar.

Text frames can also have fill colors, shadows, and other attributes, just like any other Draw object. You can rotate the frame and write the text at any angle. These options are available by right-clicking on the object.

Use the Callout tool, located on the Drawing toolbar, to create callouts (also known as captions or figure labels).

If you double-click on an object or press *F2* (or the **Text** icon in the Drawing toolbar) when an object is selected, text is written in the center of the object and remains within the object. Nearly any kind of object contains such an additional text element. These texts have slight differences to those in text frames concerning position and hyphenation.

For more about text, see Chapter 2 (Drawing Basic Shapes) and Chapter 10 (Advanced Draw Techniques) in the *Draw Guide*.

Gluepoints and connectors

All Draw objects have associated invisible *gluepoints*. Most objects have four gluepoints, as shown in Figure 166.

Figure 166: Four gluepoints

Gluepoints are different from handles (the small blue or green squares around an object). Use the handles to move or resize an object; use the gluepoints to attach connectors to an object.

You can add more gluepoints, and customize gluepoints, using the toolbar of the same name. Gluepoints become visible when you click the **Gluepoints** icon on the Drawing toolbar and then move the end of a connector over the object.

Connectors are a type of line or arrow whose ends dock to glue points on other objects. When you move the other object, the connector moves with it. Connectors are particularly useful for making organizational charts. You can reorganize the blocks of your chart and all the connected objects stay connected.

Figure 167 shows two Draw objects and a connector.

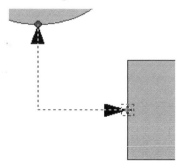

Figure 167: A connector between two objects

Draw has a range of advanced connector functions. You can change connector types using the context menu or by opening the floating Connectors toolbar (click on the **Connector** icon ⌐▪). For more about connectors and gluepoints, see Chapter 9 (Organization Charts, Flow Diagrams, and More) in the *Draw Guide*.

Drawing geometric shapes

Geometric shapes include basic shapes, symbol shapes, block arrows, flowcharts, callouts, and stars.

Figure 168 shows part of the Drawing toolbar with the icons necessary for the following sections. They open floating toolbars with the relevant work tools. The use of all these tools is similar to that of the Rectangle tool, even though they produce different geometric shapes.

Figure 168: Part of the main Drawing toolbar

Basic shapes

The **Basic Shapes** icon ◇ ▪ makes available the range of tools for drawing basic shapes.

If you choose the rectangle tool from this toolbar, it looks the same as a rectangle drawn using the Rectangle tool on the Drawing toolbar. The only differences you will see are in the information field in the status bar.

Symbol shapes

The **Symbol Shapes** icon ☺ ▪ brings you to an array of tools for drawing the various symbol shapes.

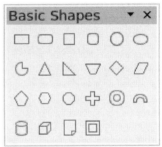

Block arrows

The **Block Arrows** icon opens the Block Arrows toolbar.

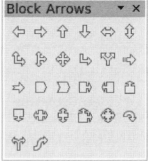

Flowcharts

The tools for drawing flowcharts are accessed by clicking on the **Flowcharts** icon.

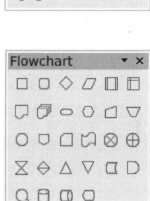

The creation of flowcharts, organization charts, and similar planning tools are described in Chapter 9 (Organization Charts, Flow Diagrams, and More) in the *Draw Guide*.

Callouts

Use the **Callouts** icon to open the Callouts toolbar.

Stars and banners

These tools are associated with the **Stars** icon.

You can add text to all these shapes. See Chapter 2 (Drawing Basic Shapes) and Chapter 10 (Advanced Draw Techniques) in the *Draw Guide* for details.

Selection modes

There are three selection modes: moving and changing size, rotating, and editing points.

The default mode for selecting objects depends on whether the **Points** button on the Drawing toolbar is active (appears lit) 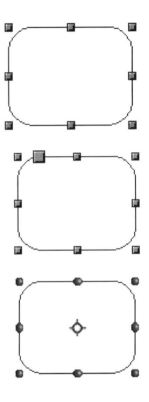 or not inactive (appears dark or dimmed) . .

In standard mode (when you begin a new drawing), the **Points** button is not active, and the default mode is for selections to be moved or changed in size; these selections are indicated by small green squares.

When the **Points** button is active, the default mode is for selections to be edited; these selections are indicated by blue squares. Some objects will have one or more extra handles, which are larger or colored differently. This is explained in more detail in the *Draw Guide*.

Selections for rotating objects are indicated by small red circles and a symbol representing the center of rotation. To choose these selections, click on the **Effects** drop-down button from the Drawing toolbar.

Changing the selection mode

To go from one mode to another, you can do one of the following:

- Toggle the **Points** button on the Drawing toolbar to switch from the simple selection mode to the Points mode . . You can also use the keyboard shortcut *F8* (Points).

- Choose the **Effects** drop-down button from the Drawing toolbar to activate the Rotation mode for a selected object.

- If you often work in Rotation mode, you can choose the **Rotation Mode after Clicking Object** button from the Options bar, you can cycle through normal and rotation modes just by clicking on the object. This can be more convenient than clicking the object, then clicking the **Rotate** button from the Drawing Toolbar.

Selecting objects

Direct selection

To select an object, the easiest way is to click directly on it. For objects that are not filled, click directly on the object's outline to select it.

Selection by framing

You can select several objects by using the mouse to drag a large rectangle around the objects, as shown. For this to work, the **Select** ⬚ icon on the Drawing toolbar must be active. Only objects that lie entirely within the rectangle are selected.

Selecting hidden objects

Even if objects are located behind others and not visible, they can still be selected. To select an object that is covered by another object, hold down the *Alt* key and click the object. To select an object that is covered by several objects, hold down the *Alt* key and click through the objects until you reach the required underlying object. To cycle through the objects in reverse order, hold down the *Alt+Shift* keys when you click. To help in making accurate selections, you can check the number and type of the selected objects, shown at the left of the status bar.

Note	There may be some variation in the use of the *Alt* key on different operating systems. In general the *Alt* key on a Windows computer functions as described above, but on a Linux system it usually does not. If the *Alt* key on your system does not operate as described above, use the *Tab* key method described below.

To select an object that is covered by another object using the keyboard, press *Tab* to cycle through the objects, stopping at the object you wish to select. To cycle through the objects in reverse order, press *Shift+Tab*. This may not be practical if you have a large number of objects in your drawing.

When you click on the selected object, its outline appears briefly through the objects on top of the selected object.

In the illustration to the right, the square located beneath the circle was selected in this way (the circle was made transparent in order to see the square).

Arranging objects

In a complex drawing, you may have objects stacked up, one on top of the other, with the result that a particular object is hidden by one or more other objects above it. You can rearrange the stacking order of objects (move an object to the front or to the back of the stack) by selecting the object, clicking **Modify > Arrange** and selecting the appropriate **Bring Forward** or **Send Backward** option, or by right-clicking the object and selecting **Arrange** from the context menu, then selecting from the list of **Bring Forward** or **Send Backward** options.

On the Drawing toolbar, the Arrange tear-off menu on the  button contains the above options. A keyboard shortcut is *Shift+Ctrl++* to bring an object to the top, and *Shift+Ctrl+−* to send an object to the bottom.

Draw also provides tools for aligning multiple objects; details are given in the *Draw Guide*.

Selecting several objects

To select or deselect several objects one by one, press the *Shift* key and click on the various objects to be selected or deselected. One click on an object selects it; a second click deselects it.

Moving and dynamically adjusting an object's size

There are several ways of moving or changing the size of an object. The method described here will be called *dynamic* in the sense that it is carried out using the mouse.

When you dynamically change an object, remember to check the central area of the status bar at the bottom of your screen. This area shows detailed information about the ongoing manipulation. For example, during resizing, you will see the following information displayed. This information changes when the mouse is moved.

Object position   Object dimensions   Current proportional page size

Dynamic movement of objects

To move an object, select it and then click within the object's border and hold down the left mouse button while moving the mouse. To drop the object at its new location, release the mouse button.

During movement, the shape of the object appears as dotted lines to help with repositioning.

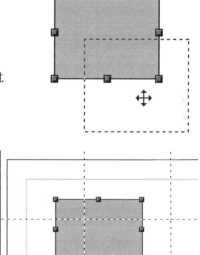

If you have selected **Guides when moving** in **Tools > Options > OpenOffice.org Draw > View**, then during movement, dotted lines appear, to help with repositioning.

Dynamic size modification of objects

To change the size of an object (or group of selected objects) with the mouse, you need to move one of the handles located around the selection. As shown in the following illustration, the outline of the resulting new object appears as a dotted line.

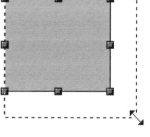

The results differ depending on which handle you use. If you choose a corner handle, you will resize the object along two axes at the same time. If you use a side handle, the objects will only be resized along one axis.

Note	If you press the *Shift* key at the same time as you carry out the resizing operation, the size change will be carried out symmetrically with respect to the two axes; this enables you to keep the aspect (height/length) ratio of the object.

Rotation

Rotating an object lets you move the object around an axis. To do this dynamically, use the red handles, as you do when changing the size of the object.

Note	Rotation works in a slightly different way for 3D objects because the rotation occurs in 3D space and not in one plane. See Chapter 7 (Working with 3D Objects) in the *Draw Guide* regarding rotation when Edit Points mode is active.

To rotate an object (or a group of objects), drag the red corner handle points of the selection with the mouse. The mouse cursor takes the shape of an arc of a circle with an arrow at each end. A dotted outline of the object being rotated appears and the current angle of rotation is dynamically shown in the status bar.

Rotations are made about an axis which is displayed as a small symbol. You can move the axis of rotation with the mouse, as shown in Figure 169.

If you hold down the *Shift* key during the rotation, the operation will be carried out in increments of 15°.

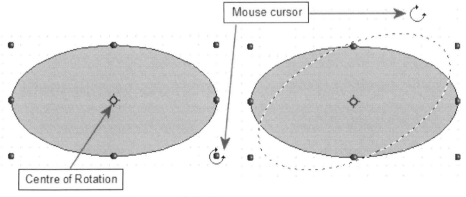

Figure 169: Rotating an object

Inclination and perspective

To slant or shear objects, use the red handles located at the midpoint of an edge of the selected objects. The mouse pointer changes to a ⇌ when the pointer hovers over one of these midpoint handles. Not every object can be slanted—basic shapes can be rotated but not slanted.

The slant axis is the point directly opposite the midpoint handle to be used for shearing the object. This point stays fixed in location; the other sides and edges move in relation to it as the mouse is dragged (make sure that the ⇌ handle icon is showing before dragging).

As with rotation, you can set the inclination to occur as steps of 15° by pressing the *Shift* key while moving the handle.

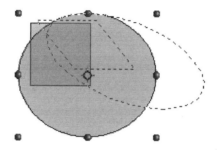

Editing objects

To change an object's attributes (such as color, border width, among others) you can use the Line and Filling toolbar or the context menu.

If the Line and Filling toolbar (Figure 170) is not visible, you can display it using **View > Toolbars > Line and Filling**. From here you can edit the most common object attributes. You can also open the Line dialog by clicking on the Line ⬧ icon and the Area dialog by clicking on the Area ⬧ icon to see more options.

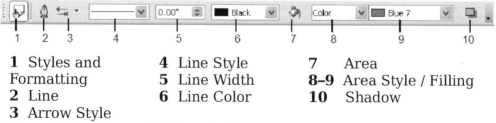

1 Styles and Formatting	**4** Line Style	**7** Area
2 Line	**5** Line Width	**8–9** Area Style / Filling
3 Arrow Style	**6** Line Color	**10** Shadow

Figure 170: Line and Filling toolbar

When you select text, this toolbar changes to show text formatting options (Figure 171).

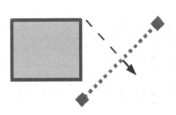

Figure 171: Line and Filling toolbar (when text is selected)

The context menu

When an object is selected, you can right-click on the object to bring up a context menu, which provides additional access to the options shown above and another way to change an object's attributes. The entries with a small arrow on the right-hand side contain a submenu.

Editing lines and borders

Lines (like arrows) and the borders of an object are managed through the same dialog. An object's border is just another type of line.

You can change some properties from the **Line and Filling** toolbar. To see more options, select the object and click on the Line 🖋 icon or right-click on the object and choose **Line** from the context menu. This opens the Line dialog.

Common line properties

In most cases the property you want to change is the line's style (solid, dashed, invisible, and so on), its color, or its width. These options are all available from the Line and Filling toolbar (Figure 170).

You can also edit these properties from the Line dialog, where you can also change the line's transparency. Figure 175 illustrates different degrees of transparency.

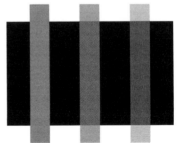

Figure 172: The vertical lines have different levels of transparency (0%, 25%, and 50%).

Drawing arrows

Arrowheads (and other line endings, usually referred to collectively as arrows) are a line property. Select a line and click on the **Arrow Style** ⬅ · icon. This opens the Arrowheads menu.

Several types of arrowheads are available. Each end of the line can have a different arrowhead (or no arrowhead).

Arrowheads are only applicable to lines. They have no effect on an object's border.

Customizing line and arrow styles

You can modify the line and arrow styles and create your own. See Chapter 4 (Changing Object Attributes) in the *Draw Guide* for details.

Editing the inside (fill) of an object

The OpenOffice.org term for the inside of an object is **Area fill**. The area fill of an object can be a uniform color, a gradient, a hatching, or a pattern from an image. It can be made partly or wholly transparent and can throw a shadow.

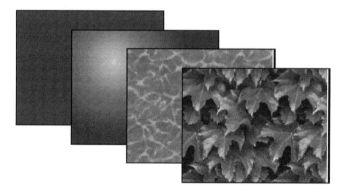

In most cases, you will choose one of the standard fill options, which are all available from the Line and Filling toolbar. You can also define your own area fills; see Chapter 4 of the *Draw Guide* for details.

Adding a shadow

In Draw, shadows are considered an area property. Click on the Shadow  icon on the **Line and Filling** toolbar.

You can customize the position, distance, color, and transparency of shadows.

Adding transparency

You can make objects partly or fully transparent, or even with a varying degree of transparency (as a gradient).

Using styles

Suppose that you want to apply the same area fill, line thickness, and border to a set of objects. This repetitive process can be greatly simplified by the use of styles. Styles allow you to define a formatting template (a style) and then to apply that style to multiple objects. For more about styles, see Chapter 3 (Using Styles and Templates) for more information.

Special effects

With Draw, you can apply many special effects to objects and groups of objects. This section describes a few of these effects. Others include distorting, shadows, and transparency. See the *Draw Guide* for examples of the many effects available.

Flip an object

Select an object and click on the **Flip** icon 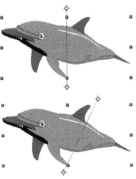. You will see a dashed line through the middle of the object.

This dashed line is the **axis of symmetry**. The object will be reflected about this line. Move one or both ends of the line with your mouse to set the axis.

Then, grab any one of the eight green handles and move it across to the other side of the dashed line. The new position of the figure is shown dashed until the mouse is released.

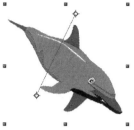

Note	If you hold down the *Shift* key while moving the line, the line will rotate in 45-degree increments.

Mirror copies

Officially, this useful command does not (yet) exist in Draw. It can, however, be easily emulated.

Move the axis of symmetry to the desired location of the mirror axis. Copy the object to the clipboard. Flip the object, then click on an empty area of the Draw screen in order to deselect the object. Paste from the clipboard to put a copy of the object in its original location and now you have a mirror copy.

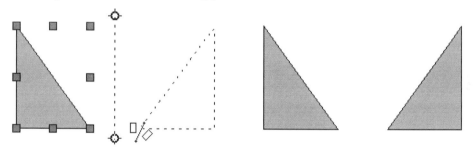

Distorting an image

There are three tools on the **Effects** menu that let you drag the corners and edges of an object to distort the image.

The **Distort** tool distorts an object in perspective, the **Set to Circle (slant)** and **Set in Circle (perspective)** tools both create a pseudo three-dimensional effect. See Chapter 4 of the *Draw Guide* for details.

Dynamic gradients

You can control transparency gradients in the same manner as color gradients. Both types of gradient can be used together. With a transparency gradient, the direction and degree of an object's fill color changes from opaque to transparent (in a regular gradient, the fill changes from one color to another, but the degree of transparency remains the same). See Chapter 4 of the *Draw Guide* for details.

Duplication

Duplication makes copies of an object while applying a set of changes (such as color or rotation) to the duplicates. The result of a duplication is a new group.

To start duplication, click on an object or group and choose **Edit > Duplicate**. The dialog shown in Figure 173 appears.

The options chosen in Figure 173 applied to a blue rectangle produce the result on the right.

Figure 173: Duplicating an object

Cross-fading

Cross-fading transforms a shape from one form to another, with OpenOffice.org handling all of the intermediate transitions. The result is a new group of objects including the two end points and the intermediate steps.

To carry out a cross-fade, select both objects (hold the *Shift* key while selecting each object in turn) and then choose **Edit > Cross-fading** The following dialog appears.

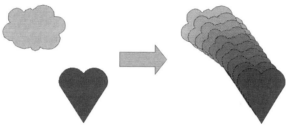

On the dialog choose the number of increments (transition steps). You probably want to have *Cross-fade attributes* and *Same orientation* both checked. The end result is shown in Figure 174.

Figure 174: Cross-fading example

Combining multiple objects

Using Draw, you can combine drawing objects together in two distinct ways: *grouping* and *combining*. These two methods allow you to treat multiple objects as one unit, or to merge objects to form a new shape.

Grouping is like putting objects in a container. You can move them as a group and apply global changes to them. A group can always be undone and the objects that make up the group can always be manipulated separately.

A *combination* is a permanent fusion of objects leading to a new object. The original objects are no longer available as individual entities and the operation is not reversible.

Grouping by common selection

When several objects are selected, any operations you carry out are applied to all of the objects. For example, you can rotate a group of objects in its entirety. Groups obtained through common selection of several objects are undone as soon as you click outside the group. However, you can group objects and keep those selected objects grouped together.

Maintaining groups and undoing groups

To group selected objects, right-click and choose **Group** from the pop-up menu. You can also use the keyboard shortcut *Control+Shift+G* or choose **Modify > Group** from the menu bar.

When objects are grouped, any editing operations carried out on that group are applied to all members of the group. If you click on one member of the group, the whole group is selected.

The objects of a group retain their own individual properties. To undo a group, right-click and choose **Ungroup** from the pop-up menu, use the keyboard shortcut *Control+Alt+Shift+G* or choose **Modify > Ungroup** from the menu bar.

You can edit a member of a group individually without breaking the group. To do this, right-click and choose **Enter group** or double-click on the group.

Combining objects

In contrast to grouping functions, *combinations* create a new object; subsequent "un-combining" in the same manner as ungrouping is not possible. Select a collection of objects, then right-click and choose **Combine** from the pop-up menu.

After you have selected more than one object, the Merge, Subtract, and Intersect functions can be reached in the **Modify > Shapes** menu or though the group's right-click menu under the heading **Shapes**.

Aids for positioning objects

Draw has various tools to help you arrange the objects with respect to each other:

- Moving an object to the front or to the back
- Aligning objects with respect to each other
- Distributing the distance and space between objects

See Chapter 5 (Combining Multiple Objects) in the *Draw Guide* for more information.

Editing pictures

Draw contains a number of functions for editing raster graphics (bitmaps)—for example, photos, scanned pictures, and so on—including import and and export as well as conversion from one format to another. Draw can read in all the usual range of graphic file formats. However, it does not have the same capabilities as the specialized raster graphics programs like Adobe Photoshop or The Gimp.

See Chapter 6 (Editing Pictures) in the *Draw Guide* for details.

Working with 3D objects

Although Draw does not match the functionality of the leading drawing or picture editing programs, it does offer a wide array of tools and methods to produce and edit very good 3D drawings and pictures.

Draw offers two types of 3D objects: the ones carried forward from OOo version 1, *3D bodies*, and the ones newly introduced in version 2, *3D shapes*. Depending on which type you choose, there are different possibilities for further editing of the object (rotation, illumination, perspective). Setting up and editing 3D objects is simpler with 3D shapes than with 3D bodies, but 3D bodies currently allow for more customizing than 3D shapes.

See Chapter 7 (Working with 3D Objects) in the *Draw Guide* for details.

Inserting pictures from other sources

You can add pictures from several sources:

* The Gallery—see Chapter 11 (Graphics, the Gallery, and Fontwork)

* Directly from a scanner (**Insert > Picture > Scan**)

* Images created by another program, including photographs from a digitial camera (**Insert > Picture > From File**)

Draw provides tools for working with bitmap images such as photographs: the Picture toolbar and the bitmap image management palette. See the *Draw Guide* for details and examples.

Exchanging objects with other programs

To save a Draw image in a foreign format, use **File > Export**. Draw can save to many graphic file formats, as listed in Chapter 3 (File Management).

You can also export Draw files to HTML, PDF, or Flash. PDF export is the same as for any part of OpenOffice.org, as described in Chapter 10 (Printing, E-mailing, and Exporting). Flash export creates a .swf file.

HTML export uses a conversion wizard that creates as many web pages as there are pages in your Draw document. You can optionally choose to display the pages in frames with a navigator and can set an index page. For more information, see Chapter 12 (Creating Web Pages: Saving Documents as HTML Files).

Chapter *8*
Getting Started with Base

OpenOffice.org's database component

A data source, or database, is a collection of pieces of information that can be accessed or managed by OpenOffice.org (OOo). For example, a list of names and addresses is a data source that could be used for producing a mail merge letter. A shop stock list could be a data source managed through OOo.

Note	OpenOffice.org uses the terms "Data Source" and "Database" to refer to the same thing, which could be a database such as MySQL or dBase or a spreadsheet or text document holding data.

This chapter covers creating a database, showing what is contained in a database and how the different parts are used by OOo. It also covers using the Base component of OOo to register other data sources. A data source can be a database, spreadsheet, or text document.

Data sources are only introduced in this chapter. For more detailed information about the use of databases, see the *Database Guide*.

Note	OOo Base uses the HSQL database engine. All of the files created by this engine are kept in one zipped file. The database forms are included in this zipped file.

A *database* consists of a number of *fields* that contain the individual pieces of data. Each *table* of the database is a group of fields. When creating a table, you also determine the characteristics of each field in the table. *Forms* are for data entry into the fields of one or more tables associated with the form. They can also be used for viewing fields from one or more tables associated with the form. A *query* creates a new table from the existing tables based upon how you create the query. A *report* organizes the information of the fields of a query in a document according to your requirements.

Caution	The database in OOo requires Java Runtime Environment (JRE). If you do not have it on your computer, you can download it from www.java.com and install it following the instructions on the site. It should be Java 5.0 or higher. In OOo, use **Tools > Options > OpenOffice.org > Java** to register Java. Windows' version of JRE can **not** be used, while there are other versions that can.

Base creates *relational databases*. This makes it fairly easy to create a database in which the fields of the database have relationships with each other.

For example: Consider a database for a library. It will contain a field for the names of the authors and another field for the names of the books. There is an obvious relationship between the authors and the books they have written. The library may contain more than one book by the same author. This is what is known as a one-to-many relationship: one author and more than one book. Most if not all the relationships in such a database are one-to-many relationships.

Consider an employment database for the same library. One of the fields contains the names of the employees while others contain the social security numbers, and other personal data. The relationship between the names and social security numbers is one-to-one: only one social security number for each name.

If you are acquainted with mathematical sets, a relational database can easily be explained in terms of sets: elements, subsets, unions, and intersections. The fields of a database are the elements. The tables are subsets. Relationships are defined in terms of unions and intersections of the subsets (tables).

To explain how to use a database, we will create one for automobile expenses. In the process, we will be explaining how a database work.

Planning a database

The first step in creating a database is to ask yourself many questions. Write them down, and leave some space between the questions to later write the answers. At least some of the answers should seem obvious after you take some time to think.

You may have to go through this process a few times before everything becomes clear in your mind and on paper. Using a text document for these questions and answers makes it easier to move the questions around, add additional questions, or change the answers.

Here are some of the questions and answers I developed before I created a database for automobile expenses. I had an idea of what I wanted before I started, but as I began asking questions and listing the answers, I discovered that I needed additional tables and fields.

What are the fields going to be? My expenses divided into three broad areas: fuel purchases, maintenance, and vacations. The annual cost for the car's license plate and driver's license every four years did not fit into any of these. It will be a table of its own: license fees.

What fields fit the fuel purchases area? Date purchased, odometer reading, fuel cost, fuel quantity, and payment method fit. (Fuel economy can be calculated with a query.)

What fields fit the maintenance area? Date of service, odometer reading, type of service, cost of service, and next scheduled service of this type (for example, for oil changes list when the next oil change should be). But it would be nice if there was a way to write notes. So, a field for notes was added to the list.

What fields fit the vacations area? Date, odometer reading, fuel (including all the fields of the fuel table), food (including meals and snacks), motel, total tolls, and miscellaneous. Since these purchases are made by one of two bank cards or with cash, I want a field to state which payment type was used for each item.

What fields fit into the food category? Breakfast, lunch, supper, and snacks seem to fit. Do I list all the snacks individually or list the total cost for snacks for the day? I chose to divide snacks into two fields: number of snacks and total cost of snacks. I also need a payment type for each of these: breakfast, lunch, supper, and total cost of snacks.

What are the fields that are common to more than one area? Date appears in all of the areas as does odometer reading and payment type.

How will I use this information about these three fields? While on vacation, I want the expenses for each day to be listed together. The date fields suggest a relationship between the vacation table and the dates in each of these tables: fuel and food, This means that the date fields in these tables will be linked as we create the database.

The type of payment includes two bank cards and cash. So, we will create a table with a field for the type of payment and use it in list boxes in the forms.

Tip	While we have listed fields we will create in the tables of the database, there is one more field that may be needed in a table: the field for the primary key. In some tables, the field for the primary key has already been listed. In other tables such as the payment type, an additional field for the primary key must be created.

Creating a new database

To create a new database, click the arrow next to the **New** icon. In the drop-down menu, select **Database** (Figure 175). This opens the Database Wizard. You can also open the Database Wizard using **File > New > Database**.

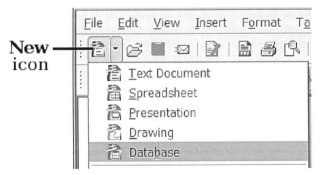

Figure 175: Creating a new database

The first step of the Database Wizard has one question with two choices: **Create a new database** or **Connect to an existing database**. For this example, select **Create a new database** and then click **Next**.

The second step has two questions with two choices each. The default choice for the first question is **Yes, register the database for me** and the default choice for the second question is **Open the database for editing**. Make sure these choices are selected and click **Finish**.

Note	If the database is not registered, it will not be accessible to the other OOo components such as Writer and Calc. If the database is registered, other components can access it.

Save the new database with the name *Automobile.* This opens the Automobile – OpenOffice.org Base window. Figure 176 shows part of this window.

Tip	Every time the *Automobile* database is opened, the Automobile – OpenOffice.org Base window opens. Changes can then be made to the database. The title for this window is always (database name) – OpenOffice.org.

| **Caution** | As you create a database, you should save your work regularly. This means more than just saving what you have just created. You must save the whole database as well. |
| | For example, when you create your first table, you must save it before you can close it. If you look at the **Save** icon in the Standard toolbar at the top after closing the table, it will be active. Click the **Save** icon, and this icon will be grayed out again. Not only the table has been saved, but it also been made a part of the database. |

Creating database tables

Note	In a database, a table stores information for a group of things we call fields. For example, a table might hold an address book, a stock list, a phone book or a price list. A database can have from one to several tables.

To work with tables, click the *Tables* icon in the *Database* list, or use *Alt+a.* The three tasks that you can perform on a table are in the *Task* list (see Figure 176).

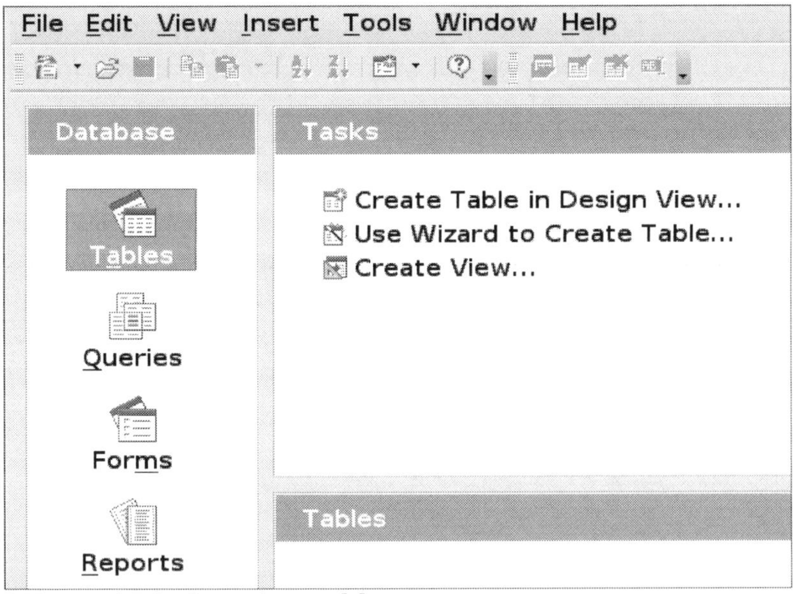

Figure 176: Creating tables

Using the Wizard to create a table

Caution

Every table requires a *Primary key field*. (What this field does will be explained later.) We will use this field to number our entries and want that number to automatically increase as we add each entry.

Since none of the fields we need for our Automobile database are contained in any of the wizard tables, we will create a simple table using the wizard that has nothing to do with our database. This section is an exercise in explaining how the Wizard works.

The Wizard permits the fields of the table to come from more than one suggested table. We will create a table with fields from three different suggested tables in the Wizard.

Click *Use Wizard to Create Table*. This opens the Table Wizard.

Note

A field in a table is one bit of information. For example, in a price list table, there might be one field for item name, one for the description and a third for the price. More fields may be added as needed.

Step 1: Select fields.

You have a choice of two categories of suggested tables: Business and Personal. Each category contains its own suggested tables from which to choose. Each table has a list of available fields. We will use the *CD-Collection* Sample table in the Personal category to select the fields we need.

1) *Category*: Select *Personal*. The *Sample Tables* drop down list changes to a list of personal sample tables.

2) *Sample Tables*: Select *CD-Collection*. The *Available* fields window changes to a list of available fields for this table.

3) *Selected Fields*: Using the **>** button, move these fields from the *Available fields* window to the *Selected fields* window in this order: *CollectionID, AlbumTitle, Artist, DatePurchased, Format, Notes,* and *NumberofTracks*.

4) *Selected Fields from another sample* table. Click Business as the Category. Select *Employees* from the dropdown list of sample tables. Use the **>** button to move the *Photo* field from the *Available fields* window to the *Selected fields* window. It will be at the bottom of the list directly below the *NumberofTracks* field.

5) If a mistake is made in the order as listed above, click on the field name that is in the wrong order to highlight it. Use the **Up** or **Down** arrow on the right side of the *Selected Fields* list (see Figure 177) to move the field name to the correct position. Click **Next**.

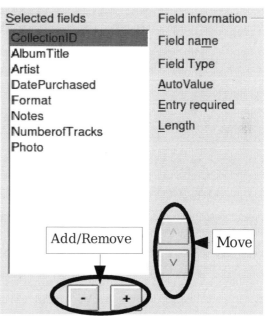

Figure 177: Order of fields

Caution

⚠

Below the *Selected Fields* list are two buttons: one with a **+**, and one with a **–**. These buttons are used to add or to remove fields from the *Selected Fields* list. Be careful when using these buttons until well acquainted with how to create tables (Figure 177).

Step 2: Set field types and formats.

In this step you give the fields their properties. When you click a field, the information on the right changes. You can then make changes to meet your needs. (See Figure 178.) Click each field, one at a time, and make the changes listed below.

Selected fields	Field information	
CollectionID	Field name	CollectionID
AlbumTitle		
Artist	Field Type	Integer [INTEGE ▼
DatePurchased	AutoValue	No ▼
Format	Entry required	No ▼
Notes	Length	10
NumberofTracks		
Photo		

Figure 178: Changing field types

Note	If any of these fields requires an entry, set *Entry required* to **Yes**. If *Entry required* is set to Yes, this field must have something in it. For example if FirstName has E*ntry required* set to Yes, having an entry with the first name missing will not be allowed. In general, only set *Entry required* to **Yes** if something must always be put in that field. By default, *Entry required* is set to **No**.

- *CollectionID:* Change *AutoValue* from **No** to **Yes**.
- *AlbumTitle*:
  - *Entry required*: If all of your music is in albums, change *Entry required* to *Yes*. Otherwise, leave *Entry required* as *No*.
  - *Length*: Unless you have an album title that exceeds 100 characters in length counting the spaces, do not change the length.

Note	In Base the maximum length of each field must be specified on creation. It is not easy to change this later, so if in doubt specify a greater length. Base uses VCHAR as the field format for text fields. This format only uses the actual number of characters in a field up to the limit set. So, a field containing 20 characters will only use space for 20 characters even if the limit is set at 100. Two album titles containing 25 and 32 characters respectively will use space for 25 and 32 characters and not 100 characters.

- *Artist*: Use the Default setting. And since music has authors, set *Entry Required* to *Yes.*

- *Date Purchased*: *Length*: default setting. *Entry required* should be *No.* (You may not know the date.)

- *Format*: Only change the *Entry Required* setting: from *No* to *Yes.*

- *Notes*: No changes are required.

- *NumberofTracks*: Change the *Field Type* to *Tiny Integer [TINYINT]*. Your allowable number of tracks will be 999. Small Integer [SMALLINT] would allow 99999 tracks if you needed more than 999 tracks.

- *Photo:* Use the default settings.

When you have finished, click **Next**.

Note	Each field also has a *Field Type*. In Base the field type must be specified. These types include text, integer, date and decimal. If the field is going to have general information in it (for example a name or a description), then you want to use text. If the field will always contain a number (for example a price), the type should be decimal or another appropriate numerical field. The wizard picks the right field type, so to get an idea of how this works, see what the wizard has chosen for different fields.

Step 3: Set primary key.

1) *Create a primary key* should be checked.
2) Select option *Use an existing field as a primary key.*
3) In the *Fieldname* drop down list, select *CollectionID.*
4) Check *Auto* value if it is not already checked.
5) Click **Next**.

Note	A primary key uniquely identifies an item (or record) in the table. For example, you might know two people called "Randy Herring" or three people living at the same address and the database needs to distinguish between them.
	The simplest method is to assign a unique number to each one: number the first person 1, the second 2, and so on. Each entry has one number and every number is different, so it is easy to say "record ID 172". This is the option chosen here: CollectionID is just a number

assigned automatically by Base to each record of this table.

There are more complex ways of doing this, all answering the question "How do I make sure that every single record in my database can be uniquely identified?"

Step 4: Create the table.

1) If desired, rename the table at this point. If you rename it, make the name meaningful to you. For this example, make no changes.

2) Leave the option *Insert data immediately* checked.

3) Click **Finish** to complete the table wizard. Close the window created by the table wizard. You are now back to the main window of the database with the listing of the tables, queries, forms, and reports.

Creating a table by copying an existing table

If you have a large collection of music, you might want to create a table for each type of music you have. Rather than creating each table from the wizard, you can make a copy of the original table. Each table can be named according to the type of music contained in it. Possible names could include Classical, Pop, Country and Western, and Rock, among others.

1) Click on the **Tables** icon in the Database pane to see the existing tables.

2) Right-click on the *CD-Collection* table icon. Select **Copy** from the context menu.

3) Move the mouse pointer below this table, right-click, and select **Paste** from the context menu. The *Copy table* window opens.

4) Change the table name to *Pop* and click **Next**.

5) Click the **>>** button to move all the Fields from the left window to the right window and click **Next**.

6) Since all the Fields already have the proper File Type formating, no changes should be needed. However, this is the time and place to make these changes if they are needed. (See **Caution** below for the reason why.) Click **Create**. The new table is created.

Caution

Once tables have been created using the wizard and data has been entered, editing them should be very limited if any editing is done at all. Fields can be added or deleted. But adding a field requires taking the time to enter the data for that one field for every record having an entry for that field. Deleting a field deletes **all the data** once contained in that field. Changing the field type of a field can lead to data being lost either partially or completely. When creating a new table, it pays to create the fields with the correct names, length and format before data is added.

Caution

Tables can be deleted in a very simple way. But doing so removes all of the data contained in every field of the table. Unless you are sure, do not delete a table.

To delete a table, right-click it in the list of tables. Select **Delete** from the context menu. A popup window asks if you are sure you want to delete the table. Once you click *Yes*, the table and its data are gone forever unless you have a backup.

Creating tables in Design View

Design View is a more advanced method for creating a new table. It allows you to directly enter information about each field in the table. We will use this method for the tables of our database.

Note

While the *Field type* and *formatting* are different in *Design View*, the concepts are the same as in the Wizard.

The first table to be created is *Fuel*. Its fields are *FuelID, Date, FuelCost, FuelQuantity, Odometer*, and *PaymentType*. *FuelCost* uses currency and two decimal places. *FuelQuantity* and *Odometer* use the number format with 3 decimal places and 1 decimal place respectively. *PaymentType* uses the text format.

1) Click *Create Table in Design View*.
2) *FuelID* entries:
   a) Enter *FuelID* as the first *Field Name*.
   b) Select *Integer [INTEGER]* as the *Field Type* from the dropdown list. (The default setting is Text [VARCHAR].)

Tip	Shortcut for selecting from the Field Type dropdown list: use the key for the first letter of the choice. This might require using the letter more than once to get the choice you want. You can cycle through the choices for a given letter by repeatedly using that letter. After typing the name of the field in the Fields column, use the *Tab* key to move to the Field Type column. This will enter the field name and highlight the dropdown list. You can then use the key for the first letter of your choice to select the field type. Just remember to use it the correct number of times if necessary.

c) Change the *Field Properties* in the bottom section.

Change *AutoValue* from *No* to *Yes* (Figure 179).

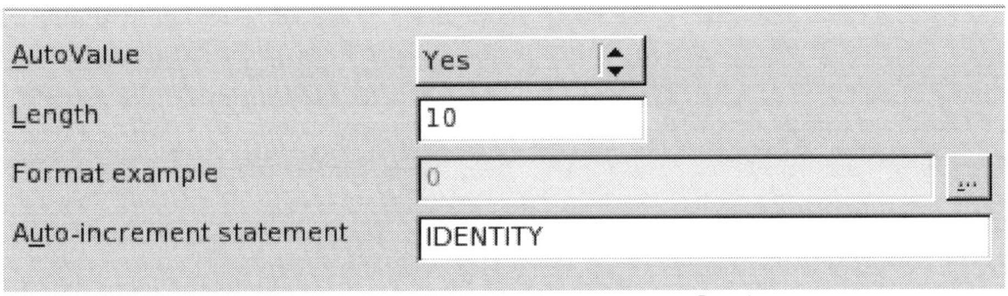

AutoValue	Yes
Length	10
Format example	0
Auto-increment statement	IDENTITY

Figure 179: Field Properties section (AutoValue)

d) Set *FuelID* as the *Primary key*.

Right-click on the green triangle to the left of *FuelID* (Figure 180).

Field Name	Field Type
▸ FuelID	Integer [INTEGER]

Figure 180: Primary key field

Click *Primary Key* in the context menu. This places a key icon in front of *FuelID*.

Note	The primary key serves only one purpose. Any name can be used for this field. It is not necessary to use *FuelID* as the name of the primary key field. We have used it so we know to which table it belongs by its name.

3) All other entries:

- Enter the next field name in the first column (*Field Name* column).

- Select the *Field Type* for each field.
  - For *Date* use Date[DATE]. (Use the *D* key once to select it.)
  - PaymentType uses Text [VARCHAR], the default setting.
  - All other fields use Number [NUMERIC]. (Use the *N* key once to select it.)
- Select the *Field Properties* (Figure 181).

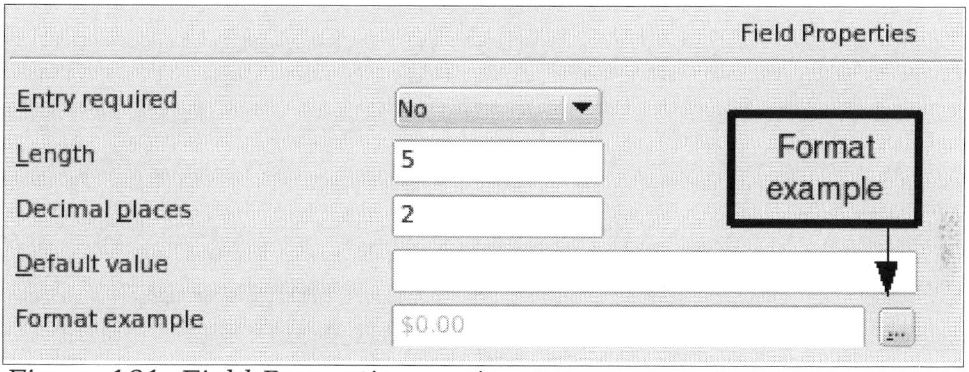

Figure 181: Field Properties section

> *FuelCost, FuelQuantity,* and *Odometer* need changes in the Field Properties section (Figure 181).
>
> - *FuelQuantity*: Change *Length* to 6 and *Decimal places* to 3. (Many fuel pumps measure fuel to thousands of a gallon in the USA where I live.)
>
> - *Odometer*: Change the *Length* to 10 and the *Decimal places* to 1.
>
> - *FuelCost*: Change the Length to 5 and Decimal places to 2. Click the Format example button (Figure 181). This opens the Field Format window (Figure 182).
>
> Use *Currency* as the Category and your currency as the Format. My currency has two decimal places. Use what is appropriate for your currency.

4) Repeat these steps for each field in the table.
5) To access additional formatting options, click the button to the right of the Format example panel (*Format example* button in Figure 181).
6) *Description* can be anything, or can be left blank. **(Figure 183 is an example of this.)**
7) To save and close the table, select **File** > **Close**. Name the table *Fuel*.

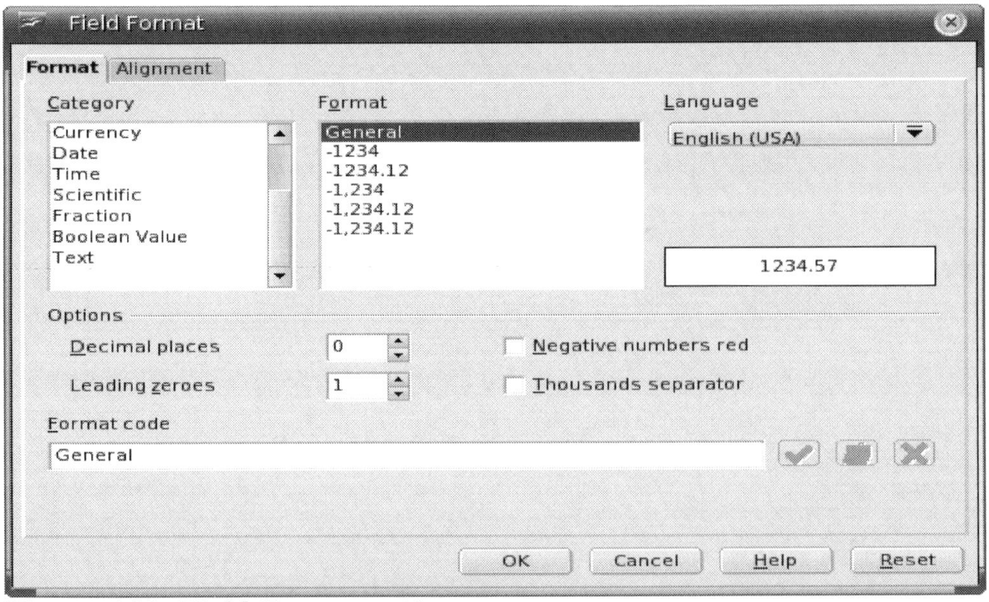

Figure 182: Field Format options

Follow the same steps to create the *Vacations* table. The fields and their field types are listed in Figure 183. Make sure you make the Date field the primary key before closing. (Right click the Grey box to the left of Date. Select Primary key from the context menu.) Name the table *Vacations*, and save it.

	Field Name	Field Type	
🔑	Date	Date [DATE]	
	Odometer	Number [NUMERIC]	Odometer reading
	Motel	Number [NUMERIC]	
	Tolls	Number [NUMERIC]	total tolls
	Breakfast	Number [NUMERIC]	
	BPayment	Text [VARCHAR]	payment type
	Lunch	Number [NUMERIC]	
	LPayment	Text [VARCHAR]	payment type
	Supper	Number [NUMERIC]	
	SPayment	Text [VARCHAR]	payment type
	SnackNo	Number [NUMERIC]	
	SnackCost	Number [NUMERIC]	
	SnPayment	Text [VARCHAR]	payment type for snacks
▶	Miscellaneous	Number [NUMERIC]	misc. costs
	MPayment	Text [VARCHAR]	payment type for motel
	MiscNotes	Memo [LONGVARCHA	
	MiscPayment	Text [VARCHAR]	payment type for miscellaneous

Figure 183: Example of Description entries

Creating tables for the list box

When the same information can be used in several fields, design a table for each type of information. Each table will contain two fields: the information field, and *ID* in this order.

Caution 	You **must create** these tables with the information field listed **first** and the and the ID field listed **last.** Failure to do so will produce the wrong results. For my Payment table, I use *Name* and ID as my fields, with *Dan*, *Kevin*, and *Cash* being the Name entries. The corresponding ID entries are *0, 1, 2*. When the Name field is listed first in the table, one of the three names will appear in the payment field of the Fuel table. If the ID field is listed first, *0, 1,* or *2* appear in the payment field instead.

1) Follow the directions in "Creating tables in Design View" on page 241. In the table we will create, the two fields can be *Type* and *PaymentID*. Make sure that the *AutoValue* is set to **Yes** for the *PaymentID* field. Set the *PaymentID* field as the primary key. (See Figure 184.)
2) Save the table using the name *Payment Type*.

	Field Name	Field Type
▶	Type	Text [VARCHAR]
🔑	PaymentID	Integer [INTEGER]

Figure 184: Table in Design View

Note:	If you have several tables to create with the same fields, design one table and produce the other tables by cutting and pasting. (See "Creating a table by copying an existing table" on page 240.)

Adding data to the list table

List tables do not require a form. Instead, add their data directly to the table. In this example, use the names of the two people with a bank card and Cash for cash purchases.

1) In the main database window, click on the *Tables* icon (Figure 176). Right-click on *Payment Type* and select **Open** from the context menu.

a) Enter *Dan* in the first row. Use the tab key to move to the
second row.

b) Enter *Kevin* in the second row.

c) Enter *Cash* in the third row.

2) Save and close the table window.

Tip	The *Enter* key can also be used to move from field entry to field entry. For this example, enter Jan. in the first *Name* field. *Enter* moves the cursor to the *ID* field. *Enter* then moves the cursor to the second *Name* field. The *Down Arrow* key can also be used to move from row to row.

Note	The *PaymentID* field contains *<AutoField>* until you use the *Enter* key to move to the second row. Then it becomes a 0. As you add the entries to each row, the rows of the *PaymentID* field change to consecutive whole numbers. For example the first three numbers in this field are 0,1,2.

Creating a View

A View is a query. Because of this, the details of how to create and
use a View are in the Creating queries section.

Date	Breakfast	Lunch	Supper	SnackCosts
▶ 04/12/07	$11.23	$12.56	$14.95	$7.34

Figure 185: View of some fields from the Vacations table

A View is also a table. Its fields come from the fields of one or more
tables of the database. It provides a way to look at a number of fields
without regard to the table to which any of the fields belong. A View
can consists of some of the fields of one table as in Figure 185. Or, it
can consist of fields from more than one field as in Figure 186.

Date	FuelCost	FuelQuanity	Who
▶ 04/12/07	24.99	8.299	Dan
04/12/07	26.45	11.650	Kevin
04/13/07	27.50	12.557	Cash
04/15/07	35.12	10.233	Kevin

Figure 186: View of fields from the Fuel and Payment Type tables

Caution	Data can not be entered into a View like it can be added to a table. It is strictly for viewing data which has already been entered into the table.

Defining relationships

Now that the tables have been created, what are the relationships between our tables? This is the time to define them based upon the questions we asked and answered in the beginning.

When on vacation, we want to enter all of our expenses all at one time each day. Most of these expenses are in the Vacations table, but the fuel we buy is not. So, we will relate these two tables using the Date fields. Since the Fuel table may have more than one entry per date, this relationship between the Vacations and Fuel tables is one to many. (It is designated 1:n.)

The Vacations tables also contains several fields for the type of payment used. For each field listing the payment type, there is only one entry from the Payment Type table. This is a one to one relationship: one field in one table to one entry from the other table. (It is designated 1:1.) Other tables also contain fields for the type of payment. The relationship between these fields of those tables and the Payment Type table are also 1:1.

Since the Payment Type table only provides a static list, we will not be defining a relationship between the Payment Type table and the fields of the other tables which use the entries of the Payment Type table. That will be done when the forms are created.

The Fuel and Maintenance tables do not really have a relationship even though they share similar fields: Date, and Odometer. Unless a person is in a habit of regularly getting fuel and having their vehicle serviced, the entries in these tables do not share anything in common.

Tip	As you create your own databases, you need to also determine where tables are related and how.

1) We begin defining relationships by **Tools > Relationships**. The Automobile – OpenOffice.org Base: Relation design window opens (Figure 187). The icons we will use are **Add Tables** and **New Relation**.

Add Tables   New Relation icon

Figure 187: Relation design window

2) Click the **Add Tables** icon. The Add Tables window opens.

3) Use one of these ways to add a table to the Relation design window:

   • Double-click the name of the table. In our case, do this for both Vacations and Fuel.

   • Or, click the name of the table and then click Add for each table.

4) Click **Close** when you have added the tables you want (Figure 248).

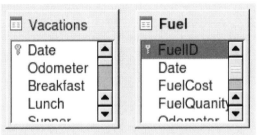

Figure 188: Added table lists

5) Defining the relationship between the Vacations and Fuel tables. Two ways exist to do this:

   • Click and drag the *Date* field in the Fuel table to the *Date* field in the Vacations table. When you release the mouse button, a connecting line forms between the two date fields (Figure 189).

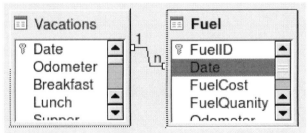

Figure 189: Designation for a 1:n relationship

- Or, click the **New Relation** icon. This opens the Relations window (Figure 190). Our two tables are listed in the *Tables involved* section.

Figure 190: Setting the relationship between tables

- In the *Fields involved* section, click the dropdown list under the Fuel label.
- Select *Date* from the Fuel table list.
- Click in the cell to the right of this dropdown list. This opens a dropdown list for the Vacations table.
- Select *Date* from the Vacations table list. It should now look like Figure 191.
- Click **OK**.

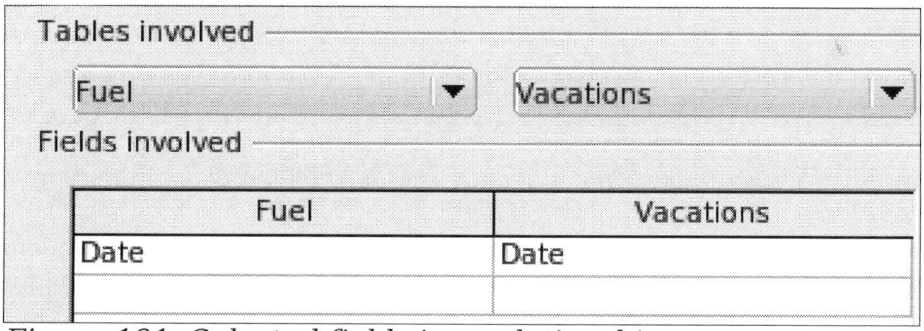

Figure 191: Selected fields in a relationship

6) Modifying the *Update options* and *Delete options* section of the Relation window.

   a) Right-click the line connecting the Date fields in the two table lists to open a context menu.

   b) Select **Edit** to open the Relation window (Figure 192).

   c) Select **Update cascade**.

   d) Select **Delete cascade**.

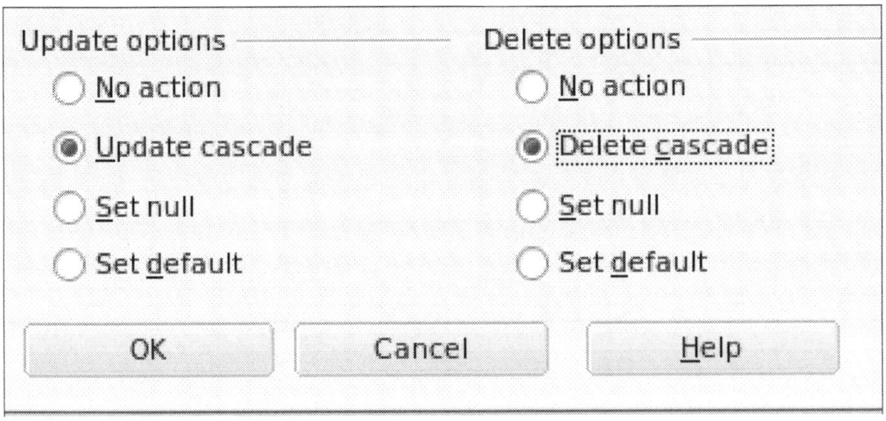

Figure 192: Update options and Delete options section

While these options are not absolutely necessary, they do help. Having these options selected permits you to update a table that has a relationship defined with another table. It also permits you to delete a field from the table.

Creating a database form

Databases are used to store data. But, how is the data put into the database? Forms are used to do this. In the language of databases, a form is a front end for data entry and editing.

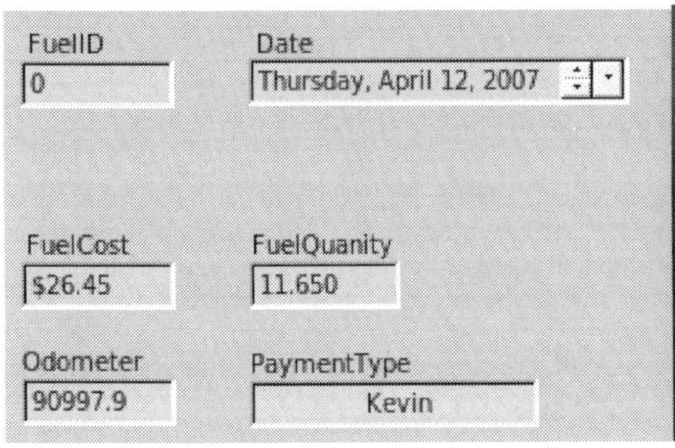

Figure 193: Fields of a simple form

Figure 194: Simple Form with additions

A simple form consists of the fields from a table (Figure 193). More complex forms can contain much more. These can contain additional text, graphics, selection boxes and many other elements. Figure 194 is made from the same table with a text label (Fuel Purchases), a list box placed in PaymentType, and a graphic background.

Using the Wizard to create a form

We will use the Form Wizard to create two forms: CD Collection and Vacations. The CD Collection form will be a simple form, while the Vacations form will contain a form and a subform. We will create the Vacations form with its subform and let you modify the CD Collection form using the same process.

In the main database window (Figure 176), click the **Form** icon. Double-click **Use Wizard to Create Form** to open the wizard (Figure 195). Simple forms require only some of these steps, while more complex forms may use all of them.

Step 1: Select fields.

1) Under Tables or queries, select Vacations as the table. *Available fields* lists the fields for the Vacations table.

2) Click the right double arrow to move all of these fields to the *Fields in the form* list. Click **Next**.

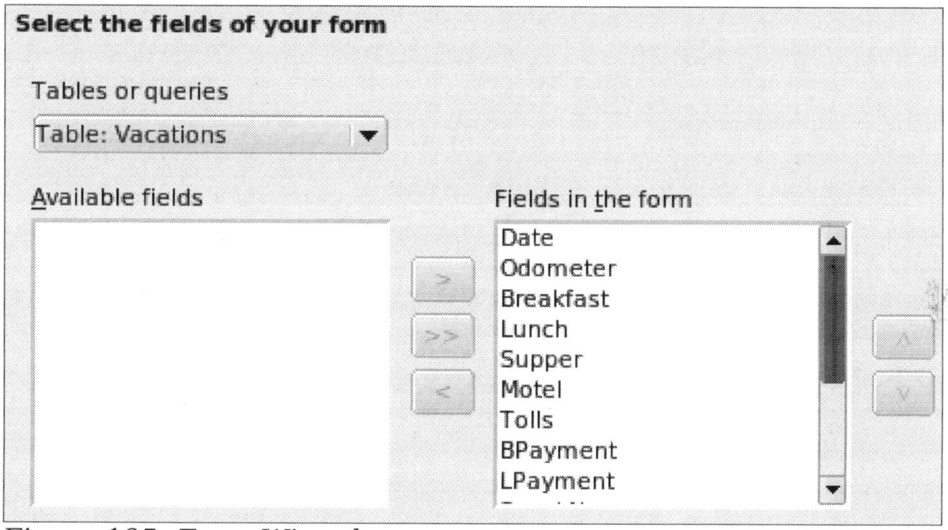

Figure 195: Form Wizard steps

Step 2: Set up a subform.

Since we have already created a relationship between the Fuel and Vacations tables, we will use that relationship. If no relationship had been defined, this would be done in step 4.

1) Click the box labeled *Add Subform*.

2) Click the radio button labeled *Subform based upon existing relation*.

3) Fuel is listed as a relation we want to add. So, click Fuel to highlight it, as in Figure 196. Click **Next**.

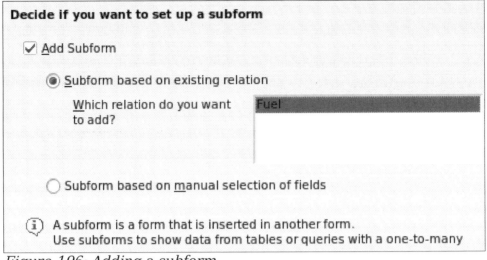

Figure 196: Adding a subform

Step 3: Add subform fields.

This step is exactly the same as step 1. The only difference is that not all of the fields will be used in the subform.

1) Select Fuel under *Tables or queries*.
2) Use the **>>** button to move all the fields to the right.
3) Click the FuelID field to highlight it.
4) Use the **<** button to move the FuelID to the left (Figure 197).
5) Click **Next**.

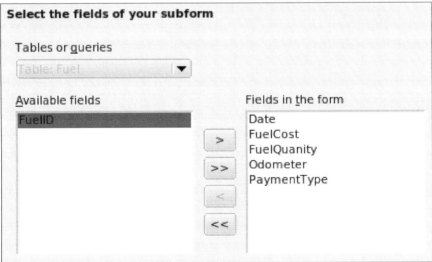

Figure 197: Selecting fields of a subform

Step 4: Get joined fields.

This step is for tables or queries for which no relationship has been defined. Since we want to list all expenses by the day they occur in both the form and subform, we will joint the Date fields of these two tables (Figure 198).

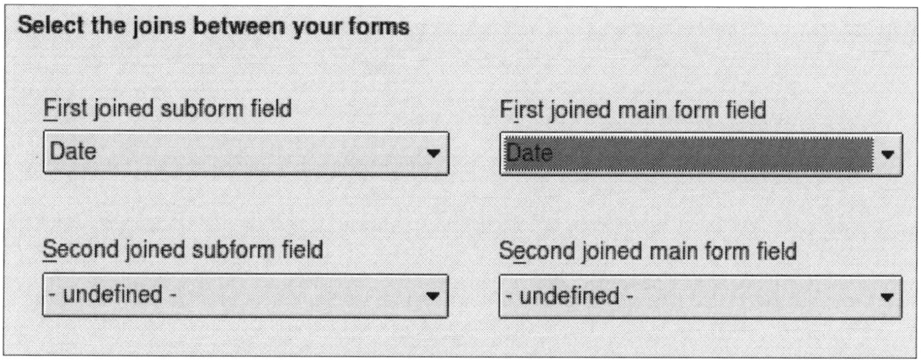

Select the joins between your forms

First joined subform field
Date

First joined main form field
Date

Second joined subform field
- undefined -

Second joined main form field
- undefined -

Figure 198: Selection of joined subform and main form fields

1) Select Date from the *First joined subform field* dropdown list. This is the Date field in the Fuel table. This is **not** the Primary key for the Fuel table, but it is known as a Foreign key.

2) Select Date from the *First joined main form field* dropdown list. This is the Date field in the Vacations table. This **is** the Primary key for the Vacations table. Click **Next**.

Note	It is possible to create a relationship between two tables that is based upon more than one pair of fields. How to do that and why is discussed in the *Base Guide*.

Caution	When selecting a pair of fields from two tables to use as a relationship, they have to have the same field type. That is why we used the Date field from both tables: both their field types are Date[DATE].
	Whether a single pair of fields from two tables are chosen as the relationship or two or more pairs are chosen, certain requirements must be met for the form to work.

• No field from the subform can be the Primary key for its table. (FuelID cannot be used.)

• Each pair of joined fields must have the same file type.

• One of the fields from the main form must be the Primary key for its table. (Date would have to be used.)

Step 5: Arrange controls.

Note	Each control in a form consists of two parts: label and field. This step in creating the form determines where a control's label and field are placed in relationship with each other. The four choices from left to right are *Columnar left, Columnar - Labels on top*, As *Data Sheet*, and *In Blocks - Labels Above* (Figure 199).

1) Arrangement of the main form: Click *Columnar - Labels on top*. The labels will be placed above their field.

2) Arrangement of the subform: Click *As Data Sheet*. (The labels are column headings and the field entries are in spreadsheet format.) Click **Next**.

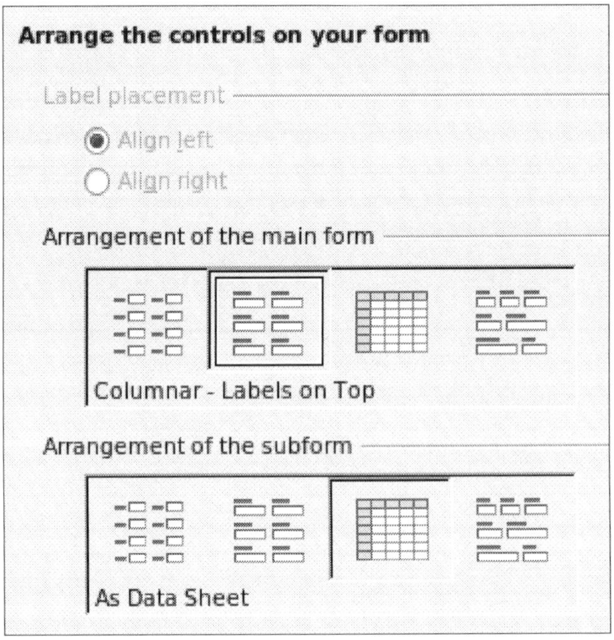

Figure 199: Control arrangements

Step 6: Set data entry.

Unless you have a need for any of these entries to be checked, accept the default settings. Click **Next**.

Step 7: Apply styles.

1) Select the color you want in the *Apply Styles* list. (I chose the beige which is Orange 4 in the Color table.)

2) Select the Field border you want. (I prefer the 3-D look. You might want to experiment with the different possible settings.)

3) Click **Next**.

Step 8: Set name.

1) Enter the name for the form. In this case, it is *Fuel*.

2) Click the circle in front of *Modify the form*. (This circle is called a radio button.)

3) Click **Next**. The form opens in Edit mode.

Modifying a form

We will be moving the controls to different places in the form and changing the background to a picture. We will also modify the label for the PaymentType field as well as change the field to a list box.

First, we must decide what we want to change and to what. The discussion will follow this ten step outline.

1) The Date field in the main form needs a dropdown capability. It also needs to be lengthened to show the day of the week, month, day, and year.

2) Shorten the length of the payment fields (all fields containing the word payment).

3) The controls need to be move into groups: food, fuel subform, and miscellaneous.

4) Some of the labels need to have their wording changed. Some single words should be two words. Some abbreviations should be used if possible (Misc. for miscellaneous).

5) The widths of several fields and labels need to be changed. Only Lunch, Supper, Motel, and Tolls have acceptable lengths. But for a better appearance, changes will be made to these as well.

6) All the fields whose label ends in *Payment* will be replaced with a list box. This box contains the entries from the Payment Type table.

7) The Note field needs to be lengthened vertically and a scroll bar added. It also needs to be moved.

8) Changes need to be made in the Date and PaymentType columns of the subform that are similar to the changes in the main form.

9) Headings need to be added for each group in the main form.

10) The background needs to be changed to a picture. Some of the labels will have to be modified so that they can be read clearly. The font color of the headings needs to be changed as well.

Here are some pointers that we will be using in these steps. The controls in the main form consists of a label and its field. Sometimes we want to work with the entire control, and other times we want to work with only the label or the field. There are times when we want to work with a group of controls.

- Clicking a label or field selects the entire control. A border appears around the control with eight green handles (Figure 200). You can then drag and drop it where you want.

- *Control+click* a label or field selects only the label or the field (Figure 201).

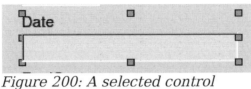

Figure 200: A selected control

- By using the *Tab* key, you can change the selection from the field to the label or the label to the field.

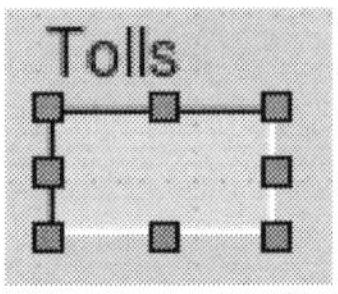

Figure 201: Selecting a field of a control

- Moving a group of controls is almost as easy as moving one of them.
  1) Click the field of the top left control to be moved, to select it.
  2) Move the cursor to just above and to the left of the selected control.
  3) Drag the cursor to the bottom right of the group of controls and release the mouse button.

     As you drag the cursor, a dashed box appears showing what is contained in your selection. Make sure it is big enough to include the entire length of all the controls.

     When you release the mouse button, a border with its green handles appears around the controls you selected (Figure 202).

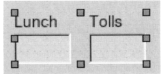

Figure 202: Selecting multiple controls

Move the cursor over one of the fields. It changes to a double arrow (Figure 203).

Figure 203: Double arrow

Drag the group of controls to where you want them.

Before changing the Date field, we will move the Lunch and Tolls controls to the right 5 cm (2 inches).

Tip	When either changing a size or moving a control, two properties of the Form Design toolbar should be selected: *Snap to Grid*, and *Guides when Moving*. Your controls will line up better, and an outline of what you are moving moves as the cursor moves.
	You should also have both rulers active (**Tools > Options > OpenOffice.org Writer > View**). Since the form is created in Writer, that is where you have to make sure both horizontal and vertical rulers have a check in the box in front of them.

Note	I use centimeters when making changes in a form because centimeters are more accurate than inches. When moving controls (fields and their labels), placement is also more accurate. You can change your rulers from inches to centimeters by right-clicking each ruler and selecting centimeter from the context menu. You do not have to understand what centimeters are. You only have to match your controls, labels, or fields to specific numerals on a ruler.

Step 1: Change the Date field.

1) *Control+click* the Date field to select it (Figure 201).
2) Move the cursor over the middle green handle on the right side. It should change to a single arrow (Figure 204).

Figure 204: Single arrow

3) Hold the left mouse button down as you drag the cursor to the right until the length is 6 cm. The vertical dashed line is lined up

---

with the 6. (This is approximately 2.4 inches.) Release the mouse button.

4) Click the Control icon in the Form Controls toolbar (Figure 205). It is the one circled in red. The *Properties: Date Field* window opens. Each line contains a property of the field.

Figure 205: Form Controls toolbar

- Go to the *Date format* property. This is a dropdown list with Standard (short) as the default setting.

  Click the default *Standard (short)* to open the list. Click the *Standard (long)* entry to select it.

- Scroll down to the *Dropdown* property. Its default setting is No. It is also a dropdown list.

  Click the default *No* setting to open the list. Click *Yes* to select it.

Tip | To see what the Date field will look like, click the **Form Mode On/Off** icon (the second icon from the left in Figure 205). You can do this any time you want to see the form with the changes you have made.

Step 2: Shorten the width of a field.

All of the fields whose label contains the word payment are too wide. They need shortening before the controls are moved.

1) *Control+click* the BPayment field (Figure 206).

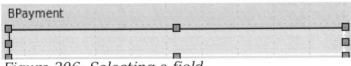

Figure 206: Selecting a field

2) Move the cursor over the middle green handle on the right. The cursor becomes a single arrow.

3) Drag the cursor to the left until the field is 2.5 cm wide (1 inch).

Tip | If you have the *Snap to Grid* and *Guides when moving* icons selected in the Design Format toolbar, you will see how wide the field is as you shorten it.

---

4) Repeat these steps to shorten these fields: Lpayment, SPayment, SnPayment, Mpayment, and MiscPayment.

Step 3: Move the controls to group them by category.

We want to move the controls so that they look like Figure 207.

1) Click the first control you want to move. A border appears around the control with eight green handles.

2) Move the cursor over the label or field of the control. It becomes a double arrow (Figure 203).

3) Drag and drop the control to where you want it.

4) Use the same steps to move the rest of the controls to where they belong.

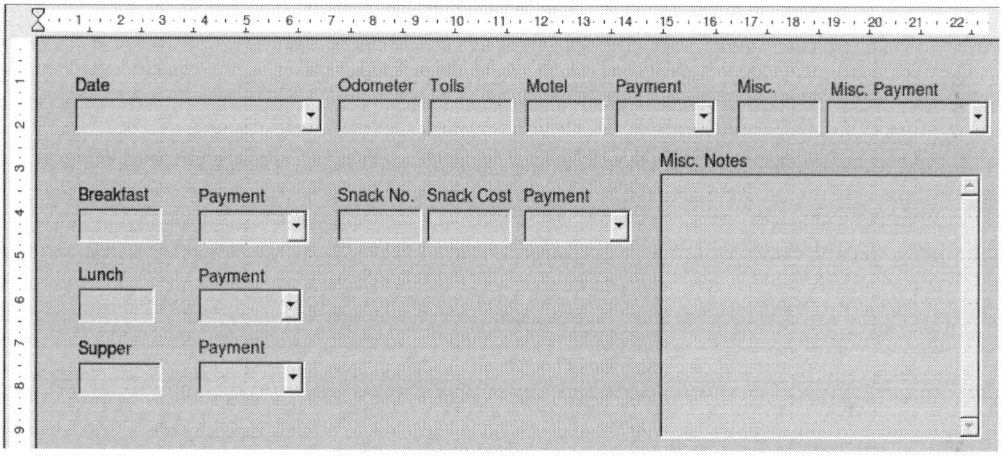

Figure 207: Positioning of Controls

| **Caution** | Do not use *Control+click* when moving a field. It moves either the field or the label but not both. To move both, use a *mouse click* and drag to the desired spot. |

| **Note** | The only way to learn to do these two steps well is to practice them. Another way exists which will place controls where you want them, but this is a more advanced feature and will be explained in the *Base Guide*. |

Step 4: Change the label wording.

Field names need to be single words. However, the labels for the fields can be more than one word. So, we will change them. To do so, we will be editing the text in the label.

1) *Control+click* the SnackNo label. Do one of the following:

   • Right-click the SnackNo label.

      – Select **Control** from the context menu (Figure 208). The window that opens is labeled Properties: Label field. It contains all of the properties of the selected label.

      – In the Label selection, click between the k and N in SnackNo.

      – Use the spacebar to make SnackNo into two words. Place a . (period) after the No. (Figure 209).

      – Close the properties window.

Figure 208: Context menu

Snack No.

Figure 209: Multi-word label

   • Or, click the Control icon in the Form Control toolbar (Figure 210). The Properties window opens. The rest of the steps are the same.

Figure 210: Form Controls toolbar

2) Use the same procedure to change these labels as well: BPayment to Payment, LPayment to Payment, SPayment to Payment, Miscellaneous to Misc., SnackCost to Snack Cost, MPayment to Payment, MiscPayment to Misc. Payment, and MiscNotes to Misc. Notes.

3) Close the Properties window.

Tip   All of the listings in the Properties window can be modified by you. For example, by changing the Alignment from Left to Center, the word or words in the label are centered within the Label. When you have some time, you might want to experiment with different settings just to see the results you get.

Step 5: Change the widths of the labels and fields.

We want the following controls to be 2 cm wide (0.8 inches): Breakfast, Lunch, Supper, Odometer, Snack No., Tolls, Snack Cost, Motel, and Misc. All of the payment fields were changed in step 2, but Misc. Payment needs to be changed to 3 cm (1.2 inches).

1) Click Breakfast. The border around it appears with eight green handles.

2) Move the cursor over the middle green handle on the right. The cursor changes into a single arrow.

3) Drag and drop the cursor to the left to shorten the control or to the right to lengthen the control. Use the guide lines to determine the width.

4) Repeat for the other listed controls.

Step 6: Replace fields with other fields.

We want to replace the PaymentType field with a List Box. Then we can choose the type of payment from the Payment Type table rather than having to manually enter the type. In my case, each of my payment types begins with a different letter. If I enter the first letter of the payment type, the rest of the word automatically appears. I can then go to the next field.

---

1) *Control+click* the Payment field for Breakfast. The green handles appear around the field but not around the Label (Figure 211).

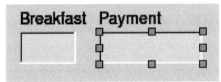

Figure 211: Selecting a field of a control

2) *Right-click* within the green handles and select **Replace with > List Box. (**Figure 208 is the context menu which contains the **Replace with** selection, and Figure 212 is the list of replacement fields.)

3) *Click* the Control icon in the Form Controls toolbar (Figure 210) to open the Properties window.

4) On the General tab, scroll down to the Dropdown selection. Change the *No* to *Yes* in this dropdown list (Figure 213).

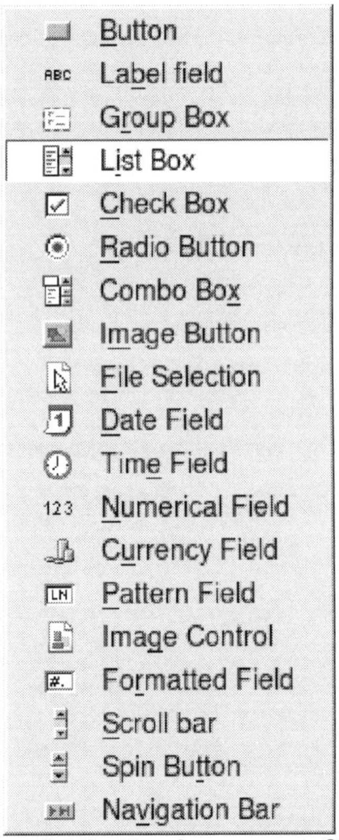

▭	<u>B</u>utton
ᴀʙᴄ	La<u>b</u>el field
▤	<u>G</u>roup Box
▤	L<u>i</u>st Box
☑	<u>C</u>heck Box
◉	<u>R</u>adio Button
▤	Combo Bo<u>x</u>
▨	I<u>m</u>age Button
▨	<u>F</u>ile Selection
▥	<u>D</u>ate Field
◷	Tim<u>e</u> Field
123	<u>N</u>umerical Field
⚖	C<u>u</u>rrency Field
LN	<u>P</u>attern Field
▤	Imag<u>e</u> Control
▦	For<u>m</u>atted Field
▤	<u>S</u>croll bar
▤	Spin Bu<u>t</u>ton
▶ꟾ	Na<u>v</u>igation Bar

Figure 212: Replacement fields

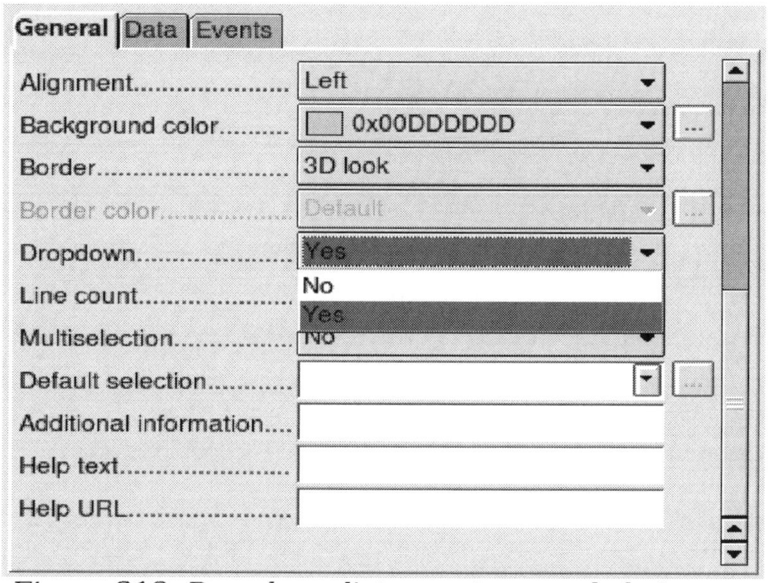

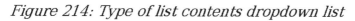

Figure 213: Dropdown list open to reveal choices

5) Click the **Data** tab.

- *Type of list contents* is a dropdown list. Change it to *Sql.*

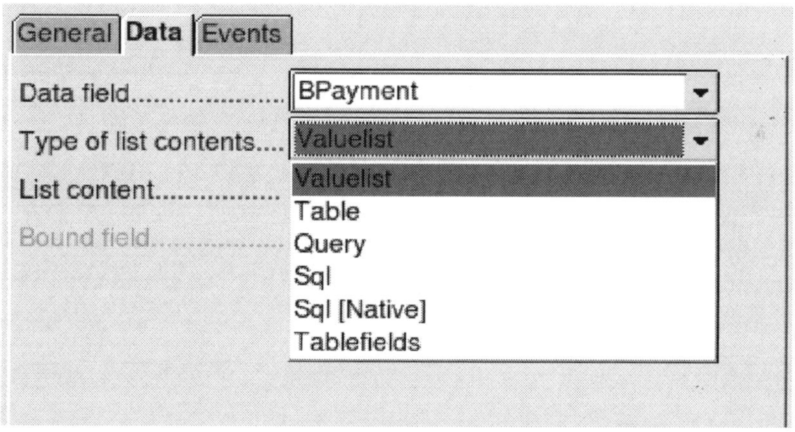

Figure 214: Type of list contents dropdown list

- Type the following **exactly** as it is in the *List contents* box:

  SELECT "Type", "Type" FROM "Payment Type"

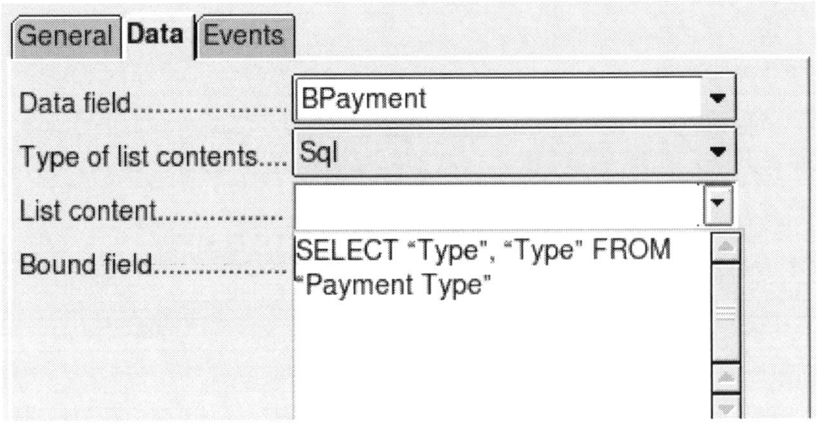

Figure 215: List content for payment type fields

Tip	You should be able to copy and paste *SELECT "Type", "Type" FROM "Payment Type"* from above directly into the *List content* box. Just make sure you copy from the *S* in SELECT to the double quotation mark after the phrase *Payment Type* and no more than this.

Note	What you wrote is called an SQL command. The words *SELECT* and *FROM* are written in capital letters because they are commands. When the command SELECT is used, it requires a field name within quotation marks and then the field's alias, also within quotation marks. In this case, the field and its alias are the same. The FROM command requires the name of the table which contains the field. Single-word table names do not require quotation marks, but multiple-word table names do.

- Repeat these steps for the payment fields for Lunch, Supper, Motel, Snacks, and Misc. The main form should look like Figure 216 as far as where the controls are located. It also shows what the Note control should look like. Those changes are explained in the next step.

- Close the Properties window.

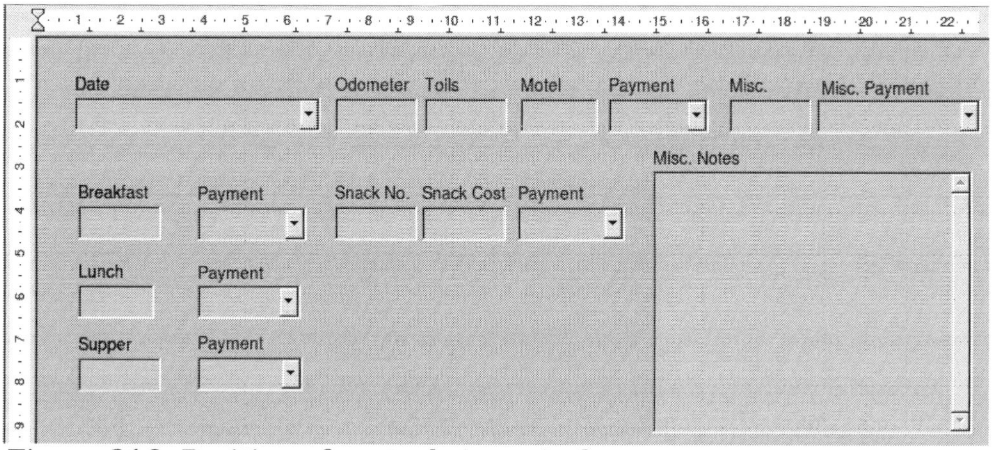

Figure 216: Position of controls in main form

Step 7: Change the Note field.

We want the Note control where it is located in Figure 216. Since it has a memo field type, it needs a vertical scrollbar for additional text space if desired.

1) *Control+click* the *Note* field. The green handles should surround the Note field but not its label.

2) Click the **Control** icon to open the Properties window (Figure 217).

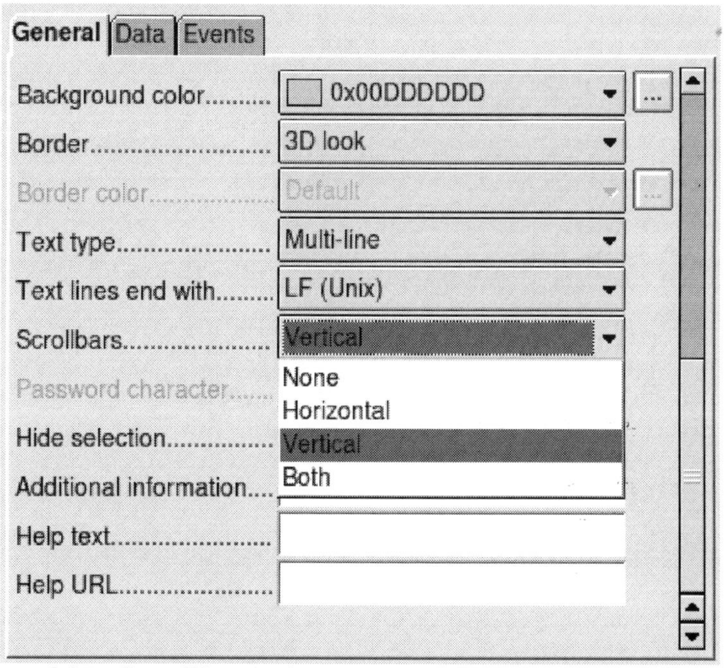

Figure 217: Scrollbar selections in the Properties window

3) Scroll down to the *Scrollbars* setting. Change the selection from *None* to *Vertical* in this dropdown list.

4) Close the Properties window.

5) Lengthen the Note field.

    a) Move the cursor over the middle green handle at the bottom of the Note field. It becomes a vertical single arrow.

    b) Drag the cursor down until the length is 6 cm (2.4 inches).

Step 8: Change labels and fields in a subform.

The Date column needs to be widened. The field in the PaymentType column needs to be changed to a list box. The label for PaymentType column needs to be two words.

Change the PaymentType column:

1) Right-click the label PaymentType to open a context menu (Figure 218).

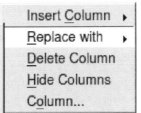

Figure 218: Choices for modifying a control in a subform

2) Select **Replace with**, and then select **List box** from the context menu.

3) Again right-click the label PaymentType to open a context menu.

4) Select **Column**. This opens the Properties window (Figure 219).

5) In the *Label* box, change PaymentType to Payment Type.

6) Click the **Data** tab.

7) From the *Type of list contents* dropdown list, select *sql*.

8) Type the following exactly as it is written:

    `SELECT "Type", "Type" FROM "Payment Type"`

9) Close the Properties window.

Tip	Step 6: Replace fields with other fields., beginning with part 5, contains more detailed instruction.

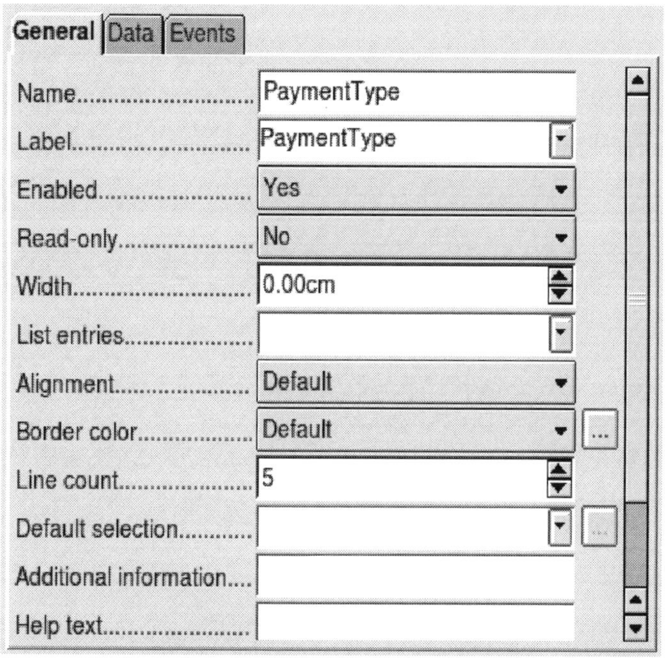

General	Data	Events

Name	PaymentType
Label	PaymentType
Enabled	Yes
Read-only	No
Width	0.00cm
List entries	
Alignment	Default
Border color	Default
Line count	5
Default selection	
Additional information	
Help text	

Figure 219: Properties window for control in a subform

Step 9: Add headings to groups.

1) Make sure the cursor in in the upper left corner. If it is not, click in that corner to move it there.

2) Use the *Enter* key to move the cursor down to the fifth line from the top.

3) Change the *Apply Styles* dropdown list from *Default* to *Heading 2*.

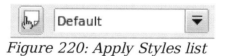

Figure 220: Apply Styles list

4) Use the spacebar to move the cursor to where you want the heading to start.

5) Type the heading *Meals*.

6) Use the spacebar to move the cursor to the center of snack area.

7) Type the heading *Snacks*.

8) Use the *Enter* key to move the cursor between the Supper control and the subform.

9) Use the spacebar to move the cursor to the center of the subform.

10) Type the heading *Fuel Data*.

	If you know how to use styles, you can open the Styles and Formatting window using *F11*. Right-clicking the Heading 2 paragraph style allows you to modify the appearance of all three headings. See the *Writer Guide* Chapter 6.
Note	

Step 10: Change the background of a form.

The background for a form can be a color, or a graphic (picture). You can use any of the colors in the Color Table at **Tools > Options > OpenOffice.org > Colors**. If you know how to create custom colors, you can use them. You can also use a picture (graphic file) as the background. We will use a picture found in OOo: sky.gif (Figure 221). Since the background is dark in places, many of the labels and headings will need changing in order to be seen.

Figure 221: background graphic

1) Select the labels of the top row of controls.
   a) *Control+click* the Date label.
   b) *Control+shift+click* the rest of the labels of the top row. The border will gradually grow to the right as you do this until all the labels are enclosed in it.

Date		Odometer	Tolls	Motel	Payment	Misc.	Misc. Payment

Figure 222: Selecting multiple labels at one time

   c) Click the **Control** icon in the Design Form toolbar to open the Properties window.
   d) Change the *Background* selection from *Default* to *Light cyan*. (This is a dropdown list.)
2) Select the other labels in the same way and then change their background color.
3) Close the Properties window.

4) Press the *F11* key to open the Styles and Formatting window (Figure 223). Notice the left icon has a black outline around it. This is the *Paragraph Styles* icon. Below it is a list of paragraph styles including headings.

Note	I have chosen to use Light cyan as the background color for my labels. You are free to choose whatever color you wish, including a custom color you earlier created.

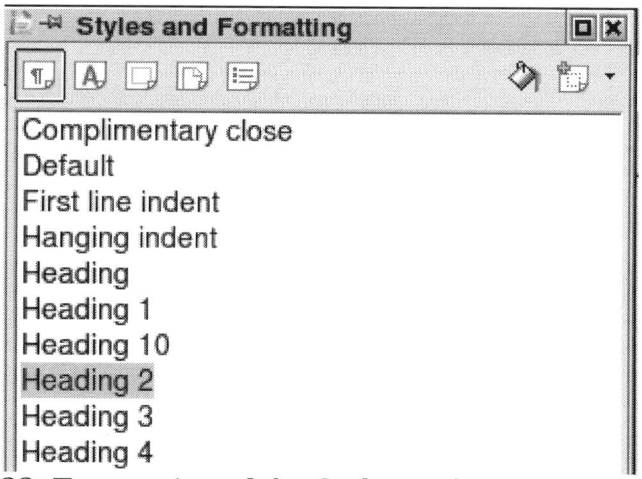

Figure 223: Top portion of the Styles and Formatting window

a) Right-click *Heading 2* and select **Modify** from the context menu.

b) On the Paragraph Style dialog (Figure 224), click the **Font Effects** tab.

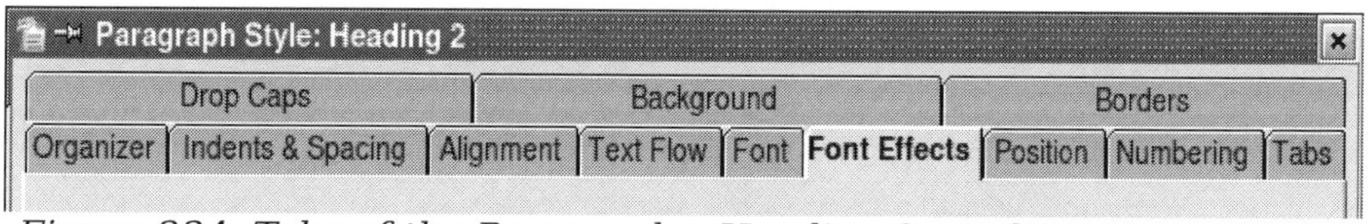

Figure 224: Tabs of the Paragraphs: Heading 2 window

c) Change the *Font color* dropdown list to *Light cyan*.

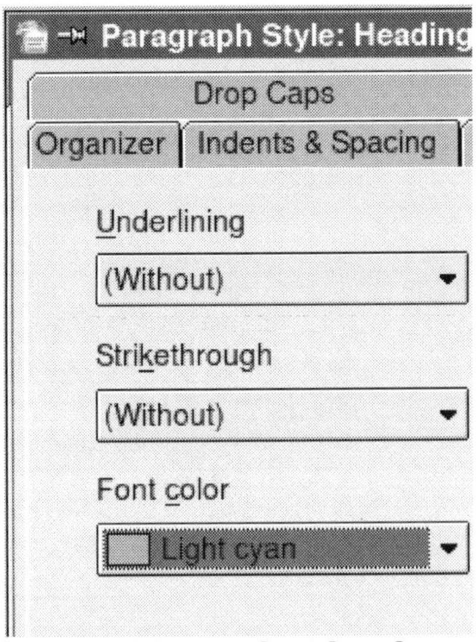

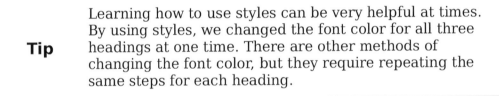

Figure 225: Left side of
Font Effects tab

    d) Click **OK** to close the Paragraph Style: Heading 2 dialog.

    e) Press the *F11* key to close the Formatting and Styles window.

Tip	Learning how to use styles can be very helpful at times. By using styles, we changed the font color for all three headings at one time. There are other methods of changing the font color, but they require repeating the same steps for each heading.

5) Right-click the background and select **Page** from the context menu.

6) Click the Background tab (Figure 226).

    a) Change the *As* dropdown list from *Color* to *Graphic.*

    b) Search for this file: sky.gif. It is located in the Gallery folder of OOo.

    c) Click the **Browse** button in the File section. Browse to the folder containing sky.gif.

    d) Select this file and click **Open**.

    e) In the Type section, select *Area.*

    f) Click **OK** to close the Page Style: Default window.

The form should look like Figure 227.

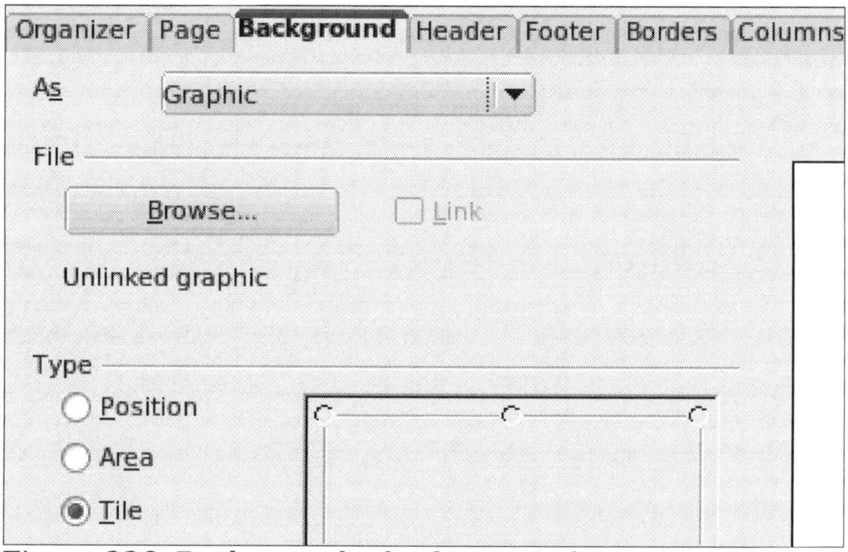

Figure 226: Background tab of Page Styles

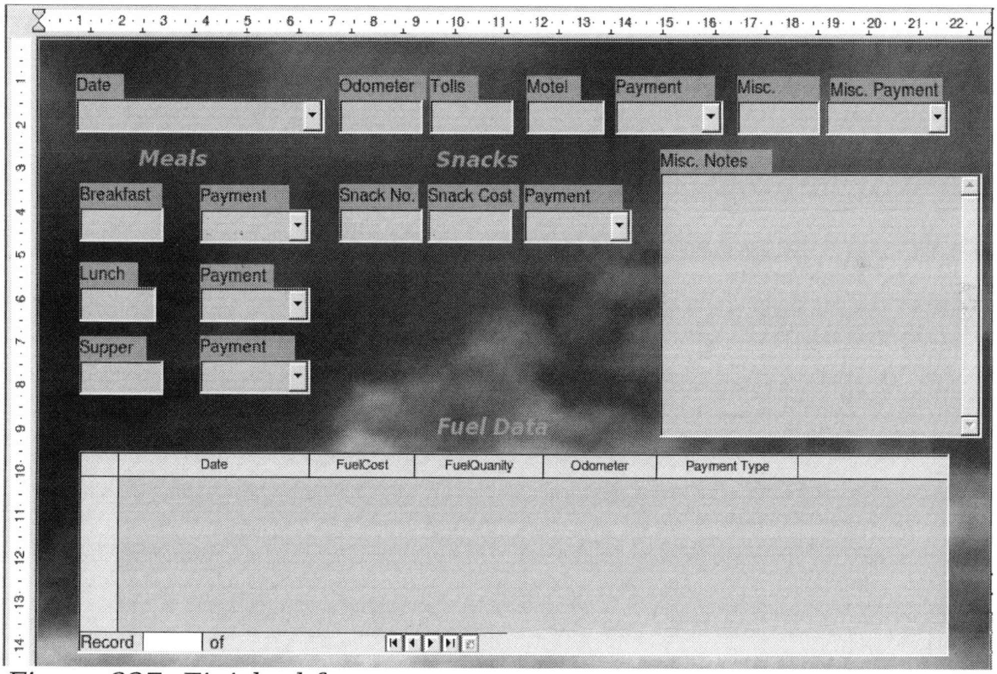

Figure 227: Finished form

Step 11: Change the tab order.

The *Tab* key moves the cursor from field to field. This is much easier to do than to click each field to enter data into it. It also permits us to group our expenses into areas before we begin entering data. For

---

example, all of our meal receipts can be grouped together as can our snacks and also our fuel purchases.

1) *Control+click* the Date field.

2) Click the **Form Design** icon in the Form Controls toolbar to open the Form Design toolbar (Figure 228). Or, use **View > Toolbars > Form Design** to open this toolbar.

3) Click the **Activation Order** icon.

Figure 228: Form Design toolbar with Activation Order icon circled

4) Rearrange the order of the fields in the Tab Order window (Figure 229).

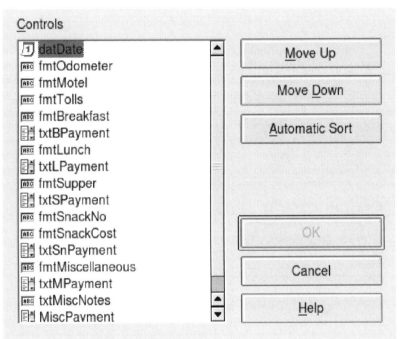

Figure 229: Tab Order window

- Find the txtMPayment listing near the bottom of the list and click it.

- Click the **Move Up** button until txtPayment is just below fmtMotel.

- Use the same two steps to put the fields in the same order as in Figure 230. Click **OK**.

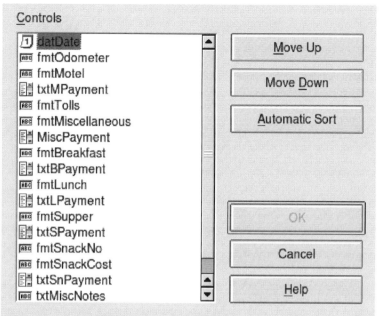

Figure 230: Tab order for the main form

5) Save and close the form.

6) Save the database.

Creating forms in Design View

This method requires using the *Form Controls* and *Form Design* toolbars extensively. These techniques are beyond the scope of this document. Instructions for creating forms using Design view will be described in the *Database Guide*.

Creating subforms in Design View

Again, this is beyond the scope of this document. Creation of subforms in Design View will be described in the *Database Guide*.

Accessing other data sources

OpenOffice.org allows data sources to be accessed and then linked into OOo documents. For example, a mail merge links an external document containing a list of names and addresses into a letter, with one copy of the letter being generated for each entry.

To register a data source, choose **File > New > Database** to open the *Database Wizard*. Select **Connect to an existing database**. This allows access to the list of data sources that can be registered with

OOo. These data sources can be accessed similarly to a dBase database as explained in the next section.

Once a data source has been registered, it can be used in any other OOo component (for example Writer or Calc) by selecting **View > Data Sources** or pressing the *F4* key.

Tip	Mozilla Address Books and dBase databases (among others) can be accessed, and entries can be added or changed.

Caution	Spreadsheets can be accessed, but no changes can be made in the spreadsheet entries. All changes in a spreadsheet sheet must be made in the spreadsheet itself. Update the database and save it. Afterwards you see in your database the changes you made and saved in the spreadsheet. If you create and save an additional sheet in your spreadsheet, the database will have a new table the next time you access it.

Accessing a dBase database

1) **File > New > Database** opens the *Database Wizard* window.

Note	Clicking the *New* icon and *Database* in the drop-down menu also open the *Database Wizard* window. (See Figure 175.)

2) Select **Connect to an existing database**. Pressing the *Tab* key highlights the *Database type* drop-down list. Typing *D* selects *dBase.* Click **Next.**

Note	Clicking the arrows opens a menu from which you can select *dBase* (Figure 231).

⦿ Connect to an existing database

Database type | dBASE ▼ | Database

Figure 231: Database type selection

3) Click *Browse* and select the folder containing the database. Click **Next**.

4) Accept the default settings: *Register the database for me,* and *Open the database for editing.* Click **Finish**. Name and save the database in the location of your choice.

5) Create the *Form* using the *Form Wizard* as explained in "Creating a database form" beginning on page 250.

Accessing a Mozilla address book

Accessing a Mozilla Address Book is very similar to accessing a dBase database.

1) Select **File > New >** Database.

2) Select *Connect to an existing database.* Select *Mozilla Address Book* as the database type (Figure 231).

3) Register this data source.

These are steps 1, 2 and 4 of "Accessing a dBase database".

Accessing spreadsheets

Accessing a spreadsheet is also very similar to accessing a dBase database.

1) Select **File** > **New** > **Database**.

2) Select *Connect to an existing database.* Select *Spreadsheet* as the *Database type* (Figure 231).

3) Click **Browse** to locate the spreadsheet you want to access. If the spreadsheet is password protected, check the *Password required* box. Click **Next**.

4) If the spreadsheet requires a user's name, enter it. If a password is also required, check its box. Click **Next**.

| **Caution** | This method of accessing a spreadsheet does not allow you to change anything in the spreadsheet. All modifications must be made in the spreadsheet itself. This method only allows you to view the contents of the spreadsheet, run queries, and create reports based upon the data already entered into the spreadsheet. |

Registering databases created by OOo2.x and later

This is a simple procedure. **Tools > Options > OpenOffice.org Base > Databases.** Under *Registered databases,* there is a list of these databases. Below this list are three buttons: **New, Delete, Edit.** To register a database created by OOo2.x or later:

1) Click **New.**
2) Browse to where the database is located.
3) Make sure the registered name is correct.
4) Click **OK.**

Using data sources in OpenOffice.org

Having registered the data source, whether a spreadsheet, text document, external database or other accepted data source, you can use it in other OpenOffice.org components including Writer and Calc.

Viewing data sources

Open a document in Writer or Calc. To view the data sources available, press *F4* or select **View > Data Sources** from the pull-down menu. This brings up a list of registered databases, which will include Bibliography and any other database registered.

To view each database, click on the **+** to the left of the database's name. (This has been done for the Automobile database in Figure 232.) This brings up Tables and Queries. Click on the **+** next to Tables to view the individual tables created. Now click on a table to see all the records held in it.

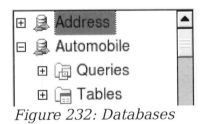

Figure 232: Databases

Editing data sources

Some data sources can be edited in the View Data Sources dialog. A spreadsheet can not. A record can be edited, added or deleted.

The data is displayed on the right side of the screen. Click in a field to edit the value.

Beneath the records are five tiny buttons. The first four move backwards or forwards through the records, or to the beginning or end. The fifth button, with a small star, inserts a new record (Figure 233).

Insert new record

Figure 233: View Data Sources navigation buttons

To delete a record, right-click on the gray box to the left of a row to highlight the entire row, and select **Delete Rows** to remove the selected row.

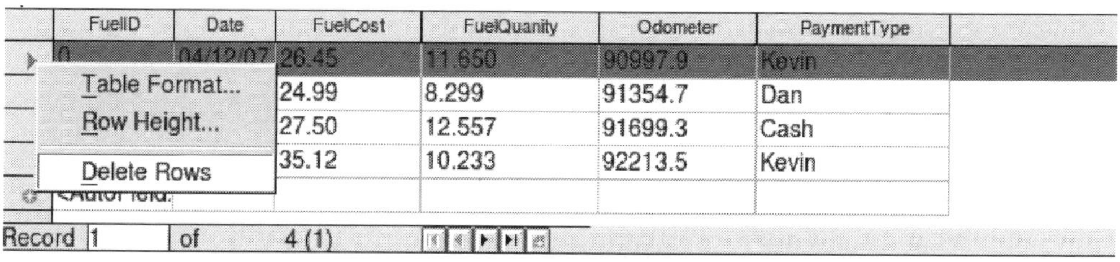

FuelID	Date	FuelCost	FuelQuanity	Odometer	PaymentType
0	04/12/07	26.45	11.650	90997.9	Kevin
		24.99	8.299	91354.7	Dan
		27.50	12.557	91699.3	Cash
		35.12	10.233	92213.5	Kevin

Table Format...
Row Height...
Delete Rows

Record 1 of 4 (1)

Figure 234: Deleting a row in the Data View window

Launching Base to work on data sources

You can launch OOo Base at any time from the View Data Source pane. Just right-click on a database or the Tables or Queries icons and select **Edit Database File**. Once in Base, you can edit, add and delete tables, queries, forms, and reports.

Using data sources in OOo documents

Data can be placed into Writer and Calc documents from the tables in the data source window. In Writer, values from individual fields can be inserted. Or, a complete table can be created in the Writer document. One common way to use a data source is to perform a mail merge.

Tip	Selecting **Tools > Mail Merge Wizard** or clicking on the Mail Merge icon (a small paper-and-envelope icon on the View Data Source pane) launches the Mail Merge wizard which steps through creating a mail merge document. This is discussed in Chapter 11 (Using Mail Merge) in the *Writer Guide*.

Writer documents

To insert a field from a table opened in the data source window into a Writer document , click on the field name (the gray square at the top of the field list) and, with the left mouse button held down, drag the field onto the document. In a Writer document, it will appear as <FIELD> (where FIELD is the name of the field you dragged).

For example: enter the cost of meals and who paid for them on a certain date of a vacation. Make a sentence of this data: "On (date), our breakfast cost (amount) paid by (name), our lunch cost (amount) paid by (name), and our supper cost (amount) paid by (name). Write the words of the sentence with the exception of the words in parentheses. Use the correct field names in the place of the words in parentheses.

1) Replacing (data)

   • Begin the sentence by typing the word *On*.

   • Click the field name Data in the data source window and drag it to the right of the word *On*.

   • The sentence becomes: On <Date>. If you have Field shadings turned on (**View > Field shading**), <Date> has a gray background. Otherwise it does not.

2) Replacing first (amount)

   • Continue typing after <Date>: *our breakfast cost*.

   • Click the Breakfast field name and drag it to the right of what you have just typed.

   • Make sure you have the proper spacing between the field names and the words before and after them.

   • Results so far: On <Date> our breakfast costs <Breakfast>,

3) Replacing the first name:

   • Continue typing after <Breakfast>: *paid by* making sure to add a space afterward.

   • Click the Bpayment field name and drag it to the right of what you just typed.

   • Place a comma after <Bpayment>.

   • Results so far: On <Date> our breakfast cost <Breakfast> paid by <BPayment>,

4) Follow these examples to fill in the rest of the fields in the sentence.

   • Use <Lunch> and <Lpayment> for the second set of (amount) and (name) in the sentence.

   • Use <Supper> and <Spayment> for the third set of (amount) and (name) in th sentence.

- Final results: On <Date> our breakfast cost <Breakfast> paid by <BPayment>, our lunch cost <Lunch> paid by <LPayment>, our supper cost <Supper> paid by <SPayment>.

5) Add data to the fields of the sentence:
   - Click the gray box to the left of the row of data you want to add. That row should be highlighted like the second row of Figure 61.
   - Click the *Data to Fields* icon (circled in black in Figure 61).This should fill the fields with the data from the row you chose.
   - Click another row and then click this icon again. The data in the sentence changes to this selected row of data.
   - Save the document.

Adding data in table format is a little easier and takes perhaps a few less steps. Some of the steps will be quite similar.

Note	Data can be added this way as a fields or text. Following the following steps. I leave this to the reader with which to experiment by changing the selections in the *Insert Database Columns* to see what results you can get.

	Date	Odometer	Motel	Tolls	Breakfast	BPayment
	Friday, M	530.0	$50.00		$11.00	Dan
	Saturday	778.5	$48.00	$4.00	$13.00	Dan

Figure 235: Selected row in data source window

1) Navigate to the place you want to place the table and click the location.
2) Click the gray box to the left of each row of the data source that you want to be a row in your table.
3) Click the *Data to text* icon to open the Insert Database Columns dialog (Figure 236). (The *Data to text* icon is in the left circle in Figure 235.)

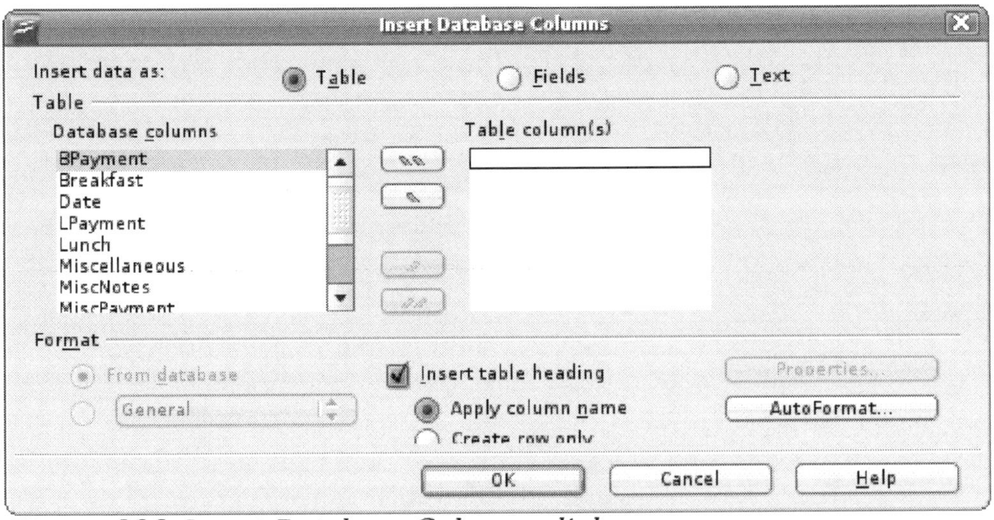

Figure 236: Insert Database Columns dialog

4) Move the fields you want in your table from the *Database Columns* list to the *Table column(s)* list.

- To place the fields in the order you select, click the field and use the *single arrow* to move the fields in the order you desire. You can also limit the fields you use to less than all of the fields available.

- If you want to use all of the fields, use the *double arrow* pointing to the right to move all of them at one time. The order of the fields in the table you create will be the same as in the data source table.

- If you want to remove a single field from the *Table Column(s)* list, click the field and use the *single arrow* pointing to the left.

- If you want to start over by moving all of the fields back to the *Database Columns* list, click the *double arrow* pointing to the left.

5) Select the settings for your table. Use the default settings as in Figure 236.

6) Click **OK**. Save the document.

Calc spreadsheets

There are two ways to enter data in a Calc spreadsheet. One enters the data into the spreadsheet cells. The other creates records in the spreadsheet just like they are done in creating a form in a database. While you can directly access the data in the spreadsheet cells, you can only see the data in the records created in the spreadsheet.

Entering data directly to the spreadsheet cells uses the *Data to Text* icon as we did to make a table in a Writer document. But differences exist in these two situations.

The steps are straightforward.

1) Click the cell of the spreadsheet which you want to be the top left of your data including the column names.

2) Use F4 to open the database source window and select the table whose data you want to use.

3) Select the rows of data you want to add to the spreadsheet:

   • Click the gray box to the left of the row you want to select if only selecting one row. That row is highlighted.

   • To select multiple rows, hold down the *shift* key while clicking the gray box of the rows you need. Those rows are highlighted.

   • To select all the rows, click the gray box in the upper left corner. All rows are highlighted.

4) Click the *Data to text* icon to insert the data into the spreadsheet cells.

5) Save the spreadsheet.

Adding records to a spreadsheet is fairly easy. You need to have the Data Source window open, your spreadsheet open, and the table you want to use selected.

1) Click the gray box above the field name you wish to use to highlight it.

2) Drop and drag the gray box to where you want the record to appear in the spreadsheet.

3) Repeat until you have moved all of the fields you need to where you want them.

4) Close the Data Source window: use *F4*.

5) Save the spreadsheet and click the *Edit File* button to make the spreadsheet read only. All of the fields will show the value for the data of the first record you selected.

6) Add the *Form Navigation* toolbar: **View > Toolbars > Form Navigation**.

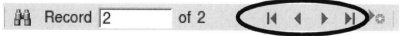

Figure 237: Navigation arrows of a form

7) Click the arrows on the Form Navigation toolbar to view the different records of the table. (The arrows are circled in red.)

The number in the box changes when you change the record number by clicking an arrow. The data in the fields changes correspondingly to the data for that particular record number.

Entering data in a form

Records are used to organize the data we enter into a form. They also organize the data we enter into a subform (Figure 238).

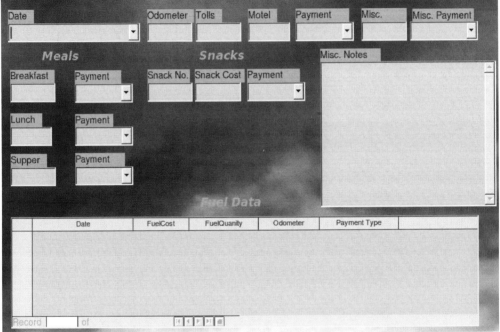

Figure 238: Single Record

Each type of field allows a different method to enter the data. In most if not all cases, more than one method can be used.

The first step to entering data in a form is to open it from the main database window.

1) Click the Forms icon in the *Database* list.
2) Find the form's name in the *Forms* list (Vacations).
3) Double-click the form's name.

The quickest way to enter a date in the Date field is to click the arrow that opens the dropdown calendar. Then click the day the you want (Figure 239). To change the month use the following steps. Then use the *Tab* key to go to the Odometer field.

* Click the left arrow before September to go back one month (August 2008).

- Click the right arrow after 2008 to go forward one month (October 2008).

- Multiple clicks in either direction will change the month the same number of times as the number of clicks. (The year also changes as you move from January back to December or December forward to January each time.)

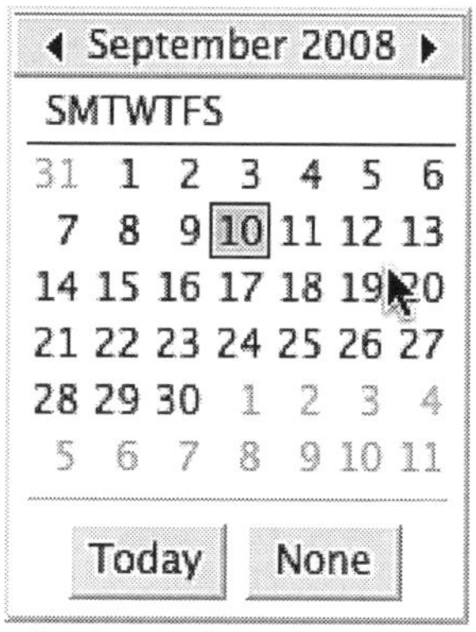

◀ September 2008 ▶
S M T W T F S
31 1 2 3 4 5 6
7 8 9 [10] 11 12 13
14 15 16 17 18 19 20
21 22 23 24 25 26 27
28 29 30 1 2 3 4
5 6 7 8 9 10 11
Today   None

Figure 239: Calendar dropdown

The Odometer, Tolls, and Motel fields are numerical fields. Enter values directly into them, or use the *up* and *down arrows*. When the value is entered, use the *Tab* key to go to the next field.

- Clicking the *up arrow* increases the value, and the *down arrow* decreases the value one unit.

- These two arrows only change the numerals to the left of the decimal place.

- Numerals to the right of the decimal place must be changed by deleting them and typing the desired ones.

The Motel's Payment field is a dropdown list. If as in my case, all of the elements of the list start with different letters, typing the first letter selects the desired letter.

- If two or more elements of the list have the same first letter, repeated typing of the first letter will cycle through the elements with this same first letter. So, if you accidentally go past the the element you wanted, you can keep typing the first letter until it reappears again.

- When the selection is correct, use the *Tab* key to go to the Misc. field.

The rest of the fields of the main form are either numerical fields or dropdown lists until we reach the Misc. Notes field. It is a text field. Type anything you desire in this field just as you would any simple text editor.

Caution ⚠️	Since the *Tab* key is used to move between fields, it can not be used in a text field. All spacing must be done by the *spacebar*. Finally, the *Enter* key only acts as a line break to move the cursor to the next line. While the *Enter* key will move from non-text fields to non-text fields, it will not do so from a text field. Use the *Tab* instead.

Note	If we did not have a subform for fuel data, using the *Tab* key in the last field would save all of the fields, clear them, and make the form ready to accept data on the second record.

Since we have a subform form, using the *Tab* key places the cursor in the first Date field of the subform with the date automatically entered to match the Date field of the main form.

The FuelCost, FuelQuantity, and Odometer fields are numerical fields. The Payment field is a dropdown list. Enter the data just as you did in the main form, and use the *Tab* key to go to the next field.

When you use the *Tab* key to leave the Payment field, it goes to the Date field of the next line and automatically enters the date. Now you can enter your second set of fuel data for this day.

To move to another record when the form has a subform, click any of the fields of the main form. In this case, click the Date field of the main form. Then use the directional arrows at the bottom. There are four of them from left to right: *First Record, Previous Record, Next Record*, and *Last Record* (Figure 237). To the right of these arrows is the *New Record* icon.

To create a new record while in another record in the main form, use one of these choices:

- Click the *Next Record* icon.

- Or, click the *New Record* icon.

Tip	The number in the Record box is the number of the record whose data is shown in the form. (The data from the second record of the Vacations form was displayed when I took the screenshot for Figure 240.)
	If you know the number of the record you want, you can enter it into the record box and then use the *Enter* key to take you to that record.

Figure 240 is a record with data inserted in its fields. Note that not all fields have data in them. It is only necessary to have data in every field if you determine ahead of time to require all fields contain data.

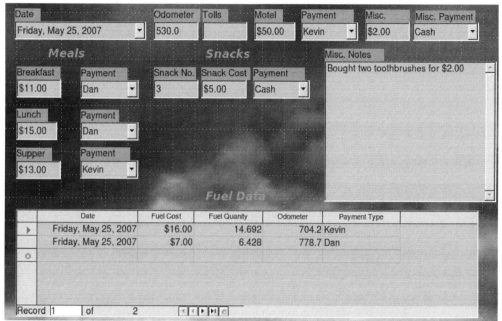

Figure 240: Sample record of the Vacation form and subform

Caution

If you required data be entered for a particular field and you do not have data for that field, you can no longer create a new record. You have to edit the table containing that field and change the *Entry Required*. Save the table **and** the database. This could also cause you to lose data in the particular field.

Creating queries

Queries are used to get specific information from a database. Using our CD-Collection table, we will create a list of albums by a particular artist. We will do this using the Wizard. The information we might want from the Fuel table includes what our fuel economy is. We will do this using the Design View.

Note	Queries blur the differences between a database and a data source. A database is only one type of data source. However, searching for usable information from a data source requires a query. Since the query (one part of a database) does this, the data source appears to become one part of that database: its table or tables. Query results, themselves, are special tables within the database.

Using the Wizard to create a query

Queries created by the wizard provide a list or lists of information based upon what one wants to know. It is possible to obtain a single answer or multiple answers, depending upon the circumstances. Queries which require calculations are best created with the Design view.

In the main database window (Figure 176), click the Queries icon in the Databases section, then in the Tasks section, click *Use Wizard to Create Query*. The Query Wizard window opens (Figure 241). The information we want is what albums are by a certain musical group or individual (the album's author). We can include when each album was bought.

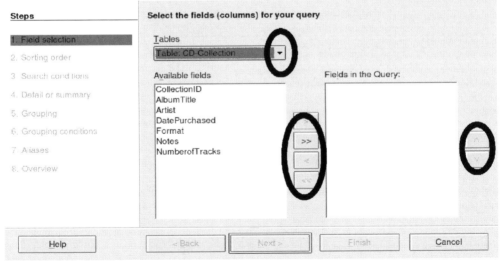

Figure 241: First page of the Query Wizard

Note	When working with a query, more than one table can be used. Since different tables may contain the same field names, the format for naming fields in a query is Table name and field name. A period (.) is placed between the table name and the field name. For example, The Lunch field of the Vacation table used in a query has the name *Vacation.Lunch*.

Step 1: Select the fields.

1) Select the CD-Collection table from the dropdown list of tables.

   - If the Tables selection is not *Table: CD-Collection*, click the arrow (top circle in Figure 241).

   - Click *Table: CD-Collection* in the list to select it.

2) Select fields from the CD-Collection table in the *Available fields* list.

   a) Click *AlbumTitle*, and use the > button (center oval in Figure 241) to move it to the *Fields in Query* list.

   b) Move the Artist and DatePurchased fields in the same manner.

   c) Use the up arrow to change the order of the fields: artist, album, and date purchased.

      - Click the *CD-Collection.Artist* field.

      - Click the up arrow to move it above *CD-Collection.AlbumTitle*.

   d) Click **Next**.

Tip	To change the order of the fields, select the field you want to move and click the up or down arrow to move it up or down (left circle in Figure 241).

Fields in the Query:

CD-Collection.Artist
CD-Collection.AlbumTitle
CD-Collection.DatePurchased

Figure 242: List of fields added to the query

Step 2: Select the sorting order.

Up to four fields can be used to sort the information of our query. A little simple logic helps at this point. Which field is most important?

In our query, the artist is most important. The album title is less important, and the date purchased is of least importance. Of course, if we were interested in what music we bought on a given day, the date purchased would be the most important.

Figure 243: Sorting order page

1) Click the first *Sort by* dropdown list.
   - Click *CD-Collection.Artist* to select it.
   - If you want the artists to be listed in alphabetical order (a-z), select *Ascending* on the right. If you want the artist listed in reverse order (z-a), select *Descending* on the right (Figure 243).

2) Click the second *Sort by* dropdown list.
   - Click *CD-Collection.ArtistTitle.*
   - Select *Ascending* or *Descending* according to the order you want.

3) Repeat this process for *CD-Collection.DatePurchased.*

4) Click **Next**.

Step 3: Select the search conditions.

The search conditions available are listed below. They allow us to compare the name we entered with the names of the artist in our database and decide whether to include a particular artist in our query or not.

- *is equal to*: the same as

- *is not equal to*: not the same as

- *is smaller than*: comes before

- *is greater than*: comes after
- *is equal or less than*: the same as or comes before
- *is equal or greater than*: the same as or comes after
- *like*: similar to in some way

Note	These conditions apply to numbers, letters (using the alphabetical order), and dates.

1) Since we are only searching for one thing, we will use the default setting of *Match all of the following*.
2) We are looking for a particular artist, so select *is equal to*.
3) Enter the name of the artist in the *Value* box. Click **Next**.

Step 4: Select type of query.

We want simple information, so the default setting: *Detailed query* is what we want. Click **Next** at the bottom of the window.

Note	Since we have a simple query, the *Grouping* and *Grouping conditions* are not needed. Those two steps are skipped in our query.

Step 5: Assign aliases if desired.

We want the default settings. Click **Next**.

Step 6: Overview.

Name the query (suggestion: *Query_Artists*). To the right of this are two choices. Select *Display Query*. Click **Finish**.

Step 7: Modify the query.

We are skipping this step since we have nothing to modify. If you select the Modify Query choice, the query would open in Design view. To make modifications, follow the instructions in the next section, "Using the Design View to create a query".

Using the Design View to create a query

Creating a query using Design View is not as hard as it may first seem. It may take multiple steps, but each step is fairly simple.

What fuel economy is our vehicle getting (miles per gallon in the USA)? This question requires creating two queries, with the first query being used as part of the second query.

Caution	The procedures we will be using only work with relational databases. This is because of how relational databases are constructed. The elements of a relational database are unique. (The primary key insures this uniqueness.) That is, there are no two elements which are exactly alike. This allows us to select specific elements to place into our queries. Without the elements of the relational database being unique from all other elements, we could not perform these procedures.

Step 1: Open the first query in Design View.

Click **Create Query in Design View.**

Step 2: Add tables.

1) Click *Fuel* to highlight it.
2) Click **Add. Click Close.**

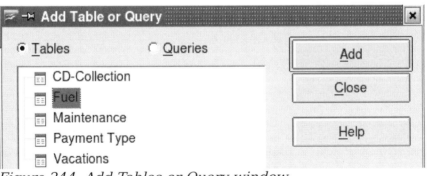

Figure 244: Add Tables or Query window

Tip	Move the cursor over the bottom edge of the fuel table (Figure 245). The cursor become a single arrow with two heads. Drag the bottom of the table to make it longer and easier to see all of the fields in the table.

Figure 245: Fuel table in query

Step 3: Add fields to the table at the bottom.

1) Double-click the *FuelID* field in the Fuel table.
2) Double-click the Odometer field.
3) Double-click the FuelQuantity field.

The table at the bottom of the query window should now have three columns (Figure 246).

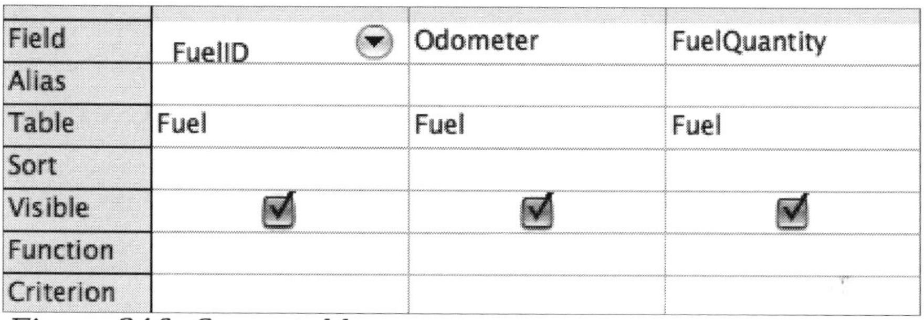

Field	FuelID		Odometer	FuelQuantity
Alias				
Table	Fuel		Fuel	Fuel
Sort				
Visible	☑		☑	☑
Function				
Criterion				

Figure 246: Query table

Step 4: Set the criterion for the query.

We want to the query's FuelID to begin with the numeral 1.

1) Type *>0* in the Criterion cell under FuelID in the query table
2) Click the *Run Query* icon in the Query Design toolbar. This icon is circled in Figure 247.

Figure 247: Query Design toolbar

Figure 248 contains the Fuel table with my entries and the query results based upon the Fuel table.

FuelID	Date	FuelCost	FuelQuantity	Odometer
0	Friday, M	$16.00	14.690	704.2
1	Friday, M	$7.00	6.430	778.7
2	Saturday	$20.00	19.570	1032.3
3	Saturday	$16.00	15.150	1239.4
4	Sunday, I			
<AutoFie				

FuelID	Odometer	FuelQuantity
1	778.7	6.430
2	1032.3	19.570
3	1239.4	15.150
4		
<AutoFie		

Figure 248: Fuel table and query of the fuel table

Step 5: Save and close the query.

Since this query contains the ending odometer reading for our calculations, name it End-Reading when saving it. Then close the query.

Step 6: Create the query to calculate the fuel economy.

1) Click **Create Query in Design View** to open a new query.
2) Add the Fuel table to the query just as you did in step 2: Add tables. But, **do not** close the Add Tables window.
3) Add the End-Reading query to this query.
   a) Click the *Query* radio button to get the list of queries in the database (Figure 249).

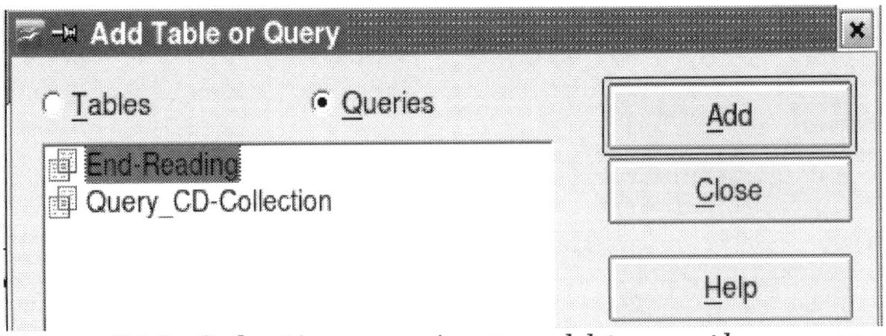

Figure 249: Selecting queries to add to another query

   b) Click End-Reading.
   c) Click **Add**, and then click **Close**.

Step 7: Add fields to the table at the bottom of the query.

We are going to calculate the fuel economy. To do this we need the FuelQuantity and distance traveled. Since the FuelQuantity we want to use is at the ending odometer reading, we will use the End-Reading query to get it. We will also use the Odometer field from the Fuel table and End-Reading query.

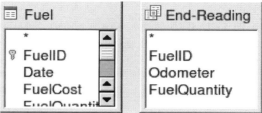

Figure 250: Tables in this query

1) Double-click *FuelQuantity* in the End-Reading query.
2) Double-click *Odometer* in the End-Reading query.
3) Double-click *Odometer* in the Fuel table.

Field	FuelQuantity ▾	Odometer	Odometer
Alias			
Table	End-Reading	End-Reading	Fuel
Sort			
Visible	☒	☒	☒
Function			
Criterion			
Or			

Figure 251: Added fields to the query

Step 8: Enter the FuelID difference field.

We want the difference between the FuelID value of the Fuel table and FuelID value of the End-Reading query to equal one (1).

1) Type `"End-Reading".FuelID - Fuel.FuelID` in the field to the right of the Odometer field of the Fuel Table (Figure 252).

   Type the numeral 1 (one) in the Criterion cell of this column.

Field	FuelQuantity	Odometer	Odometer	"End-Reading"."FuelID" - "Fuel"."FuelID" ▾
Alias				
Table	End-Reading	End-Reading	Fuel	
Sort				
Visible	☒	☒	☒	☒
Function				
Criterion				1

Figure 252: Typing in calculation of fields

2) Calculate the distance traveled (Figure 253):

- Type "End-Reading".Odometer − Fuel.Odometer in the Field cell.
- Type >0 in the Criterion cell.

Field	"End-Reading"."Odometer" - "Fuel"."Odometer"
Alias	
Table	
Sort	
Visible	☒
Function	
Criterion	>0|
Or	

Figure 253: Field for distance traveled calculations

3) Calculate fuel economy (Figure 254):

Type ("End-Reading".Odometer − Fuel.Odometer)/"End-Reading".FuelQuantity in the Field in the next column to the right.

Field	("End-Reading"."Odometer" - "Fuel"."Odometer") / "End-Reading"."FuelQuantity"
Alias	
Table	
Sort	
Visible	☒
Function	
Criterion	
Or	

Figure 254: Fuel economy calculation field

Caution

When entering fields for these calculations, you must follow this format: table or query name followed by a period follow by the field name. For hyphenated or multiple-word names (table or query), use double quotes around the table or query name. The query will then add the rest of the double quotes as in Figure 252.

Use the arithmetical symbol between the two. More than one calculation can be done by using parentheses to group the arithmetical operations.

Step 9: Run the query and make some modification.

After we run the query to make sure it works correctly, we will hide all of the fields that we do not need.

1) Click the Run Query icon in the Design Query toolbar (Figure 247). The results are in Figure 255.

FuelQuantity	Odometer	Odometer1	"End-Reading"."FuelID" - "Fuel"."FuelID"	Distance	("End-Reading"."Odometer" - "Fuel"."Odometer") / "End-Reading"."FuelQua
6.430	778.7	704.2	1	74.5	11.59
19.570	1032.3	778.7	1	253.6	12.96
15.150	1239.4	1032.3	1	207.1	13.67

Figure 255: Result of running the fuel economy query

Notice that not all of the last column label is visible because some of the labels are long. We can fix this problem by using an alias for many of the fields. The labels are replaced by their aliases.

2) Add Aliases:

Type in the aliases as they are listed in Figure 256.

FuelQuantity	Odometer	Odometer	"End-Reading	("End-Reading"."
Quanity	Begin	End		Fuel Economy
End-Reading	End-Reading	Fuel		

Figure 256: Query table with aliases added

3) Run the query again. The results are in Figure 257.

Quanity	Begin	End	"End-Reading"."FuelID" - "Fuel"."FuelID"	Distance	Fuel Economy
6.430	778.7	704.2	1	74.5	11.59
19.570	1032.3	778.7	1	253.6	12.96
15.150	1239.4	1032.3	1	207.1	13.67

Figure 257: Query run with aliases

We really do not need the column showing the difference between the FuelID fields from the table and query. So, we will hide it. While it will not be visible, it will still be used in the calculations.

4) Hide a field that does not need to be seen.

Remove the check in the box of the Visible cell as in Figure 258.

Field	FuelQuantity	Odometer	Odometer	"End-Reading"."FuelID" - "Fuel"."FuelID"
Alias	Quanity	Begin	End	
Table	End-Reading	End-Reading	Fuel	
Sort				
Visible	☒	☒	☒	☐

Figure 258: Making a field invisible in a query run

---

5) Rerun the query (Figure 259).

Quanity	Begin	End	Distance	Fuel Economy
6.430	778.7	704.2	74.5	11.59
19.570	1032.3	778.7	253.6	12.96
15.150	1239.4	1032.3	207.1	13.67

Figure 259: Query run with aliases

Step 10: Close, save, and name the query.

My suggestion for a name is *Fuel Economy*.

There are obviously other calculations that can be made in this query such as cost per distance traveled and how much of the cost belongs to each of the payments types.

Note	To fully use queries requires a knowledge of mathematics and specifically set operations (*unions, intersections, and, or, complements,* and any combinations of these). For example, we listed all of our criteria in one row. That means that all of these criteria have to be met before a row of values will be created in the query. This is how the *and* operator works on sets.
	It also requires having a copy of the *Hsqldb User Guide* available from http://hsqldb.org/.

Creating reports

Reports provide information found in the database in a useful way. In this they are similar to queries. Reports are generated from the database's tables or queries. They can contain all of the fields of the table or query or just a selected group of fields. Reports can be static or dynamic. Static reports contain the data in the selected fields at the time the report was created. Dynamic reports can be updated to show the latest data.

Caution	Dynamic reports update only the data that is changed or added to a table or query. It does **not** show any modifications made to a table or query. For example, open the fuel economy query you just created. For the "End-Reading"."Odometer – Fuel."Odometer" column, change the number 1 to the number 3 **after** creating the report below. The report will be identical before and after you make the change.

For example, a report on vacation expenses divided into categories should probably be a static report because it is based upon specific data that does not change. However, a report on the fuel data should probably be a dynamic report, because this report depends upon data that does change.

Caution	All reports are based upon a single table or query. So you need first to decide what fields you want to use in the report. If you want to use fields from different tables, you must first combine these fields in a single query. Then you can create a report on this query.

An example of this caution is creating a report on vacation expenses. Fuel costs are one part of that report as are meal costs. These values are contained in fields of two different tables: Vacations and Fuel. So this report requires creating a query.

Creating a static report

We will create a report on vacation expenses. Certain questions need to be asked before creating the report.

* What information do we want in the report?

* How do we want the information arraigned?

* What fields are required to provide this information?

* Will a query have to be created because these fields are in different tables?

* Are there any calculations required in the data before being added to the report?

The expenses for our vacation are motel, tolls, miscellaneous, breakfast, lunch, supper, snacks, and fuel. One possible report would simply list the totals of each of these expense groups. Another possible report would list the expense totals for each day of the vacation. A third possible report would list the totals for each expense group for each type of payment. (This would let us know where the money came from to pay the expenses.) At the present time, using the data from the queries in a spreadsheet is the best way to handle reports like this. In the near future, the report feature will include these abilities.

For our purposes, we will create two reports. The first one will list the expenses each day other than fuel. The second report will list the fuel costs each day.

The fields we will need for the first report from the Vacations table are: Date, Motel, Toll, Breakfast, Lunch, Supper, SnackCost, and Miscellaneous. This report will not require an additional query.

The second report involves the Fuel table. Since fuel was purchased and entered into this table at times other than during the vacation, a query needs to be created that contains only the fuel purchased during the vacation.

Vacations table report

1) Create a new report.
   a) Click the *Reports* icon in the Database list in the Automobile – OpenOffice.org window.
   b) In the Tasks list, click **Use Wizard to Create Report**. The Report Wizard window opens.
2) Select the fields.
   a) Select Table: Vacations in the Tables or Queries dropdown list.
   b) Use the **>** to move these fields from the *Available fields* list to the *Fields in report* list: Date, Motel, Tolls, Miscellaneous, Breakfast, Lunch, Supper, and SnackCost (Figure 260). Click **Next**.

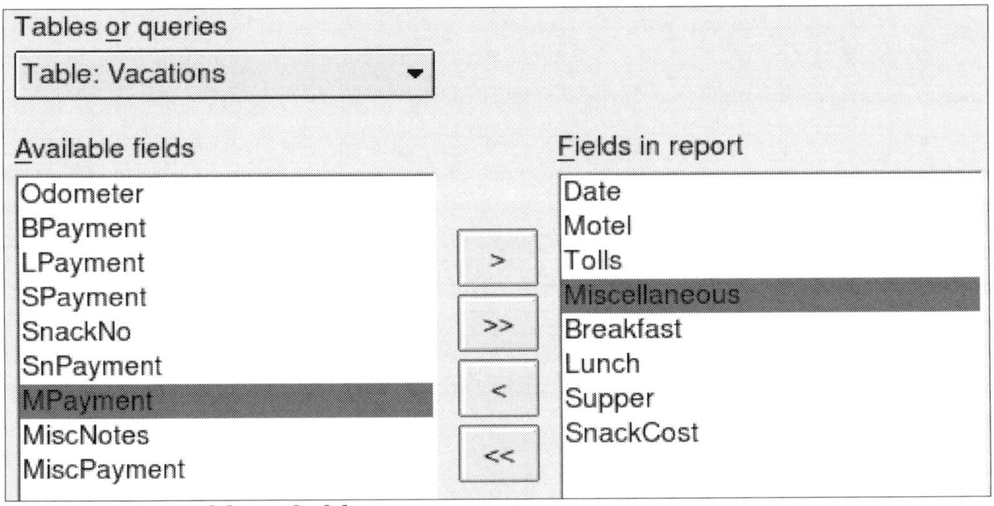

Figure 260: Adding fields to a report

3) Label the fields: answering the question How do you want to label the fields.
   - Click the field label you want to change and make your changes as you would in any text box.
   - Shorten Miscellaneous to Misc. Click **Next**.

5) Since we are grouping by the date, use the **>** button to move the *Date* field to the Grouping list. Click **Next**.

Figure 261: Selecting fields for grouping data

6) Sort options.

We do not want to do any additional sorting. Click **Next**.

7) Choose layout.

We will be using the default settings for the layout. Click **Next**.

8) Create report.

- Label the report: Vacation Expenses.
- Select Static report.
- Click **Finished**.

Note   If you feel adventurous, try selecting some of the other layout choices. After selecting a choice, drag and drop the Report Wizard window so that you can see what you have selected. (Move the cursor over the Heading of this window, and then drag and drop.)

Vacation fuel report

1) Create a query containing only fuel bought on the days of the vacation.

a) Open a query in Design View.

b) Follow the steps for adding tables in Add tables. Add the Fuel table.

c) Double-click these fields in the Fuel table listing: Date and FuelCost to enter them in the table at the bottom of the query.

d) In the Criterion cell of the Date field, type the following:
BETWEEN #5/25/2007# AND #5/26/2007#

Field	Date	▼	FuelCost
Alias			
Table	Fuel		Fuel
Sort			
Visible	☒		☒
Function			
Criterion	BETWEEN #05/25/2007# AND #05/26/2007#		

Figure 262: Setting the criterion for a query

2) Save, name, and close the query. (Suggestion: *Vacation Fuel Purchases.*)

Tip
When using dates in a query, enter them in numerical form MM/DD/YYYY or DD/MM/YYYY depending upon your language's default setting for dates (my default setting is MM/DD/YYYY).

All dates must have a # before and after it. Hence, May 25, 2007 is written #05/25/2007# or #25/5/2007depending upon your language's default setting.

---

3) Open a new report.

   • Right-click the *Vacation Fuel Purchases* query.

   • Select *Report Wizard* from the context menu.

Note
When a new report is opened in this way, the query used to open it is automatically selected in the Tables or Queries dropdown list.

---

4) Create the report.

   Use >> to move both fields from the Available Fields to the Fields in Report list. Click **Next**.

5) Label fields.

   Add a space to FuelCost to make it Fuel Cost (two words). Click **Next**.

6) Group fields.

   Click Date to highlight it. Use > to move the Date field to the Groupings list. Click **Next**.

7) Choose layout.

   We will be making no changes in the layout. Click **Next**.

8) Create report (final settings).

- Use the suggested name, which is the same as the query.
- Select Static report.
- Click **Finish**.

Creating a dynamic report

We will create a report with some statistics on our fuel consumption. To do this, we have to modify two queries: End-Reading and Fuel Economy. We will be adding the FuelCost field to the End-Reading query. Then we will add the FuelCost field from the End-Reading query to the Fuel Economy query.

Tip	When opening a query to edit it, it might appear as in Figure 263. If you move your cursor over the black line (circled), it becomes a double-headed arrow. Drag and drop it to a lower position.

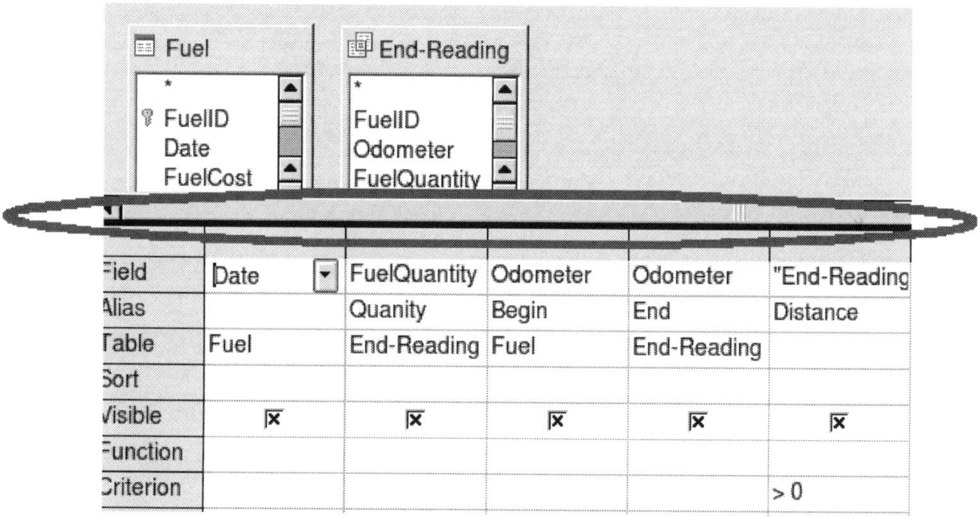

Field	Date	▾	FuelQuantity	Odometer	Odometer	"End-Reading
Alias			Quanity	Begin	End	Distance
Table	Fuel		End-Reading	Fuel	End-Reading	
Sort						
Visible	x̄		x̄	x̄	x̄	x̄
Function						
Criterion						> 0

Figure 263: Appearance of query when opened for editing

1) Add the *FuelCost* field to the End-Reading query:
   - In the Fuel table list, double-click to add *FuelCost* to the bottom table (Figure 264).
   - Save and close the query.

2) Right-click the *End-Reading* query and select **Edit** from the context menu.

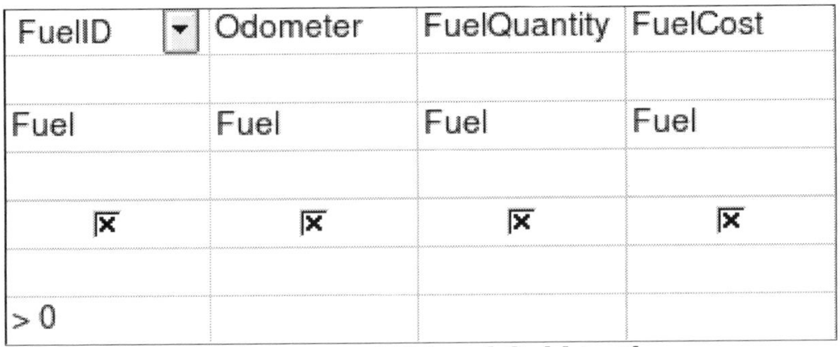

FuelID ▼	Odometer	FuelQuantity	FuelCost
Fuel	Fuel	Fuel	Fuel
☒	☒	☒	☒
> 0			

Figure 264: Adding an additional field to the query

3) Add the *FuelCost* field from the End-Reading query to the Fuel Economy query:

   - Right-click the *Fuel Economy* query and select **Edit** from the context menu.

   - Double-click the *FuelCost* field in the End-Reading query list to add it to the query table at the bottom.

4) Add a calculation field to the right of the FuelCost field.

   - Type the following in an Field cell in the table at the bottom:`"End-Reading".FuelCost/("End-Reading".Odometer − Fuel.Odometer)`

   - Type the following in its Alias cell: **cost per mile.**

Note   If you use the metric system, **cost per km** is the appropriate alias.

---

5) Save and close the query.

6) Open a new report.

   Right-click the Fuel Economy query and select **Report Wizard**.

7) Select fields.

   Move all the fields from the Available fields to the Fields in report list. Use the >> to do so. Click **Next**.

8) Label fields.

   Change FuelCost to Fuel Cost by placing a space between the words. Click **Next**.

9) Group fields.

   Use > to move the Date field to the Groupings list. Click **Next**.

10) Sort options: the wizard skipped this one.

11) Choose layout.

    Accept the default. Click **Next**.

12) Create the report.

- Change the report name to Fuel Statistics.
- The default setting is Dynamic report, so no change is necessary.
- Select Modify report layout.
- Click **Finish**.

Modifying a report

At the end of the last section, we left the Fuel Statistics report open in the edit mode (Figure 265). We will be working on that report. These same steps can be used with any report that you open for editing.

Author:	Dan Lewis							
Date:	4/26/02							

Date	05/20/16							
	Quantity	*Begin*	*End*		*Distance*	*Fuel Economy*	*Fuel Cost*	*Cost per mile*
					9876	9876	9876	9876
	9876.5	9876.5	9876.5		.54	.54	.5	.54

Figure 265: A report in edit mode

The Author is the name you listed in **Tools > Options > OpenOffice.org > User Data**. The date is not correct. The columns need to be moved to the left to give a better appearance. None of the numbers are correct, but their only purpose is to show the number of decimal places.

Step 1: Change the date.

1) Click to the right of the date (4/26/20) so that the cursor is next to the field. Use the *Backspace* key to erase the date.
2) **Insert > Fields > Date**. This places today's date where the original date was.
3) Changing the date formating:
   a) Double-click the date field you just inserted. The Edit Fields: Document window opens (Figure 266).
   b) Since this is a dynamic report, change the Select field from Date (fixed) to Date.
   c) Change the Format to what you desire. (I use the Friday, December 31, 1999 choice.) Click **OK**.

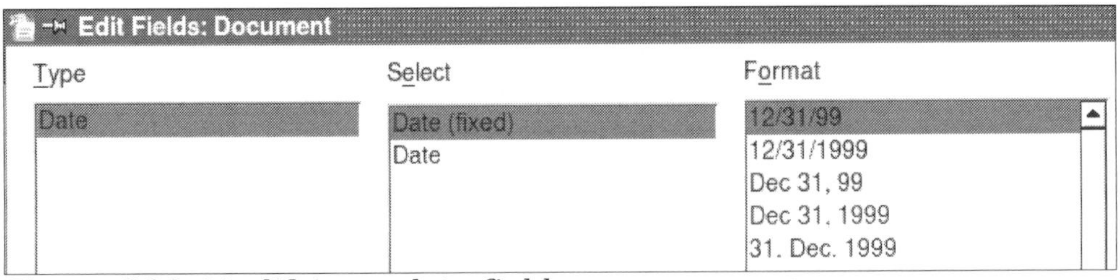

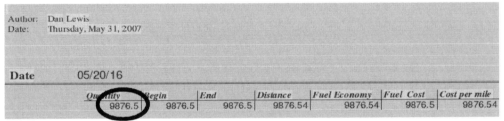

Figure 266: Modifying a date field

Step 2: Change the column widths.

The column widths can be changed by moving the cursor over the right border of each column so that it becomes a double-headed arrow. Then drag and drop it to where you want it. This has to be done for each column in each table in the report. This can also be done with the last column on the right even though there is no black border. It should now look something like Figure 267.

Figure 267: Realigned columns in a report

Step 3: Change the number formating in the cells.

The fuel quantity should have three decimal places. The Begin, End, and Distance should have one decimal place. Fuel Cost should be currency and have two decimal places, and Cost per mile should have three decimal places.

1) Right-click the cell below Quantity to open the context menu. (The cell is circled in red in Figure 267.)
2) Select **Number format.**
3) In the *Options* section (Figure 268),
   a) Change the number of Decimal places to 3.
   b) Click the green checkmark. Click **OK**.
4) Change the Cost per mile field.
   a) Right-click in the cell below *Fuel Cost*.
   b) Select **Number Format**.
   c) In the Category list, select *Currency*. Click **OK**.

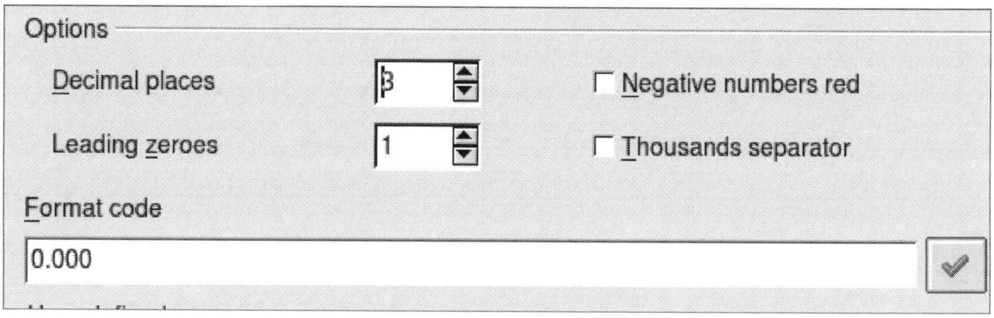

Figure 268: Option section of the Number Formating window

5) Change the Fuel Cost field.

    a) Right-click in the cell below *Cost per mile*.

    b) Select **Number Format**.

    c) In the Category list, select *Currency*.

    d) In the Option section:

       • Set the number of decimal places to 3.

       • Click the green checkmark.

    e) Click **OK**.

Step 4: Save and close the report.

Double-click the report. It should now look like Figure 269.

More ways to create reports

An extension is available to assist in report creation. *Sun Report Builder* creates stylish, complex database reports. You can define group and page headers, group and page footers, and calculation fields. It is available from http://extensions.services.openoffice.org/.

To install this extension, follow these steps:

1) Select **Tools > Extension Manager** from the menu bar. In the Extension Manager dialog, click **Get more extensions here...**.

2) The OOo extensions page opens in your browser window. Find and select the extension you want to install and follow the prompts to install it. During installation, you will be asked to accept a license agreement.

3) When the installation is complete, the extension is listed in the Extension Manager dialog.

For more about extensions, see Chapter 14 (Customizing OpenOffice.org).

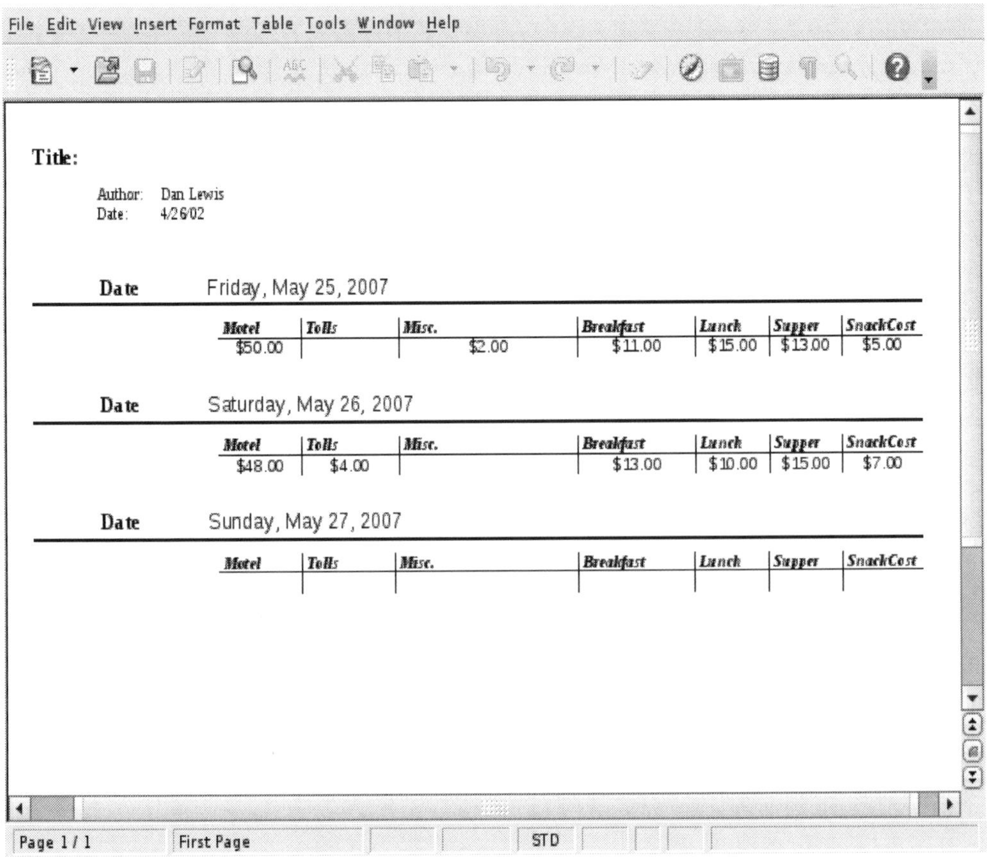

Title:

Author: Dan Lewis
Date: 4/26/02

Date	Friday, May 25, 2007						
	Motel	*Tolls*	*Misc.*	*Breakfast*	*Lunch*	*Supper*	*SnackCost*
	$50.00		$2.00	$11.00	$15.00	$13.00	$5.00

Date	Saturday, May 26, 2007						
	Motel	*Tolls*	*Misc.*	*Breakfast*	*Lunch*	*Supper*	*SnackCost*
	$48.00	$4.00		$13.00	$10.00	$15.00	$7.00

Date	Sunday, May 27, 2007						
	Motel	*Tolls*	*Misc.*	*Breakfast*	*Lunch*	*Supper*	*SnackCost*

Figure 269: Final report

Chapter *9*
Getting Started with Math

OpenOffice.org's equation editor

What is Math?

Math is OpenOffice.org (OOo)'s component for writing mathematical equations. It is most commonly used as an equation editor for text documents, but it can also be used with other types of documents or stand-alone. When used inside Writer, the equation is treated as an object inside the text document.

Note	The equation editor is for writing equations in symbolic form (as in equation 1). If you want to evaluate a numeric value, see the *Calc Guide*.

$$\frac{df(x)}{dx} = \ln(x) + \tan^{-1}(x^2) \tag{1}$$

Getting started

To insert an equation, go to **Insert > Object > Formula**.

The equation editor opens at the bottom of the screen, and the floating Selection window appears. You will also see a small box (with a gray border) in your document, where the formula will be displayed, as shown in Figure 270.

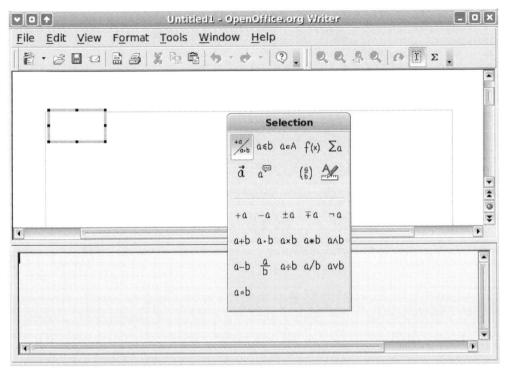

Figure 270. Equation Editor, Selection window, and location of resulting equation.

The equation editor uses a markup language to represent formulas. For example, *%beta* creates the Greek character beta (β). This markup is designed to read similar to English whenever possible. For example, *a over b* produces a fraction: $\frac{a}{b}$.

Entering a formula

There are three ways to enter a formula:

- Select a symbol from the Selection window.
- Right-click on the equation editor and select the symbol from the context menu.
- Type markup in the equation editor.

The context menu and the Selection window insert the markup corresponding to a symbol. Incidentally, this provides a convenient way to learn the OOoMath markup.

Note	Click on the document body to exit the formula editor. Double-click on a formula to enter the formula editor again.

The Selection window

The simplest method for entering a formula is the Selection window, shown in Figure 270.

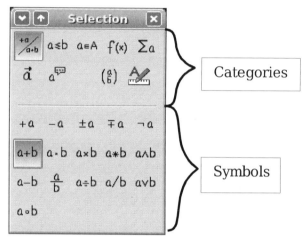

Figure 271. Symbols are divided into categories

The Selection window is divided into two main portions.

- The **top** shows the symbol categories. Click on these to change the list of symbols.

- The **bottom** shows the symbols available in the current category.

Tip	You can hide (or unhide) the Selection window with **View > Selection**.

Example 1: 5×4

For this example we will enter a simple formula: 5×4 On the Selection window:

1) Select the top-left button of the categories (top) section (Figure 272).

2) Click on the multiplication symbol (shown in Figure 272).

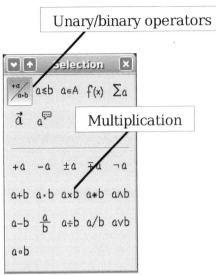

Figure 272. Unary/binary operators

When you select the multiplication symbol on the Selection window, two things happen:

- The equation editor shows the markup: *<?> times <?>*

- The body of the document shows a gray box with the figure: $\square \times \square$

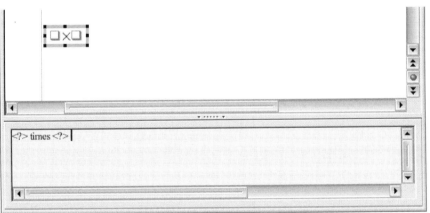

Figure 273. The multiplication symbol

The " *<?>* " symbols (Figure 273) are placeholders that you can replace by other text. The equation will update automatically, and the result should resemble Figure 274.

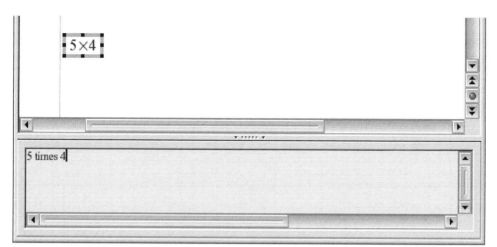

Figure 274. Result of entering "5" and "4" next to the "times" operator

Tip	To keep the equation from updating automatically, select **View >AutoUpdate display**.
	To update a formula manually, press *F9* or select **View > Update**.

Right-click menu

Another way to access mathematical symbols is to right-click on the equation editor. This produces a menu as shown in Figure 275.

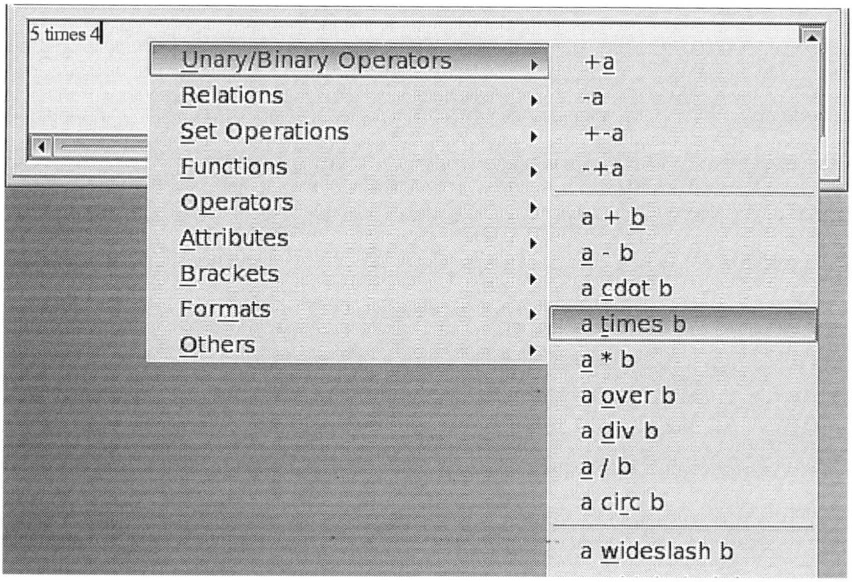

Figure 275. Right-click menu

Note	The entries in this menu correspond exactly to those in the Selection window.

Markup

You can type the markup directly on the equation editor. For example, you can type "5 times 4" to obtain 5×4. If you know the markup, this can be the fastest way to enter a formula.

Tip	As a mnemonic, the formula markup resembles the way the formula reads in English.

Below is a short list of common equations and their corresponding markup.

Display	Command	Display	Command
$a = b$	a = b	$\sqrt{a}$	sqrt {a}
a^2	a^2	a_n	a_n
$\int f(x)\,dx$	int f(x) dx	$\sum a_n$	sum a_n
$a \leq b$	a <= b	∞	infinity
$a \times b$	a times b	$x \cdot y$	x cdot y

Greek characters

Greek characters ($\alpha, \beta, \gamma, \theta$, etc) are common in mathematical formulas. *These characters are not available in the selection box or the right-click menu.* Fortunately, the markup for Greek characters is simple: Type a % sign followed the name of the character, in English.

- To type a *lowercase* character, write the name of the character in lowercase.

- To type an *uppercase* character, write the name of the character in uppercase.

See the table below for some examples.

Note	A complete table of Greek characters is included in Chapter 16 (Math Objects) in the *Writer Guide*.

Lowercase		Uppercase	
%alpha	$\rightarrow$ α	%ALPHA	$\rightarrow$ A
%beta	$\rightarrow$ β	%BETA	$\rightarrow$ B
%gamma	$\rightarrow$ γ	%GAMMA	$\rightarrow$ Γ
%psi	$\rightarrow$ ψ	%PSI	$\rightarrow$ Ψ
%phi	$\rightarrow$ ϕ	%PHI	$\rightarrow$ Φ
%theta	$\rightarrow$ θ	%THETA	$\rightarrow$ Θ

Another way to enter Greek characters is by using the catalog window. Go to **Tools > Catalog**. The catalog window is shown in Figure 276. Under "Symbol Set" select "Greek" and double-click on a Greek letter from the list.

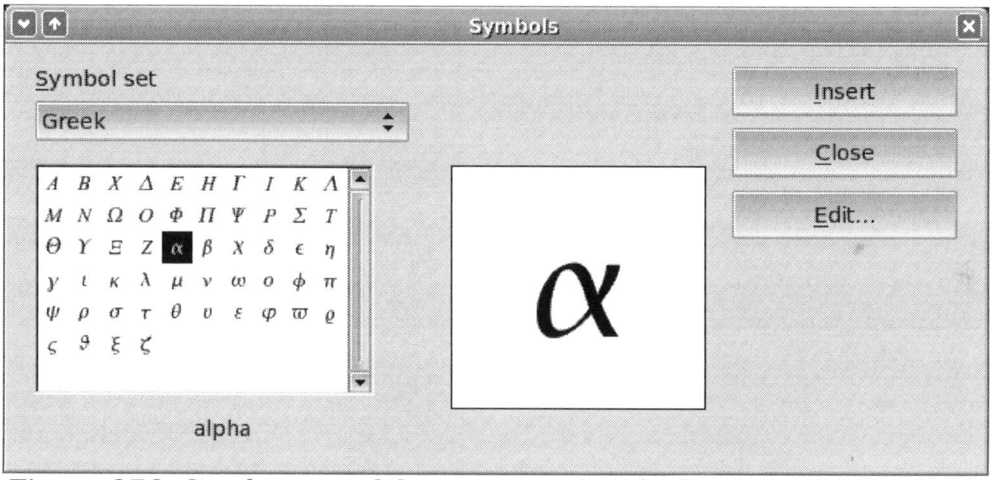

Figure 276. Catalog - used for entering Greek characters

Example 2: $\pi \simeq 3.14159$

For this example we will suppose that:

- We want to enter the above formula (the value of pi rounded to 5 decimal places).

- We know the name of the Greek character ("pi").

- But we do not know the markup associated with the $\simeq$ symbol.

Step 1: Type "%" followed by the text "pi". This displays the Greek character π .

Step 2: Open the Selection window (**View > Selection**).

Step 3: The $\simeq$ symbol is a relation, so we click on the relations button $a{\leq}b$. If you hover the mouse over this button you see the tooltip "Relations" (Figure 277).

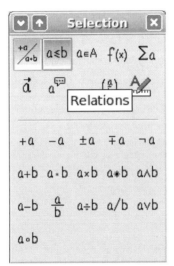

Figure 277. Tooltip indicates the "Relations" button.

Step 4: Delete the <?> text and add "3.14159" at the end of the equation. Hence we end up with the markup " %pi simeq 3.14159 ". The result is shown in Figure 278.

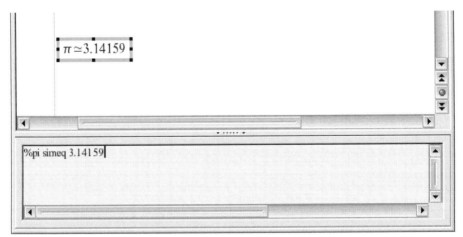

Figure 278. Final result

Customizations

Formula editor as a floating window

As seen in Figure 271, the formula editor can cover a large part of the Writer window. To turn the formula editor into a floating window, do this:

1) Hover the mouse over the editor frame, as shown in Figure 279.
2) Hold down the *Control* key and double-click.

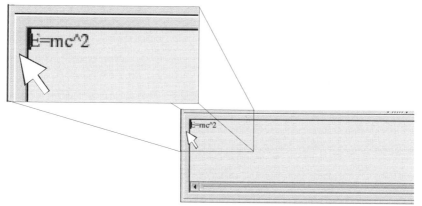

Figure 279. Hold down the Control key and double-click on the border of the math editor to turn it into a floating window.

Figure 280 shows the result. You can make the floating window back into an embedded frame, using the same steps. Hold down the *Control* key and double-click the window frame.

Figure 280. Equation editor as a floating window

How can I make a formula bigger?

This is one of the most common questions people ask about OOoMath. The answer is simple, but not intuitive:

1) Start the formula editor and go to **Format > Font size**.

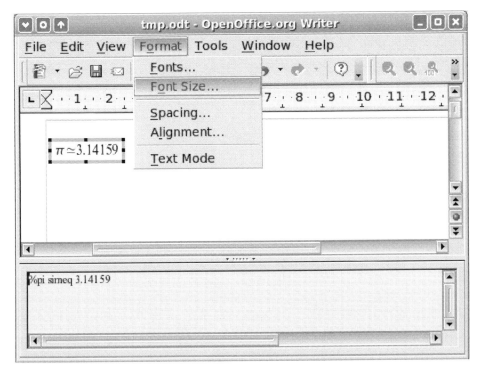

Figure 281. Changing the font size for a formula

2) Select a larger font size under "Base Size" (top-most entry), as shown in Figure 281.

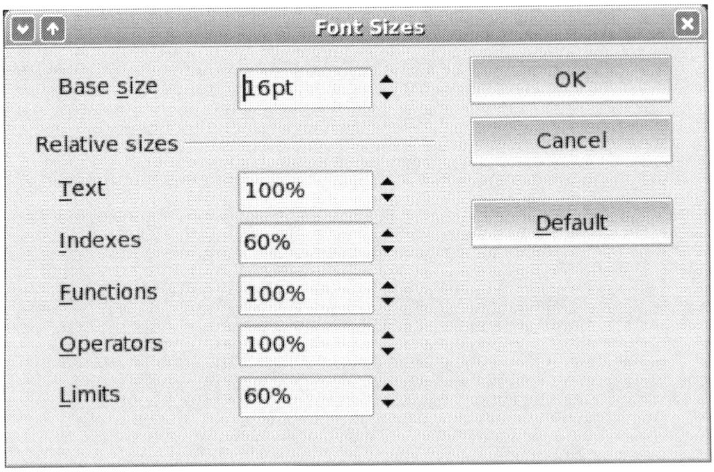

Figure 282. Edit "Base size" (top) to make a formula bigger.

The result of this change is illustrated in Figure 282.

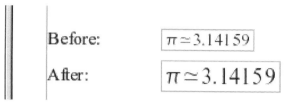

Figure 283. Result of changing the base font size.

Formula layout

The most difficult part of using OOoMath comes when writing complicated equations. This section provides some advice about writing complex formulas.

Brackets are your friends

OOoMath knows nothing about order of operation. You must use brackets to state the order of operations explicitly. Consider the following example:

Markup	Result
2 over x + 1	$\frac{2}{x}+1$
2 over {x + 1}	$\frac{2}{x+1}$

Equations over more than one line

Suppose you want to type an equation covering more than one line.

For example: $\begin{aligned} x &= 3 \\ y &= 1 \end{aligned}$

Your first reaction would be to simply press the *Enter* key. However, if you press the *Enter* key, though the markup goes to a new line, the resulting equation does not. You must type the newline command explicitly. This is illustrated in the table below.

Markup	Result
x = 3 y = 1	$x = 3 \ y = 1$
x = 3 newline y = 1	$x = 3$ $y = 1$

Common problem areas

How do I add limits to my sum/integral?

The "sum" and "int" commands can (optionally) take in the parameters "from" and "to". These are used for lower and upper limits respectively. These parameters can be used singly or together. Limits for integrals are usually treated as subscripts and superscripts.

Markup	Result
sum from k = 1 to n a_k	$\displaystyle\sum_{k=1}^{n} a_k$
int from 0 to x f(t) dt or int_0^x f(t) dt	$\displaystyle\int_0^x f(t)\,dt$ or $\displaystyle\int_0^x f(t)\,dt$
int from Re f	$\displaystyle\int_{\Re} f$
sum to infinity 2^{-n}	$\displaystyle\sum^{\infty} 2^{-n}$

Note   For more details on integrals and sums, see Chapter 16 (Math Objects) in the *Writer Guide*.

Brackets with matrices look ugly!

For background, we start with an overview of the matrix command:

Markup	Result
`matrix { a # b ## c # d }`	$\begin{matrix} a & b \\ c & d \end{matrix}$

Note Rows are separated by two #'s and entries within each row are separated by one #.

The first problem people have with matrices is that brackets do not "scale" with the matrix.

Markup	Result
`(  matrix { a # b ## c # d }  )`	$(\begin{smallmatrix} a & b \\ c & d \end{smallmatrix})$

OOoMath provides "scalable" brackets. That is, the brackets grow in size to match the size of their contents. Use the commands *left(* and *right)* to make scalable brackets.

Markup	Result
`left(  matrix { a # b ## c # d }  right)`	

Tip Use *left[* and *right]* to obtain square brackets.

How do I make a derivative?

Making derivatives essentially comes down to one trick: *Tell OOo it's a fraction.*

In other words, you have to use the "over" command. Combine this with either the letter "d" (for a total derivative) or the "partial" command (for a partial derivative) to achieve the effect of a derivative.

Markup	Result
{df} over {dx}	$\dfrac{df}{dx}$
{partial f} over {partial y}	$\dfrac{\partial f}{\partial y}$
{partial^2 f} over {partial t^2}	$\dfrac{\partial^2 f}{\partial t^2}$

Note Notice that we had to use squiggly brackets to make the derivative.

Numbering equations

Equation numbering is one of OOoMath's best hidden features. The steps are simple, but obscure:

1) Start a new line.
2) Type "fn" and then press *F3*.

The "fn" is replaced by a numbered formula:

$$E = mc^2 \tag{2}$$

Now you can double-click on the formula to edit it. For example, here is the Riemann Zeta function:

$$\zeta(z) = \sum_{n=1}^{\infty} \frac{1}{n^z} \tag{3}$$

You can reference an equation ("as shown in Equation (2)") with these steps:

1) **Insert > Cross-reference**..
2) Click on the *References* tab (Figure 283).
3) Under *Type*, select *Text*.
4) Under *Selection*, pick the equation number.
5) Under *Format*, choose *Reference*.
6) Click **Insert**.

Done! If you later add more equations to the paper before the referenced equation, all the equations will automatically renumber and the cross-references will update.

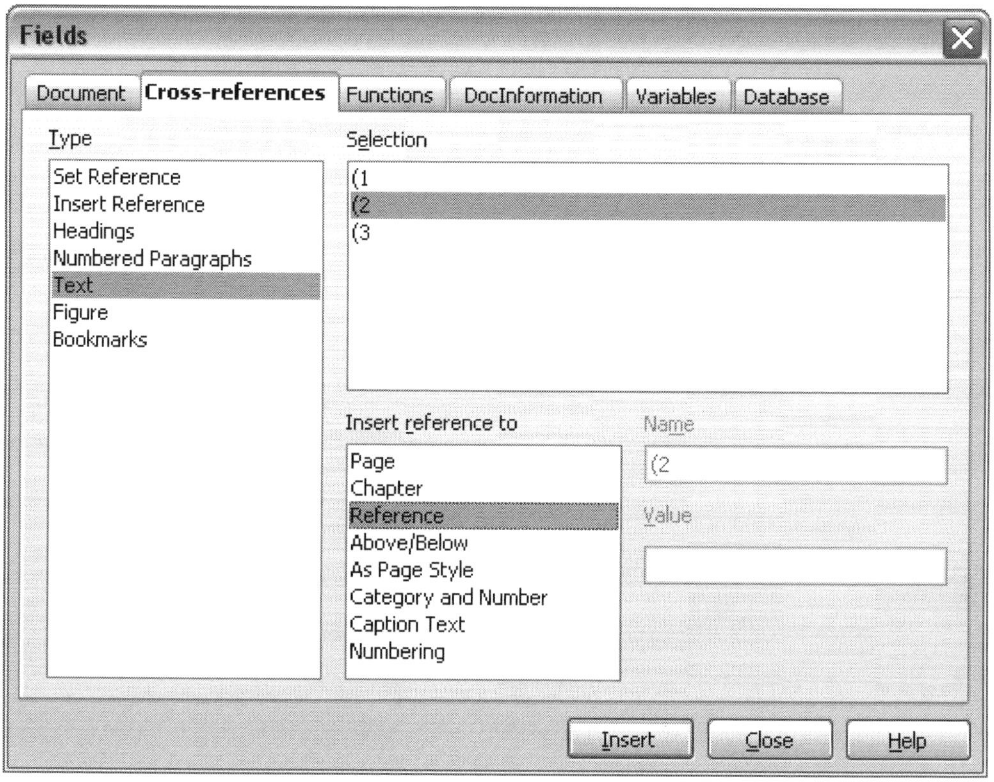

Figure 284. Inserting a cross-reference to an equation number

Tip	To insert the equation number without parenthesis around it, choose *Numbering* instead of *Reference* under *Format*.

Chapter *10*
Printing, Exporting, and E-mailing

This chapter provides general information about printing, exporting, and e-mailing documents from OOo.

Quick printing

Click the **Print File Directly** icon to send the entire document to the default printer defined for your computer.

Note	You can change the action of the **Print File Directly** icon to send the document to the printer defined for the document instead of the default printer for the computer. Go to **Tools > Options > Load/Save > General** and select the **Load printer settings with the document** option.

Controlling printing

For more control over printing, use **File > Print** to display the Print dialog.

On the Print dialog, you can choose:

- Which printer to use (if more than one are installed on your system) and the properties of the printer—for example, orientation (portrait or landscape), which paper tray to use, and what paper size to print on. The properties available depend on the selected printer; consult the printer's documentation for details.

- What pages to print, how many copies to print, and in what order to print them. Use dashes to specify page ranges and commas or semicolons to separate ranges; for example: 1, 5, 11–14, 34–40. *Selection* is the highlighted part of a page or pages.

- What items to print. Click the **Options** button to display the Printer Options dialog.

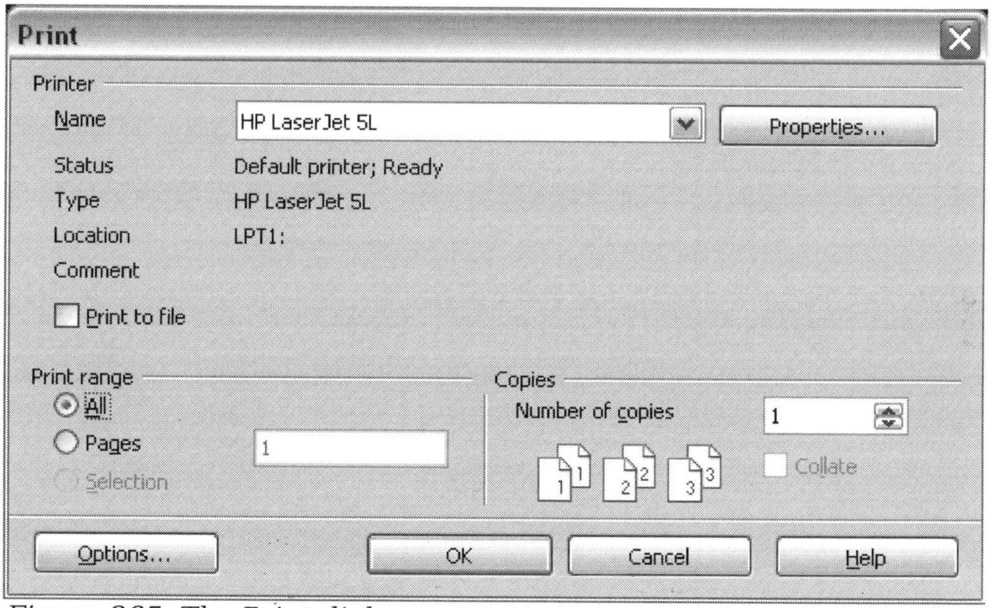

Figure 285. The Print dialog

Selections on the Printer Options dialog are different in Writer, Calc, Impress, and Draw, but in all cases they apply to this printing of this document only. For details, see the chapters on the various OOo components.

To specify default printing options, see Chapter 2 (Setting up OpenOffice.org) and the chapters on the various OOo components.

Exporting to PDF

OpenOffice.org can export documents to PDF (Portable Document Format). This industry-standard file format is ideal for sending the file to someone else to view using Adobe Reader or other PDF viewers.

The process and dialogs are the same for Writer, Calc, Impress, and Draw, with a few minor differences mentioned in this section.

Quick export to PDF

Click the **Export Directly as PDF** icon ▣ to export the entire document using your default PDF settings. You are asked to enter the file name and location for the PDF file, but you do not get a chance to choose a page range, the image compression, or other options.

Controlling PDF content and quality

For more control over the content and quality of the resulting PDF, use **File > Export as PDF**. The PDF Options dialog opens. This dialog has five pages (General, Initial View, User Interface, Links, and Security). Make your selections, and then click **Export**. Then you are asked to enter the location and file name of the PDF to be created, and click **Save** to export the file.

General page of PDF Options dialog

On the *General* page, you can choose which pages to include in the PDF, the type of compression to use for images (which affects the quality of images in the PDF), and other options.

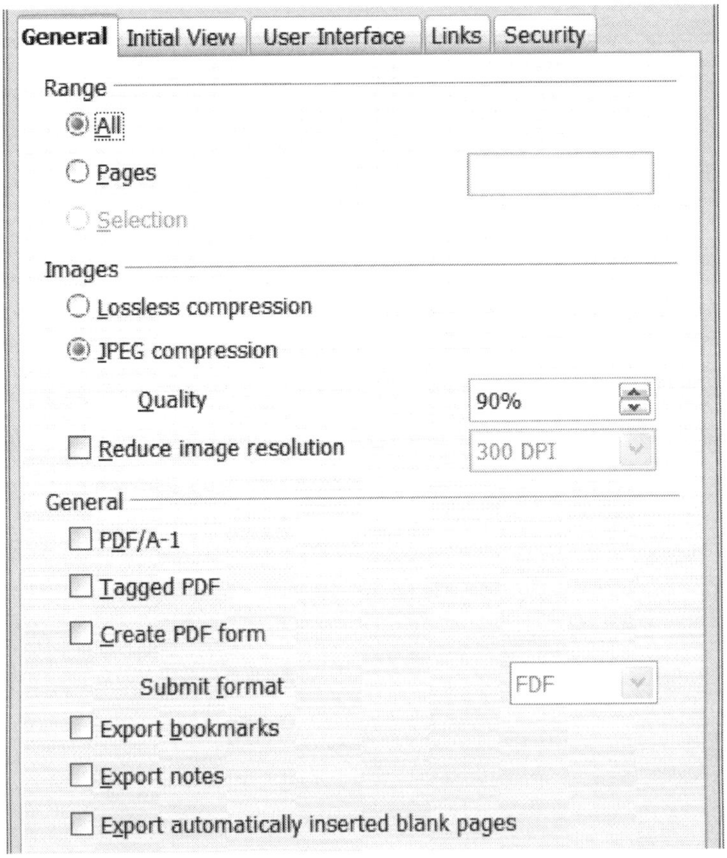

Figure 286: General page of PDF Options dialog

Range section

- **All**: Exports the entire document.

- **Pages**: To export a range of pages, use the format **3-6** (pages 3 to 6). To export single pages, use the format **7;9;11** (pages 7, 9, and 11). You can also export a combination of page ranges and single pages, by using a format like **3-6;8;10;12**.

- **Selection**: Exports whatever material is selected.

Images section

- **Lossless compression**: Images are stored without any loss of quality. Tends to make large files when used with photographs. Recommended for other images.

- **JPEG compression**: Allows for varying degrees of quality. A setting of 90% tends to work well with photographs (small file size, little perceptible loss of quality).

- **Reduce image resolution**: Lower-DPI (dots per inch) images have lower quality.

Note	EPS images with embedded previews are exported only as previews. EPS images without embedded previews are exported as empty placeholders.

General section

- **PDF/A-1**: PDF/A is an ISO standard established in 2005 for long-term preservation of documents, by embedding all the pieces necessary for faithful reproduction (such as fonts) while forbidding other elements (including forms, security, encryption, and tagged PDF). If you select PDF/A-1, the forbidden elements are greyed-out (not available).

- **Tagged PDF**: Exports special tags into the corresponding PDF tags. Some tags that are exported are table of contents, hyperlinks, and controls. This option can increase file sizes significantly.

- **Export bookmarks:** Exports headings in Writer documents, and page names in Impress and Draw documents, as "bookmarks" (a table of contents list displayed by some PDF readers, including Adobe Reader).

- **Export notes**: Exports notes in Writer and Calc documents as PDF notes. You may not want this!

- **Create PDF form - Submit format:** Choose the format of submitting forms from within the PDF file. This setting overrides the control's URL property that you set in the document. There is only one common setting valid for the whole PDF document: PDF (sends the whole document), FDF (sends the control contents), HTML, and XML. Most often you will choose the PDF format.

- **Export automatically inserted blank pages**: If selected, automatically inserted blank pages are exported to the PDF. This is best if you are printing the PDF double-sided. For example, books usually have chapters set to always start on an odd-numbered (right-hand) page. When the previous chapter ends on an odd page, OOo inserts a blank page between the two odd pages. This option controls whether to export that blank page.

Initial View page of PDF Options dialog

On the *Initial View* page, you can choose how the PDF opens by default in a PDF viewer. The selections should be self-explanatory.

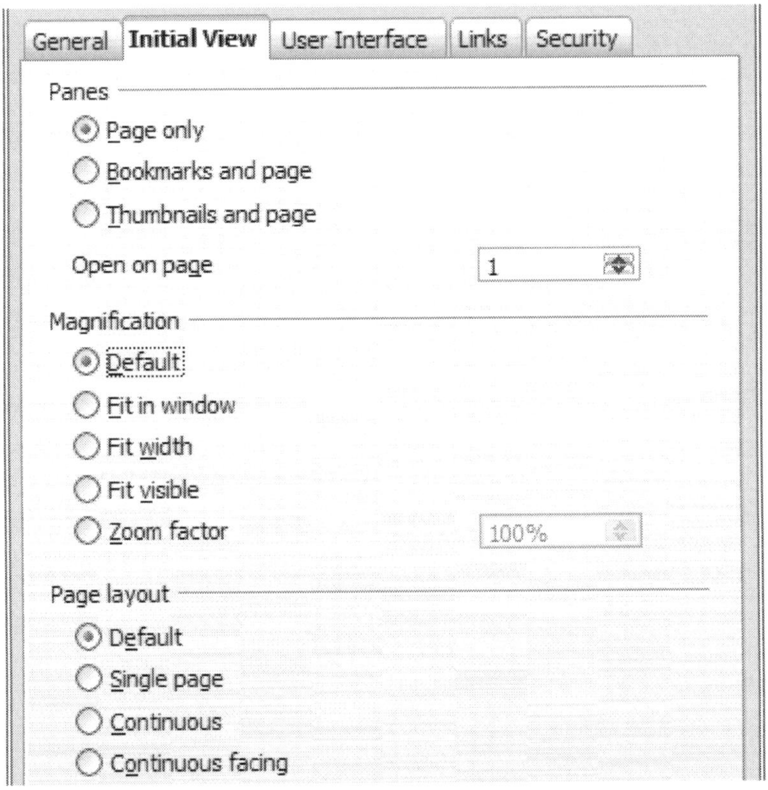

Figure 287: Initial View page of PDF Options dialog

User Interface page of PDF Options dialog

On the *User Interface* page, you can choose more settings to control how a PDF viewer displays the file. Some of these choices are particularly useful when you are creating a PDF to be used as a presentation or a kiosk-type display.

Window options section

- **Resize window to initial page.** Causes the PDF viewer window to resize to fit the first page of the PDF.

- **Center window on screen.** Causes the PDF viewer window to be centered on the computer screen.

- **Open in full screen mode.** Causes the PDF viewer to open full-screen instead of in a smaller window.

- **Display document title.** Causes the PDF viewer to display the document's title in the title bar.

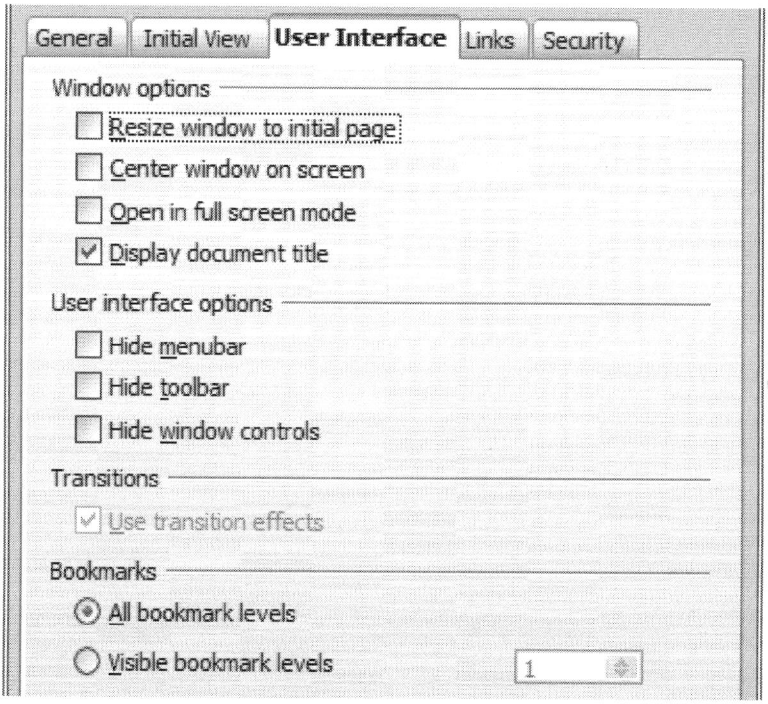

Figure 288: User Interface page of PDF Options dialog

User interface options section

- **Hide menubar.** Causes the PDF viewer to hide the menu bar.

- **Hide toolbar.** Causes the PDF viewer to hide the toolbar.

- **Hide window controls.** Causes the PDF viewer to hide other window controls.

Transitions

In Impress, displays slide transition effects as their respective PDF effects.

Bookmarks

Select how many heading levels are displayed as bookmarks, if *Export bookmarks* is selected on the General page.

Links page of PDF Options dialog

On this page you can choose how links are exported to PDF.

Export bookmarks as named destinations

If you have defined Writer bookmarks, Impress or Draw slide names, or Calc sheet names, this option exports them as "named destinations" to which Web pages and PDF documents can link.

Convert document references to PDF targets

If you have defined links to other documents with OpenDocument extensions (such as .ODT, .ODS, and .ODP), this option converts the files names to .PDF in the exported PDF document.

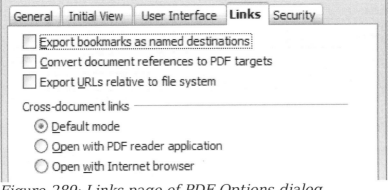

Figure 289: Links page of PDF Options dialog

Export URLs relative to file system

If you have defined relative links in a document, this option exports those links to the PDF.

Cross-document links

Defines the behavior of links clicked in PDF files.

Security page of PDF Options dialog

PDF export includes options to encrypt the PDF (so it cannot be opened without a password) and apply some digital rights management (DRM) features.

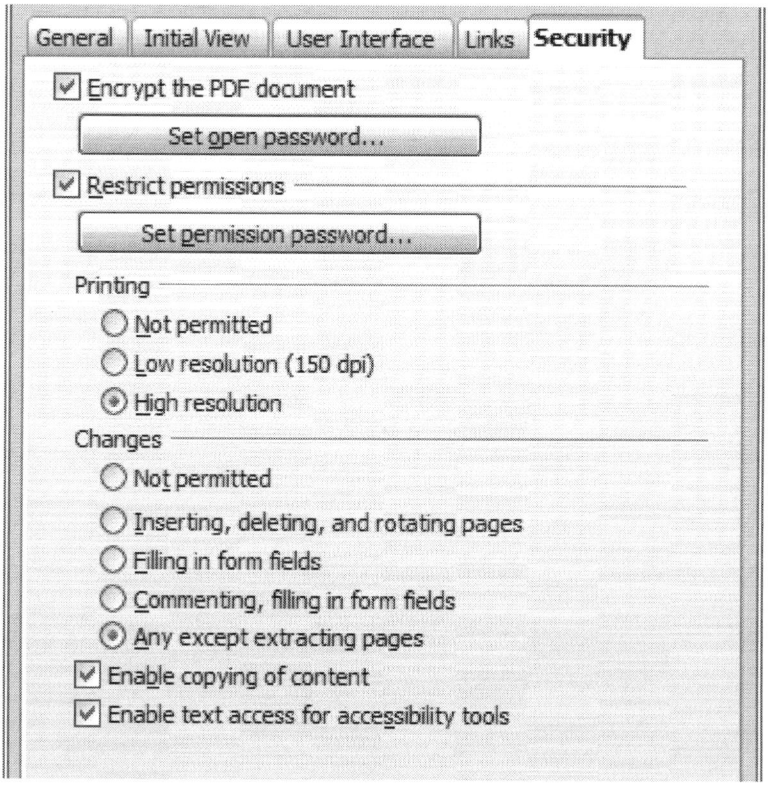

Figure 290: Security page of PDF Options dialog

- With an *open password* set, the PDF can only be opened with the password. Once opened, there are no restrictions on what the user can do with the document (for example, print, copy, or change it).

- With a *permissions password set*, the PDF can be opened by anyone, but its permissions can be restricted. See Figure 290.

- With *both* the *open password* and *permission password* set, the PDF can only be opened with the correct password, and its permissions can be restricted.

Note   Permissions settings are effective only if the user's PDF viewer respects the settings.

Figure 291 shows the pop-up dialog displayed when you click the **Set open password** button on the Security page of the PDF Options dialog.

After you set a password for permissions, the other choices on the Security page (shown in Figure 290) become available. These selections should be self-explanatory.

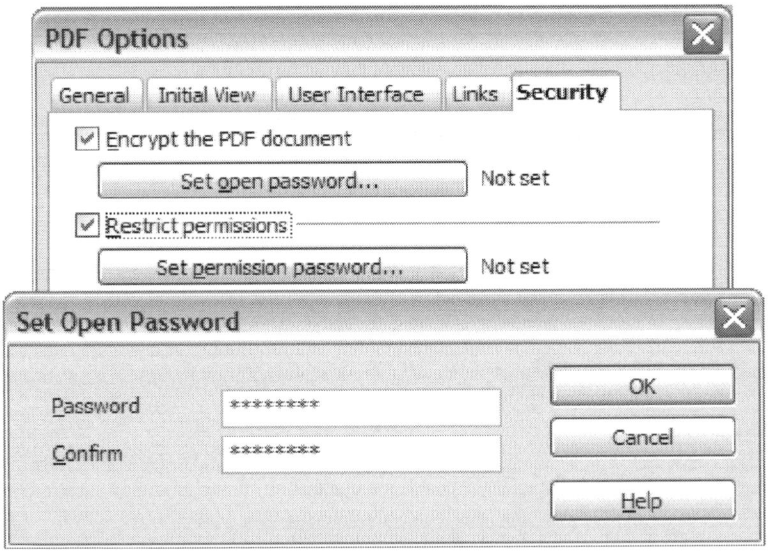

Figure 291: Setting a password to encrypt a PDF

Exporting to other formats

OOo uses the term "export" for some file operations involving a change of file type. If you cannot find what you want under **Save As**, look under **Export** as well.

OpenOffice.org can export files to XHTML. In addition, OOo Writer can export to BibTeX (.bib), LaTeX 2e (.tex) and MediaWiki (.txt). OOo Draw and OOo Impress can export to Macromedia Flash (.swf).

To export to one of these formats, choose **File > Export**. On the Export dialog, specify a file name for the exported document, then select the required format in the *File format* list and click the **Export** button.

E-mailing documents

OOo provides several ways to quickly and easily send documents as an e-mail attachment in one of three formats: OpenDocument (OOo's default format), Microsoft Office formats, or PDF.

To send the current document in OpenDocument format:

1) Choose **File > Send > Document as E-mail**. OpenOffice.org opens the e-mail program specified in **Tools > Options > Internet > E-mail**. The document is attached.

2) In your e-mail program, enter the recipient, subject and any text you want to add, then send the e-mail.

File > Send > E-mail as OpenDocument Text (or Spreadsheet or Presentation) has the same effect.

If you choose **E-mail as Microsoft [Word**, **Excel**, or **Powerpoint]**, OOo first creates a file in one of those formats and then opens your e-mail program with the file attached.

Similarly, if you choose **E-mail as PDF**, OOo first creates a PDF using your default PDF settings (as when using the **Export Directly as PDF** toolbar button) and then opens your email program with the .PDF file attached.

E-mailing a document to several recipients

To e-mail a document to several recipients, you can use the features in your e-mail program or you can use OOo's mail merge facilities to extract email addresses from an address book.

You can use OOo's mail merge to send e-mail in two ways:

- Use the Mail Merge Wizard to create the document and send it. See Chapter 11 (Using Mail Merge) of the *Writer Guide* for details.

- Create the document in Writer without using the Wizard, then use the Wizard to send it. This method is described here.

To use the Mail Merge Wizard to send a previously-created Writer document:

1) Click **Tools > Mail Merge Wizard**. On the first page of the wizard (Figure 292), select **Use the current document** and click **Next**.

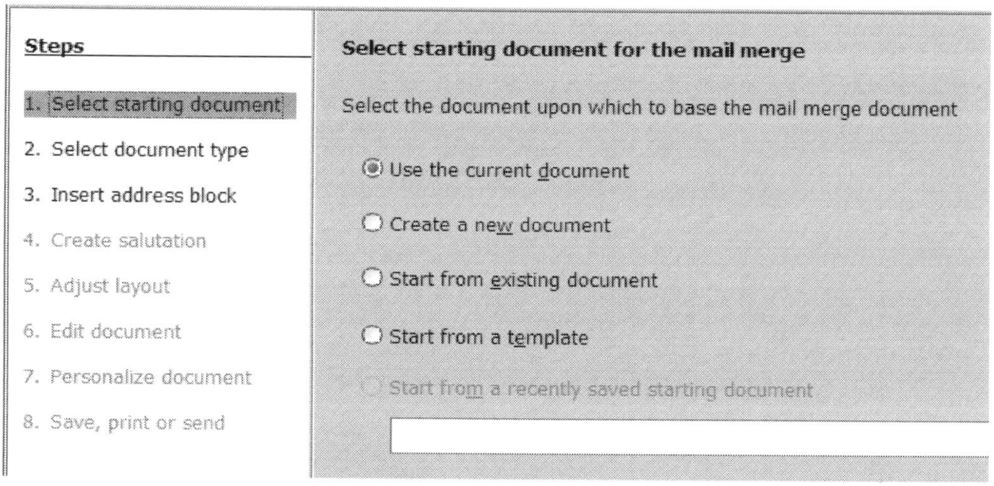

Figure 292: Select starting document

---

2) On the second page (Figure 293), select **E-mail message** and click **Next**.

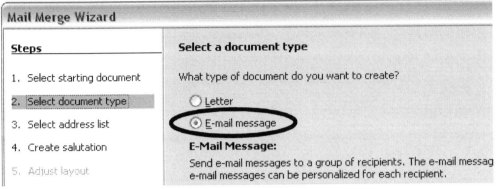

Figure 293: Select document type

3) On the third page (Figure 294), click the **Select Address List** button. Select the required address list (even if only one is shown) and then click **OK**. (If the address list you need is not shown here, you can click **Add** to find it and add it to the list.)

4) Back on the Select address list page, click **Next**. On the Create salutation page (Figure 295), deselect **This document should contain a salutation**.

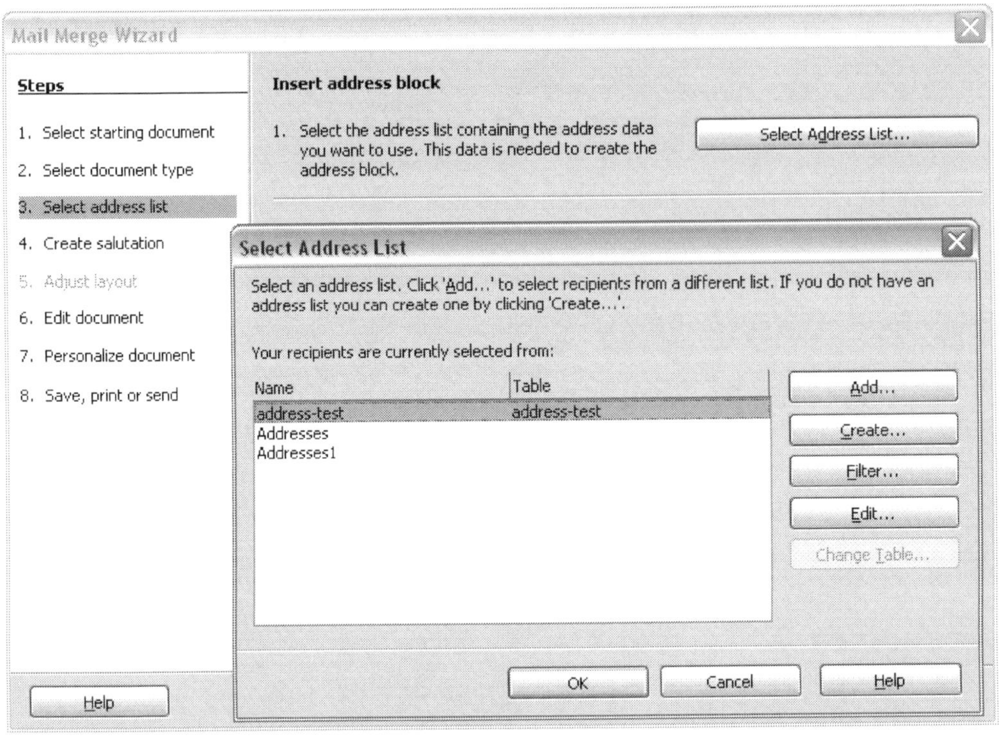

Figure 294: Selecting an address list

5) In the left-hand list, click **8. Save, print or send**. OOo displays a "Creating documents" message and then displays the *Save, print or send* page of the Wizard.

6) Select **Send merged document as E-Mail**. The lower part of the page changes to show e-mail settings choices (see Figure 296).

7) Type a subject for your email and click **Send documents**. OOo sends the e-mails.

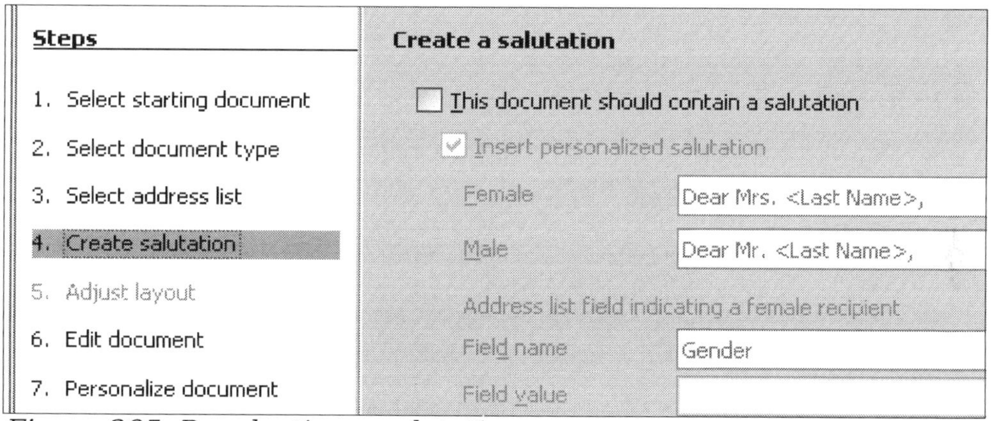

Figure 295: Deselecting a salutation

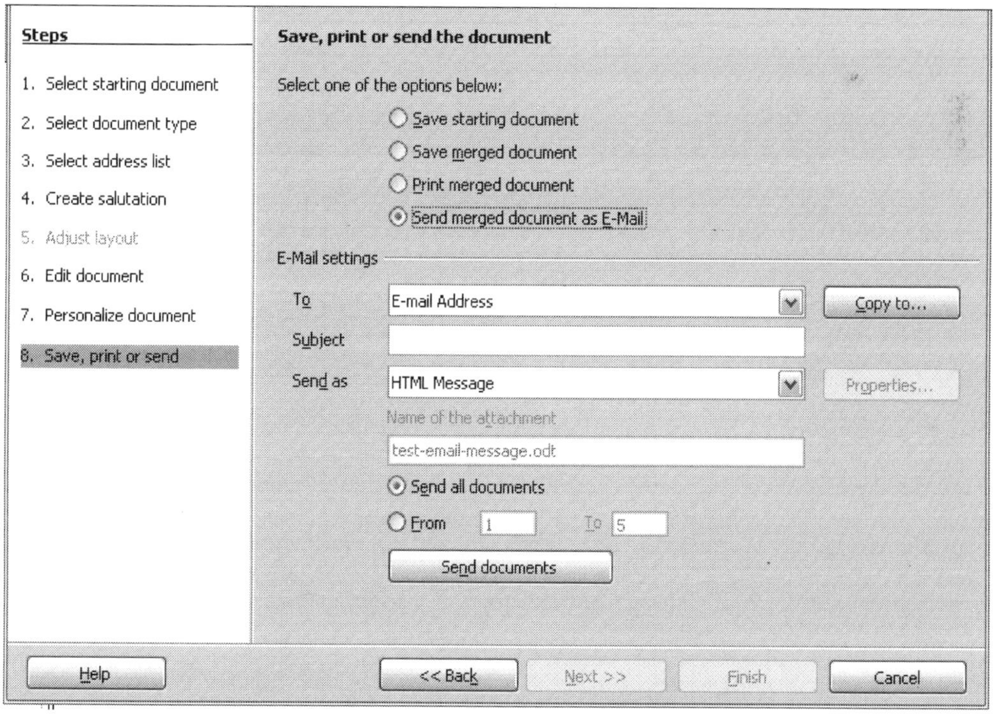

Figure 296: Sending a document as an email message

Digital signing of documents

To sign a document digitally, you need a personal key, the certificate. A personal key is stored on your computer as a combination of a private key, which must be kept secret, and a public key, which you add to your documents when you sign them. You can get a certificate from a certification authority, which may be a private company or a governmental institution.

When you apply a digital signature to a document, a kind of checksum is computed from the document's content plus your personal key. The checksum and your public key are stored together with the document.

When someone later opens the document on any computer with a recent version of OpenOffice.org, the program will compute the checksum again and compare it with the stored checksum. If both are the same, the program will signal that you see the original, unchanged document. In addition, the program can show you the public key information from the certificate. You can compare the public key with the public key that is published on the web site of the certificate authority.

Whenever someone changes something in the document, this change breaks the digital signature.

On Windows operating systems, the Windows features of validating a signature are used. On Solaris and Linux systems, files that are supplied by Thunderbird, Mozilla or Firefox are used. For a more detailed description of how to get and manage a certificate, and signature validation, see "Using Digital Signatures" in the OOo Help.

To sign a document:

1) Choose **File > Digital Signatures**.
2) If you have not saved the document since the last change, a message box appears. Click **Yes** to save the file.
3) After saving, you see the Digital Signatures dialog. Click **Add** to add a public key to the document.
4) In the Select Certificate dialog, select your certificate and click **OK**.
5) You see again the Digital Signatures dialog, where you can add more certificates if you want. Click **OK** to add the public key to the saved file.

A signed document shows an icon 🔏 in the status bar. You can double-click the icon to view the certificate.

Chapter *11*
Graphics, the Gallery, and Fontwork

You can add graphic and image files, including photos, drawings, scanned images, and others, to OpenOffice.org documents. OOo can import various vector (line drawing) and raster (bitmap) file formats. The most commonly used graphic formats are GIF, JPG, PNG, and BMP.

Inserting an image from a file

To insert an image from a file, the file must be already stored in a directory (folder) on the computer.

1) Determine the destination for the image. Place the cursor at or near the appropriate location in the document.

2) On the main menu, select **Insert > Picture > From File**. This displays the dialog shown in Figure 297.

3) Navigate to the file to be inserted, select it, and click **Open**.

Note	At the bottom of the Insert picture dialog are two checkboxes. If **Preview** is checked, the selected graphic file is previewed in a pane, as shown in Figure 297, so you can verify that you have the correct file. The **Link** option is discussed below.

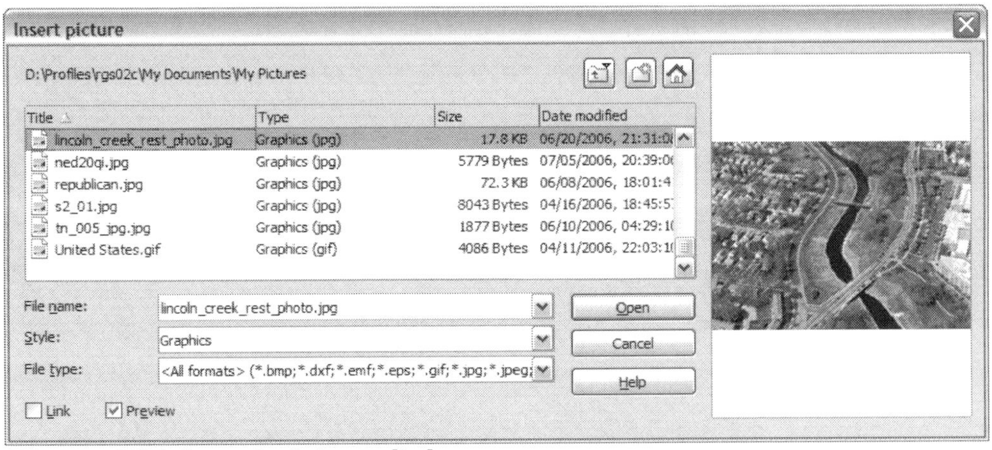

Figure 297. Insert picture dialog

Linking an image file

If the **Link** option in the Insert picture dialog is selected, OOo creates a link to the file containing the image, instead of saving a copy of the image in the document. The result is that the image is displayed in the document, but when the document is saved, it contains only a reference to the image file—not the image itself. The document and the image remain as two separate files, and they are merged together only when you open the document again.

Linking an image has two advantages and one disadvantage:

- Advantage – Linking can reduce the size of the document when it is saved, because the image file itself is not included. File size is usually not a problem on a modern computer with a reasonable amount of memory, unless the document includes many large graphics files; OOo can handle quite large files.

- Advantage – You can modify the image file separately without changing the document because the link to the file remains valid, and the modified image will appear when you next open the document. This can be a big advantage if you (or someone else, perhaps a graphic artist) is updating images.

- Disadvantage – If you send the document to someone else, or move it to a different computer, you must also send the image files, or the receiver will not be able to see the linked images. You need to keep track of the location of the images and make sure the recipient knows where to put them on another machine, so the document can find them. For example, you might keep images in a subfolder named Images (under the folder containing the document); the recipient of the file needs to put the images in a subfolder with the same name (under the folder containing the document).

Note	When inserting the same image several times in the document it would appear beneficial to create links; however, this is not necessary as OOo embeds in the document only one copy of the image file.

Embedding linked images

If you originally linked the images, you can easily embed one or more of them later if you wish. To do so:

1) Open the document in OpenOffice.org and choose **Edit > Links**.
2) The Edit Links dialog (Figure 298) shows all the linked files. In the *Source file* list, select the files you want to change from linked to embedded.
3) Click the **Break Link** button.
4) Save the document.

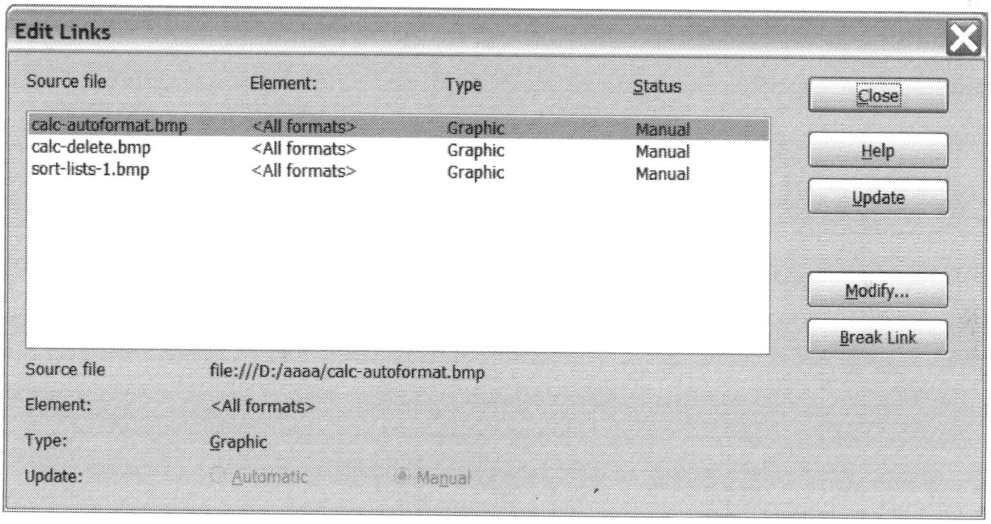

Figure 298: The Edit Links dialog

Note	Going the other way, from embedded to linked, is not so easy—you must delete and reinsert each image, one at a time, selecting the **Link** option when you do so.

Inserting images from a graphics program

You can use many different graphics programs to edit a graphic file. From these programs, you can select, copy, and paste an image or part of a graphic into an OpenOffice.org document. Figure 299 shows an example of this procedure.

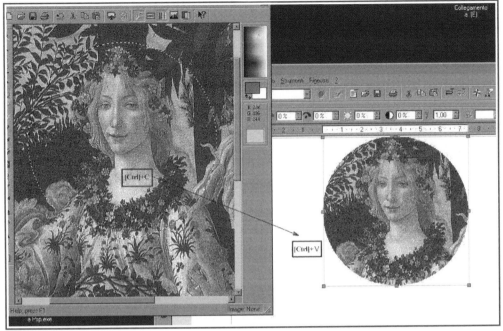

Figure 299. Inserting an image from a graphics program

1) In the graphics program window, select an area of the image to be copied.
2) Move the cursor over the selected area and press *Control+C* to copy.
3) Switch to the OpenOffice.org window.
4) Click to place the cursor where the graphic is to be inserted.
5) Press *Control+V* to paste the image.

Inserting images using a scanner

If a scanner is connected to your computer, OOo can call the scanning application and inserted the scanned item into the OOo document page as an image. To start this procedure, place the cursor where the graphic is to be inserted and select **Insert > Picture > Scan > Select Source**.

Although this practice is quick and easy, it is unlikely to result in a high-quality image of the correct size. You may get better results by scanned material into a graphics program and cleaning it up there before inserting the resulting image into OOo.

Modifying and positioning graphics

OpenOffice.org provides many tools for resizing, modifying, filtering, and positioning graphics; wrapping text around graphics; and using graphics as backgrounds and watermarks. These tools are described in relevant chapters of the other guides. Some sophisticated adjustments of the graphics are best done in an image manipulation program and the results brought into OOo, rather than using OOo's inbuilt tools.

Using the OpenOffice.org Gallery

The **Gallery** contains objects (graphics and sounds) that you can insert into your documents. The Gallery is available in all components of OpenOffice.org.

To open the Gallery, choose **Tools > Gallery**, or click the Gallery icon
. If the Gallery is open, these choices close it.

Graphics in the Gallery are grouped by themes, such as Bullets, Rulers, and Backgrounds. You can create other groups or themes. The box on the left of the gallery window lists the available themes. Click on a theme to see its graphics displayed in the Gallery window.

Figures 300 and 301 show two views of one of the themes supplied with OpenOffice.org.

You have the option of *Icon View* or *Detailed View* for the Gallery, and you can hide or show the Gallery by clicking on the *Hide* button.

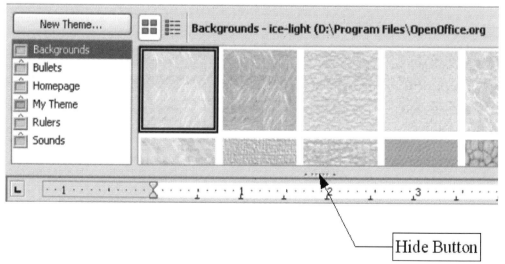

Figure 300. Icon view of one theme in the Gallery

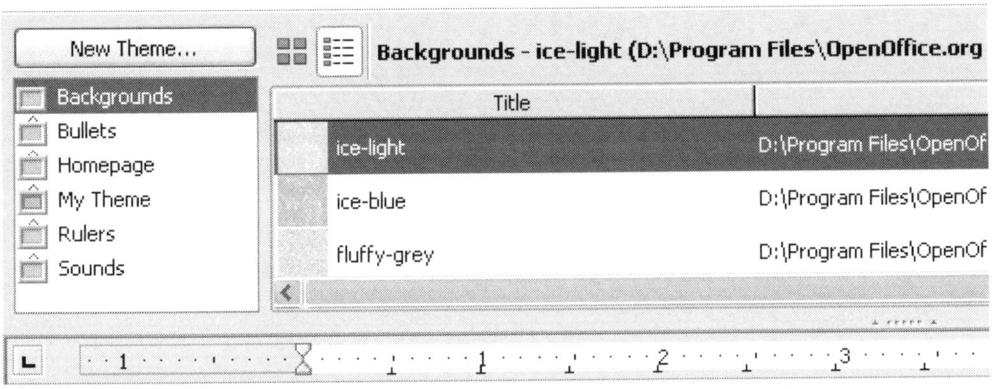

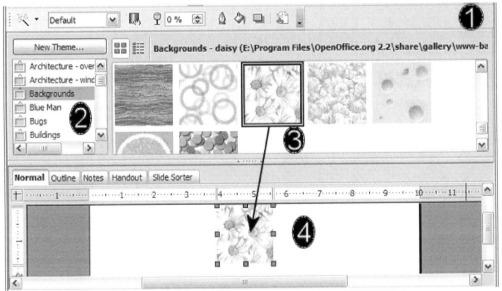

Figure 301. Detailed view of the same theme in the Gallery

Inserting images into a document

You can copy or link an object from the Gallery into a document.

To insert an object:

1) Choose **Tools > Gallery** and select a theme.

2) Select an object with a single click, then drag and drop the image into the document. (See Figure 302.)

   You can also right-click on the object and select **Insert > Copy**.

Figure 302. Copying a graphic object from the Gallery into a document

Inserting objects as links

To insert an object as a link:

1) Choose **Tools > Gallery** and select a theme.
2) Select an object with a single click, then while pressing the *Shift* and *Ctrl* keys, drag and drop the object into the document.

Inserting an object as a background

To insert an object as the background to a page or paragraph:

1) Choose **Tools > Gallery** and select a theme.
2) Select an object with a single click, right-click on the object and choose **Insert > Background > Page or Paragraph**.

Managing the Gallery

The default themes are locked; no items can be added or deleted from these themes. The locked themes are easily recognizable by right-clicking on them; the only available option in the pop-up menu is **Properties**.

In a default installation, only the *My themes* theme is customizable, although new themes can be added as explained in "Adding a new theme to the Gallery" on page 342.

Adding objects to the Gallery

You may wish to add to the Gallery any images that you use frequently, for example, a company logo. You can then very easily insert these graphics into a document later. You can add images only to "My Theme" or to any other theme that you have created; these are indicated by a green icon in the list of themes. You cannot add images to the built-in themes, indicated by an icon of another color.

Method 1 (selecting a file):

1) In the theme's Properties, on the *Files* page, click the **Find Files** button. The Select path dialog opens.
2) You can enter the path for the file's directory in the *Path* text box, or you can navigate to locate the file's directory. Use the *File type* drop-down list to help limit the search.
3) Click the **Select** button to start the search.
4) A list of graphic files is then displayed in the window. You can use the *File type* filter again to further limit the search.
5) Select the files to add. To select more than one file, hold the *Control* key down while you click on each file.
6) Finally, click **Add**.

Method 2 (drag and drop):

1) Open the document containing an image you want to add to the Gallery, and display the Gallery theme to which you want to add it.

2) Position the mouse pointer above the image, without clicking.

3) If the mouse pointer changes to a hand symbol, the image refers to a hyperlink. In this case, press the *Alt* key while you click the image, to select it without activating the link. If the mouse pointer does not change to a hand symbol, you can simply click the image to select it.

4) Once the image is selected, evident from the green selection handles around it, release the mouse button. Click again on the image, keeping the mouse button pressed for more than two seconds. Without releasing the mouse button, drag the image into the document.

5) Release the mouse button.

Deleting images from the Gallery

To delete an image from a theme:

1) Right-click on the name of the image file or its thumbnail in the Gallery.

2) Click **Delete** on the pop-up menu. A message appears, asking if you want to delete this object. Click **Yes.**

Note	Deleting the name of a file from the list in the Gallery does not delete the file from the hard disk or other location.

Adding a new theme to the Gallery

To add a new theme to the Gallery:

1) Click the **New Theme** button above the list of themes (Figure 300).

2) In the Properties of New Theme dialog, click the *General* tab and type a name for the new theme.

3) Click the *Files* tab and add images to the theme, as described earlier.

Deleting a theme from the Gallery

You can delete only theme that you have added to the Gallery; you cannot delete any of the inbuilt themes. To delete a theme from the Gallery:

1) Go to **Tools > Gallery.**
2) In the left part of the Gallery, select in the list the theme you wish to delete.
3) Right-click on the theme, then click **Delete** on the pop-up menu.

Location of the Gallery and the objects in it

Graphics and other objects shown in the Gallery can be located anywhere on your computer's hard disk, on a network drive, or on a CD-ROM. Listings in the Gallery refer to the location of each object. When you add graphics to the Gallery, the files are not moved or copied; only the location of each new object is added as a reference.

In a workgroup situation, you may have access to a shared Gallery (where you cannot change the contents unless authorized to do so) and a user Gallery, where you can add, change, or delete objects.

The location of the user Gallery is specified in **Tools > Options > OpenOffice.org > Paths**. You can change this location, and you can copy your gallery files (*.sdv) to other computers.

Gallery contents provided with OOo are stored in a different location. You cannot change this location.

What is Fontwork?

With Fontwork you can create graphical text art objects for making your work more attractive. There are many different settings for text art objects (line, area, position, size, and more), so you have a large choice. You will surely find one that fits your document.

Fontwork is available with each component of OOo, but you will notice small differences in the way that each component displays it.

The Fontwork toolbars

You can use two different toolbars for creating and editing a Fontwork object.

• Go to **View > Toolbars > Fontwork**.

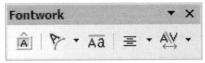

Figure 303. The floating Fontwork toolbar

- If you click on an existing Fontwork object, the Formatting toolbar changes to display the Fontwork options as shown in Figure 307. The contents of this toolbar vary depending on the OOo component with which it is being used.

Creating a Fontwork object

1) On the Drawing or Fontwork toolbar, click the Fontwork Gallery icon. If the Drawing toolbar is not visible, go to **View > Toolbars > Drawing** to display it.

2) In the Fontwork Gallery dialog (Figure 304), select a Fontwork style, then click **OK**.

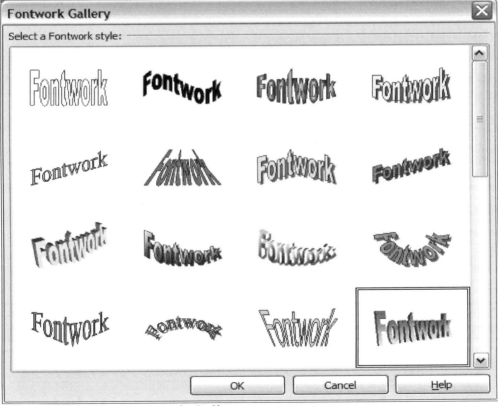

Figure 304. The Fontwork Gallery

The Fontwork object will appear in your document. Notice the blue squares around the edge (indicating that the object is selected) and the yellow dot; these are discussed in "Moving and resizing Fontwork objects" on page 351.

3) Double-click the object to edit the Fontwork text. Type your own text in place of the black *Fontwork* text that appears over the object (Figure 305).

Figure 305. Editing Fontwork text

4) Click anywhere in a free space or press *Esc* to apply your changes.

Editing a Fontwork object

Now that the Fontwork object is created, you can edit some of its attributes. To do this, you can use the Fontwork toolbar, the Formatting toolbar, or menu options as described in this section.

Using the Fontwork toolbar

Make sure that the Fontwork toolbar, shown in Figure 303, is visible. If you do not see it, go to **View > Toolbars > Fontwork**.

Click on the different icons to edit Fontwork objects.

 Fontwork Shape: Edits the shape of the selected object. You can choose from a palette of shapes.

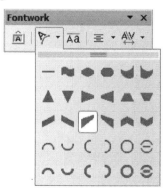

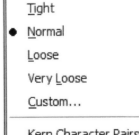 **Fontwork Same Letter Heights**: Changes the height of characters in the object. Toggles between normal height (some characters taller than others, for example capital letters, d, h, l and others) and all letters the same height.

Figure 306. Left: normal letters; right: same letter heights

Fontwork Alignment: Changes the alignment of characters. Choices are left align, center, right align, word justify, and stretch justify. The effects of the text alignment can only be seen if the text spans over two or more lines. In the stretch justify mode, all the lines are filled completely.

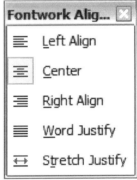

Fontwork Character **Spacing**: Changes the character spacing and kerning in the object. For custom spacing, input a percentage value: 100% is normal spacing; less than 100% is tight spacing; more than 100% is expanded spacing.

Using the Formatting toolbar

Now let us go further and customize the Fontwork object with several more attributes.

Click on the Fontwork object. The Formatting toolbar changes to show all the options for editing the object. (For example, the toolbar shown in Figure 307 appears when you use Fontwork in Writer.)

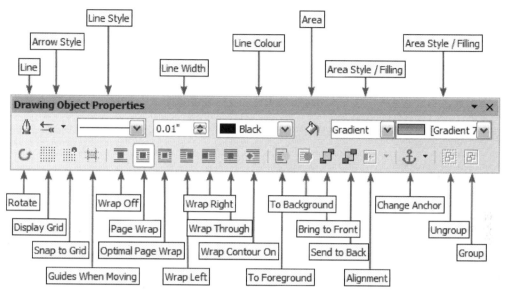

Figure 307. Formatting toolbar with a Fontwork object selected in Writer

Note that in this figure the toolbar has been undocked for ease of illustration: unless you have chosen to float the toolbar in this way, it appears in its default, docked position somewhere below the menu bar.

On the Formatting toolbar you have a large choice of options for customizing your object. These choices are the same as the ones for other drawing objects. You can read about them in more detail in the *Draw Guide*.

Line options

Line icon: Opens a dialog (Figure 308) with three tabs: **Line, Line Styles, Arrow Styles**.

Use the **Line** tab to edit the most common properties of the line around the selected Fontwork object, by choosing from previously-defined attributes including line style, line color, and arrow styles.

Use the **Lines Styles** and **Arrow Styles** tabs to edit the properties of line and arrow styles, and define new styles.

Arrow Style icon: Choose from the different arrow styles.

Line Style box: Choose from the available line styles.

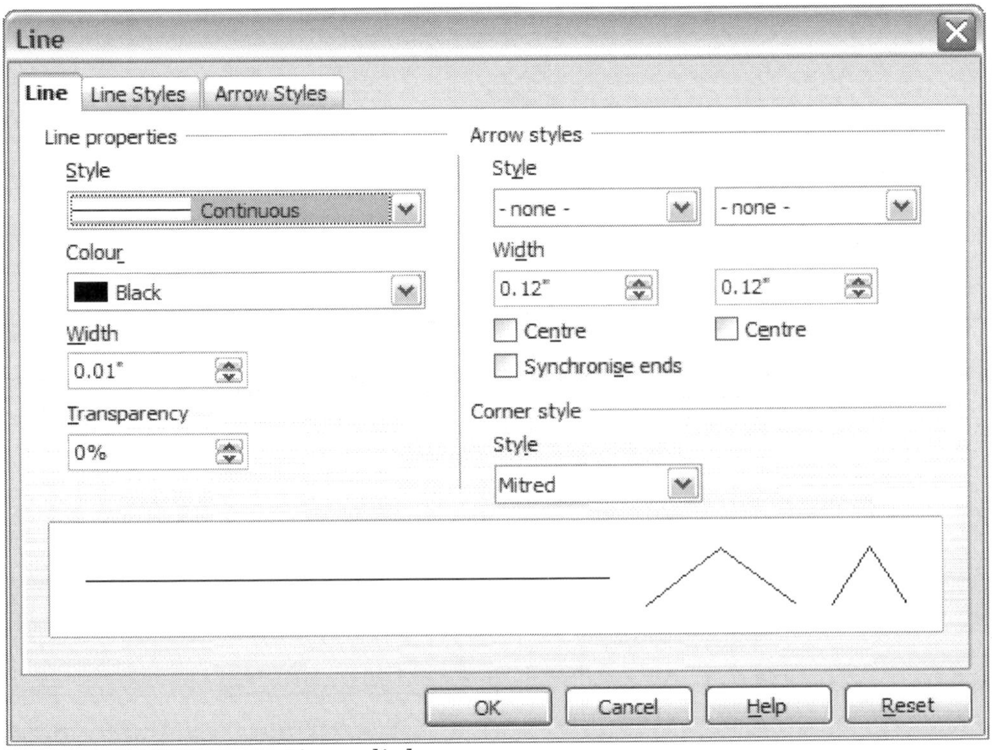

Figure 308. Line options dialog

Line Width box: Set the width of the line.

Line Color box: Select the color of the line.

Area options

Area icon: Opens a dialog (Figure 309) with seven tabs: **Area**, **Shadow**, **Transparency**, **Colors**, **Gradients**, **Hatching**, **Bitmaps**.

- **Area** tab: Choose from the predefined list a color, bitmap, gradient or hatching pattern to fill the selected object.

- **Shadow** tab: Set the shadow properties of the selected object.

- **Transparency** tab: Set the transparency properties of the selected object.

- **Colors** tab: Modify the available colors or add new ones to appear on the Area tab.

- **Gradients** tab: Modify the available gradients or add new ones to appear on the Area tab.

- **Hatching** tab: Modify the available hatching patterns or add new ones to appear on the Area tab.

- **Bitmaps tab:** Create simple bitmap patterns and import bitmaps, to make them available on the Area tab.

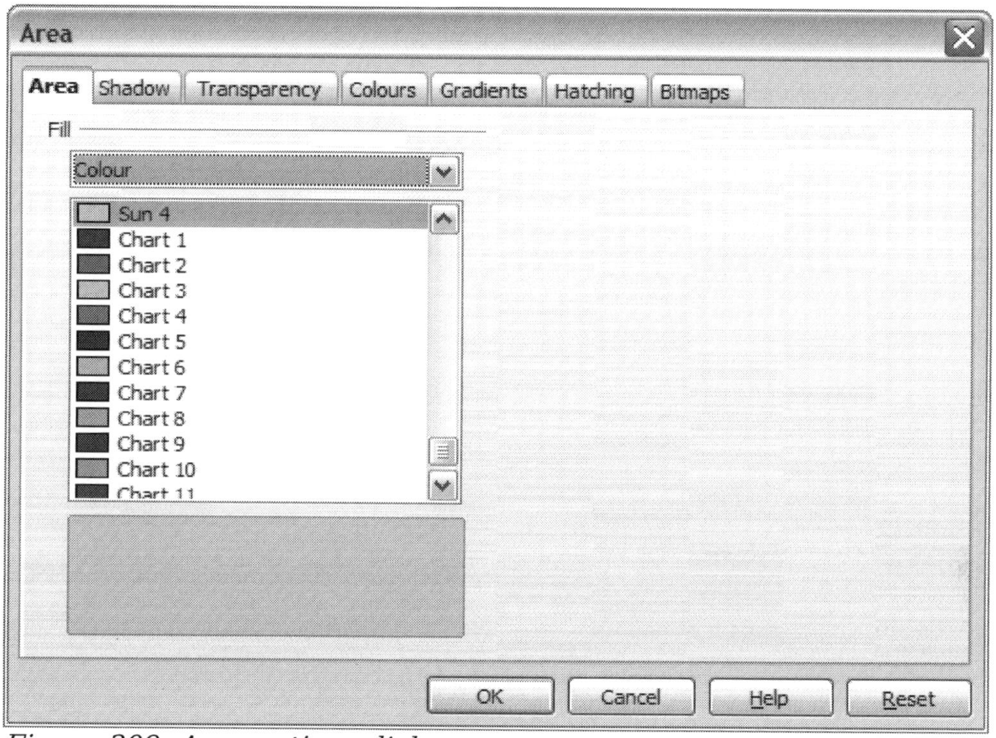

Figure 309. Area options dialog

Area Style / Filling boxes: Select the type of the fill of the selected object. For more detailed settings, use the Area icon.

Positioning options

Rotate icon: Rotate the selected object manually using the mouse to drag the object.

To Foreground icon: Moves the selected object in front of the text.

To Background icon: Moves the selected object behind the text.

Alignment icon: Modifies the alignment of the selected objects.

Bring to front icon: Moves the selected object in front of the others.

Send to back icon: Moves the selected object behind the others.

Change Anchor icon: Switch between anchoring options:

- To Page - The object keeps the same position in relation to the page margins. It does not move as you add or delete text.

- To Paragraph - The object is associated with a paragraph and moves with the paragraph. It may be placed in the margin or another location.

- To Character - The object is associated with a character but is not in the text sequence. It moves with the paragraph but may be placed in the margin or another location. This method is similar to anchoring to a paragraph.

- As Character - The object is placed in the document like any character and moves with the paragraph as you add or delete text before the object.

Ungroup icon: Ungroups the selected objects, so you can manage them individually.

Group icon: Groups the selected objects, so you can manage them as a single object.

Using menu options

You can use some the choices on the **Format** menu to anchor, align, arrange and group selected Fontwork objects, wrap text around them, and flip them horizontally and vertically.

You can also right-click on a Fontwork object and choose many of the same options from the pop-up menu. In addition, the pop-up menu provides quick access to the Line, Area, Text, and Position and Size dialogs. The Line and Area dialogs are described on pages 347 and 348. The Text dialog offers only a few options for Fontwork objects and is not discussed here.

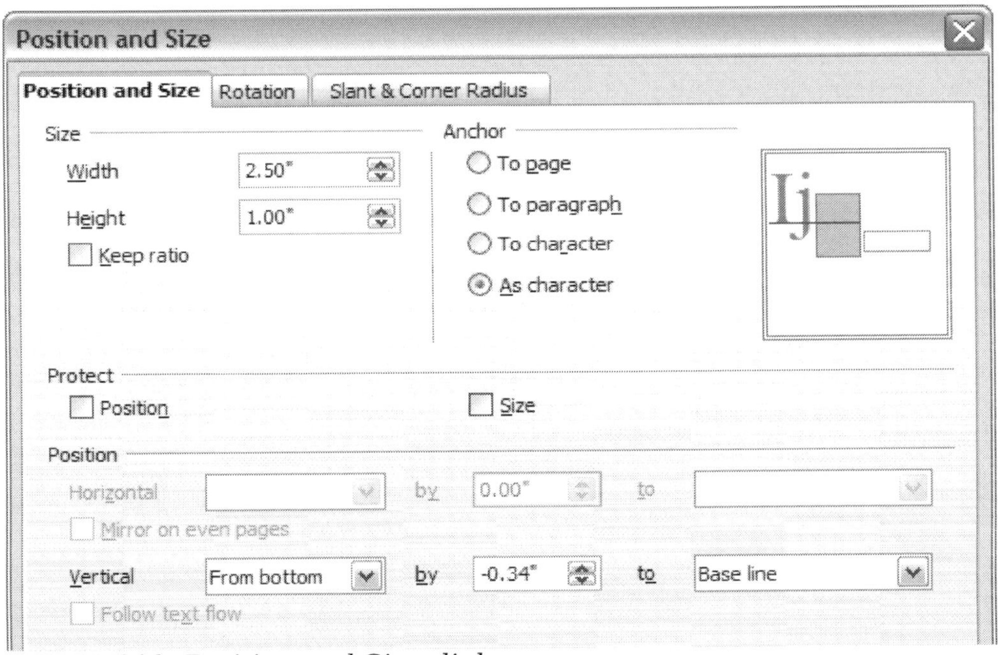

Figure 310. Position and Size dialog

On the Position and Size dialog (Figure 310), you can enter precise values concerning size and position. For more information, see the *Draw Guide*.

Moving and resizing Fontwork objects

When you select a Fontwork object, eight blue squares (known as *handles*) appear around the edge of the object, as shown below. You can drag these handles to resize the object.

A yellow dot also appears on the object. This dot may be along an edge of the object, or it may be somewhere else; see figure to right for an example. If you hover the pointer over this yellow dot, the pointer turns into a hand symbol. You can drag the dot in different directions to distort the object.

Hovering the pointer over other parts of the object turns the pointer into the usual symbol for dragging the object to another part of the page.

For precise control of the location and size of the object, use the Position and Size dialog (Figure 310).

Chapter *12*
Creating Web Pages

Saving documents as HTML files

This chapter describes how to save documents as web pages from Writer, Calc, Draw and Impress.

Note	Cross references do not become hyperlinks in an HTML document.

Inserting hyperlinks

When you type text (such as a website addresses or URL) that can be used as a hyperlink, OOo formats it automatically, creating the hyperlink and applying to the text a color and underlining. If this does not happen, you can enable this feature using **Tools > AutoCorrect > Options** and selecting **URL Recognition**.

Tips	If you do not want OOo to convert a specific URL to a hyperlink, select **Edit > Undo Insert** from the menu bar or press *Control+Z* immediately after the formatting has been applied.
	To change the color of hyperlinks, go to **Tools > Options > OpenOffice.org > Appearance**, scroll to *Unvisited links* and/or *Visited links*, pick the new colors and click **OK**. Caution: this will change the color for all hyperlinks in all components of OpenOffice.org—this may not be what you want.
	In Writer and Calc (but not Draw or Impress), you can also change the *Internet link* character style or define and apply new styles to selected links.

You can also insert and modify links using the Hyperlink dialog (Figure 311). To display the dialog, click the **Hyperlink** icon ⬚ on the Standard toolbar or select **Insert > Hyperlink** from the menu bar. To turn existing text into a link, highlight it before opening the Hyperlink dialog.

On the left hand side, select one of the four types of hyperlinks:

- **Internet**: a web address, normally starting with http://
- **Mail & News**: for example an email address.
- **Document**: the hyperlink points to another document or to another place in the presentation.
- **New document**: the hyperlink creates a new document.

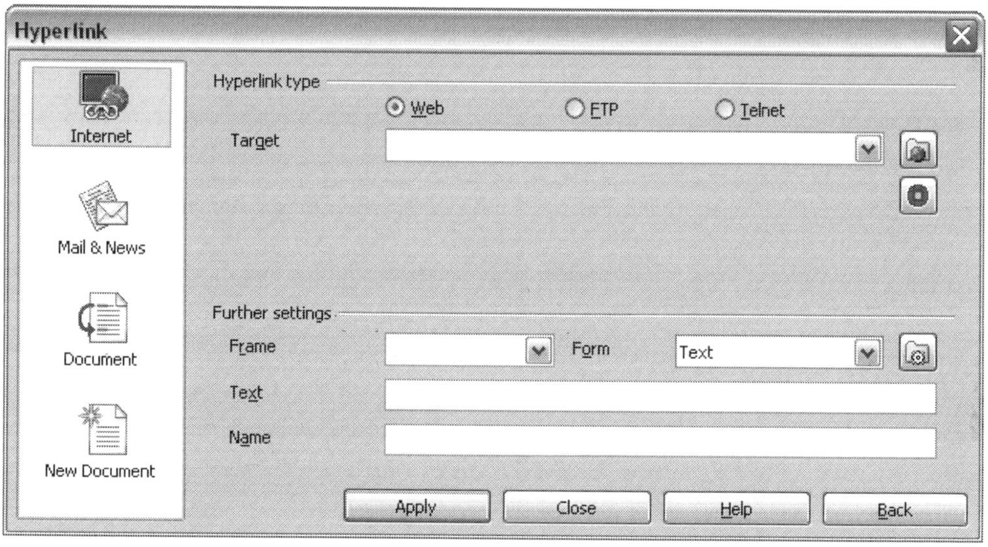

Figure 311. Hyperlink dialog showing details for Internet links

The top right part of the dialog changes according to the choice made for the hyperlink type. A full description of all the choices, and their interactions, is beyond the scope of this chapter. Here is a summary of the most common choices used in presentations.

For an *Internet* type hyperlink, choose the type of hyperlink (choose between Web, FTP or Telnet), and enter the required web address (URL).

For a *Mail and News* type hyperlink, specify whether it is a mail or news link, the receiver address and for email, also the subject.

For a *Document* type hyperlink, specify the document path (the **Open File** button opens a file browser); leave this blank if you want to link to a target in the same presentation. Optionally specify the target in the document (for example a specific slide). Click on the **Target** icon to open the Navigator where you can select the target, or if you know the name of the target, you can type it into the box.

For a *New Document* type hyperlink, specify whether to edit the newly created document immediately or just create it (**Edit later**) and the type of document to create (text, spreadsheet, etc.). For a presentation, **Edit now** is the more likely choice. The **Select path** button opens a directory picker.

The *Further settings* section in the bottom right part of the dialog is common to all the hyperlink types, although some choices are more relevant to some types of links.

*   Set the value of **Frame** to determine how the hyperlink will open. This applies to documents that open in a Web browser.
*   **Form** specifies if the link is to be presented as text or as a button.
*   **Text** specifies the text that will be visible to the user.
*   **Name** is applicable to HTML documents. It specifies text that will be added as a NAME attribute in the HTML code behind the hyperlink.
*   **Event** button: this button will be activated to allow OOo to react to events for which the user has written some code (macro). This function is not covered in this book.

Editing hyperlinks

To edit an existing link, place the cursor anywhere in the link and click **Edit > Hyperlink**. The Hyperlink dialog (Figure 311) opens. Make your changes and click **Apply**. If you need to edit several hyperlinks, you can leave the Hyperlink dialog open until you have edited all of them. Be sure to click **Apply** after each one. When you are finished, click **Close**.

The standard (default) behavior for activating hyperlinks is to use *Ctrl+click*. This behavior can be changed in Tools **> Options > OpenOffice.org > Security > Options**, by deselecting the option **Ctrl-click required to follow hyperlinks**. If clicking in your links activates them, check that page to see if the option has been deselected.

Saving Writer documents as web pages

Writer's HTML capabilities include saving existing documents in HTML format, creating new documents as HTML and creating several different types of web pages using a wizard.

The easiest way to create HTML documents is to start with an existing Writer document. You can view it as it will appear on a web page by using **View > Web Layout**.

Saving a document as a single web page

To save a document as a single web page (HTML format), select **Save As** from the **File** menu and specify **HTML Document** as the file type.

Note	Writer does not replace multiple spaces in the original document with the HTML code for non-breaking spaces. If you want to have extra spaces in your HTML file or web page, you need to insert non-breaking spaces in OOo. To do this, press *Control+Spacebar* instead of just *Spacebar*.

Saving a document as a series of web pages

Writer can save a large document as a series of web pages (HTML files) with a table of contents page. To do this:

1) Decide which headings in the document should start on a new page and make sure all those headings have the same style (for example, Heading 1).
2) Select **File > Send** and click on **Create HTML Document**.
3) In the dialog (Figure 312), enter the file name to save the pages under. Also specify which style indicates a new page (as decided in step 1).
4) Click **Save** to create the multi-page HTML document. (For those who may be interested, the resulting HTML files conform to the HTML 4 Transitional.)

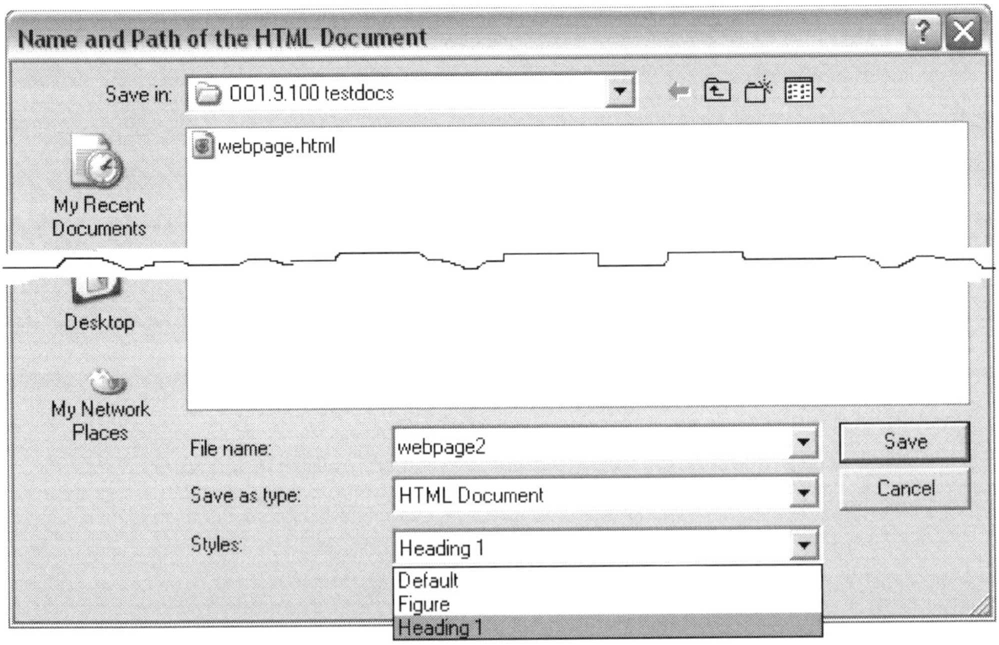

Figure 312. Creating a series of web pages from one document

Creating web pages using a Wizard

OOo's Web wizard allows you to create several types of standard web pages. To use it:

1) Select **File > Wizards > Web Page**. On the first page of the Wizard, choose settings and click **Next**.

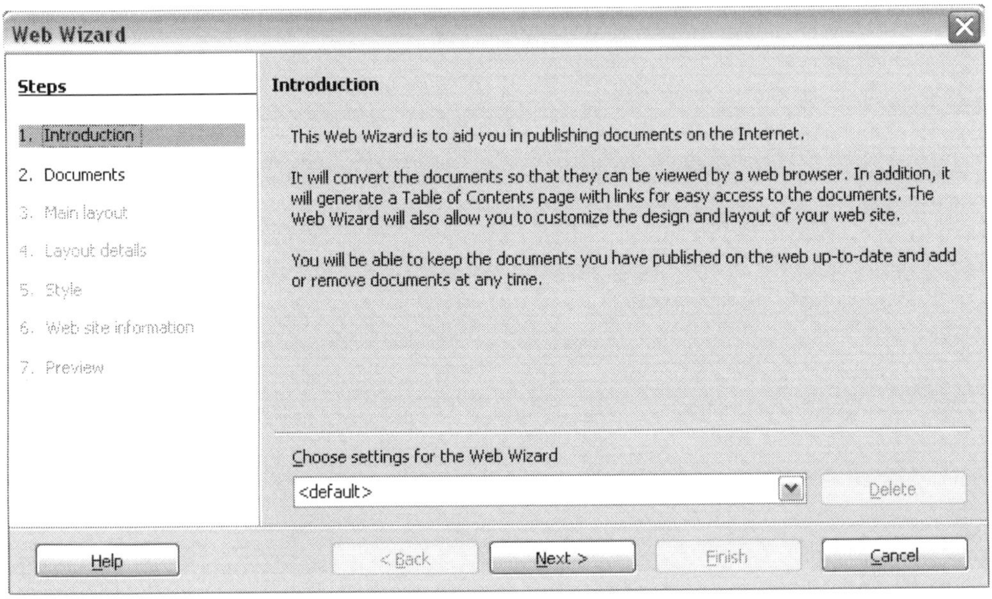

Note	If this is your first web page, the only settings option is Default.

2) Choose or browse to the document you would like to format. The *Title*, *Summary* and *Author* information is picked up from the document's properties; if necessary, edit it. Click **Next.**

Web Wizard

Steps

1. Introduction
2. Documents
3. Main layout
4. Layout details
5. Style
6. Web site information
7. Preview

Select the documents you want to publish

Web site content

0117GS-CreatingWebPages.sxw

Export to file format:

HTML

Document information

Title:

Creating Web Pages

Summary:

Fields to edit:

Chapter Title :   Description
tab > Title
Chapter Subtitle : User Defined

Author:

Add... Remove

3) Chose a layout for the web site by clicking on the layout boxes. Click **Next.**

Web Wizard

Steps

1. Introduction
2. Documents
3. Main layout
4. Layout details
5. Style
6. Web site information
7. Preview

Choose a layout for the table of contents of your web site

Layouts:

Simple

Help   < Back   Next >   Finish   Cancel

4) Chose the information to be listed and the screen resolution. Click **Next.**

Web Wizard

Steps

1. Introduction
2. Documents
3. Main layout
4. Layout details
5. Style
6. Web site information
7. Preview

Customize the selected layout

Include the following information for each document in the table of contents:

- ☐ File name
- ☑ Description
- ☐ Author
- ☐ Creation date
- ☐ Last change date

- ☐ File format
- ☑ File format icon
- ☐ Number of pages
- ☑ Size in KB

Optimize the layout for screen resolution:

- ○ 640x480
- ⦿ 800x600
- ○ 1024x768

[Help]   [< Back] [Next >] [Finish]   [Cancel]

5) Select a style for the page. Use the drop-down list to choose different styles and color combinations. You can browse to a background image and icon set from the Gallery. Click **Next.**

Web Wizard

Steps

1. Introduction
2. Documents
3. Main layout
4. Layout details
5. Style
6. Web site information
7. Preview

Select a style for the table of contents page

Style: Water   ▼

Background image: <no background image>   [Choose...]

Icon set: <no icon set>   [Choose...]

The icon set is used for presentations in HTML format.

Site title

Document
Creation Date
Last Change Date
Filename

[Help]   [< Back] [Next >] [Finish]   [Cancel]

6) Enter general information such as Title and HTML Metadata information. Click **Next.**

7) Chose where to save the file and preview the page if you wish. Click **Finish**.

To edit or view the document's underlying HTML code, click **View > HTML Source** or click the **HTML Source** icon on the Main toolbar.

Saving Calc spreadsheets as web pages

Calc can save files as HTML documents. As for Writer, use **File > Save As** and select **HTML Document**, or **File > Wizards > Web Page**.

If the file contains more than one sheet, the additional sheets will follow one another in the HTML file. Links to each sheet will be placed at the top of the document. Calc also allows the insertion of links directly into the spreadsheet using the Hyperlink dialog.

Saving Impress presentations as web pages

You can export presentations as Macromedia Flash files: select **File > Export** and choose Macromedia Flash for the file type.

You can also convert presentations into a series of web pages, as described below.

Note	Saving as web pages (HTML format) does not retain animation and slide transitions.

1) To begin, select **File > Export** and choose **HTML Document** as the file type.
2) Create a folder for the files, supply a name for the resulting HTML file, and click **Save**. The HTML Export Wizard opens.

Note	Depending on the size of your presentation and the number of graphics it contains, the HTML export function creates many HTML, JPG, and GIF files. If you simply save to your desktop (not in a specific folder), these separate HTML and graphics files will be all over your desktop. So be sure to create a folder to hold all the files.

3) Choose the design for all of the pages, either from an existing design or by creating a new one. If you have not previously saved a design, the *Existing Design* choice is not available.

4) Click **Next** to select the type of web pages to create.

- *Standard HTML*: one page for each slide, with navigation links to move from slide to slide.

- *Standard HTML with frames*: one page with a navigation bar on the left-hand side; uses slide title as navigation links. Click on links to display pages in right-hand side.

- *Automatic*: one page for each slide, with each page set with the Refresh meta tag so a browser automatically cycles from one page to the next.

- *WebCast*: generates an ASP or Perl application to display the slides. Unfortunately OOo has no direct support for PHP as yet.

5) Decide how the images will be saved (PNG, GIF, or JPG) and what resolution to use.

When choosing a resolution, consider what the majority of your viewers might have. If you use a high resolution, then a viewer with a medium-resolution monitor will have to scroll sideways to see the entire slide—probably not desirable.

6) If *Create title page* was chosen in step 4, supply the information for it on the next page. The title contains an author name, e-mail address and home page, along with any additional information you want to include.

This page of the Wizard does not display if *Create title page* was not chosen.

7) Choose the navigation button style to use to move from one page to another. If you do not choose any, OOo will create a text navigator.

8) Select the color scheme for the web pages. Available schemes include the document's existing scheme, one based upon browser colors, and a completely user-defined scheme. You can save a new scheme so that it will appear on the first page of the HTML export wizard.

9) Click **Create** to generate the HTML files. If this is a new design, a small dialog pops up. If you might want to reuse this design, you can give it a name and save it. Otherwise, click **Do Not Save**.

Name HTML Design	⊠
Save	Do Not Save

Saving Draw documents as web pages

Exporting drawings from OpenOffice.org's Draw application is similar to exporting a presentation from Impress. Use **File > Export** and select **HTML Document** as the file type.

When using the wizard, you can choose to create the web page at any time by clicking the **Create** button.

Chapter *13*
Getting Started with Macros

Using the macro recorder

Your first macro

A macro is a saved sequence of commands or keystrokes that are stored for later use. An example of a simple macro is one that "types" your address. The OpenOffice.org macro language is very flexible, allowing automation of both simple and complex tasks. Macros are especially useful to repeat a task the same way over and over again.

OpenOffice.org macros are usually written in a language called StarBasic, or just abbreviated Basic. Although you can learn Basic and write macros, there is a steep learning curve to writing macros from scratch. The usual method for a beginner is to use the built-in macro recorder, which records your keystrokes and saves them for use.

Most tasks in OpenOffice.org are accomplished by "dispatching a command" (sending a command), which is intercepted and used. The macro recorder works by recording the commands that are dispatched (see "The dispatch framework" on page 375).

Creating a simple macro

Imagine repeatedly entering simple information. Although you can store the information in the clipboard, if you use the clipboard for something else, the contents are changed. Storing the contents as a macro is a simple solution. (In some simple cases, including the example used here, a better solution is to use AutoText.)

1) Use **Tools > Macros > Record Macro** to start recording a macro.

A small window is displayed so you know that OpenOffice.org is recording.

2) Type the desired information or perform an appropriate series of operations. In this case, I typed my name, *Andrew Pitonyak*.

3) Click the **Stop Recording** button to stop recording, save the macro, and display the OpenOffice.org Basic Macros dialog (see Figure 313).

4) Be certain to open the library container named *My Macros*. Find the library named *Standard* under My Macros. Be warned, *every* library container has a library named Standard. Select the Standard library and click **New Module** to create a new module to contain the macro.

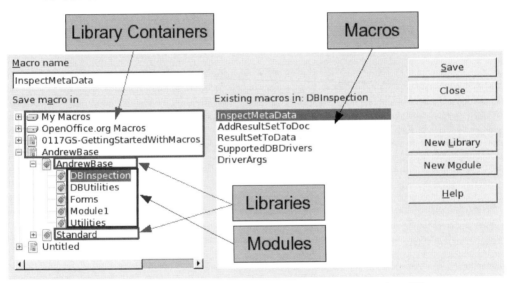

Figure 313: OOo Macro Organizer dialog, DBInspection library selected

5) The default module name is Module1; choose a better name. Although it is still not descriptive, I used Recorded. Type a descriptive name and click **OK** to create the module. The OpenOffice.org Basic Macros dialog is displayed again, showing the new module.

Figure 314: Give your module a meaningful name

6) Highlight the newly created module. In the upper left corner, type the macro name to use, such as "EnterMyname", and then click **Save** to save the macro.

If you followed all of the steps, the Standard library now contains a module named Recorded, which contains the EnterMyName macro, as shown in Figure 315. When OOo creates a new module, it automatically adds the macro named Main; as seen in Figure 315.

Running the macro

Use **Tools > Macros > Run Macro** to open the Macro Selector dialog (see Figure 315). Select the newly created macro and click **Run**.

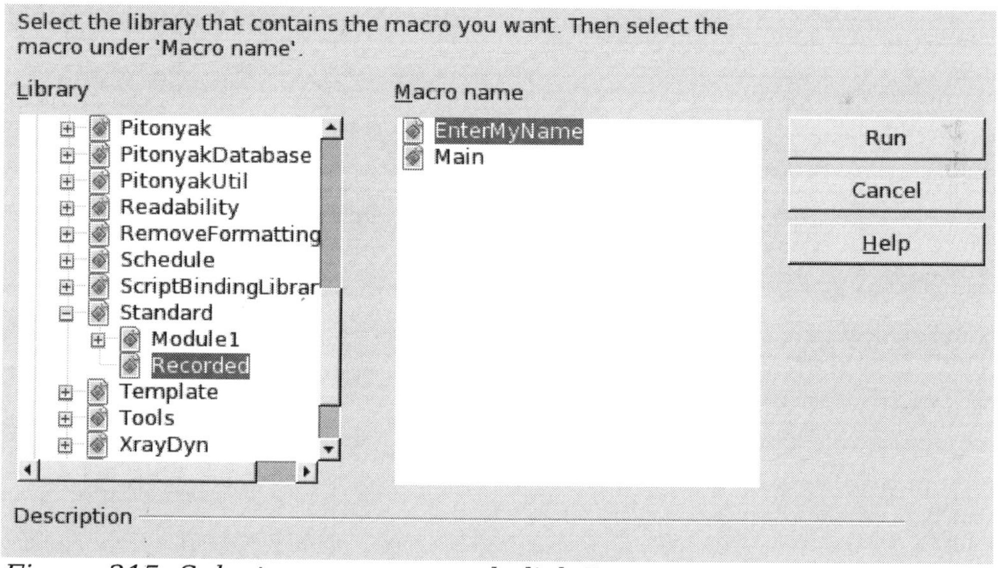

Figure 315: Select your macro and click Run

There are other methods to run a macro. For example, use **Tools > Macros > Organize Macros > OpenOffice.org Basic** to open the macro organizer, which contains a **Run** button as well. The author, an avid macro writer, prefers the macro organizer because the dialog usually opens faster, but the selection process may be slightly slower.

Viewing and editing the macro

You can view and edit the macro that was just created. Use **Tools > Macros > Organize Macros > OpenOffice.org Basic** to open the OpenOffice.org Basic Macros dialog (see Figure 315). Select the new macro and click **Edit** to open the macro in the Basic IDE (Integrated Development Environment).

Listing 1: Generated "EnterMyname" macro.

```
REM  *****  BASIC  *****
Sub Main

End Sub

sub EnterMyName
rem ------------------------------------------------------
rem define variables
dim document    as object
dim dispatcher as object
rem ------------------------------------------------------
rem get access to the document
document    = ThisComponent.CurrentController.Frame
dispatcher = createUnoService("com.sun.star.frame.DispatchHelper")

rem ------------------------------------------------------
dim args1(0) as new com.sun.star.beans.PropertyValue
args1(0).Name = "Text"
args1(0).Value = "Andrew Pitonyak"

dispatcher.executeDispatch(document, ".uno:InsertText", "", 0, args1())
end sub
```

The macro in Listing 1 is not as complicated as it first appears. Learning a few things helps significantly in understanding the generated macros. The discussion starts with features near the top of the macro listing and describes them. If you like to avoid details, then simply change the text "Andrew Pitonyak" to what you want to insert at the current cursor position.

Comments start with REM

The keyword REM, short for *remark*, starts a macro comment. All text after REM (on the same line) is ignored. As a short cut, the single quote character can also be used to start a comment.

Tip	StarBasic is not case-sensitive for keywords, so REM, Rem, and rem all start a comment. If you use symbolic constants defined by the API, it is safer to assume that the names are case-sensitive—symbolic constants are an advanced topic not usually needed by people that use the macro recorder.

Defining subroutines with SUB

Individual macros are stored in subroutines defined with the keyword SUB. The end of a subroutine is indicated by the words END SUB. The code starts by defining the subroutine named Main, which is empty and does nothing. The next subroutine, EnterMyName, contains the generated code.

Tip	OpenOffice.org creates an empty subroutine named Main when it creates a module.

There are advanced topics that are beyond the scope of this document, but knowing about them might be of interest:

- You can write a macro so that values can be passed to the subroutine. The values are called arguments. Recorded macros do not accept arguments.

- Another kind of subroutine is called a function. A function is a subroutine that returns a value. The keyword FUNCTION is used rather than SUB to define a function. Generated macros are always of type SUB.

Defining variables using DIM

You can write information on a piece of paper so that you can look at it later. A variable, like a piece of paper, contains information that can be changed and read. The DIM statement is similar to setting aside a piece of paper to be used to store a message or note.

The EnterMyName macro defines the variables *document* and *dispatcher* as type *object*. Other common variable types include *string*, *integer*, and *date*. A third variable, named *args1*, is an array of property values. A variable of type *array* allows a single variable to contain multiple values, similar to storing multiple pages in a single book. Values in an array are usually numbered starting from zero. The number in the parentheses indicates the highest usable number to access a storage location. In this example, there is only one value, and it is numbered zero.

Pulling the macro together

The following details are very complete; it is not important to understand all of the details. The first line defines the start of the macro.

```
sub EnterMyName
```

Declare two variables:

```
dim document   as object
dim dispatcher as object
```

ThisComponent refers to the current document.

The CurrentController property of a document refers to a service that "controls" the document. For example, when you type, it is the current controller that notices. The current controller then dispatches the changes to the document's frame.

The Frame property of a controller returns a main frame for a document. Therefore, the variable named *document* refers to a document's frame, which receives dispatched commands.

```
document = ThisComponent.CurrentController.Frame
```

Most tasks in OpenOffice.org are accomplished by dispatching a command. OOo version 2.0 introduced the dispatch helper service, which does most of the work to use dispatches in macros. The method CreateUnoService accepts the name of a service and it tries to create an instance of that service. On completion, the dispatcher variable contains a reference to a DispatchHelper.

```
dispatcher = createUnoService("com.sun.star.frame.DispatchHelper")
```

Declare an array of properties. Each property has a name and a value. In other words, it is a name/value pair. The created array has one property at index zero.

```
dim args1(0) as new com.sun.star.beans.PropertyValue
```

Give the property the name "Text" and the value "Andrew Pitonyak", which is the text that is inserted when the macro is run.

```
args1(0).Name = "Text"
args1(0).Value = "Andrew Pitonyak"
```

This is where the magic happens. The dispatch helper sends a dispatch to the document's frame (stored in the variable named document) with the command .uno:InsertText. The next two arguments, *frame name* and *search flags*, are beyond the scope of this document. The last argument is the array of property values to be used while executing the command InsertText.

```
dispatcher.executeDispatch(document, ".uno:InsertText", "", 0, args1())
```

Finally, the end of the subroutine.

```
    end sub
```

Creating a macro

I usually ask two questions before recording a macro:

1) Can the task be written as a simple set of commands?
2) Can the steps be arranged such that the last command leaves the cursor ready for the next command?

A complicated example

I frequently copy rows and columns of data from a web site and format them as a table in a text document. First, I copy the table from the web site to the clipboard. To avoid strange formatting and fonts, I paste the text into a Writer document as unformatted text. I reformat the text with tabs between columns so that I can use **Table > Convert > Text to Table** to convert to a table.

I inspect the text to see if I can record a macro to format the text (remember the two questions that I ask). As an example, I copied the FontWeight constants group from the OpenOffice.org web site. The first column indicates the constant name. Each name is followed by a space and a tab.

DONTKNOW	The font weight is not specified/known.
THIN	specifies a 50% font weight.
ULTRALIGHT	specifies a 60% font weight.
LIGHT	specifies a 75% font weight.
SEMILIGHT	specifies a 90% font weight.
NORMAL	specifies a normal font weight.
SEMIBOLD	specifies a 110% font weight.
BOLD	specifies a 150% font weight.
ULTRABOLD	specifies a 175% font weight.
BLACK	specifies a 200% font weight.

I want the first column to contain the numeric value, the second column the name, and the third column the description. The desired work is easily accomplished for every row except for DONTKNOW and NORMAL, which do not contain a numeric value—but I know that the values are 0 and 100, so I will enter those manually.

The data can be cleaned in multiple ways—all of them easy. The first example uses keystrokes that assume the cursor is at the start of the line with the text THIN.

1) Use **Tools > Macros > Record Macro** to start recording.
2) Press *Ctrl+Right Arrow* to move the cursor to the start of "specifies".
3) Press *Backspace* twice to remove the tab and the space.

4) Press *Tab* to add the tab without the space after the constant name.

5) Press *Delete* to delete the lower case s and then press *S* to add an upper case S.

6) Press *Ctrl+Right Arrow* twice to move the cursor to the start of the number.

7) Press *Ctrl+Shift+Right Arrow* to select and move the cursor before the % sign.

8) Press *Ctrl+C* to copy the selected text to the clipboard.

9) Press *End* to move the cursor to the end of the line.

10) Press *Backspace* twice to remove the two trailing spaces.

11) Press *Home* to move the cursor to the start of the line.

12) Press *Ctrl+V* to paste the selected number to the start of the line.

13) Pasting the value also pasted an extra space, so press *Backspace* to remove the extra space.

14) Press *Tab* to insert a tab between the number and the name.

15) Press *Home* to move to the start of the line.

16) Press *down arrow* to move to the next line.

17) Stop recording the macro and save the macro.

It takes much longer to read and write the steps than to record the macro. Work slowly and think about the steps as you do them. With practice this becomes second nature.

The generated macro has been modified to contain the step number in the comments to match the code to the step above.

Listing 2: Copy the numeric value to the start of the column.

```
sub CopyNumToCol1
rem ----------------------------------------------------------------
rem define variables
dim document    as object
dim dispatcher as object
rem ----------------------------------------------------------------
rem get access to the document
document    = ThisComponent.CurrentController.Frame
dispatcher = createUnoService("com.sun.star.frame.DispatchHelper")

rem (2) Press Ctrl+Right Arrow to move the cursor to the start of
rem "specifies".
dispatcher.executeDispatch(document, ".uno:GoToNextWord", "", 0, Array())

rem (3) Press Backspace twice to remove the tab and the space.
dispatcher.executeDispatch(document, ".uno:SwBackspace", "", 0, Array())

rem ----------------------------------------------------------------
```

```
dispatcher.executeDispatch(document, ".uno:SwBackspace", "", 0, Array())

rem (4) Press Tab to add the tab without the space after the constant
rem name.
dim args4(0) as new com.sun.star.beans.PropertyValue
args4(0).Name = "Text"
args4(0).Value = CHR$(9)

dispatcher.executeDispatch(document, ".uno:InsertText", "", 0, args4())

rem (5) Press Delete to delete the lower case s ....
dispatcher.executeDispatch(document, ".uno:Delete", "", 0, Array())

rem (5) ... and then press S to add an upper case S.
dim args6(0) as new com.sun.star.beans.PropertyValue
args6(0).Name = "Text"
args6(0).Value = "S"

dispatcher.executeDispatch(document, ".uno:InsertText", "", 0, args6())

rem (6) Press Ctrl+Right Arrow twice to move the cursor to the number.
dispatcher.executeDispatch(document, ".uno:GoToNextWord", "", 0, Array())

rem ------------------------------------------------------------------
dispatcher.executeDispatch(document, ".uno:GoToNextWord", "", 0, Array())

rem (7) Press Ctrl+Shift+Right Arrow to select the number.
dispatcher.executeDispatch(document, ".uno:WordRightSel", "", 0, Array())

rem (8) Press Ctrl+C to copy the selected text to the clipboard.
dispatcher.executeDispatch(document, ".uno:Copy", "", 0, Array())

rem (9) Press End to move the cursor to the end of the line.
dispatcher.executeDispatch(document, ".uno:GoToEndOfLine", "", 0, Array())

rem (10) Press Backspace twice to remove the two trailing spaces.
dispatcher.executeDispatch(document, ".uno:SwBackspace", "", 0, Array())

rem ------------------------------------------------------------------
dispatcher.executeDispatch(document, ".uno:SwBackspace", "", 0, Array())

rem (11) Press Home to move the cursor to the start of the line.
dispatcher.executeDispatch(document, ".uno:GoToStartOfLine", "", 0, _
    Array())

rem (12) Press Ctrl+V to paste the selected number to the start of the
rem line.
dispatcher.executeDispatch(document, ".uno:Paste", "", 0, Array())

rem (13) Press Backspace to remove the extra space.
dispatcher.executeDispatch(document, ".uno:SwBackspace", "", 0, Array())

rem (14) Press Tab to insert a tab between the number and the name.
dim args17(0) as new com.sun.star.beans.PropertyValue
args17(0).Name = "Text"
args17(0).Value = CHR$(9)

dispatcher.executeDispatch(document, ".uno:InsertText", "", 0, args17())
```

```
rem (15) Press Home to move to the start of the line.
dispatcher.executeDispatch(document, ".uno:GoToStartOfLine", "", 0, _
    Array())

rem (16) Press down arrow to move to the next line.
dim args19(1) as new com.sun.star.beans.PropertyValue
args19(0).Name = "Count"
args19(0).Value = 1
args19(1).Name = "Select"
args19(1).Value = false

dispatcher.executeDispatch(document, ".uno:GoDown", "", 0, args19())
end sub
```

Cursor movements are used for all operations (as opposed to searching). If run on the DONTKNOW line, the word *weight* is moved to the front of the line, and the first "The" is changed to "She". This is not perfect, but I should not have run the macro on the lines that did not have the proper format; I need to do these manually.

Running the macro quickly

It is tedious to repeatedly run the macro using **Tools > Macros > Run Macro** (see Figure 315). The macro can be run from the IDE. Use **Tools > Macros > Organize Macros > OpenOffice.org Basic** to open the Basic Macro dialog. Select your macro and click **Edit** to open the macro in the IDE.

The IDE has a **Run Basic** icon in the toolbar that runs the first macro in the IDE. Unless you change the first macro, it is the empty macro named Main. Modify Main so that it reads as shown in Listing 3.

Listing 3: Modify Main to call CopyNumToCol1.

```
Sub Main
    CopyNumToCol1
End Sub
```

Now, you can run CopyNumToCol1 by repeatedly clicking the **Run Basic** icon in the toolbar of the IDE. This is very fast and easy, especially for temporary macros that will be used a few times and then discarded.

Sometimes the macro recorder fails

Understanding the OpenOffice.org internals helps to understand how and why the macro recorder frequently fails. The primary offender is related to the dispatch framework and its relationship to the macro recorder.

The dispatch framework

The purpose of the dispatch framework is to provide a uniform access to components (documents) for commands that usually correspond to menu items. I can use **File > Save** from the menu, the shortcut keys *Ctrl+S*, or click on the **Save** toolbar icon. All of these commands are translated into the same "dispatch command", which is sent to the current document.

The dispatch framework can also be used to send "commands" back to the UI (User Interface). For example, after saving the document, the File Save command is disabled. As soon as the document has been changed, the File Save command is enabled.

If we see a dispatch command, it is text such as .uno:InsertObject or .uno:GoToStartOfLine. The command is sent to the document's frame, and the frame passes on the command until an object is found that can handle the command.

How the macro recorder uses the dispatch framework

The macro recorder records the generated dispatches. The recorder is relatively simple to implement and the same commands that are issued are recorded for later use. The problem is that not all dispatched commands are complete. For example, inserting an object generates the following code:

```
dispatcher.executeDispatch(document, _
    ".uno:InsertObject", "", 0, Array())
```

It is not possible to specify what kind of object to create or insert. If an object is inserted from a file, you cannot specify which file to insert.

I recorded a macro and used **Tools > Options** to open and modify configuration items. The generated macro does not record any configuration changes; in fact, the generated code is commented so it will not even be run.

```
rem dispatcher.executeDispatch(document, _
    ".uno:OptionsTreeDialog", "", 0, Array())
```

If a dialog is opened, the command to open the dialog is likely to be generated. Any work done inside the dialog is not usually recorded. Examples include macro organization dialogs, inserting special characters, and similar types of dialogs. Other possible problems using the macro recorder include things such as inserting a formula, setting user data, setting filters in Calc, actions in database forms, and exporting a document to an encrypted PDF file. You never know for certain what will work unless you try it, however. The actions from the search dialog are properly captured, for example.

Other options

When the macro recorder is not able to solve a specific problem, the usual solution is to write code using the OpenOffice.org objects. Unfortunately, there is a steep learning curve for the OOo objects. It is usually best to start with simple examples and then branch out slowly as you learn more. Learning to read generated macros is a good place to start.

If you record Calc macros, and the recorder can correctly generate a macro, there is an add-in created by Paolo Mantovani, which converts Calc macros when they are recorded. The final code manipulates OpenOffice.org objects rather than generating dispatches. This can be very useful for learning the object model.

You can download the macro recorder from Paolo's web site directly or from the OOo Macros web site. You should check both places to see which contains the latest version.

http://www.paolo-mantovani.org/downloads/ DispatchToApiRecorder/

http://www.ooomacros.org/user.php

Macro organization

In OpenOffice.org, macros are grouped in modules, modules are grouped in libraries, and libraries are grouped in library containers. A library is usually used as a major grouping for either an entire category of macros, or for an entire application. Modules usually split functionality, such as user interaction and calculations. Individual macros are subroutines and functions.

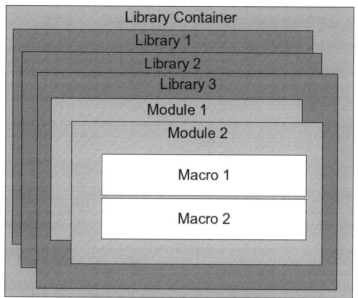

Figure 316: Macro Library hierarchy

A computer scientist would use Figure 317 to precisely describe the situation. The text "1..*" means one or more, and "0..*" means zero or more. The black triangle means composed of or contains.

- A library container contains one or more libraries, and each library is contained in one library container.

- A library contains zero or more modules, and each module is contained in one library.

- A module contains zero or more macros, and each macro is contained in one module.

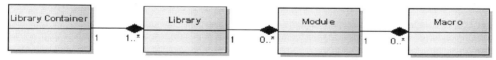

Figure 317: Macro Library hierarchy

Use **Tools > Macros > Organize Macros > OpenOffice.org Basic** to open the OpenOffice.org Basic Macros dialog (see Figure 318). All available library containers are shown in the *Macro from* list. Every document is a library container, capable of containing multiple libraries. The application itself acts as two library containers, one container for macros distributed with OpenOffice.org called OpenOffice.org Macros, and one container for personal macros called My Macros. As shown in Figure 318, only two documents are currently open.

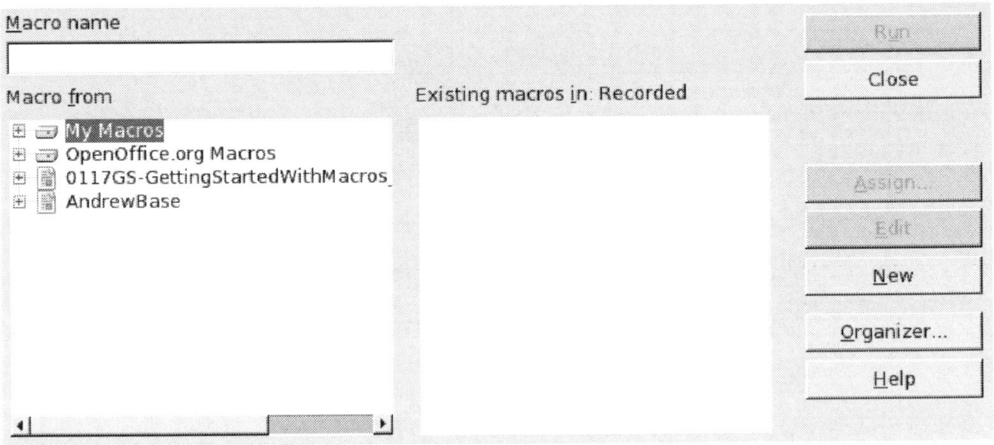

Figure 318: Library containers are shown on the left

The OpenOffice.org Macros are stored with the application runtime code, which may not be editable to you unless you are an administrator. This is just as well since these macros should not be changed and you should not store your own macros in the OOo container.

Unless your macros are applicable to a single document, and only to a single document, your macros will probably be stored in the My Macros container. The My Macros container is stored in your user area or home directory.

If a macro is contained in a document, then a recorded macro will attempt to work on that document; primarily because it uses "ThisComponent" for its actions.

Every library container contains a library named *Standard*. It is better to create your own libraries with meaningful names than to use the Standard library. Not only are meaningful names easier to manage, but they can also be imported into other library containers whereas the Standard library cannot.

Caution ⚠	OpenOffice.org allows you to import libraries into a library container, but it will not allow you to overwrite the library named Standard. Therefore, if you store your macros in the Standard library, you cannot import them into another library container.

Just as it makes good sense to give your libraries meaningful names, it is prudent to use meaningful names for your modules. By default, OpenOffice.org uses names such as Module1. Feel free to use your own meaningful name.

As you create your macros, you must decide where to store them. Storing a macro in a document is useful if the document will be shared and you want the macro to be included with the document. Macros stored in the application library container named My Macros, however, are globally available to all documents.

Macros are not available until the library that contains them is loaded. The Standard library and Template library, however, are automatically loaded. A loaded library is displayed differently from a library that is not loaded. To load the library and the modules it contains, double-click on the library.

Where are macros stored?

OpenOffice.org stores user-specific data in a directory under the user's home directory. For example, on Windows, this is `C:\Documents and Settings\<name>\Application Data`. User macros are stored in OpenOffice.org2\user\basic. Each library is stored in its own directory off the basic directory.

It is not important to understand where macros are stored for casual use. If you know where they are stored, however, you can create a backup, share your macros, or inspect them if there is an error. For example, on one or more of my OpenOffice.org upgrades, all of my macros disappeared. Although the macros were still on disk, the macros were not copied to the new directories. The solution was to import the macros into the new installation.

Use **Tools > Macros > Organize Dialogs** to open the OpenOffice.org Macros organizer dialog. Another common way to open this dialog is to use **Tools > Macros > Organize Macros > OpenOffice.org Basic** to open the OpenOffice.org Macros dialog and then click the **Organizer** button (see Figure 319).

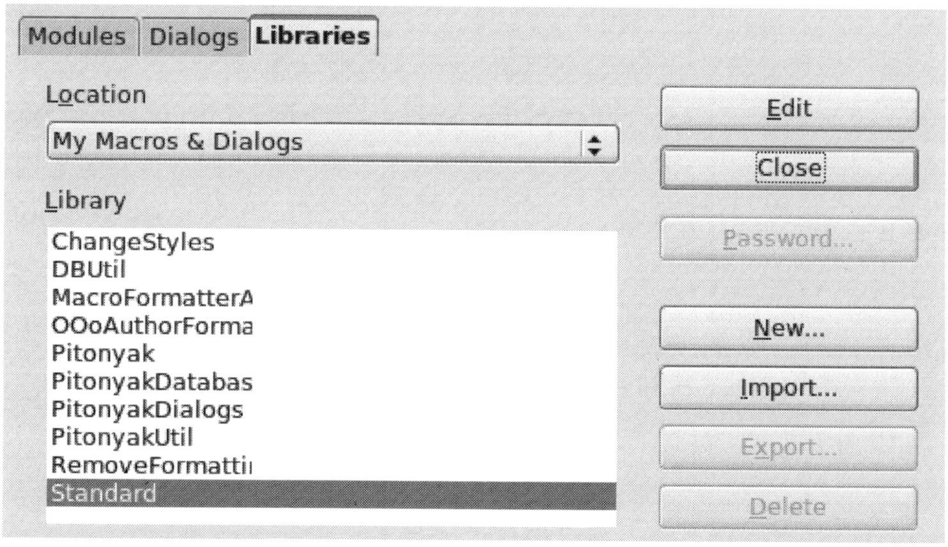

Figure 319: The macro organizer dialog

Importing macros

The OpenOffice.org Macro Organizer dialog provides functionality to create, delete, and rename libraries, modules, and dialogs. Select the library container to use and then click the **Import** button to import macro libraries (see Figure 320).

Tip	You cannot import the library named Standard.

Tip	On Linux, the OpenOffice.org-specific files are stored in a directory whose name begins with a period. Directories and files with names beginning with a period are not shown in a normal selection dialog. To open the directory, I navigated to the parent directory, entered the name .openoffice.org2.0, and then clicked **Open**. This opened the directory, which was not initially shown.

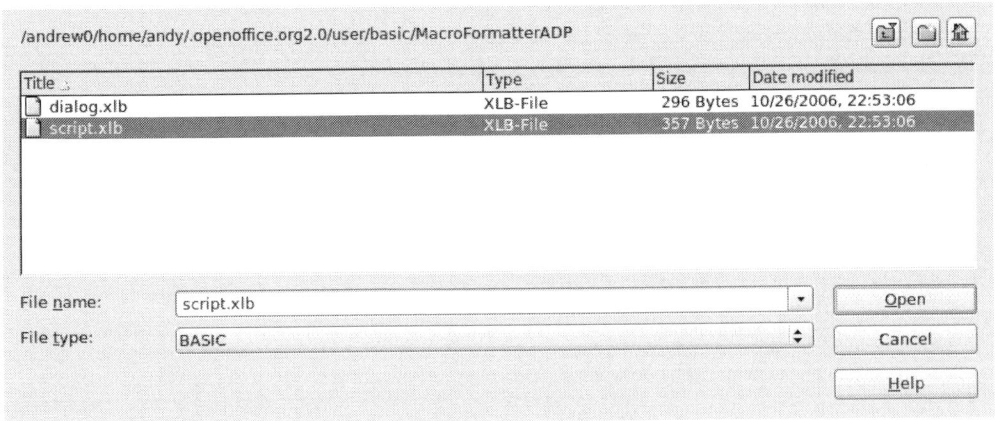

Figure 320: Select a macro library to import

Navigate to the directory containing the library to import. There are usually two files from which to choose, dialog.xlb and script.xlb. It does not matter which of these two files you select; both will be imported. Select a file and click **Open** to continue (see Figure 321).

If the library already exists, it will not be replaced unless **Replace existing libraries** is checked. If **Insert as reference** is checked, the library is referenced in its current location, but you cannot edit the library. If **Insert as reference** is not checked, however, the library is copied to the user's macro directory.

Figure 321: Choose library import options

Macros can be stored in libraries inside OpenOffice.org documents. Select a document rather than a directory on disk (as shown in Figure 320) to import libraries contained in a document.

Downloading macros to import

Macros are available for download. Some macros are contained in documents, some as regular files that you must select and import, and some as macro text that should be copied and pasted into the Basic IDE; use **Tools > Macros > Organize Macros > OpenOffice.org Basic** to open the OpenOffice.org Macros dialog, choose the macro to edit, and then click **Edit** to open the macro in the Basic IDE.

Some macros are available as free downloads on the Internet (see Table 3).

Table 3. Places to find macro examples.

Location	Description
http://www.ooomacros.org/	Excellent collection of packaged macros.
http://www.pitonyak.org/oo.php	Reference materials regarding macros.
http://www.pitonyak.org/database/	Reference materials regarding database macros.
http://development.openoffice.org/	Lots of links to everything.
http://www.oooforum.org/	Many examples and help.

How to run a macro

A typical method to run a macro is as follows:

1) Use **Tools > Macros > Run Macro** to open the Macro Selector dialog (see Figure 322).

2) Select the library and module in the Library list (left hand side).

3) Select the macro in the Macro name list (right hand side).

4) Click **Run** to run the macro.

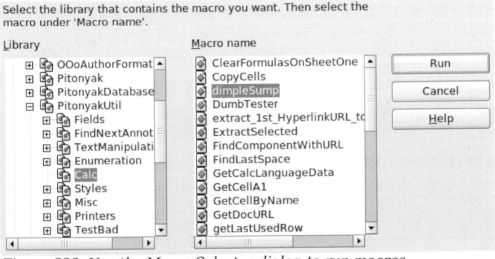

Figure 322: Use the Macro Selector dialog to run macros

Although you can use **Tools > Macros > Run Macro** to run all macros, this is not efficient for frequently run macros. A more common technique is to assign a macro to a toolbar button, menu item, keyboard shortcut, or a button embedded in a document. While choosing a method, it is also good to ask questions such as:

- Should the macro be available for only one document, or globally for all documents?

- Does the macro pertain to a specific document type, such as a Calc document?

- How frequently will the macro be used?

The answers will determine where to store the macro and how to make it available. For example, you will probably not add a rarely used macro to a toolbar. To help determine your choices, see Table 4.

Table 4. Methods for starting a macro.

Type	OpenOffice.org	Document Type	Document
Toolbar	No	Yes	Yes
Menu	No	Yes	Yes
Shortcut	Yes	Yes	No
Event	Yes	No	Yes

To add a menu item, keyboard shortcut, or toolbar icon that calls a macro, use the Customize dialog (see Figure 324). Open this dialog in either of these ways:

- Choose **Tools > Customize** from the main menu bar.

- Each toolbar has an icon ▾ that opens a menu; choose the **Customize Toolbar** option.

Tip   Complete coverage of the Customize dialog is beyond the scope of this document. Click the **Help** button to access the help pages included with OpenOffice.org.

The Customize dialog contains tabs to configure menus, keyboard bindings, toolbars, and events.

Toolbar

Macros can be added to toolbars. For more about modifying toolbars, see Chapter 14 (Customizing OpenOffice.org).

Menu item

Use **Tools > Customize** to open the Customize dialog, and select the Menus tab. You can modify an existing menu, or create new menus that call macros. For more about modifying menus, see Chapter 14.

Keyboard shortcuts

Use **Tools > Customize** to open the Customize dialog, and select the Keyboard tab. Assigning keyboard shortcuts is discussed in Chapter 14.

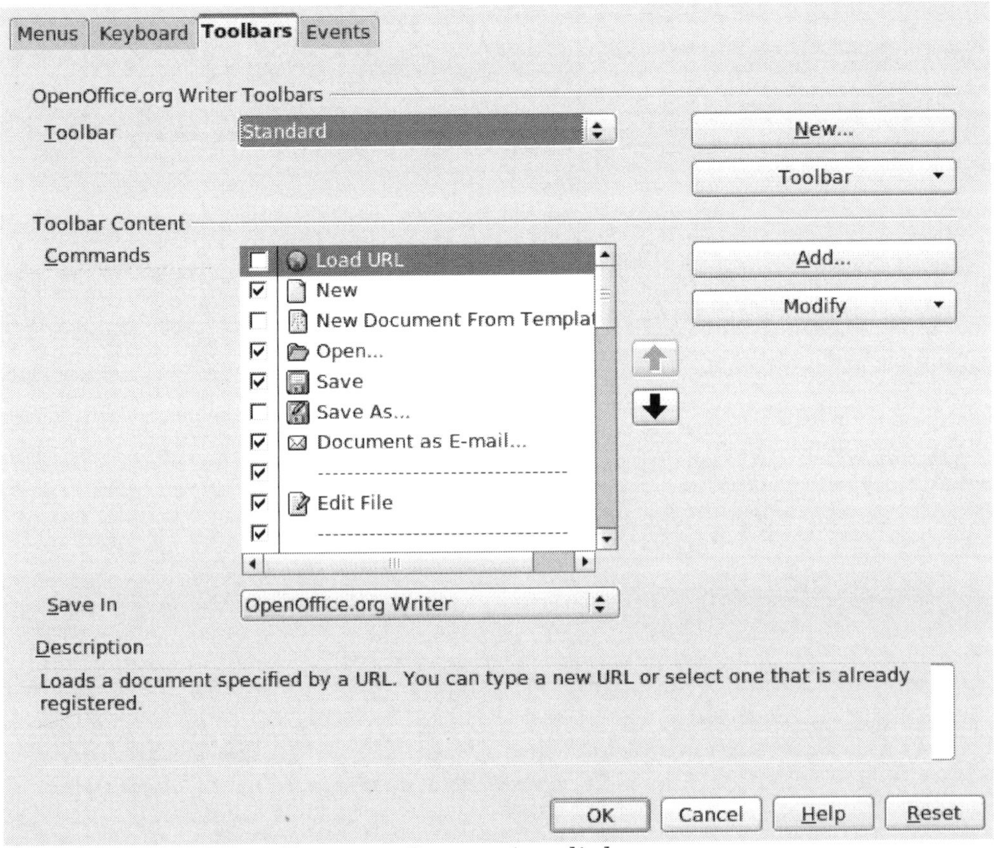

Figure 323: OpenOffice.org Customize dialog

Event

In OpenOffice.org, when something happens, we say that an event occurred. For example, a document was opened, a key was pressed, or the mouse moved. OpenOffice.org allows events to cause a macro to be called; the macro is then called an event handler. Full coverage of event handlers is well beyond the scope of this document, but a little knowledge can accomplish much.

Caution ⚠	Be careful when you configure an event handler. For example, assume that you write an event handler that is called every time that a key is pressed, but you make a mistake so the event is not properly handled. One possible result is that your event handler will consume all key presses, forcing you to forcibly terminate OpenOffice.org.

Use **Tools > Customize** to open the Customize dialog, and select the Events tab (see Figure 324). The events in the Customize dialog are related to the entire application and specific documents. Use the Save In box to choose OpenOffice.org, or a specific document.

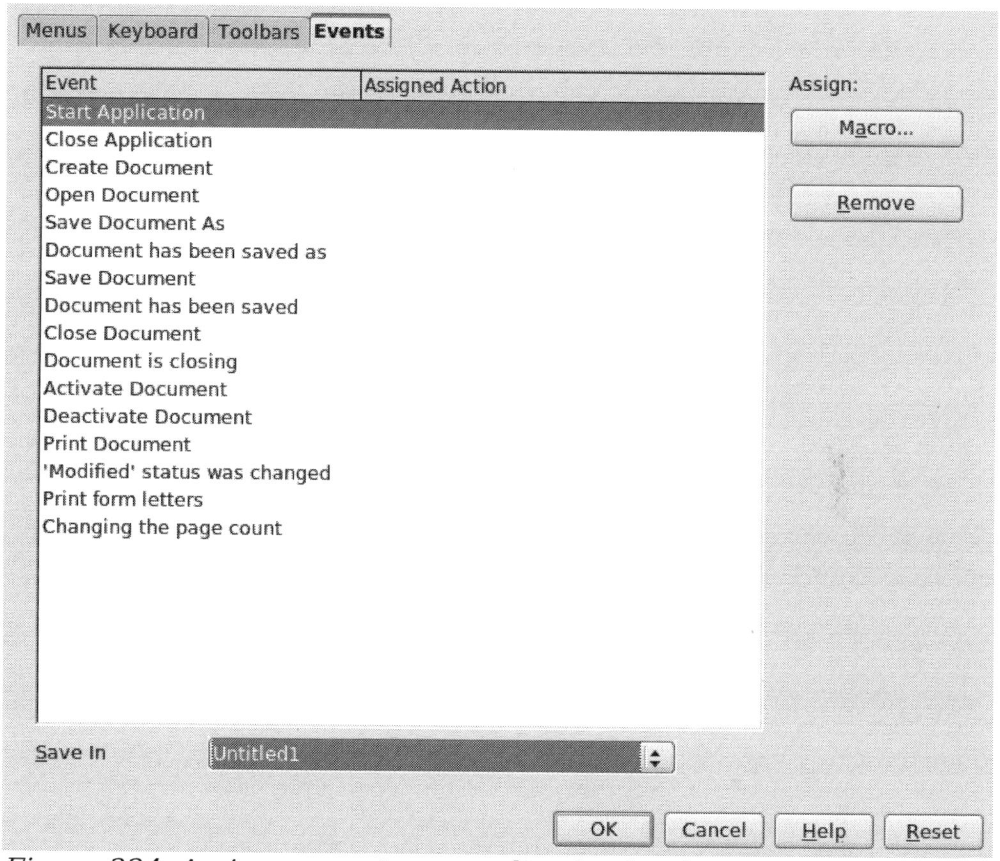

Figure 324: Assign macro to an application level event

A common use is to assign the Open Document event to call a specific macro. The macro then performs certain setup tasks for the document. Select the desired event and click the **Macro** button to open the Macro Selector dialog (see Figure 325).

Select the desired macro and click **OK** to assign the macro to the event. The Events tab shows that the event has been assigned to a macro (see Figure 326). When the document opens, the PrintHello macro is run.

Many objects in a document can be set to call macros when events occur. The most common usage is to add a control, such as a button, into a document. Even double-clicking on a graphic opens a dialog with a Macros tab that allows you to assign a macro to an event.

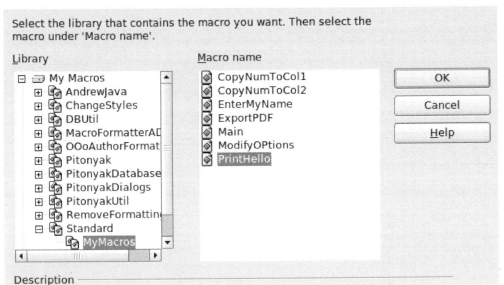

Select the library that contains the macro you want. Then select the
macro under 'Macro name'.

Library	Macro name

☐ ⊟ My Macros
  ⊞ 🔲 AndrewJava
  ⊞ 🔲 ChangeStyles
  ⊞ 🔲 DBUtil
  ⊞ 🔲 MacroFormatterAD
  ⊞ 🔲 OOoAuthorFormat
  ⊞ 🔲 Pitonyak
  ⊞ 🔲 PitonyakDatabase
  ⊞ 🔲 PitonyakDialogs
  ⊞ 🔲 PitonyakUtil
  ⊞ 🔲 RemoveFormattin
  ⊟ 🔲 Standard
    🔲 MyMacros

CopyNumToCol1
CopyNumToCol2
EnterMyName
ExportPDF
Main
ModifyOPtions
PrintHello

OK
Cancel
Help

Description

Figure 325: Assign macro to the document open event

Event	Assigned Action
Start Application	
Close Application	
Create Document	
Open Document	▶ Standard.MyMacros.PrintHello
Save Document As	

Assign:
Macro...
Remove

Figure 326: PrintHello is assigned to the Open Document event

Extensions

An extension is a package that can be installed into OpenOffice.org to
add new functionality. Extensions can be written in almost any
programming language and may be simple or sophisticated.
Extensions can be grouped into types:

- Calc Add-Ins, which provide new functionality for Calc, including
  new functions that act like normal built-in functions

- New components and functionality, which normally include some
  level of UI integration such as new menus or toolbars

- Data pilots that are used directly in Calc

- Chart Add-Ins with new chart types

- Linguistic components such as spell checkers

- Document templates and images

       Getting Started with OpenOffice.org 3

Although individual extensions can be found in different places, there is an extension repository at: http://extensions.services.openoffice.org/.

For more about obtaining and installing extensions, see Chapter 14 (Customizing OpenOffice.org).

Writing macros without the recorder

The examples covered in this chapter are created using the macro recorder and the dispatcher. You can also write macros that directly access the objects that comprise OpenOffice.org. In other words, you can directly manipulate a document.

Directly manipulating OOo's internal objects is an advanced topic that is beyond the scope of this chapter. A simple example, however, demonstrates how this works.

Listing 4: Append the text "Hello" to the current document.

```
Sub AppendHello
  Dim oDoc
  Dim sTextService$
  Dim oCurs

  REM ThisComponent refers to the currently active document.
  oDoc = ThisComponent

  REM Verify that this is a text document
  sTextService = "com.sun.star.text.TextDocument"
  If NOT oDoc.supportsService(sTextService) Then
    MsgBox "This macro only works with a text document"
    Exit Sub
  End If

  REM Get the view cursor from the current controller.
  oCurs = oDoc.currentController.getViewCursor()

  REM Move the cursor to the end of the document
  oCurs.gotoEnd(False)

  REM Insert text "Hello" at the end of the document
  oCurs.Text.insertString(oCurs, "Hello", False)
End Sub
```

Finding more information

Numerous resources are available that provide help with writing macros. Use **Help > OpenOffice.org Help** to open the OOo help pages. The upper left corner of the OOo help system contains a drop-down list that determines which help set is displayed. To view the help for Basic, the drop-down must display *Help about OpenOffice.org Basic*.

Included material

Many excellent macros are included with OOo. Use **Tools > Macros > Organize Macros > OpenOffice.org Basic** to open the Macro dialog. Expand the Tools library in the OpenOffice.org library container. Inspect the Debug module—some good examples include WritedbgInfo(document) and printdbgInfo(sheet).

Online resources

The following links and references contain information regarding macro programming:

http://www.openoffice.org (the main link)

http://codesnippets.services.openoffice.org/ (categorized examples)

http://user.services.openoffice.org/ (OOo forums, well supported)

http://www.oooforum.org (OOo forums, well supported)

http://api.openoffice.org/docs/common/ref/com/sun/star/module-ix.html (official IDL reference, here you'll find almost every command with a description)

http://wiki.services.openoffice.org/wiki/Documentation/DevGuide/OpenOffice.org_Developers_Guide (official documentation that contains a detailed explanation)

http://www.pitonyak.org/oo.php (Andrew Pitonyak's macro page)

http://www.pitonyak.org/AndrewMacro.odt (numerous examples of working macros)

http://www.pitonyak.org/book/ (Andrew Pitonyak wrote a book on macros)

http://www.pitonyak.org/database/ (numerous macro examples using Base)

http://docs.sun.com/app/docs (Sun wrote a book on macro programming—very well written and laid out) http://documentation.openoffice.org (contains content related to macros)

http://ooextras.sourceforge.net/ (examples)

http://sourceforge.net/project/showfiles.php?group_id=43716 (examples)

http://homepages.paradise.net.nz/hillview/OOo/ (numerous excellent macros, including reveal codes macros, key macros, and information on converting from MS Office)

Published material

The following published sources contain macro examples. The most obvious example is the documentation from Sun. Start from Sun's documentation site http://docs.sun.com/app/docs and search for StarOffice documentation.

Andrew Pitonyak wrote a book called *OpenOffice.org Macros Explained*. Two chapters are available as direct downloads from the publisher. See http://www.pitonyak.org/book/.

Dr. Mark Alexander Bain wrote *Learn OpenOffice.org Spreadsheet Macro Programming* (see http://www.packtpub.com/openoffice-ooobasic-calc-automation/book).

Chapter *14*
Customizing OpenOffice.org

This chapter describes some common customizations that you may wish to do.

You can customize menus, toolbars, and keyboard shortcuts in OpenOffice.org, add new menus and toolbars, and assign macros to events. However, you cannot customize context (right-click) menus.

Other customizations are made easy by extensions that you can install from the OpenOffice.org website or from other providers.

Note	Customizations to menus and toolbars can be saved in a template. To do so, first save them in a document and then save the document as a template as described in Chapter 3 (Styles and Templates).

Customizing menu content

In addition to changing the menu font (described in Chapter 2), you can add and rearrange items on the menu bar, add items to menus, and make other changes.

To customize menus:

1) Choose **Tools > Customize.**
2) On the **Customize** dialog, pick the **Menus** page (Figure 327).
3) In the Save In drop-down list, choose whether to save this changed menu for the application (for example, Writer) or for a selected document.

4) In the section **OpenOffice.org <name of the program (example: Writer) > Menus**, select from the **Menu** drop-down list the menu that you want to customize. The list includes all the main menus as well as sub-menus, that is menus that are contained under another menu. For example, in addition to *File*, *Edit*, *View*, and so on, there is *File | Send* and *File |Templates*. The commands available for the selected menu are shown in the central part of the dialog.

5) To customize the selected menu, click on the **Menu** or **Modify** buttons. You can also add commands to a menu by clicking on the **Add** button. These actions are described in the following sections. Use the up and down arrows next to the Entries list to move the selected menu item to a different position.

6) When you have finished making all your changes, click **OK** to save them.

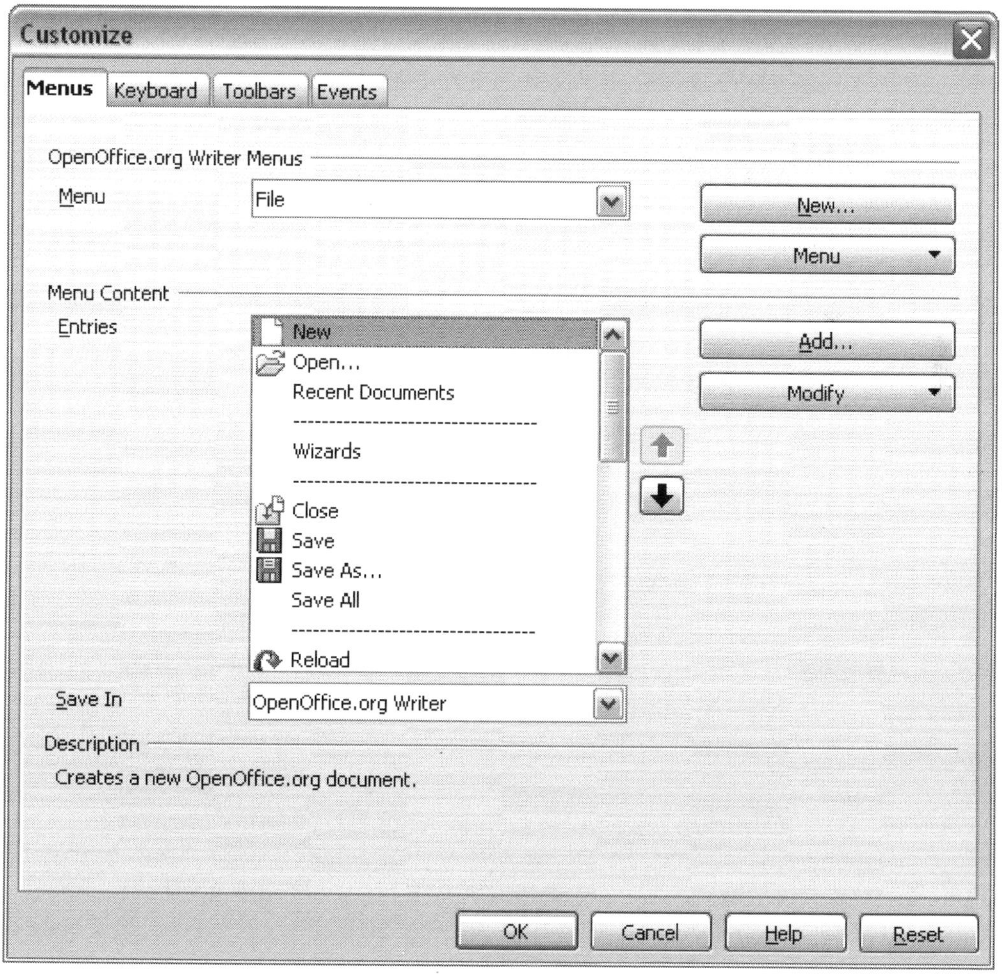

Figure 327. The Menus page of the Customize dialog

Creating a new menu

In the Customize dialog, click **New** to display the dialog shown in Figure 328.

1) Type a name for your new menu in the **Menu name** box.
2) Use the up and down arrow buttons to move the new menu into the required position on the menu bar.
3) Click **OK** to save.

The new menu now appears on the list of menus in the Customize dialog. (It will appear on the menu bar itself after you save your customizations.)

After creating a new menu, you need to add some commands to it, as described in "Adding a command to a menu" on page 393.

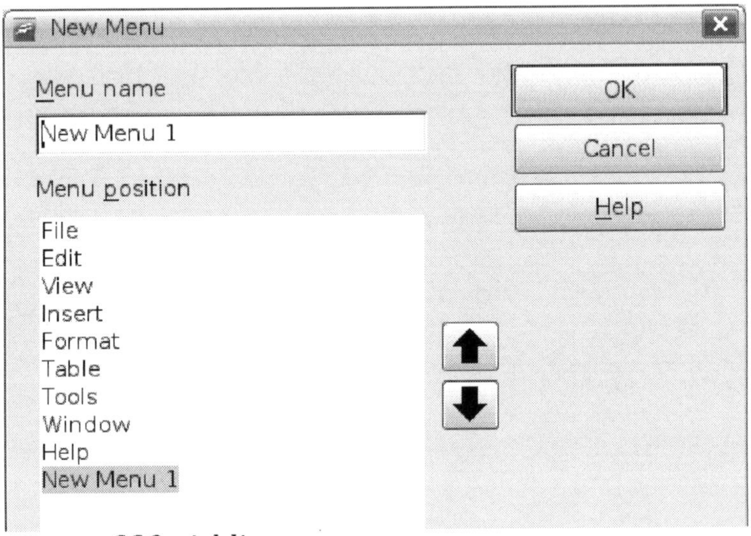

Figure 328: Adding a new menu

Modifying existing menus

To modify an existing menu, select it in the Menu list and click the **Menu** button to drop down a list of modifications: **Move, Rename, Delete**. Not all of these modifications can be applied to all the entries in the Menu list. For example, **Rename** and **Delete** are not available for the supplied menus.

To move a menu (such as *File*), choose **Menu > Move**. A dialog similar to the one shown in Figure 328 (but without the **Menu name** box) opens. Use the up and down arrow buttons to move the menu into the required position.

To move submenus (such as *File | Send*), select the main menu (File) in the Menu list and then, in the Menu Content section of the dialog, select the submenu (Send) in the Entries list and use the arrow keys to move it up or down in the sequence. Submenus are easily identified in the Entries list by a small black triangle on the right hand side of the name.

In addition to renaming, you can specify a keyboard shortcut that allows you to select a menu command when you press *Alt+* an underlined letter in a menu command.

1) Select a menu or menu entry.
2) Click the **Menu** button and select **Rename**.
3) Add a tilde (~) in front of the letter that you want to use as an accelerator. For example, to select the Save All command by pressing *Alt+V*, enter `Sa~ve All`.

Adding a command to a menu

You can add commands to the supplied menus and to menus you have created. On the Customize dialog, select the menu in the Menu list and click the **Add** button in the Menu Content section of the dialog.

On the Add Commands dialog, select a category and then the command, and click **Add**. The dialog remains open, so you can select several commands. When you have finished adding commands, click **Close**. Back on the Customize dialog, you can use the up and down arrow buttons to arrange the commands in your preferred sequence.

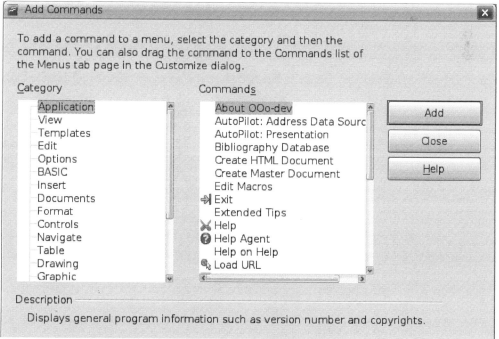

Figure 329: Adding a command to a menu

Modifying menu entries

In addition to changing the sequence of entries on a menu or submenu, you can add submenus, rename or delete the entries, and add group separators.

To begin, select the menu or submenu in the Menu list near the top of the Customize page, then select the entry in the Entries list under Menu Content. Click the **Modify** button and choose the required action from the drop-down list of actions.

Most of the actions should be self-explanatory. **Begin a group** adds a separator line after the highlighted entry.

Customizing toolbars

You can customize toolbars in several ways, including choosing which icons are visible and locking the position of a docked toolbar, as described in Chapter 1 (Introducing OpenOffice.org). This section describes how to create new toolbars and add other icons (commands) to the list of those available on a toolbar.

To get to the toolbar customization dialog, do any of the following:

- On the toolbar, click the arrow at the end of the toolbar and choose **Customize Toolbar**.

- Choose **View > Toolbars > Customize** from the menu bar.

- Choose **Tools > Customize** from the menu bar and pick the **Toolbars** page (Figure 330).

To customize toolbars:

1) In the Save In drop-down list, choose whether to save this changed toolbar for the application (for example, Writer) or for a selected document.

2) In the section **OpenOffice.org <name of the program (example: Writer) > Toolbars**, select from the **Toolbar** drop-down list the toolbar that you want to customize.

3) You can create a new toolbar by clicking on the **New** button, or customize existing toolbars by clicking on the **Toolbar** or **Modify** buttons, and add commands to a toolbar by clicking on the **Add** button. These actions are described below.

4) When you have finished making all your changes, click **OK** to save them.

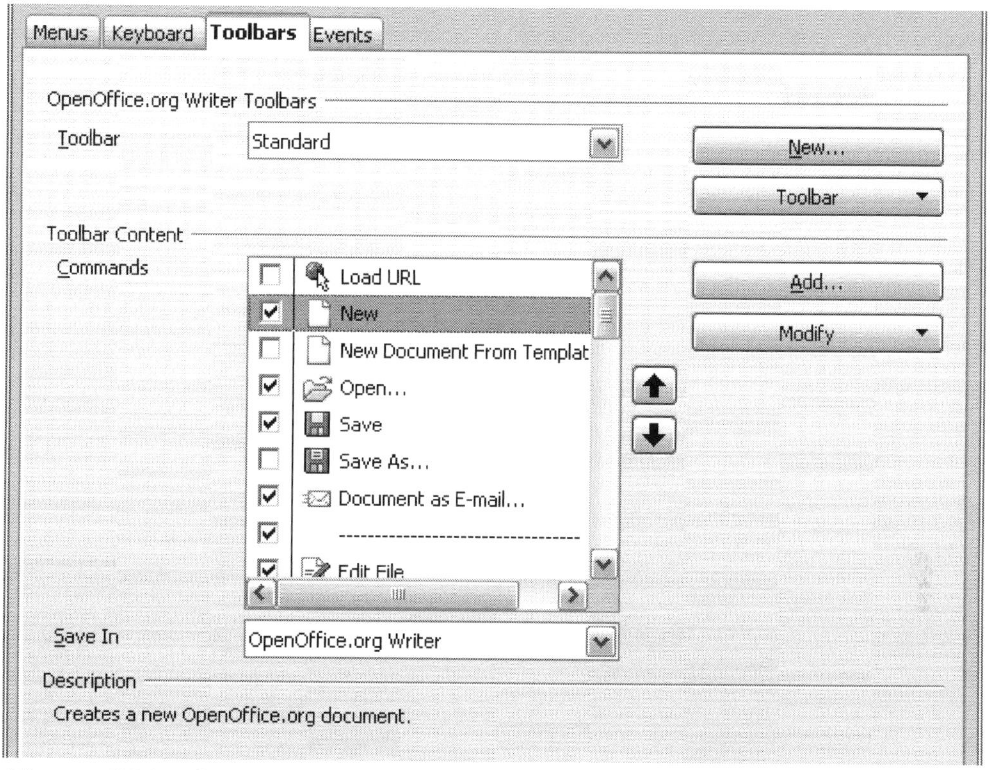

Figure 330. The Toolbars page of the Customize dialog

Creating a new toolbar

To create a new toolbar:

1) Choose **Tools > Customize > Toolbars** from the menu bar.

2) Click **New**. On the Name dialog, type the new toolbar's name and choose from the Save In drop-down list where to save this changed menu: for the application (for example, Writer) or for a selected document.

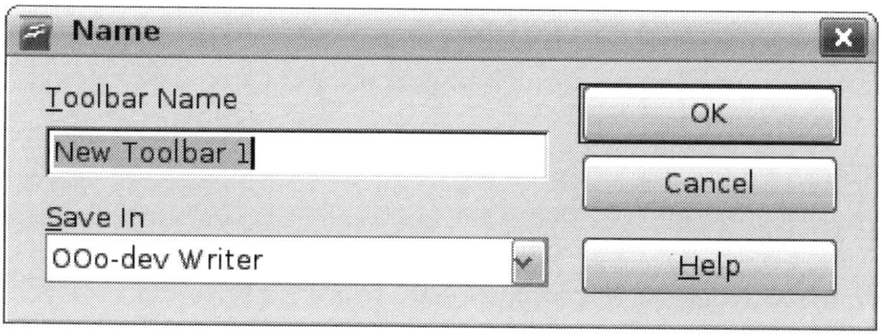

The new toolbar now appears on the list of toolbars in the Customize dialog. After creating a new toolbar, you need to add some commands to it, as described below.

Adding a command to a toolbar

If the list of available buttons for a toolbar does not include all the commands you want on that toolbar, you can add commands. When you create a new toolbar, you need to add commands to it.

1) On the Toolbars page of the Customize dialog, select the toolbar in the Toolbar list and click the **Add** button in the Toolbar Content section of the dialog.

2) The Add Commands dialog is the same as for adding commands to menus (Figure 329). Select a category and then the command, and click **Add**. The dialog remains open, so you can select several commands. When you have finished adding commands, click **Close**. If you insert an item which does not have an associated icon, the toolbar will display the full name of the item: the next section describes how to choose an icon for a toolbar command.

3) Back on the Customize dialog, you can use the up and down arrow buttons to arrange the commands in your preferred sequence.

4) When you are done making changes, click **OK** to save.

Choosing icons for toolbar commands

Toolbar buttons usually have icons, not words, on them, but not all of the commands have associated icons.

To choose an icon for a command, select the command and click **Modify > Change icon**. On the Change Icon dialog, you can scroll through the available icons, select one, and click **OK** to assign it to the command.

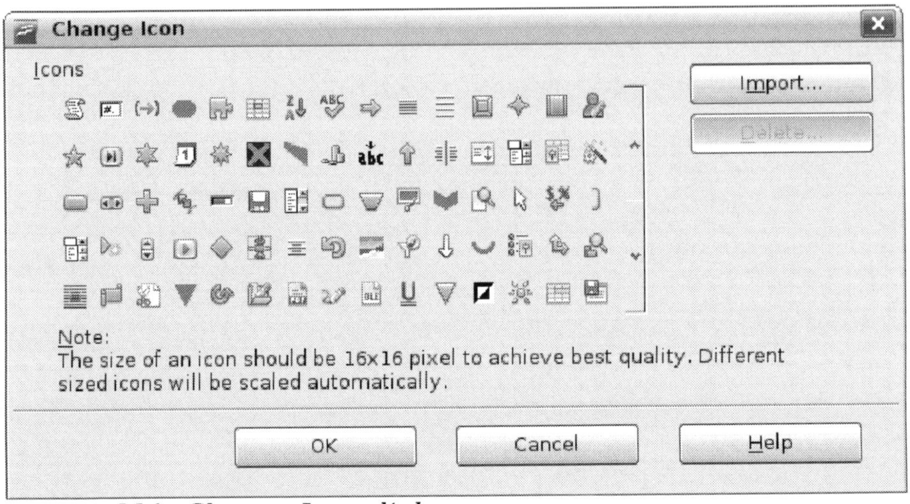

Figure 331: Change Icon dialog

To use a custom icon, create it in a graphics program and import it into OOo by clicking the **Import** button on the Change Icon dialog. Custom icons must be 16 x 16 or 26 x 26 pixels in size and cannot contain more than 256 colors.

Example: Adding a Fax icon to a toolbar

You can customize OpenOffice.org so that a single click on an icon automatically sends the current document as a fax.

1) Be sure the fax driver is installed. Consult the documentation for your fax modem for more information.

    a) Choose **Tools > Options > OpenOffice.org Writer > Print**. The dialog shown in Figure 332 opens.

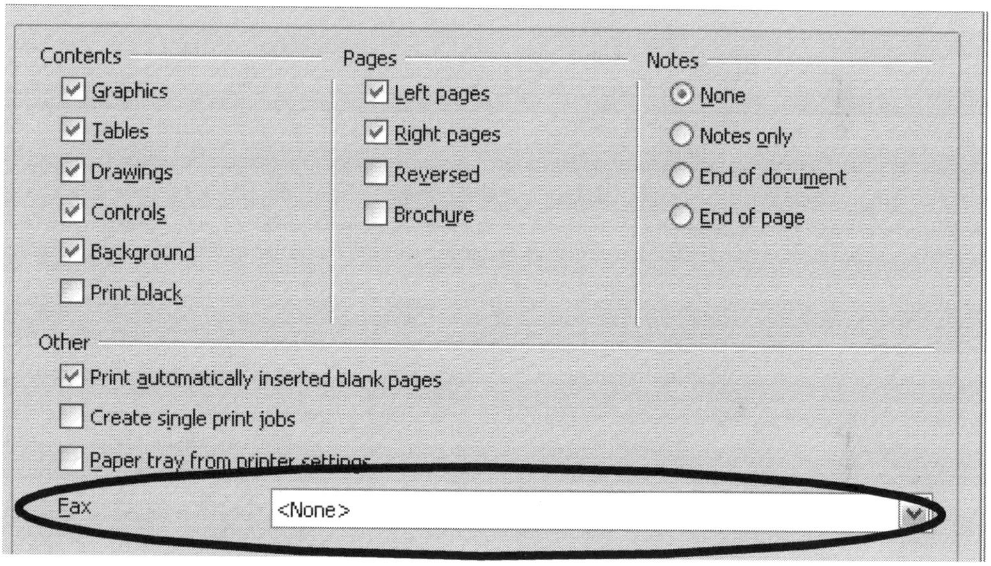

Figure 332: Setting up OOo for sending faxes

    b) Select the fax driver from the **Fax** list and click **OK**.

2) Click the arrow icon at the end of the Standard toolbar. In the drop-down menu, choose **Customize Toolbar**. The Toolbars page of the Customize dialog appears (Figure 330). Click **Add**.

3) On the Add Commands dialog (Figure 333), select *Documents* in the Category list, then select *Send Default Fax* in the Commands list. Click **Add**. Now you can see the new icon in the Commands list.

4) In the Commands list, click the up or down arrow button to position the new icon where you want it. Click **OK** and then click **Close**. Your toolbar now has a new icon to send the current document as a fax.

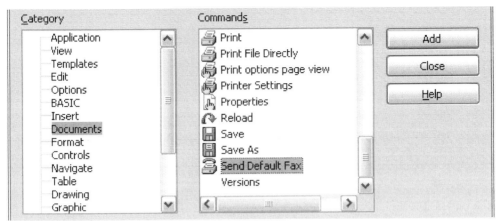

Figure 333: Adding a Send Fax command to a toolbar

Assigning shortcut keys

In addition to using the built-in keyboard shortcuts (listed in Appendix A), you can define your own. You can assign shortcuts to standard OOo functions or your own macros and save them for use with the entire OpenOffice.org suite.

Caution	Be careful when reassigning your operating system's or OOo's predefined shortcut keys. Many key assignments are universally understood shortcuts, such as *F1* for Help, and are always expected to provide certain results. Although you can easily reset the shortcut key assignments to the OOo defaults, changing some common shortcut keys can cause confusion, frustration and possible data loss or corruption, especially if other users share your computer.

To adapt shortcut keys to your needs, use the Customize dialog, as described below.

1) Select **Tools > Customize > Keyboard**. The Customize dialog opens.

2) To have the shortcut key assignment available in all components of OpenOffice.org select the **OpenOffice.org** button.

3) Next select the required function from the *Category* and *Function* lists.

4) Now select the desired shortcut keys in the *Shortcut keys* list and click the **Modify** button at the upper right.

5) Click **OK** to accept the change. Now the chosen shortcut keys will execute the function chosen in step 3 above whenever they are pressed.

Note	All existing shortcut keys for the currently selected *Function* are listed in the *Keys* selection box. If the *Keys* list is empty, it indicates that the chosen key combination is free for use. If it were not, and you wanted to reassign a shortcut key combination that is already in use, you must first **Delete** the existing *Key*. Shortcut keys that are greyed-out in the listing on the Customize dialog, such as *F1* and *F10,* are not available for reassignment.

Example: Assigning styles to shortcut keys

You can configure shortcut keys to quickly assign styles in your document. Some shortcuts are predefined, such as *Ctrl+0* for the *Text body* paragraph style, *Ctrl+1* for the *Heading 1* style, and *Ctrl+2* for *Heading 2*. You can modify these shortcuts and create your own.

1) Click **Tools > Customize > Keyboard**. The Keyboard page of the Customize dialog (Figure 334) opens.

2) To have the shortcut key assignment available only with one component (for example, Writer), select that component's name in the upper right corner of the page; otherwise select **OpenOffice.org** button to make it available to every component.

3) Choose the shortcut keys you want to assign a style to. In this example, we have chosen *Ctrl+9*.

4) In the *Functions* section at the bottom of the dialog, scroll down in the Category list to Styles. Click the + sign to expand the list of styles.

5) Choose the category of style (our example uses a paragraph style). The *Function* list will display the names of the available styles for the selected category. The example shows some of OOo's predefined styles.

6) To assign *Ctrl+9* to be the shortcut key combination for the List 1 style, select *List 1* in the *Function* list, and then click **Modify**. *Ctrl+9* now appears in the *Keys* list.

7) Make any other required changes, and then click **OK** to save these settings and close the dialog.

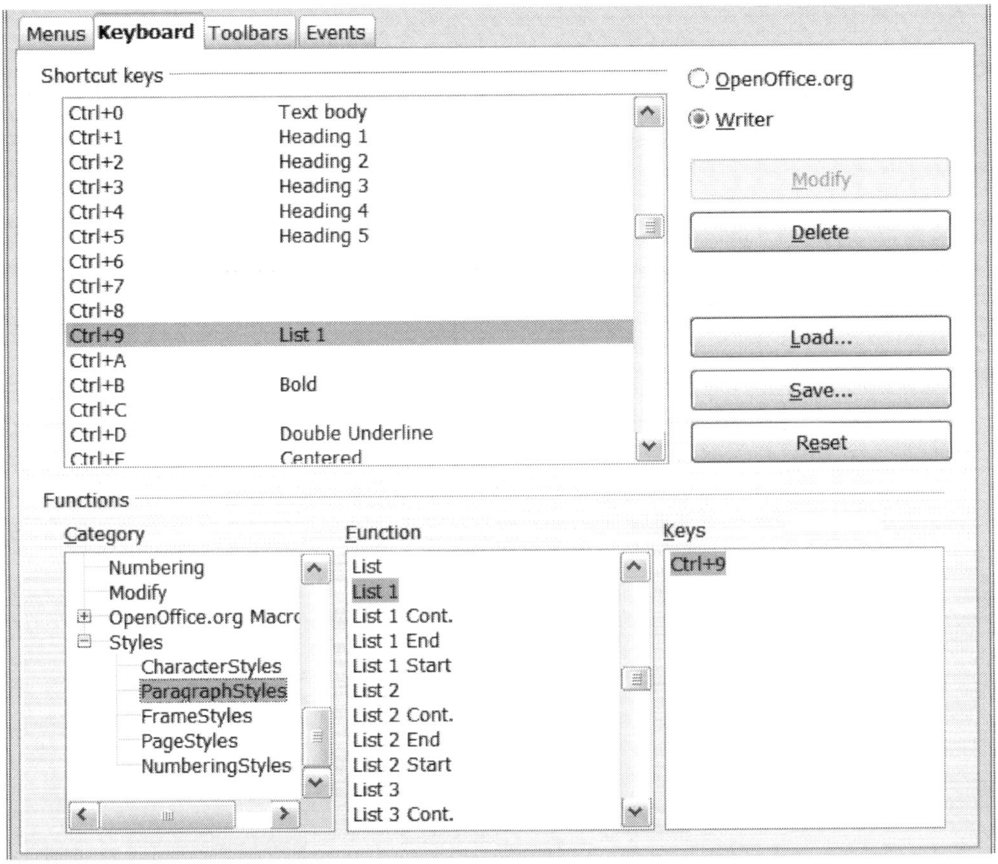

Figure 334. Defining keyboard shortcuts for applying styles

Saving changes to a file

Changes to the shortcut key assignments can be saved in a keyboard configuration file for use at a later time, thus permitting you to create and apply different configurations as the need arises. To save keyboard shortcuts to a file:

1) After making your keyboard shortcut assignments, click the **Save** button near the bottom right of the Customize dialog (Figure 334).

2) In the Save Keyboard Configuration dialog, select *All files* from the **Save as Type** list.

3) Next enter a name for the keyboard configuration file in the **File name** box, or select an existing file from the list. If you need to, browse to find a file from another location.

4) Click **Save**. A confirmation dialog appears if you are about to overwrite an existing file, otherwise there will be no feedback and the file will be saved.

Loading a saved keyboard configuration

To load a saved keyboard configuration file and replace your existing configuration, click the **Load** button near the bottom right of the Customize dialog, and then select the configuration file from the Load Keyboard Configuration dialog.

Resetting the shortcut keys

To reset all of the keyboard shortcuts to their default values, click the **Reset** button near the bottom right of the Customize dialog. Use this feature with care as no confirmation dialog will be displayed; the defaults will be set without any further notice or user input.

Assigning macros to events

In OOo, when something happens, we say that an event occured. For example, a document was opened, a key was pressed, or the mouse moved. You can associate a macro with an event, so the macro is run when the event occurs. For example, a common use is to assign the "open document" event to run a macro that performs certain setup tasks for the document.

To associate a macro with an event, use the Events page of the Customize dialog. For more information, see Chapter 13 (Getting Started with Macros).

Adding functionality with extensions

An extension is a package that can be installed into OpenOffice.org to add new functionality.

Although individual extensions can be found in different places, the official OpenOffice.org extension repository is at http://extensions.services.openoffice.org/. Some extensions are free of charge; others are available for a fee. Check the descriptions to see what licenses and fees apply to the ones that interest you.

Installing extensions

To install an extension, follow these steps:

1) Download an extension and save it anywhere on your computer.
2) In OOo, select **Tools > Extension Manager** from the menu bar. In the Extension Manager dialog (Figure 335), click **Add**.

3) A file browser window opens. Find and select the extension you want to install and click **Open**. The extension begins installing. You may be asked to accept a license agreement.

4) When the installation is complete, the extension is listed in the Extension Manager dialog.

Tip	To get extensions that are listed in the repository, you can open the Extension Manager and click the **Get more extensions here** link. You do not need to download them separately as in step 1 above.

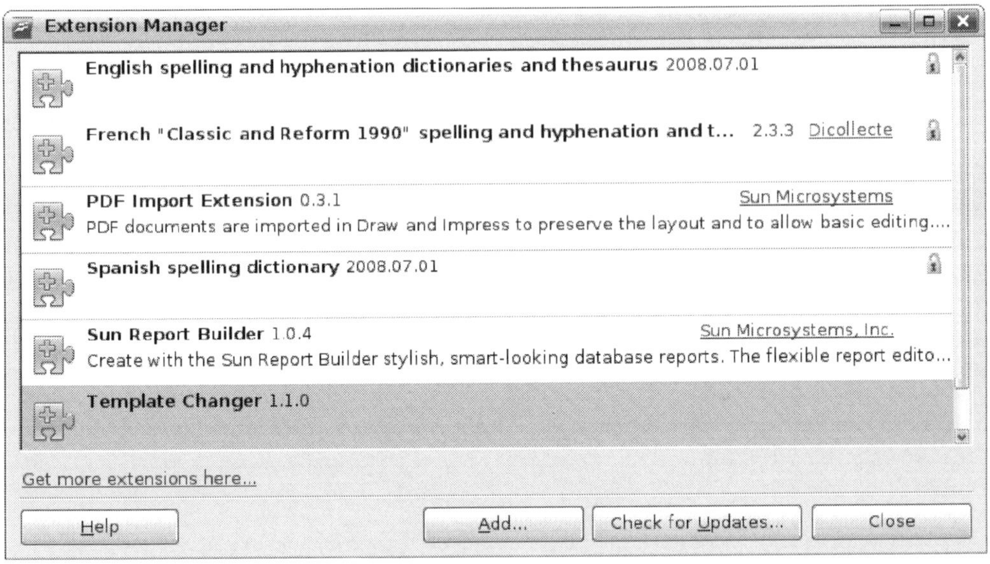

Figure 335: Installing an extension

Note	To install a *shared* extension, you need write access to the OpenOffice.org installation directory.

Using extensions

This section describes several of the more important and popular extensions to OpenOffice.org. In each case, you need to first install the extension as described in the previous section.

PDF Import

Enables you to make minor modifications to the text of existing PDF files when the original source files do not exist or you are unable to open the source files. (Whenever possible, modify the source and regenerate the PDF to obtain the best results.)

When the extension is installed, PDF is listed as a choice in the File Type drop-down list in the **File > Open** dialog. PDF documents open in Draw. Depending on the complexity of the layout, changes may be easy or difficult to make, and the saved result may or may not preserve the original layout. Font substitution may occur.

Each line of text appears in a separate text box. If part of the text is in a different font or font variation (for example, bold or italic), that part of the line is in a separate text box. Thus a single line of text may contain several separate text boxes. If you edit the text in one box, the result may overlap the text in the following box or leave a conspicuous gap between the two portions of text. If this occurs, you need to manually adjust the spacing between the boxes.

Graphics with transparent backgrounds are imported with black backgrounds, and these black backgrounds remain when the edited PDF is saved again. Graphics and frames anchored "to paragraph" may move away from their positions during import; any incorrect positioning remains when the PDF is saved again.

From Sun Microsystems. Open source.

Presenter Console

Provides extra control over slide shows (presentations); for example, the presenter has ability to see the upcoming slide, the slide notes, and a presentation timer—while the audience sees only the current slide. The Presenter Console displays the elements in three easily changeable views:

- The first view displays the current slide, including the effects, and the upcoming slide.
- The second view shows the speaker's notes in large, clear, and scalable type, plus the current and upcoming slide.
- The third view is a slide sorter view with the slide thumbnails.

From Sun Microsystems. Open source.

| **Note** | The Presenter Console works only on an operating system that supports multiple displays. |

Report Builder

Creates stylish, complex database reports from Base. You can define group and page headers, group and page footers, and calculation fields. Export your reports into PDF or OpenDocument formats, or send them as email attachments. From Sun Microsystems. Open source.

Professional Template Pack II

More than 120 templates for Writer, Calc, and Impress. Available in several languages. After you have installed this Extension, you will find the templates under **File > New > Templates and Documents**. From Sun Microsystems. Freeware.

Template Changer

Adds two new items to the **File > Templates** menu that allow you to assign a new template to the current document or to a folder of documents. All styles and formatting will be loaded from that template and the document will behave as it was created using that template. Open source.

Appendix A
Keyboard Shortcuts

You can use OpenOffice.org (OOo) without requiring a pointing device, such as a mouse or trackball, by using its built-in keyboard shortcuts. Tasks as varied and complex as docking and un-docking toolbars and windows, or changing the size or position of objects, can all be accomplished with only a keyboard.

OOo has a general set of keyboard shortcuts, available in all components, and a component-specific set directly related to the work of that component (Writer, Calc, Impress, Draw, and Base). This appendix lists the general set. For component-specific shortcuts, see the relevant component guide.

For help with OOo's keyboard shortcuts, or using OOo with a keyboard only, search the OOo Help using the "shortcut" or "accessibility" keywords.

In addition to using the built-in keyboard shortcuts listed in this Appendix, you can define your own. See Chapter 14 (Customizing OpenOffice.org) for instructions.

Note	Some of the shortcut keys may be assigned to your desktop system. Keys that are assigned to the desktop system are not available to OOo. Try to assign different keys either for OOo (described in Chapter 14), or for your desktop system (see your system's documentation).

Function key shortcuts

Shortcut Keys	Result
F1	Starts the OpenOffice.org Help. In the OpenOffice.org Help: jumps to main help page.
Shift+F1	Activates *What's This?* (extended tip) help for the mouse pointer, which turns into a question mark. Move the pointer over an item (command, icon or control) to view the extended tip.
Shift+F2	Displays an extended tip for the item (command, icon or control) currently selected by using the keyboard.
Ctrl+F4 or Alt+F4	Closes the current document. Closes OpenOffice.org when the last open document is closed.
F6	Sets focus in next subwindow.
Shift+F6	Sets focus in previous subwindow.
F10	Activates the first menu (File menu).
Shift+F10	Opens the context (pop-up) menu.
Ctrl+F11	Opens the Style Catalog.

General shortcut keys for OpenOffice.org

Shortcut Keys	Result
Enter key	Activates the focused button in a dialog.
Esc	Terminates the action or dialog. If in OpenOffice.org Help: goes up one level.
Spacebar	Toggles the focused checkbox in a dialog.
Arrow keys	Changes the active control field in an option section of a dialog.
Tab	Advances focus to the next section or element in a dialog.
Shift+Tab	Moves the focus to the previous section or element in a dialog.

Shortcut Keys	Result
Alt+Down Arrow	Opens the list of the control field currently selected in a dialog. This shortcut applies to combo boxes and to icon buttons with pop-up menus. Close an opened list by pressing the Esc key.
Del	Deletes the selected items into the recycle bin.
Shift+Del	Deletes the selected items without putting them in the recycle bin.
Backspace	When a folder is shown: goes up one level (goes back).
Ctrl+Shift+Space bar	Removes direct formatting from selected text or objects (as in **Format > Default Formatting**).
Ctrl+Tab	When positioned at the start of a header, a tab is inserted.
Enter (if an OLE object is selected)	Activates the selected OLE object.
Enter (if a drawing object or text object is selected)	Activates text input mode.
Ctrl+O	Opens a document.
Ctrl+S	Saves the current document.
Ctrl+N	Creates a new document.
Shift+Ctrl+N	Opens the Templates and Documents dialog.
Ctrl+P	Prints the document.
Ctrl+Q	Exits the application.
Ctrl+X	Cuts the selected items.
Ctrl+C	Copies the selected items.
Ctrl+V	Pastes from the clipboard.
Ctrl+Shift+V	Opens the Paste Special dialog.
Ctrl+A	Selects all.
Ctrl+Z	Undoes last action.
Ctrl+Y	Redoes last action.
Ctrl+Shift+Y	Repeats last command.

Shortcut Keys	Result
Ctrl+F	Calls the Find & Replace dialog.
Ctrl+Shift+F	Searches for the last entered search term.
Ctrl+Shift+J	Toggles the view between fullscreen mode and normal mode in Writer or Calc.
Ctrl+Shift+R	Refreshes (redraws) the document view.
Ctrl+Shift+I	Enables or disables the selection cursor in read-only text.
Ctrl+I	Applies the Italic attribute to the selected area or the word in which the cursor is positioned.
Ctrl+B	Applies the Bold attribute to the selected area or the word in which the cursor is positioned.
Ctrl+U	Applies the Underlined attribute to the selected area or the word in which the cursor is positioned.

Shortcut keys in the Gallery

Shortcut Keys	Result
Tab	Moves between areas.
Shift+Tab	Moves between areas (backwards).

In the New Theme area of the Gallery

Shortcut keys	Result
Up arrow	Moves the selection up.
Down arrow	Moves the selection down.
Ctrl+Enter	Opens the Properties dialog.
Shift+F10	Opens a context menu.
Ctrl+U	Refreshes the selected theme.
Ctrl+R	Opens the Enter Title dialog.
Ctrl+D	Deletes the selected theme.
Insert	Inserts a new theme.

In the Gallery preview area

Shortcut keys	Result
Home	Jumps to the first entry.
End	Jumps to the last entry.
Left Arrow	Selects the next Gallery element on the left.
Right Arrow	Selects the next Gallery element on the right.
Up Arrow	Selects the next Gallery element above.
Down Arrow	Selects the next Gallery element below.
Page Up	Scrolls up one screen.
Page Down	Scrolls down one screen.
Ctrl+Shift+Insert	Inserts the selected object as a linked object into the current document.
Ctrl+I	Inserts a copy of the selected object into the current document.
Ctrl+T	Opens the Enter Title dialog.
Ctrl+P	Switches between themes view and object view.
Spacebar	Switches between themes view and object view.
Enter	Switches between themes view and object view.
Step backward	Switches back to main overview (only in object view).

Selecting rows and columns in a database table (opened by F4)

Shortcut keys	Result
Spacebar	Toggles row selection, except when the row is in edit mode.
Ctrl+spacebar	Toggles row selection.
Shift+spacebar	Selects the current column.
Ctrl+PgUp	Moves pointer to the first row.
Ctrl+PgDn	Moves pointer to the last row.

Shortcut keys for drawing objects

Shortcut keys	Result
Select the toolbar with *F6*. Use the Down Arrow and Right Arrow to select the desired toolbar icon and press *Ctrl+Enter*.	Inserts a Drawing Object.
Select the document with *Ctrl+F6* and press *Tab*	Selects a Drawing Object.
Tab	Selects the next Drawing Object.
Shift+Tab	Selects the previous Drawing Object.
Ctrl+Home	Selects the first Drawing Object.
Ctrl+End	Selects the last Drawing Object.
Esc	Ends Drawing Object selection.
Esc (in Handle Selection Mode)	Exits Handle Selection Mode and returns to Object Selection Mode.
Up/down/left/right arrow	Moves the selected point (the snap-to-grid functions are temporarily disabled, but end points still snap to each other).
Alt+Up/Down/Left/ Right Arrow	Moves the selected Drawing Object one pixel (in Selection Mode). Re-sizes a Drawing Object (in Handle Selection Mode). Rotates a Drawing Object (in Rotation Mode). Opens the properties dialog for a Drawing Object. Activates the Point Selection mode for the selected drawing object.
Spacebar	Selects a point of a drawing object (in Point Selection mode) or cancels the selection. The selected point blinks once per second.
Shift+Spacebar	Selects an additional point in Point Selection mode.

Shortcut keys	Result
Ctrl+Tab	Selects the next point of the drawing object (Point Selection mode).
	In Rotation mode, the centre of rotation can also be selected.
Shift+Ctrl+Tab	Selects the previous point of the drawing object (Point Selection mode).
Ctrl+Enter	Places a new drawing object with default size in the centre of the current view.
Ctrl+Enter at the Selection icon	Activates the first drawing object in the document.
Esc	Leaves the Point Selection mode. The drawing object is selected afterwards.
	Edits a point of a drawing object (Point Edit mode).
Any text or numerical key	If a drawing object is selected, switches to edit mode and places the cursor at the end of the text in the drawing object. A printable character is inserted.

Appendix B
Background Information

History, licensing, and file formats

OpenOffice.org is both a product and an open-source project. If you are new to OOo, its open source development, and the community that produces and supports it, you should read this appendix.

A short history of OpenOffice.org

The OpenOffice.org project began when Sun Microsystems released the source code ("blueprints") for its StarOffice® software to the open source community on October 13, 2000. This allowed Sun to use the technical expertise and rapid development times of an open-source project in the development of its own software products. All recent versions of Sun's StarOffice use source code developed by the OpenOffice.org community. However, the products do not provide exactly the same features due to the copyrights of third parties that are not compatible with open-source licensing.

OpenOffice.org 1.0, the product, was released on April 30, 2002.

Read more about OpenOffice.org's history and organization at: http://about.openoffice.org/

Information about StarOffice can be found at:
http://www.sun.com/software/star/staroffice/

The OpenOffice.org community

OpenOffice.org's Mission Statement is:

> "To create, as a community, the leading international office suite that will run on all major platforms and provide access to all functionality and data through open-component based APIs and an XML-based file format."

The OpenOffice.org project is primarily sponsored by Sun Microsystems, which is the primary contributor of code to the Project. Our other major corporate contributors include Novell, RedHat, RedFlag CH2000, IBM, and Google. Additonally over 450,000 people from nearly every curve of the globe have joined this Project with the idea of creating the best possible office suite that all can use. This is the essence of an "open source" community!

With its free software licence and active Native Language Confederation, OpenOffice.org is a key player in the drive to eradicate digital exclusion and preserve minority languages threatened by being on the wrong side of the digital divide. For tens of thousands of community members, this makes the OpenOffice.org community their volunteering opportunity of choice.

The OpenOffice.org community invites contributors. Whatever you do best, you can do it for OpenOffice.org. As well as software developers, the Community welcomes translators, artists, technical writers and editors, testers, people offering user support, sales and marketing people, lobbyists, donors... the list is long. The Community operates internationally in all time zones, linked by the internet.

How is OpenOffice.org licensed?

OpenOffice.org is distributed under the Open Source Initiative (OSI) approved Lesser General Public License (LGPL).

The LGPL can be viewed on the OOo website at:
http://www.openoffice.org/licenses/lgpl_license.html

For more general information on OOo's licensing, please refer to:
http://www.openoffice.org/license.html

What is "open source"?

The ideals of open-source software can be explained by the four essential rights, which are embodied within the Free Software Foundation's *General Public License* (GPL):

- The right to use the software for any purpose.
- Freedom to redistribute the software for free or for a fee.
- Access to the complete source code of the program (that is, the "blueprints").
- The right to modify any part of the source, or use portions of it in other programs.

Another view of this philosophy comes from the *Open Source Definiton*:

> "The basic idea behind open source is very simple: When programmers can read, redistribute, and modify the source code for a piece of software, the software evolves. People improve it, people adapt it, people fix bugs. And this can happen at a speed that, if one is used to the slow pace of conventional software development, seems astonishing."

For more information on Free and Open Source software, visit these websites:

Open Source Initiative (OSI): http://www.opensource.org

Free Software Foundation (FSF): http://www.gnu.org

What is OpenDocument?

Starting with Version 2.0, OpenOffice.org by default saves documents in Open Document Format (ODF). OpenOffice.org 3 has adopted version 1.2 of the OpenDocument standard.

OpenDocument is an XML-based file format for office documents (text documents, spreadsheets, drawings, presentations and more), developed at OASIS, an independent, international standards group.

Unlike other file formats, ODF is an open standard. It is publicly available, royalty-free, and without legal or other restrictions; therefore ODF files are not tied to a specific office suite and anybody can build a program that interprets these files. For this reason ODF is quickly becoming the preferred file format for government agencies, schools and other companies who prefer not to be too dependent on a particular software supplier.

File formats OOo can open

OpenOffice.org can open a wide variety of file formats in addition to the OpenDocument formats.

Opening text documents

In addition to OpenDocument formats (.odt, .ott, .oth, and .odm), Writer 3 can open the formats used by OOo 1.x (.sxw, .stw, and .sxg) and the following text document formats:

Microsoft Word 6.0/95/97/2000/XP) (.doc and .dot)
Microsoft Word 2003 XML (.xml)
Microsoft Word 2007 XML (.docx, .docm, .dotx, .dotm)
Microsoft WinWord 5 (.doc)
WordPerfect Document (.wpd)
WPS 2000/Office 1.0 (.wps)
.rtf, .txt, and .csv
StarWriter formats (.sdw, .sgl, .vor)
DocBook (.xml)
Unified Office Format text (.uot, .uof)
Ichitaro 8/9/10/11 (.jtd and .jtt)
Hangul WP 97 (.hwp)
T602 Document (.602, .txt)
AportisDoc (Palm) (.pdb)
Pocket Word (.psw)

When opening .htm or .html files (used for web pages), OOo customizes Writer for working with these files.

Opening spreadsheets

In addition to OpenDocument formats (.ods and .ots), Calc 3 can open the formats used by OOo 1.x (.sxc and .stc) and the following spreadsheet formats:

Microsoft Excel 97/2000/XP (.xls, .xlw, and .xlt)
Microsoft Excel 4.x–5.0/95 (.xls, .xlw, and .xlt)
Microsoft Excel 2003 XML (.xml)
Microsoft Excel 2007 XML (.xlsx, .xlsm, .xlts, .xltm)
Microsoft Excel 2007 binary (.xlsb)
Lotus 1-2-3 (.wk1, .wks, and .123)
Data Interchange Format (.dif)
Rich Text Format (.rtf)
Text CSV (.csv and .txt)
StarCalc formats (.sdc and .vor)
dBASE (.dbf)
SYLK (.slk)
Unified Office Format spreadsheet (.uos, .uof)
.htm and .html files, including Web page queries
Pocket Excel (pxl)
Quattro Pro 6.0 (.wb2)

Opening presentations

In addition to OpenDocument formats (.odp, .odg, and .otp), Impress 3 can open the formats used by OOo 1.x (.sxi and .sti) and the following presentation formats:

> Microsoft PowerPoint 97/2000/XP (.ppt, .pps, and .pot)
> Microsoft PowerPoint 2007 (.pptx, .pptm, .potx, .potm)
> StarDraw and StarImpress (.sda, .sdd, .sdp, and .vor)
> Unified Office Format presentation (.uop, .uof)
> CGM – Computer Graphics Metafile (.cgm)
> Portable Document Format (.pdf)

Opening graphic files

In addition to OpenDocument formats (.odg and .otg), Draw 3 can open the formats used by OOo 1.x (.sxd and .std) and the following graphic formats:

BMP	JPEG, JPG	PCX	PSD	SGV	WMF
DXF	MET	PGM	RAS	SVM	XBM
EMF	PBM	PLT	SDA	TGA	XPM
EPS	PCD	PNG	SDD	TIF, TIFF	
GIF	PCT	PPM	SGF	VOR	

Opening formula files

In addition to OpenDocument Formula (.odf) files, Math 3 can open the format used by OOo 1.x (.sxm), StarMath, (.smf), and MathML (.mml) files.

When opening a Word document that contains an embedded equation editor object, if the option for it is checked in **Tools > Options > Load/Save > Microsoft Office**, the object will be automatically converted to an OpenOffice.org Math object.

File formats OOo can save to

Saving in an OpenDocument format guarantees the correct rendering of the file when it is transferred to another person or when the file is re-opened with a later version of OpenOffice.org. It is strongly recommended that you use ODF as default file format. However, you can save files in other formats, if you wish.

Tip	When sharing a document that you do not expect or want the recipient to modify, the safest option is to convert the document to PDF. OOo provides a very straightforward way to convert documents to PDF.

Saving text documents

In addition to OpenDocument formats (.odt and .ott), Writer 3 can save in these formats:

OpenOffice.org 1.x Text Document (.sxw)
OpenOffice.org 1.x Text Document Template (.stw)
Microsoft Word 6.0, 95, and 97/2000/XP (.doc)
Microsoft Word 2003 XML (.xml)
Rich Text Format (.rtf)
StarWriter 3.0, 4.0, and 5.0 (.sdw)
StarWriter 3.0, 4.0, and 5.0 Template (.vor)
Text (.txt)
Text Encoded (.txt)
Unified Office Format text (.uot, .uof)
HTML Document (OpenOffice.org Writer) (.html and .htm)
DocBook (.xml)
AportisDoc (Palm) (.pdb)
Pocket Word (.psw)

Note	The .rtf format is a common format for transferring text files between applications, but you are likely to experience loss of formatting and images. For this reason, other formats should be used.

Saving spreadsheet files

In addition to OpenDocument formats (.ods and .ots), Calc 3 can save in these formats:

OpenOffice.org 1.x Spreadsheet (.sxc)
OpenOffice.org 1.x Spreadsheet Template (.stc)
Microsoft Excel 97/2000/XP (.xls and .xlw)
Microsoft Excel 97/2000/XP Template (.xlt)
Microsoft Excel 5.0 and 95 (.xls and .xlw)
Microsoft Excel 2003 XML (.xml)
Data Interchange Format (.dif)
dBase (.dbf)
SYLK (.slk)
Text CSV (.csv and .txt)

StarCalc 3.0, 4.0, and 5.0 formats (.sdc and .vor)
Unified Office Format spreadsheet (.uos)
HTML Document (OpenOffice.org Calc) (.html and .htm)
Pocket Excel (.pxl)

Note	The Java Runtime Environment is required to use the mobile device filters for AportisDoc (Palm), Pocket Word, and Pocket Excel.

Saving presentations

In addition to OpenDocument formats (.odp, .otp, and .odg), Impress 3 can save in these formats:

OpenOffice.org 1.x Presentation (.sxi)
OpenOffice.org 1.x Presentation Template (.sti)
Microsoft PowerPoint 97/2000/XP (.ppt and .pps)
Microsoft PowerPoint 97/2000/XP Template (.pot)
StarDraw, StarImpress (.sda, .sdd, and .vor)
Unified Office Format presentation (.uop)

Impress can also export to MacroMedia Flash (.swf) and any of the graphics formats listed for Draw.

Saving drawings

Draw 3 can only save in the OpenDocument Drawing formats (.odg and .otg), the OpenOffice.org 1.x formats (.sxd and .std) and StarDraw format (.sda, .sdd, and .vor).

However, Draw can also export to BMP, EMF, EPS, GIF, JPEG, MET, PBM, PCT, PGM, PNG, PPM, RAS, SVG, SVM, TIFF, WMF, and XPM.

Writer/Web can save in these formats

HTML document (.html and .htm), as HTML 4.0 Transitional
OpenOffice.org 1.0 HTML Template (.stw)
OpenOffice.org 2.x HTML Template (.oth)
StarWriter/Web 4.0 and 5.0 (.vor)
Text (OpenOffice.org Writer/Web) (.txt)
Text Encoded (OpenOffice.org Writer/Web) (.txt)

Frequently asked questions

Is this software a "demo" version?	No, this is a fully functioning software suite.
May I distribute OOo to anyone?	Yes.
How many computers may I install it on?	As many as you like.
May I sell it?	Yes.
May I use OpenOffice.org in a business?	Yes.
Is OpenOffice available in my language?	OpenOffice.org has been translated (localized) into over 40 languages, so your language probably is supported. Additionally, there are over 70 *spelling*, *hyphenation*, and *thesaurus* dictionaries available for languages, and dialects that do not have a localized program interface. The dictionaries are available from the OpenOffice.org website at: http://lingucomponent.openoffice.org/download_dictionary.html
How can you make it for free?	A large share of the development, and much of the support for the project, is currently supplied or sponsored by Sun Microsystems. There are also many other people who work on OOo as volunteers.
What if I need technical support?	Read the section titled "How to get help" in Chapter 1 (Introducing OpenOffice.org).
Who owns the software?	The copyright is shared by Sun Microsystems and all the volunteers who have contributed.
Does that mean that they can take away the software?	No. The licenses under which OOo is developed and distributed can never be revoked, so it cannot be taken away.

I am writing a software application. May I use programming code from OpenOffice.org in my program?	You may, within the parameters set in the LGPL. Read the license: http://www.openoffice.org/license.html
Why is my favorite feature from StarOffice not available in OOo?	That feature is probably a third-party add-on that Sun cannot distribute with OpenOffice.org.
Why do I need Java to run OOo? Is it written in Java?	OpenOffice.org is not written in Java; it is written in the C++ language. Java is one of several languages that can be used to extend OOo. The Java JDK/JRE is only required for some features. The most notable one is the HSQLDB relational database engine. Note: Java is available at no cost. If you don't want to use Java, you can still use nearly all of the features of OOo.
How can I contribute to OpenOffice.org?	You can help with the development of OOo in many ways, and you do not need to be a programmer. To start, check out this webpage: http://www.openoffice.org/contributing.html
What's the catch?	There really is none; you can read the licenses here: http://www.openoffice.org/license.html

Index

A

accessibility features 405
accessibility options 36
advantages of OpenOffice.org 3
antialiasing screen font 28
appearance options 35
Apply Style list 53
area fill, editing 223
arranging objects 218
arrow styles, customizing 223
arrows 223
Asian language support 45
Asian languages enabled 187
AutoCorrect 47, 87
AutoLayout 187
automatic saving 18
AutoRecovery 18, 40
AutoUpdate styles 55

B

background images from Gallery 341
Basic 365
bitmaps 229
BitTorrent 5
book preview 108
booklet printing 109
bookmarks 117, 118
borders, editing 222
brackets (Math) 317
bring forward 218
brochure printing 109
bulleted list 189
Bullets and Numbering dialog 191

C

Calc macros 376
CD or DVD of OpenOffice.org 5
check for updates automatically 37
circle, drawing 210
clipboard 29
closing a document 21
closing OpenOffice.org 22
CMYK 201
Color Bar 201
color options 31
color palette 202
color scheme 36

combining objects 228
command line, starting from 10
Community Forum (user support) 6
complex text layout (CTL) 3, 45
components of OpenOffice.org 1
conditional hyphen 95
connectors 213
consultants 7
context menu 222
context menus 16
conversion 229
copying object from Gallery 340
create document from template 60
creating a document 16
cross-fading 226
cross-references
    inserting references 117
    overview 117
Ctrl-click required to follow hyperlinks 34
custom dictionary 46
Customize dialog 383
customizing
    keyboard shortcuts 398
    menus 390
    toolbars 394

D

data source
    description 231
    editing 276
    linking 273
    registering 273
    using in OOo documents 277
    viewing 276
database
    AutoValue 242
    creating 234
    creating subforms 273
    creating tables 235
    field types and formats 238
    list table 245
    planning 233
    primary key 236, 239, 242
    registering 276
    Report Wizard 298
    Table Wizard 236
    tables 235
database form